Excel

Revise in a Month

Year 9 NAPLAN*-style Tests

PASCAL PRESS

* This is not an officially endorsed publication of the NAPLAN program and is produced by Pascal Press independently of Australian governments.

Alan Horsfield, Allyn Jones & Bianca Hewes

Reprinted 2010
Revised in 2011 for NAPLAN Test changes
New NAPLAN Test question formats added 2012
Reprinted 2014, 2015
Conventions of Language questions updated 2017
Reprinted 2017, 2018, 2019 (twice)

Revised in 2020 for the NAPLAN Online tests

Reprinted 2021 (twice), 2022, 2023

ISBN 978 1 74125 210 1

Pascal Press
PO Box 250
Glebe NSW 2037
(02) 9198 1748
www.pascalpress.com.au

Publisher: Vivienne Joannou
Project editor: Mark Dixon
Edited by Rema Gnanadickam, Mark Dixon and Rosemary Peers
Proofread and answers checked by Peter Little and Dale Little
Typeset by Precision Typesetting (Barbara Nilsson) and Grizzly Graphics (Leanne Richters)
Cover and page design by DiZign Pty Ltd
Printed by Vivar Printing/Green Giant Press

Contents

NAPLAN and NAPLAN Online

WHAT IS NAPLAN?

- NAPLAN stands for National Assessment Program—Literacy and Numeracy.
- It is conducted every year in March and the tests are taken by students in Years 3, 5, 7 and 9.
- The tests cover Literacy—Reading, Writing, Conventions of Language (spelling, grammar and punctuation)—and Numeracy.

WHAT IS NAPLAN ONLINE?

Introduction

- In the past all NAPLAN tests were paper tests.
- From 2022 all students have taken the NAPLAN tests online.
- This means students complete the NAPLAN tests on a computer or tablet.

Tailored test design

- With NAPLAN paper tests, all students in each year level took exactly the same tests.
- In the NAPLAN Online tests this isn't the case; instead, every student takes a tailor-made test based on their ability.
- Please visit the official ACARA site for a detailed explanation of the tailored test process used in NAPLAN Online and also for general information about the tests: https://nap.edu.au/online-assessment.
- These tailor-made tests mean broadly, therefore, that a student who is at a standard level of achievement takes a test mostly comprised of questions of a standard level; a student who is at an intermediate level of achievement takes a test mostly comprised of questions of an intermediate level; and a student who is at an advanced level of achievement takes a test mostly comprised of questions of an advanced level.

Different question types

- Because of the digital format, NAPLAN Online contains more question types than in the paper tests. In the paper tests there are only multiple-choice and short-answer question types. In NAPLAN Online, however, there are also other question types. For example, students might be asked to drag text across a screen, measure a figure with an online ruler or listen to an audio recording of a sentence and then spell a word they hear.
- Please refer to the next page to see some examples of these additional question types that are found in NAPLAN Online and how they compare to questions in this book. As you will see, the content tested is exactly the same but the questions are presented differently.

NAPLAN Online question types

Additional NAPLAN Online question types	Equivalent questions in this book
Drag and drop 3^3 2^5 3^2 2^3 4^2 Rearrange the cards from lowest to highest value. [ ] [ ] [ ] [ ] [ ] **smallest** … **largest**	Arrange these from lowest to highest value: 3^3 (A) 2^5 (B) 3^2 (C) 2^3 (D) 4^2 (E) [ ] [ ] [ ] [ ] [ ] **smallest** … **largest**
Online ruler A, B, C Use the online protractor to measure the size of *CBA*. The size of the angle is [ ] degrees.	What is the size of the angle *CBA*? A, B, C Write your answer in the box. [ ]
Text entry Amendments can be made to a ___________ if enough people support them. Click on the play button to listen to the missing word. 0.08 / 0.09 Type the correct spelling of the word in the box. [ ]	Please ask your parent or teacher to read to you the spelling words on page 250. Write the correct spelling of each word in the box. **Word**: 1. constitution — **Example**: Amendments can be made to a constitution if enough people support them. [ ]
Drag and drop Drag these events to show the order in which Jim did these things. Use the tab to read the text. 1 2 3 4 5 tried to force the door cowered on the veranda walked tip-toe across the lawn tried to open a window became aware of moving shadows	In which order did Jim do these things? Number the events from 1 to 5. [ ] tried to force the door [ ] cowered on the veranda [ ] walked tip-toe across the lawn [ ] tried to open a window [ ] became aware of moving shadows

Maximise your results in NAPLAN Online

STEP 1: USE THIS BOOK

How *Excel* has updated this book to help you revise

Tailored test design

- We can't replicate the digital experience in book form and offer you tailored tests, but with this series we do provide Intermediate and Advanced NAPLAN Online–style Literacy and Numeracy tests
- This means that a student using these tests will be able to prepare with confidence for tests at different ability levels.
- This makes it excellent preparation for the tailored NAPLAN Online Literacy and Numeracy tests.

Remember the advantages of revising in book form

There are many benefits to a child revising using books for the online test:

- One of the most important benefits is that writing on paper will help your child retain information. It can be a very effective way to memorise. High-quality educational research shows that using a keyboard is not as good as note-taking for learning.
- Students will be able to prepare thoroughly for topic revision using books and then practise computer skills easily. They will only succeed with sound knowledge of topics; this requires study and focus. Students will not succeed in tests simply because they know how to answer questions digitally.
- Also, some students find it easier to concentrate when reading a page in a book than when reading on a screen.
- Furthermore it can be more convenient to use a book, especially when a child doesn't have ready access to a digital device.
- You can be confident that ***Excel*** books will help students acquire the topic knowledge they need, as we have over 30 years experience in helping students prepare for tests. All our writers are experienced educators.

STEP 2: PRACTISE ON *Excel Test Zone*

How *Excel Test Zone* can help you practise online

We recommend you go to www.exceltestzone.com.au and register for practice in NAPLAN Online–style tests once you have completed this book. The reasons include:

- for optimal performance in the NAPLAN Online tests we recommend students gain practice at completing online tests as well as completing revision in book form
- students should practise answering questions on a digital device to become confident with this process
- students will be able to practise tailored tests like those in NAPLAN Online, as well as other types of tests
- students will also be able to gain valuable practice in onscreen skills such as dragging and dropping answers, using an online ruler to measure figures and using an online protractor to measure angles.

Remember that ***Excel Test Zone*** has been helping students prepare for NAPLAN since 2009; in fact we had NAPLAN online questions even before NAPLAN tests went online!

We also have updated our website along with our book range to ensure your preparation for NAPLAN Online is 100% up to date.

About the NAPLAN tests and this book

ABOUT THE TESTS

Test results

- The test results are used by teachers as a diagnostic tool. The results provide students, parents and teachers with information that can be used to improve student learning.
- The student report provides information about what students know and can do in the areas of Reading, Writing, Conventions of Language (spelling, grammar and punctuation) and the various strands of Numeracy. It also provides information on how each student has performed in relation to other students in their year group and against the national average and the national minimum standard.
- NAPLAN tests are not aptitude or intelligence tests. They focus on what has been achieved, especially on the knowledge and skills taught in the syllabus. These are often called KLAs (key learning areas).
- Official tests are trialled on selected groups to test the reliability of the questions. The questions in this book are representative of questions that you can expect to find in an official test. They have been prepared by professionals who have an understanding of teaching and of testing procedures.
- The NAPLAN results present an objective view of student performance and form the basis from which schools can make informed educational decisions about further school learning programs.
- Because NAPLAN tests are national tests they provide authorities with sufficient information to track student educational development from primary to high school, or when transferring from one Australian school to another.

TYPES OF TESTS

- There are four different types of tests in Year 9 NAPLAN Online.
  1. The Numeracy test (65 minutes)
  2. The Conventions of Language test (45 minutes)
  3. The Reading test (65 minutes)
  4. The Writing test (42 minutes)

  Tests 2–4 form the Literacy component of the test.
- The Writing test is held first, followed by the Reading test, the Conventions of Language test and finally the Numeracy test.

USING THIS BOOK

- This book is designed to be used over four weeks, with weekly exercises in various aspects of literacy and numeracy.
- Each session gives students an opportunity to Test their Skills, revise Key Points and practise a Real Test on a specific aspect of the curriculum.
- In a month the student will have covered much of the material that could be included in a NAPLAN Online test.
- Finally there are two Sample Test Papers based on the content used in past Year 9 NAPLAN test papers.
- Because NAPLAN tests are timed tests, times have been suggested for completing the various units in this book.

Week 1

This is what we cover this week:

Day 1 **Number and Algebra:**
- ◎ Whole numbers
- ◎ Fractions and decimals
- ◎ Percentages
- ◎ Chance, rates and ratio
- ◎ Using the calculator

Day 2 **Spelling:**
- ◎ Plural nouns and singular verbs, root words, compound words, irregular spelling patterns, and multi-syllable words
- ◎ Common misspellings

Grammar and Punctuation:
- ◎ Types of nouns, adjectives, adverbs, verbs and participles

Day 3 **Reading:** ◎ Understanding narratives

Day 4 **Writing:** ◎ Persuasive texts

NUMBER AND ALGEBRA
Whole numbers

1. What is the remainder when 141 is divided by 4?
A 0 B 1 C 2 D 3

2. What is the highest number that is a factor of both 18 and 28?
A 2 B 3 C 4 D 8

3. How many prime numbers are less than 20?
A 7 B 8 C 9 D 10

4. Which of these numbers is a multiple of 3?
A 47 B 58 C 75 D 83

5. The number 64 is the same as
A 1^{64} B 2^{32} C 8^8 D 2^6

6. $2^3 \times 3^2 =$
A 11 B 30 C 36 D 72

7. What two numbers is $4\frac{1}{2}^2$ between?
A 4 and 9 B 9 and 16
C 16 and 25 D 25 and 36

8. Find the value of 2^5.
A 16 B 24 C 32 D 50

9. Evaluate $\sqrt{100} + \sqrt{121}$
A 20 B 21 C 22 D $\sqrt{221}$

10. What is 4×3^2?
A 14 B 36 C 49 D 144

11. What is the value of $\sqrt{3^2 + 4^2}$?
A 5 B 7 C 10 D 14

12. $\sqrt{48}$ is closest to
A 7 B 8 C 9 D 25

13. $-5 - 3 + 8 =$?
A –16 B –8 C 0 D 8

14. Complete the number sentence:
$-7 + \_\_\_\_ = 10$
A –3 B 3 C 7 D 17

15. What is the sum of –4, –2 and 8?
A –14 B –6 C 2 D 14

16. What is the square of –4?
A –16 B –2 C 2 D 16

17. Complete the number sentence:
$\_\_\_\_ \div -4 = 6$
A –24 B –10 C –2 D 24

18. What is $(-1)^5$?
A –5 B –1 C 1 D 5

19. What is the value of $15 - 6 \times 2$?
A 3 B 4 C 18 D 22

20. Evaluate $3 - (2 - 4)$.
A –9 B –5 C 1 D 5

21. What is the value of $9 + 2 \times 0 \times 5$?
A 0 B 9 C 11 D 55

22. What is 24 divided by the product of 4 and 2?
A 3 B 4 C 6 D 12

23. Which of the following equals 4?
A $1 + 1 + 1 \div 1$ B $1 + 1 - 1 - 1$
C $(1 + 1) \times (1 + 1)$ D $-1 \times -1 - (-1 - 1)$

24. Evaluate $\frac{4+6}{2+3}$
A 1 B 2 C 10 D 11

25. Another way of writing 3 450 000 is
A 3.45×10^4 B 3.45×10^5
C 3.45×10^6 D 345×10^6

26. What number is halfway between 56 and 74?
A 18 B 64 C 65 D 66

27. What is the average of 7, 23 and 30?
A 20 B 26 C 30 D 33

28. The middle number between 1 and another number is 4. What is the other number?
A 2 B 3 C 5 D 7

☞ **Explanations on page 179**

Answers: 1 B 2 A 3 B 4 C 5 D 6 D 7 C 8 C 9 B 10 B 11 A 12 A 13 C 14 D 15 C 16 D 17 A 18 B 19 A 20 D 21 B 22 A 23 C 24 B 25 C 26 C 27 A 28 D

NUMBER AND ALGEBRA
Whole numbers

1. **Factors** are numbers that go, or divide, evenly into a given number. This means that there is no remainder.

   Example 1: Write the factors of 12.
   Solution: 12: 1, 2, 3, 4, 6, 12

   Example 2: Is 3 a factor of 19?
   Solution: As 3 into 19 gives 6 with 1 left over, it means that 3 is not a factor of 19.

2. A **prime number** has only two factors: 1 and the number itself. A composite number has more than two factors. 0 and 1 are not considered prime or composite numbers.

   Example 1: Is 21 prime or composite?
   Solution: Factors of 21 are 1, 3, 7, 21. This means that 21 is composite.

   Example 2: Write the first ten prime numbers.
   Solution: 2, 3, 5, 7, 11, 13, 17, 19, 23, 29

3. Here are some **divisibility tests**:
   - divisible by 2 (or a multiple of 2): the last digit is even or zero.
   - divisible by 3 (or a multiple of 3): sum of digits is divisible by 3.
   - divisible by 5 (or a multiple of 5): the last digit is a 5 or 0.

   Example 1: Is 276 divisible by 2?
   Yes, because the last digit 6 is even.

   Example 2: Is 513 divisible by 3?
   Yes, as $5 + 1 + 3 = 9$ which is divisible by 3.

4. **Index notation** is used when the same number is multiplied by itself.
   Example 1: Write $3 \times 3 \times 3 \times 3 \times 3$ in index form.
   $3 \times 3 \times 3 \times 3 \times 3 = 3^5$

   Example 2: True or false? $4^2 = 2^4$
   $4^2 = 4 \times 4 = 16$
   $2^4 = 2 \times 2 \times 2 \times 2 = 16$
   Therefore this is true.

5. Any number (or pronumeral) to the **power of zero** is equal to 1.
   Example 1: Find the value of 5^0.
   $5^0 = 1$
   Example 2: Evaluate $(3 \times 4)^0 + 2^0 = 12^0 + 2^0$
   $= 1 + 1$
   $= 2$

6. **Square numbers** are
   $1^2 = 1 \times 1 = 1$
   $2^2 = 2 \times 2 = 4$
   $3^2 = 3 \times 3 = 9$
   $4^2 = 4 \times 4 = 16$

   Here are the first 10 square numbers:
   1, 4, 9, 16, 25, 36, 49, 64, 81, 100

   Example: What is 7^2?
   $7^2 = 7 \times 7 = 49$

7. **Square roots:**
   Example: What is $\sqrt{64}$?
   $\sqrt{64} = 8$ as $8^2 = 64$

8. **Cubes and cube roots**:
   Example 1: What is the value of 2^3?
   $2 \times 2 \times 2 = 8$

   Example 2: Evaluate $\sqrt[3]{8}$
   $\sqrt[3]{8} = 2$, as $2^3 = 8$

9. **Directed numbers**: The number line shows the position of negative and positive numbers:

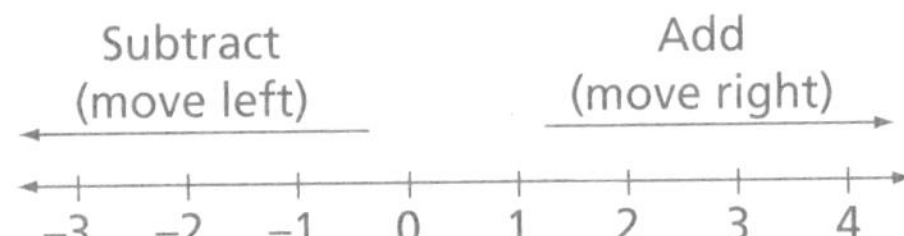

   Example 1: Evaluate $4 - 7 = -3$
   [by starting at 4 and moving 7 places to the left].

   Example 2: Evaluate $-2 + 6 = 4$
   [by starting at –2 and moving 6 places to the right].

   Other rules to use:

+ + = +	+ × + = +	+ ÷ + = +
+ − = −	+ × − = −	+ ÷ − = −
− + = −	− × + = −	− ÷ + = −
− − = +	− × − = +	− ÷ − = +

   Example 1: Evaluate $-2 - -1 = -2 + 1 = -1$
   [as − − = +]

   Example 2: Evaluate $-3 \times 6 = -18$
   [as − × + = −]

   Example 3: Evaluate $-30 \div -5 = 6$
   [as − ÷ − = +]

NUMBER AND ALGEBRA
Whole numbers

⑩ **Order of operations**: **B**rackets before **M**ultiplication or **D**ivision then **A**ddition or **S**ubtraction (**Remember:** BMDAS).

Example 1: $10 - 7 \times 2 = 10 - 14$
$= -4$

Example 2: $(12 - 7) \div 5 = 5 \div 5$
$= 1$

⑪ The average is found by adding quantities and dividing by the number of quantities.

Example 1: Find the average of 15, 8 and 7

$$\text{Average} = \frac{15 + 8 + 7}{3} = \frac{30}{3} = 10$$

Example 2: What is the middle of 86 and 128?

The middle is found by finding the average:

$$\text{Average} = \frac{86 + 128}{2} = \frac{214}{2} = 107$$

⑫ A very large number can be rewritten as a number between 1 and 10 multiplied by a power of 10. This is rewriting the number in scientific notation.

Example 1: Rewrite 360 000 in scientific notation.

$$360\,000 = 3.6 \times 100\,000 = 3.6 \times 10^5$$

Example 2: Rewrite 1.07×10^4 in normal form.

$$1.07 \times 10^4 = 1.07 \times 10\,000 = 10\,700$$

NUMBER AND ALGEBRA

Whole numbers

1 Fifty–two playing cards are placed into six equal piles. How many are left over?

A 1 B 2 C 4 D 5

2 Two warning lights are flashing. Light A flashes every 3 seconds and Light B flashes every 4 seconds. How many times will Light A flash before it flashes at the same time as Light B? *Hint 1*

A 1 B 2 C 3 D 4

3 What is the first prime number larger than 23? *Hint 2*

Write your answer in the box: ☐

4 Which cards have the same value?

3^2 2^2 2^3 4^2 2^4

A 4^2 and 2^4 B 2^2 and 2^3
C 3^2 and 2^3 D 2^2 and 4^2

5 Arrange these from lowest to highest value. *Hint 3*

3^3	2^5	3^2	2^3	4^2
A	B	C	D	E

6 What is the sum of $3^2 + 2^4$?

A 5^2 B 5^6 C 17 D 30

7 Bridgett thinks of a number. When she squares it her answer lies between 80 and 100. Bridgett's number could be between

A 3 and 4. B 5 and 6.
C 7 and 8. D 9 and 10.

8 What is the value of $4 + 5 \times 6$? *Hint 4*

A 34 B 43 C 45 D 54

9 Which number sentence matches: the difference between the product of 4 and 2 and the quotient of 12 and 6?

A $4 - 2 \times 12 \div 6$ B $4 \times 2 \div 12 - 6$
C $4 \times 2 - 12 \div 6$ D $4 - 2 + 12 \div 6$

10 What is the square root of the sum of the first three odd numbers?

A 2 B 3 C 4 D 5

11 Wendy wrote a number that was
- a multiple of 3
- even
- between 20 and 70
- divisible by 5 *Hint 5*

The number that Wendy wrote could be

A 93. B 72. C 45. D 60.

12 Which of these is the value of $4^2 - 4^0$?

A 2 B 4 C 15 D 16

13 The temperature was –3 degrees at 6 am. It then rose 8 degrees by 2 pm and then dropped 4 degrees by 7 pm. What is the temperature at 7 pm?

A –1 degree B 1 degree
C 2 degrees D 9 degrees

14 What is the middle number between –8 and 6? *Hint 6*

A 3 B 2 C 1 D –1

15

From P, add 6, subtract 4, subtract 1 and add 2. What is the answer? *Hint 7*

A –2 B 1 C 2 D 3

16 The population of Indonesia was estimated in 2019 to be 270 million. This number can be rewritten as

A 270×10^3 B 270×10^8
C 2.7×10^8 D 2.7×10^6

Hint 1: Use the lowest common multiple.
Hint 2: A prime number has exactly two factors.
Hint 3: Any number can be written as a power of 1: e.g. $4^1 = 4$.
Hint 4: Use the rules for the order of operations.
Hint 5: A large number can be shown to be a multiple of 3 (or divisible by 3) if its digits add to a multiple of 3.
Hint 6: The middle of two numbers is the average.
Hint 7: When reading a number line, the numbers to the left are less than the numbers to the right.

☞ Answers and explanations on pages 179–180

NUMBER AND ALGEBRA
Fractions and decimals

1 Change $\frac{29}{4}$ to a mixed numeral.

A $7\frac{1}{4}$ B $7\frac{1}{2}$ C $7\frac{3}{4}$ D $9\frac{3}{4}$

2 Change $2\frac{5}{9}$ to an improper fraction.

A $\frac{16}{9}$ B $\frac{4}{3}$ C $\frac{23}{5}$ D $\frac{23}{9}$

3

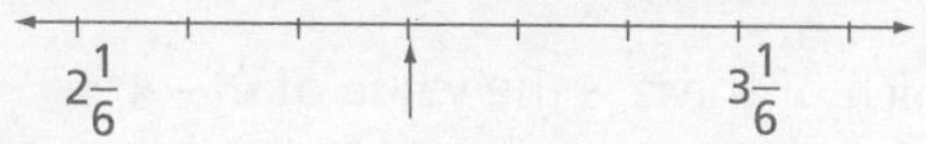

What number is the arrow pointing to?

A $2\frac{1}{3}$ B $2\frac{1}{2}$ C $2\frac{2}{3}$ D $2\frac{5}{6}$

4 Which is the largest fraction?

A $\frac{3}{4}$ B $\frac{5}{6}$ C $\frac{2}{3}$ D $\frac{7}{12}$

5 What is the reciprocal of $1\frac{2}{5}$?

A $\frac{5}{7}$ B $\frac{7}{10}$ C $2\frac{1}{2}$ D $3\frac{1}{2}$

6 What fraction is 20 minutes of 2 hours?

A $\frac{1}{10}$ B $\frac{1}{6}$ C $\frac{1}{3}$ D $\frac{2}{3}$

7 What is the sum of $\frac{1}{2}$ and $\frac{1}{3}$?

A $\frac{1}{6}$ B $\frac{2}{5}$ C $\frac{4}{5}$ D $\frac{5}{6}$

8 Find $2\frac{1}{4} + 3\frac{2}{3}$.

A $5\frac{3}{7}$ B $5\frac{11}{12}$ C $6\frac{1}{12}$ D $6\frac{1}{6}$

9 Subtract $\frac{2}{5}$ from $\frac{1}{2}$.

A $\frac{1}{10}$ B $\frac{1}{5}$ C $\frac{1}{3}$ D $\frac{3}{7}$

10 What is three-quarters of 36?

A 20 B 24 C 27 D 33

11 Evaluate $\left(2\frac{1}{2}\right)^2$.

A $4\frac{1}{4}$ B 5 C $6\frac{1}{4}$ D $6\frac{1}{2}$

12 Two-thirds of the class of 24 students have brown hair. Another 2 students have black hair. The remaining students have blonde hair. What fraction of the students in the class have blonde hair?

A $\frac{1}{20}$ B $\frac{1}{5}$ C $\frac{1}{4}$ D $\frac{3}{24}$

13 $\frac{10}{21} \div \frac{5}{6} = ?$

A $\frac{1}{6}$ B $\frac{2}{7}$ C $\frac{3}{7}$ D $\frac{4}{7}$

14 Apples are being cut into quarters. How many quarters will be cut from 8 apples?

A 16 B 24 C 32 D 36

15 $4 + \frac{2}{3}$ is closest to

A 0.423 B 4.23 C 4.6 D 4.667

16 Which is the smallest of these decimals?

A 0.3 B 0.29 C 0.049 D –0.4

17 Find the value of 0.63 + 1.2

A 0.75 B 1.83 C 1.85 D 7.5

18 What is 4 – 1.07?

A 0.75 B 2.93 C 3.93 D 7.5

19 Evaluate 0.11^2 to two decimal places.

A 0.01 B 0.012 C 0.12 D 1.21

20 What is 4 – 0.3 × 0.4?

A 1.2 B 2.2 C 3.88 D 14.8

21 Find the average of 0.3, 0.6 and 1.5.

A 0.8 B 1.2 C 1.4 D 2.4

☞ Explanations on pages 180-181

Answers: 1 A 2 D 3 C 4 B 5 A 6 B 7 D 8 B 9 A 10 C 11 C 12 C 13 D 14 C 15 D 16 D 17 B 18 B 19 A 20 C 21 A

NUMBER AND ALGEBRA
Fractions and decimals

1 A fraction is written in the form $\frac{\text{numerator}}{\text{denominator}}$. An **improper fraction** can be rewritten as a **mixed numeral**.

Example 1: Convert $\frac{21}{4}$ to a mixed numeral.

As 4 into 21 is 5 and remainder 1, then $\frac{21}{4} = 5\frac{1}{4}$.

Example 2: Convert $6\frac{2}{3}$ to an improper fraction.

As 3 times 6 plus 2 is 20, then $6\frac{2}{3} = \frac{20}{3}$.

2 Fractions can be **cancelled** (or simplified) by dividing the numerator and denominator by the same number.

Example 1: Simplify $\frac{6}{8}$.

$$\frac{6}{8} = \frac{2 \times 3}{2 \times 4} = \frac{\cancel{2}^1 \times 3}{\cancel{2}^1 \times 4} = \frac{1 \times 3}{1 \times 4} = \frac{3}{4}$$

Example 2: Simplify $\frac{24}{36}$.

$$\frac{24}{36} = \frac{12 \times 2}{12 \times 3} = \frac{\cancel{12}^1 \times 2}{\cancel{12}^1 \times 3} = \frac{1 \times 2}{1 \times 3} = \frac{2}{3}$$

3 When we **add or subtract fractions** with the same denominator, we just add or subtract the numerator.

Example 1: $\frac{3}{8} + \frac{5}{8} = \frac{8}{8} = 1$

Example 2: $1\frac{2}{5} + 2\frac{4}{5} = 3\frac{6}{5} = 3 + 1\frac{1}{5} = 4\frac{1}{5}$

Example 3: $1 - \frac{3}{5} = \frac{5}{5} - \frac{3}{5} = \frac{2}{5}$

4 When we add or subtract fractions with **different denominators**, we first make the denominators the same.

Example 1: $\frac{4}{5} + \frac{3}{10} = \frac{8}{10} + \frac{3}{10} = \frac{11}{10} = 1\frac{1}{10}$

Example 2: $\frac{2}{3} + \frac{3}{4} = \frac{8}{12} + \frac{9}{12} = \frac{17}{12} = 1\frac{5}{12}$

5 When we **multiply fractions** we multiply the numerators together then the denominators together. (We can cancel fractions if possible.)

Example 1: $\frac{3}{4} \times \frac{5}{6} = \frac{15}{24} = \frac{\cancel{3}^1 \times 5}{\cancel{3}^1 \times 8} = \frac{5}{8}$

Example 2: $\left(\frac{2}{3}\right)^3 = \frac{2}{3} \times \frac{2}{3} \times \frac{2}{3} = \frac{8}{27}$

6 The **reciprocal** of a fraction is found by turning the fraction upside down.

Example: What is the reciprocal of $\frac{3}{4}$?

Reciprocal of $\frac{3}{4}$ is $\frac{4}{3} = 1\frac{1}{3}$.

7 When we **divide by a fraction** we multiply by its reciprocal.

Example 1: $\frac{1}{2} \div \frac{1}{4} = \frac{1}{2} \times \frac{4}{1} = \frac{4}{2} = 2$

Example 2: $1\frac{1}{3} \div \frac{1}{6} = \frac{4}{\cancel{3}^1} \times \frac{\cancel{6}^2}{1} = \frac{8}{1} = 8$

8 When **adding or subtracting decimals** take care with place values.

Example 1: $32.4 + 1.76 = 32.40 + 1.76$
$= 34.16$

Example 2: $4 - 1.03 = 4.00 - 1.03$
$= 2.97$

9 When **decimals are multiplied**, the number of digits following decimal points in the question is repeated in the answer.

Example 1: 1.3×5
As $13 \times 5 = 65$, then $1.3 \times 5 = 6.5$

Example 2: 3.4×0.3 As $34 \times 3 = 102$, then $3.4 \times 0.3 = 1.02$

10 When **dividing by a decimal**, multiply both numbers so that we divide by a whole number.

Example 1: $1.5 \div 0.5 = 15 \div 5 = 3$

Example 2: $16 \div 0.04 = 1600 \div 4 = 400$

NUMBER AND ALGEBRA
Fractions and decimals

1 Which fraction has the same value as $3\frac{4}{5}$?

A $\frac{19}{5}$ B $\frac{17}{5}$ C $\frac{12}{5}$ D $\frac{32}{3}$

2 Rewrite $\frac{23}{3}$ as a mixed numeral.

A $7\frac{2}{7}$ B $7\frac{1}{3}$ C $7\frac{2}{3}$ D $8\frac{2}{3}$

3 What value is placed in the triangle to make the number sentence correct?

$\frac{3}{8} = \frac{\triangle}{48}$ *Hint 1*

A 6 B 18 C 20 D 24

4 Find the sum of $\frac{3}{5}$ and $\frac{1}{3}$.

A $\frac{4}{8}$ B $\frac{11}{15}$ C $\frac{13}{15}$ D $\frac{14}{15}$

5 $3\frac{3}{4} + \frac{1}{3} = ?$

A $3\frac{4}{7}$ B $3\frac{11}{12}$ C $4\frac{1}{12}$ D $4\frac{1}{7}$

6 $2 - \left(\frac{1}{2} - \frac{1}{4}\right) = ?$ *Hint 2*

A $\frac{7}{8}$ B $1\frac{1}{8}$ C $1\frac{1}{4}$ D $1\frac{3}{4}$

7 What is $\frac{2}{3}$ of 4 hours?

A 2 h 20 min B 2 h 30 min
C 2 h 40 min D 2 h 50 min

8 $\frac{3}{4} \times \square = \frac{1}{2}$

Which of the following replaces the square?

A $\frac{2}{3}$ B $\frac{3}{8}$ C $\frac{1}{4}$ D $\frac{3}{4}$

9 In a class of 30 students, 24 catch the bus to school. What fraction of the students in the class do not catch the bus?

A $\frac{1}{6}$ B $\frac{1}{5}$ C $\frac{1}{4}$ D $\frac{1}{3}$

10 What fraction is halfway between $\frac{1}{4}$ and $\frac{1}{3}$?
Hint 3

A $\frac{1}{7}$ B $\frac{7}{24}$ C $\frac{3}{8}$ D $\frac{5}{24}$

11 This is the working that Enoch showed for the sum of $\frac{3}{4}$ and $\frac{5}{8}$:

Line 1: Sum of $\frac{3}{4}$ and $\frac{5}{8}$ $= \frac{3}{4} + \frac{5}{8}$

Line 2: $= \frac{6}{8} + \frac{5}{8}$

Line 3: $= \frac{11}{8}$

Line 4: $= 1\frac{1}{8}$

Enoch's answer is incorrect. Where did Enoch make an error?

A Line 1 B Line 2 C Line 3 D Line 4

12 Find $\frac{3}{5} + \frac{1}{2}$ and write your answer as a decimal.

A 0.11 B 1.1 C 1.2 D 3.52

13 What is 2.3 × 0.08?

A 0.184 B 0.194 C 1.84 D 2.38

14 Evaluate $\frac{3 - 1.4}{0.2}$.

A 0.8 B 1.3 C 2.3 D 8

15 Habib wrote this number sentence:

5.2 − ____ = 3.8

Write your answer in the box: ☐

16 Arrange these expressions from largest value to smallest value.

A 2.4 ÷ 0.3 B 2.4 − 0.3
C 2.4 × 0.3 D 2.4 + 0.3

Hint 1: *First consider the denominators to find the number that is multiplying 8 to get 48.*
Hint 2: *Evaluate the expression inside the grouping symbols (brackets) first—remember the order of operations rules.*
Hint 3: *Change the fractions to equivalent fractions that have the same denominators.*

☞ **Answers and explanations on pages 181–182**

NUMBER AND ALGEBRA
Percentages

1. Rewrite $\frac{4}{5}$ as a percentage.
   A 45% B 54%
   C 80% D 85%

2. What percentage is 18 of 24?
   A 25% B 40%
   C 60% D 75%

3. What percentage is 50 cents of $2.00?
   A 20% B 25%
   C 50% D 75%

4. What percentage of the rectangle remains unshaded?
   A 75% B 80%
   C 25% D 20%

5. Change $2\frac{4}{5}$ to a percentage.
   A 2.45% B 24.5%
   C 245% D 280%

6. What percentage of the circle is shaded?
   A 75% B 70%
   C 40% D 25%

7. Which of the following is not equal to 45%?
   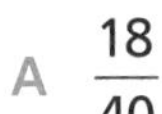
   A $\frac{18}{40}$ B $\frac{45}{100}$ C $\frac{9}{20}$ D $\frac{4}{5}$

8. The table shows the number of books read by students during a vacation.

Number of books	Students
0	4
1	9
2	5
3	2

   What percentage of students read 2 books?
   A 2% B 20% C 25% D 28%

9. What percentage is $8 of $40?
   A 5% B 20% C 32% D 48%

10. Which is the largest?
    A $\frac{2}{5}$ B 0.3 C 31% D 0.08

11. What percentage is 15 minutes of 1 hour?
    A 15% B 25% C 30% D 45%

12. What is 20% of 50?
    A 10 B 15 C 25 D 40

13. How much is 10% of $200?
    A 20c B $20 C $40 D $30

14. Find 15% of 200.
    A 15 B 25 C 30 D 35

15. What is 50% of $150?
    A $25 B $50 C $75 D $100

16. Wendy wants to shade 60% of the shape.

    How many more sections will she need to shade?
    A 1 B 2 C 3 D 4

17. If $80 is increased by 10%, what is the new amount?
    A $8 B $8.80
    C $80.80 D $88

18. The diagram shows a grid. If 80% of the grid is to be shaded, how many squares will remain unshaded?

    A 4 B 5
    C 8 D 20

19. If $70 is increased by 20%, what is the new amount?
    A $90 B $14 C $77 D $84

☞ Explanations on pages 182–183

Answers: 1 C 2 D 3 B 4 A 5 D 6 A 7 D 8 C 9 B 10 A 11 B 12 A 13 B 14 C 15 C 16 D 17 D 18 A 19 D

NUMBER AND ALGEBRA
Percentages

1 A **percentage** is a fraction with a denominator of 100.

This means that $1 = \frac{100}{100} = 100\%$.

2 Here are some **familiar conversions**:

Percentages	Fractions	Decimals
50%	$\frac{1}{2}$	0.5
25%	$\frac{1}{4}$	0.25
20%	$\frac{1}{5}$	0.2
10%	$\frac{1}{10}$	0.1
5%	$\frac{1}{20}$	0.05

Example 1: Rewrite 80% as a fraction:

As $20\% = \frac{1}{5}$, $80\% = \frac{4}{5}$ [by multiplying by 4]

Example 2: Rewrite 75% as a fraction:

As $25\% = \frac{1}{4}$, $75\% = \frac{3}{4}$ [by multiplying by 3]

Example 3: Rewrite $\frac{7}{20}$ as a percentage:

As $\frac{1}{20} = 5\%$, $\frac{7}{20} = 35\%$ [by multiplying by 7]

3 To **change a fraction or decimal to a percentage** multiply by 100.

Change to percentages:

Example 1: $\frac{7}{25} : \frac{7}{{}_1\cancel{25}} \times \frac{\cancel{100}^4}{1} = 28 \quad \therefore 28\%$

Example 2: $\frac{2}{3} : \frac{2}{3} \times \frac{100}{1} = \frac{200}{3} \quad \therefore 66\frac{2}{3}\%$

Example 3: 0.875: $0.875 \times 100 = 87.5 \therefore 87.5\%$

Example 4: 0.09: $0.09 \times 100 = 9 \therefore 9\%$

4 When writing **one quantity as a percentage of another** first express it as a fraction and then change to a percentage.

Example 1: What percentage is \$12 of \$20?

$\frac{12}{20} = \frac{3}{5} = 60\%$ or $\frac{12}{{}_1\cancel{20}} \times \frac{\cancel{100}^5}{1} = 60\%$

Example 2: Write half an hour as a percentage of 2 hours.
Change hours to min: 30 min and 120 min.

$\frac{30}{120} = \frac{1}{4} = 25\%$ or $\frac{\cancel{30}^1}{{}_4\cancel{120}} \times \frac{\cancel{100}^{25}}{1} \therefore 25\%$

5 To find a **percentage of a quantity,** we first change the percentage to a fraction or decimal.

Example 1: Find 30% of \$40.

Amount $= 0.3 \times 40$
$= 12$
$\therefore$ \$12

Example 2: What is 15% of 5 minutes?

Change 5 minutes to $5 \times 60 = 300$ seconds

Amount $= 0.15 \times 300$
$= 45$
$\therefore$ 45 seconds

6 **Increasing/decreasing a quantity by a percentage** can be found by finding the percentage and then adding it to or subtracting it from the original quantity.

Example: A magazine which costs \$3.50 increases in price by 10%. What is the new price of the magazine?

Increase = 10% of \$3.50
$= \frac{1}{10} \times 350c$
= 35c $\therefore$ price increases by 35c.

New price = \$3.50 + \$0.35
= \$3.85

[OR New price = $1.10 \times 3.50 = 3.85$]

7 To find **simple interest** on a deposit, multiply the amount of money by the interest rate, by the number of years.

Example: Find simple interest on an investment of \$4000 at 8% per annum for 3 years.

Simple interest $= 4000 \times 0.08 \times 3$
$= 960$

Simple interest of \$960.

NUMBER AND ALGEBRA
Percentages

1 A survey is held to find the types of trees in a park containing 20 trees. *Hint 1*

Trees	Number
Eucalypt	9
Oak	?
Banksia	4
Palm	3
Cedar	1

What percentage are oak trees? ☐ %

2 In a test Marcos scored 12 out of a possible 25. What is this mark as a percentage?

A 12% B 24% C 45% D 48%

3 Last year Demi saved 20% of her annual income of $61 000. The amount of Demi's savings is closest to *Hint 2*

A $12 000. B $20 000.
C $30 000. D $32 000.

4 While Phoebe was in Year 8 her height increased by 10%. At the start of the year she was 140 cm tall. What was her height at the end of the year?

A 150 cm B 152 cm C 154 cm D 164 cm

5 A salesman dropped the price of a computer game from $80 to $72. What is this saving as a percentage? *Hint 3*

A 8% B 10% C 12% D 18%

6 After a storm, water is covering a road to a depth that is shown on the post. What percentage of the post is above the water level?

4 m
3 m
2 m
1 m

A 90% B 80%
C 75% D 25%

7 Dorothy received 15 emails and she replied to 40% of them. To how many emails did she not reply?

A 9 B 6 C 4 D 3

8 Logan invested $2000 at 4% p.a. simple interest for 3 years. What was the amount of interest earned?

A $2024 B $1200
C $120 D $240

9 When Krystal purchased a pair of shoes online for $45 she paid an additional surcharge of 5% to the Internet company.

Which calculation gives the total cost of the shoes?

A 45×1.05 B 45×0.05
C $45 + 1.05$ D $45 \div 1.05$

10 A shrub in Cedric's garden was 30 cm tall. In six months it grew by 20%. What is the new height of the shrub?

A 32 cm B 35 cm C 36 cm D 45 cm

11 A school has a total of 1000 students:

Year	7	8	9	10	11	12
Students	190	190	180	170	140	130

What percentage is in year 9? ☐ %

12 In a bag of twenty-four jelly beans, Li counts 8 black, 3 green, 4 pink, 6 yellow and the remainder blue. If he eats the pink jelly beans first, what percentage of the remaining jelly beans are blue?

A 3% B 6% C 9% D 15%

13 Quentin's team won 12 of their 16 games this year. What percentage of the games were not won?

A 4% B 25% C 36% D 40%

14 When he purchased a pair of sports socks for $9.90, Simeon was given a discount of 15%. Which calculation shows the amount he paid?

A $9.9 - 0.15$ B $9.9 - 0.15 \times 9.9$
C 0.95×9.9 D $9.9 + 0.15 \times 9.9$

15 Therese's book has 100 pages. On the first night she read 20% of the book and on the second night she read 25% of the remainder. How many pages are unread?

16 A console game is bought on sale at 25% of its original price of $96. How much is paid for the game? $ ☐

Hint 1: First use subtraction to find the missing entry in the table.
Hint 2: As 20% is one-fifth, divide 5 into 60 to get an approximation.
Hint 3: Use subtraction to find the discount and then express as a fraction and then change to a percentage.

☞ Answers and explanations on pages 183–184

NUMBER AND ALGEBRA
Chance, rates and ratio

1 A die is rolled. What is the chance of rolling a number less than 6?
A $\frac{1}{5}$ B $\frac{4}{5}$ C $\frac{5}{6}$ D 1

2 A bag contains 9 identical balls, numbered 1 to 9. If a ball is selected at random, what is the probability that it is odd?
A $\frac{1}{2}$ B $\frac{5}{9}$ C $\frac{1}{5}$ D $\frac{4}{9}$

3 Twenty-five per cent of a dozen eggs are rotten. What is the chance of selecting an egg at random that is not rotten?
A 1 in 3 B 1 in 4 C 3 in 4 D 2 in 3

4 A bag contains 24 balls of various colours. Toni knows the chance of selecting a red ball is $\frac{2}{3}$. How many red balls are in the bag?
A 8 B 12 C 18 D 16

5 A tap drips three times every 10 seconds. How many times will it drip in a minute?
A 6 B 18 C 24 D 30

6 How far will a car travel in 3 hours if it has an average speed of 63 km/h?
A 21 km B 32 km C 66 km D 189 km

7 What is the average speed of a cyclist who travels 108 km in 4 hours?
A 27 km/h B 32 km/h
C 34 km/h D 35 km/h

8 How long will it take to travel 60 km at a speed of 15 km/h?
A 4 minutes B 45 minutes
C 3 hours D 4 hours

Use the table for questions 9, 10 and 11:

Distance	Speed	Time
200 km	40 km/h	X hours
180 km	Y km/h	2 hours
Z m	10 m/s	45 seconds

9 What replaces X in the table?
A 5 B 6 C 8 D 16

10 What replaces Y in the table?
A 360 B 45 C 90 D 182

11 What replaces Z in the table?
A 4.5 B 45 C 450 D 4500

12 Casey's parents give her $15 per week. She saves half of the money each week. How much will she save in 4 weeks?
A $30 B $60 C $7.50 D $35

13 A car can travel 100 kilometres on 8 litres of petrol. How many litres are used on a journey of 350 kilometres?
A 11.5 litres B 24 litres
C 28 litres D 30 litres

14 Exercise books cost $0.60. What would be the cost of 40 books?
A $2.40 B $24 C $32 D $36

15 When $200 is shared between Pete and Paul in the ratio of 2:3, how much money will Paul receive?
A $40 B $80 C $100 D $120

16 The ratio of dogs to cats is 3:4. If there are 36 dogs, how many cats are there?
A 12 B 16 C 27 D 48

17 A baker uses 400 grams of flour to make each loaf of bread. What mass of flour is needed to make 300 loaves of bread?
A 1.2 kg B 12 kg C 120 kg D 700 kg

18 There are 8 boys in the school choir. If there are twice as many girls than boys in the choir, what is the ratio of boys to total students in the choir?
A 1:3 B 1:8 C 2:3 D 2:1

19 The ratio of 10:15 is the same as
A 2:3 B 3:2 C 1:2 D 2:1

20 What is the ratio of shaded squares to unshaded?
A 1:2 B 1:1 C 6:1 D 1:6

☞ Explanations on pages 184-185

Answers: 1 C 2 B 3 C 4 D 5 B 6 D 7 A 8 D 9 A 10 C 11 C 12 A 13 C 14 B 15 D 16 D 17 C 18 A 19 A 20 B

NUMBER AND ALGEBRA
Chance, rates and ratio

1 **Probability** is the study of chance, measured as a fraction, decimal or percentage, and is expressed as a number from 0 to 1.

2 The probability of an event **P(E)** is written as

$$P(E) = \frac{\text{number of favourable outcomes}}{\text{number of possible outcomes}}$$

Example 1: A bag contains 4 red balls and 3 blue balls. If a ball is chosen at random, what is the chance that it is blue?

$P(\text{blue}) = \frac{3}{7}$ (or 3 in 7)

Example 2: Ten cards are numbered 1 to 10 and are placed in a bag. If one card is chosen at random, what is the probability that it is less than 5?

$P(\text{less than 5}) = \frac{4}{10}$ or $\frac{2}{5}$

Example 3: A box contains black and white balls. The probability of choosing a white ball at random is $\frac{3}{4}$. If there are 12 black balls in the bag, how many are white?

If $P(\text{white}) = \frac{3}{4}$, then $P(\text{black}) = \frac{1}{4}$.

As $\frac{1}{4}$ of the balls is 12, then $\frac{3}{4}$ of the balls is $3 \times 12 = 36$. There are 36 white balls.

3 A **rate** is a comparison of quantities of different units.

Example: In 20 weeks Kevin is paid \$13 460. What is his weekly pay rate?

Pay rate = 13 460 ÷ 20
= 1346 ÷ 2
= 673 ∴ \$673 per week.

4 **Speed** relates distance and time:

$\text{Speed} = \frac{\text{Distance}}{\text{Time}}$ $\text{Time} = \frac{\text{Distance}}{\text{Speed}}$

Distance = Speed × Time

Example 1: Find the speed of a motorist if she travels 200 km in 4 hours.

$\text{Speed} = \frac{200}{4} = 50$ ∴ 50 km/h

Example 2: How far will a plane travel in 6 hours if it has an average speed of 700 km/h?

Distance = 700 × 6 = 4200 ∴ 4200 km

Example 3: Jennifer leaves Adlington at 11 am and travels 240 km to Bledston at an average speed of 60 km/h. At what time will Jennifer arrive at Bledston?

$\text{Time} = \frac{240}{60} = 4$ ∴ 4 hours

Jennifer arrives at 11 am + 4 hours = 3 pm.

5 A **ratio** is a comparison between quantities of the same units. The ratio of 'a to b' is written as a : b, but can also be written as a fraction as $\frac{a}{b}$. **Ratios can be simplified** in a similar way to fractions.

Example 1: Simplify 12:16
Dividing each by 4, 12:16 = 3:4

Example 2: Simplify \$3.50 : \$5
Rewriting in cents, 350:500 = 35:50 = 7:10

6 **Quantities** can be divided in a given ratio.

Example: Share \$600 in the ratio of 3 : 2.
As 3 + 2 = 5, use fractions to find each amount.

$\frac{3}{5} \times 600 = 600 \div 5 \times 3 = 120 \times 3 = 360$

$\frac{2}{5} \times 600 = 600 \div 5 \times 2 = 120 \times 2 = 240$

The amounts are \$360 and \$240.

7 The **unitary method** can be used to solve some ratio problems.

Example 1: The ratio of rainy days to dry days throughout a holiday was 2:5. If there were 10 rainy days, how many were dry days?
As 'rainy' and '2' are mentioned first,
2 parts = 10
1 part = 10 ÷ 2 = 5
5 parts = 5 × 5 = 25
This means 25 dry days.

Example 2: The ratio of populations of towns A and B is 4:9. If town B has a population of 450, what is the population of town A?
9 parts = 450
1 part = 450 ÷ 9 = 50
4 parts = 50 × 4 = 200
This means town A has 200 people.

NUMBER AND ALGEBRA
Chance, rates and ratio

1. There are 40 marbles in a bag. Eight of the marbles are red and twelve are blue. The rest of the marbles are green. If a marble is chosen at random from the bag, what is the chance that it is green? *Hint 1*
   A 1 in 2 B 1 in 3 C 2 in 5 D 1 in 4

2. The letters of the word ISOSCELES are written on nine identical cards and placed in a bag. One card is chosen at random. What is the chance that it is an E?
   A 1 in 2 B 1 in 3 C 2 in 7 D 2 in 9

3. The table shows the colours of balls in a bag.

Colour	red	blue	yellow	green
Balls	12	4	2	6

   A ball is chosen from the bag at random. What is the chance that it is not blue?
   A 1 in 6 B 1 in 4 C 3 in 4 D 5 in 6

4. In a class there are 12 boys and 18 girls. If a student is chosen at random, what is the probability that the student is a boy?
   A $\frac{1}{2}$ B $\frac{1}{3}$ C $\frac{2}{5}$ D $\frac{3}{5}$

5. A bag contains 3 red balls and 2 blue balls. If a ball is chosen at random, what is the probability that it is blue?
   A 0.2 B 0.3 C 0.4 D 0.6

6. A bag contains 14 red, 7 blue, 8 green and 11 black jelly beans. If a jelly bean is taken from the bag, what is the chance that it is green?
   A $\frac{1}{5}$ B $\frac{1}{8}$ C $\frac{8}{41}$ D $\frac{5}{8}$

7. Belinda has given birth to three children. What is the chance that she has a girl and two boys? *Hint 2*
   A 1 in 8 B 2 in 8 C 3 in 8 D 4 in 8

8. Sowmya drove $4\frac{1}{2}$ hours at an average speed of 80 km/h. How far did she travel?
   Write your answer in the box: ☐ km

9. Bintang travelled 360 kilometres in 6 hours. She had travelled the first 2 hours at an average speed of 80 km/h. At what speed did she then travel to complete her journey?
   A 40 km/h B 50 km/h
   C 60 km/h D 70 km/h

10. Jack's car uses petrol at the rate of 9 litres per 100 kilometres. The petrol cost him 129.9 cents per litre. What calculation is used to find the cost of petrol, in dollars, for Jack to travel 200 kilometres?
    A $9 \times 2 \times 1.299$ B $9 \times 2 \times 129.9$
    C $9 \div 2 \times 129.9$ D $9 \div 2 \times 1.299$

11. James uses a small quantity of LawnKleen in a bucket of water to improve his lawn. He adds 10 mL of LawnKleen to 10 Litres of water. What is the ratio of LawnKleen to water?
    A 1:1 B 100:1 C 1:10 D 1:1000

12. In a town, the ratio of adults to children is 5:3. If the town has a population of 600, how many children live in the town? ☐

13. The ratio of boys to girls on a camp is 5:2. If there are 70 boys on the camp, how many girls are there?
    A 18 B 20 C 24 D 28

14. A shopkeeper found that the ratio of masses of oranges to lemons to mandarins sold is 3:1:4. If sales totalled 120 kilograms, what mass of oranges were sold?
    A 15 kg B 30 kg C 45 kg D 60 kg

15. The diagram shows a line divided into equal intervals. What is the ratio of RU to PS?

    P Q R S T U

    A 1:1 B 1:3 C 3:1 D 3:4

16. A bag contains 20 balls. There are red balls and blue balls in the bag in the ratio of 3:2. What is the smallest number of balls that can be added so that there are more blue balls than red balls in the bag?
    A 1 B 2 C 4 D 5

Hint 1: First find the number of green marbles in the bag.
Hint 2: There are 8 possibilities for 3 children—if boy (B) and girl (G): BBB, BBG, BGB, BGG, GGG, GGB, GBG, GBB.

☞ **Answers and explanations on pages 185–186**

NUMBER AND ALGEBRA
Using the calculator

1 What is the value of $(12 - 6) \times (2 + 2)$?
A 2 B 14 C 24 D 26

2 Find $11 - 9 \div (6 - 3)$.
A 4 B 6 C 7 D 8

3 What is the answer to $\frac{10 + 6}{2 + 2}$?
A 4 B 6 C 15 D 16

4 Evaluate $\frac{24}{4 + 2}$.
A 8 B 2 C 4 D 12

5 Evaluate $\frac{12 - 8}{2 + 6}$.
A 0.2 B 0.25 C 0.5 D 14

6 $\sqrt{9 + 16} = ?$
A 7 B 5 C 12 D 25

7 What is the average of 2, 8, 11 and 7?
A 4 B 8 C 9 D 7

8 Find the average of 0.3 and 4.5.
A 2.4 B 1.5 C 4.2 D 4.8

9 What is $\frac{5}{8}$ written as a percentage?
A 58% B 6.25% C 62.5% D 85%

10 What is the square root of 441?
A 21 B 23 C 29 D 31

11 $\sqrt{12.96} = ?$
A 6.48 B 6.92 C 3.6 D 2.88

12 $12 \times \square = 85.2$
The missing number is
A 7.1 B 8.3 C 7.6 D 8.6

13 $28 \div \square = 11.2$
The missing number is
A 2.4 B 1.4 C 1.8 D 2.5

14 What is 2.3^2?
A 5.3 B 5.29 C 4.6 D 4.9

15 What is the square root of the sum of 5^2 and 12^2?
A 17 B 13 C 8.5 D 9.5

16 What is the difference between 3 and –8?
A 5 B –5 C 11 D –11

17 Simplify the fraction $\frac{18}{48}$.
A $\frac{1}{4}$ B $\frac{1}{8}$ C $\frac{3}{8}$ D $\frac{5}{8}$

18 Express $\frac{23}{5}$ as a mixed numeral.
A $4\frac{3}{5}$ B $3\frac{4}{5}$ C $3\frac{1}{8}$ D $3\frac{2}{5}$

19 Find the sum of $\frac{4}{5}$ and $\frac{3}{10}$.
A 1.01 B 1.1 C 1.2 D 1.7

20 What is the middle of $1\frac{1}{4}$ and $2\frac{3}{4}$?
A 2 B 2.25 C 2.125 D 1.875

21 What is the average of $\frac{2}{5}$, $\frac{1}{4}$, $\frac{3}{4}$ and $\frac{1}{2}$?
A 1.9 B 0.475 C 1.525 D 0.45

22 $4 \div \frac{2}{3} = ?$
A 1.5 B 4.5 C 5 D 6

23 Calculate $2 \times \pi \times 6$, correct to 2 decimal places.
A 36.00 B 37.68 C 37.69 D 37.70

24 What is $\pi \times 4^2$ to 2 decimal places?
A 50.27 B 50.26 C 25.13 D 25.14

25 Find the value of $\pi \times 5^2 \times 8$, to the nearest whole number.
A 627 B 628 C 629 D 630

☞ Explanations on pages 186–187

Answers: 1 C 2 D 3 A 4 C 5 C 6 B 7 D 8 A 9 C 10 A 11 C 12 A 13 D
14 B 15 B 16 C 17 C 18 A 19 B 20 A 21 B 22 D 23 D 24 A 25 B

NUMBER AND ALGEBRA
Using the calculator

1 Use the **brackets** (grouping) symbols (and) to help with the order of operations.

Example 1: Find the value of $\frac{4 + 4 \times 4}{4}$

[pressing (4 + 4 × 4) ÷ 4 =]

Therefore $\frac{4 + 4 \times 4}{4} = 5$.

Example 2: Evaluate $\frac{16 - 4}{5 + 7}$

[pressing (16 – 4) ÷ (5 + 7) =]

Therefore $\frac{16 - 4}{5 + 7} = 1$.

Example 3: Find the average of 14, 87, 53 and 190.

[pressing (14 + 87 + 53 + 190) ÷ 4 =]

$$\text{Average} = \frac{14 + 87 + 53 + 190}{4} = 86$$

Therefore the average is 86.

2 On the online NAPLAN calculator, the **square root** key is pressed before the number, or expression, is entered.

Example 1: Find the answer, correct to 2 decimal places: $\sqrt{781.23} = ?$

[pressing √ 781.23 =]

Therefore $\sqrt{781.23} = 27.95$ [correct to 2 decimal places]

Example 2: $\sqrt{12.6 \times 8.02} = ?$

[pressing √ (12.6 × 8.02) =]

Therefore $\sqrt{12.6 \times 8.02} = 10.05$ [correct to 2 decimal places]

Example 3: $\frac{4}{\sqrt{3.6 - 1.7}} = ?$

[pressing 4 ÷ √ (3.6 – 1.7) =]

Therefore $\frac{4}{\sqrt{3.6 - 1.7}} = 2.90$ [correct to 2 decimal places]

3 When **squaring** a number, either multiply the number by itself or use the x^2 button.

Example: Find the value of 13.8^2

[pressing 13.8 x^2 =]

Therefore $13.8^2 = 190.44$

4 **Negative numbers** are entered into the calculator using (–).

Example: Find the value of $4 - (-3)^2$.

[pressing 4 – (–) 3 x^2 =]

Therefore $4 - (-3)^2 = -5$.

5 There is no separate fractions key on the online NAPLAN calculator. A fraction can be represented using the division key.

Example 1: Find $\frac{3}{10}$ of 750.

[pressing 3 ÷ 10 × 750 =]

Therefore $\frac{3}{10}$ of 750 = 225.

Example 2: What is the difference between $\frac{3}{4}$ and $\frac{2}{5}$?

[pressing 3 ÷ 4 – 2 ÷ 5 =]

Therefore the difference is $0.35 = \frac{7}{20}$.

Example 3: What is the middle of $\frac{1}{4}$ and $\frac{3}{10}$?

[pressing (1 ÷ 4 + 3 ÷ 10) ÷ 2 =]

$$\text{Middle} = 0.275 = \frac{275}{1000} = \frac{11}{40}$$

6 The **pi** (π) button π is used when finding the circumference and area of a circle.

Example: The area of a circle is found using the formula $A = \pi r^2$. Find the area of a circle with a radius of 8 cm, correct to 2 decimal places.

[pressing π × 8 x^2 =]

Therefore $\pi \times 8^2 = 201.06$ [correct to 2 decimal places] ∴ area is 201.06 cm^2.

NUMBER AND ALGEBRA
Using the calculator

1 In a recent census, the town of Balgal had a population of 13 876. If there were 2941 fewer people living in the town of Voss, what is the population of Voss?
A 10 827 B 10 935 C 16 815 D 16 817

2 Every morning Jamie jogs $1\frac{3}{4}$ kilometres. What is the total distance he runs in 2 mornings?
A $2\frac{6}{8}$ kilometres B $3\frac{1}{4}$ kilometres
C $3\frac{1}{2}$ kilometres D $3\frac{3}{4}$ kilometres

3 18 × ☐ = 8 *Hint 1*
What is the missing number?
A 0.75 B $0.\dot{2}$ C $0.\dot{4}$ D 2.25

4

Top	4	8	12	14
Bottom	1	2	3	

What is the missing number in the table?
Hint 2
A 3.25 B 3.5 C 3.75 D 4

5 What is the value of 260 – (160 + 50 + 25)?
A 25 B 35 C 165 D 175

6 Teri multiplied 48 by 0.93. What is Teri's answer?
A 44.46 B 44.64 C 47.07 D 48.93

7 Evaluate 180 – (25 + 25).
Write your answer in the box: ☐

8 Minh used her calculator to find the answer to $\frac{\pi \times 3^2 \times 8}{5}$. What is Minh's answer to the nearest whole number?
A 30 B 42 C 45 D 121

9 Find the value of $\frac{6^2}{9 \times 4}$. *Hint 3*
A 1 B 4 C 8 D 16

10 The daily maximum temperatures over a long weekend were –6°, –3° and 3°. What was the average maximum temperature?
A –3° B –2° C –1° D 3°

11 What is the product of –4 and –5?
A 1 B –9 C –20 D 20

12 Fiona is making pumpkin soup. Her recipe requires $1\frac{3}{4}$ kilograms of pumpkin and will make 4 servings. If Fiona increases all of her ingredients to make 12 servings, what mass of pumpkin is required?
A 3.75 kg B 4.25 kg C 4.75 kg D 5.25 kg

13 12 out of 27 people surveyed have flown overseas. The percentage of people surveyed that have **not** flown overseas is closest to
A 55%. B 56%. C 44%. D 45%.

14 Leno wrote 4050 as a product of prime factors. Which of the following is his answer?
Hint 4
A $2^4 \times 5^2 \times 3$ B $2^4 \times 10^2 \times 5$
C $3^4 \times 5^2 \times 2$ D $3^3 \times 5^2 \times 2^2$

15 Bianca wrote the following $\frac{2}{x} < \frac{3}{5}$.
Which two of these are possible values of x?
Hint 5
A 2 B 3 C 4 D 5

16 What is the best estimate for the area of a circular playground with a diameter of 6 metres? *Hint 6*
A 24 m² B 28 m² C 48 m² D 56 m²

Hint 1: The opposite, or inverse, operation of multiplication is division.
Hint 2: First find the pattern, or rule, that links the top and bottom numbers in the other pairs of numbers in the table.
Hint 3: Use the brackets (grouping symbol) buttons on the calculator.
Hint 4: A prime has only two factors: itself and 1.
Hint 5: Fractions are easily compared when they are rewritten with the same denominators.
Hint 6: Area of circle is πr^2.

☞ Answers and explanations on page 187

SPELLING

Plural nouns and singular verbs, root words, compound words, irregular spelling patterns, and multi-syllable words

Key Points

Good spelling isn't just about having a good memory, rather it's about memory supported by understanding. To help you become a better speller you should become familiar with the patterns and conventions of spelling. To be a great speller you need to know how to sound a word out (this requires an understanding of the relationship between sounds and letters) and also the small units of meaning used to make up the word (these are called morphemes).

To understand morphology (this big word just means the study of the structure of words) you need to be able to identify root words, compound words, prefixes and suffixes.

1. **Root words** are simple words that can't be broken into parts.
   Examples: cat, jump, man
   You learn how to spell these by sounding them out, although there are some special cases that need to be learned from memory, such as 'taught'.

2. **Compound words** are formed by combining two root words.
   Examples: ant + eater = anteater, thumb + print = thumbprint, hand + bag = handbag

3. The most common **suffix** that you will use is the suffix 's' to change a noun from singular to plural. For most nouns you simply add 's'.
   Examples: relationship → relationships, catalogue → catalogues

   Again, there are a couple of exceptions to this rule that you must learn, especially when trying to spell words that are unfamiliar to you. Most nouns that end in 'o' add an 'e' before adding the suffix 's'. This will help you correctly spell some of those frequently misspelled and annoying words such as 'potato' and 'hero'.
   Examples: innuendo → innuendoes, hero → heroes

   Also, nouns that end in 's', 'ss', 'sh', 'ch' and 'x' add 'es' to make the plural.
   Examples: fox → foxes, beach → beaches, dish → dishes, glass → glasses, bus → buses

   Finally, some nouns that end in 'f' change the 'f' to 'v' before adding the suffix 'es' to make the plural. *Example:* leaf → leaves

4. The words most people spell incorrectly are often longer words. These are referred to as **multi-syllable words**. Students often find these words both hard to read and hard to spell. To overcome these problems, and to give yourself a greater chance of spelling success, you must break multi-syllable words into smaller parts by sounding them out into their phonemes. Remember that each syllable contains a vowel (a, e, i, o ,u) or vowel-sounding letters such as 'y'.
   Examples: organism → or-gan-is-m, protective → pro-tec-tive

   Some common multi-syllable words are: consequence, permanent, atmosphere, imaginary, argument, explanation, accommodation, perspective, presentation, processor, classification, personification, paragraph, exclamation, vocabulary.

5. While it is possible to sound out most words into smaller chunks (e.g. intelligent → in-tell-i-gent), **some words cannot be sounded out** in this way and this causes spelling mistakes. This is because some words are not spelt the way they sound when spoken, so you need to learn these and remember them.
   Words that you may come across that have irregular spelling patterns include: phantom, rhyme, antique, pharaoh, physical, often, comfortable, enough, something, people, almost, another, answer, know.

SPELLING

Plural nouns and singular verbs, root words, compound words, irregular spelling patterns, and multi-syllable words

Test Your Skills

Learn the words below. A common method of learning and self-testing is the LOOK, SAY, COVER, WRITE, CHECK method. If you make any mistakes, you should rewrite the word three times correctly, immediately. In this way you will become familiar with the correct spelling. If the word is particularly troublesome, rewrite it several more times or keep a list of words that you can check regularly.

This week's theme word: SCIENCE

nutrient	________________	colleague	________________
nutrients	________________	answer	________________
hazard	________________	succinct	________________
hazards	________________	elicit	________________
combustion	________________	dinosaur	________________
condensation	________________	bureau	________________
vertebrate	________________	cough	________________
digestion	________________	exhibit	________________
predator	________________	stomach	________________
predators	________________	stomaches	________________
blowtorch	________________	workbench	________________
bench	________________	guess	________________
benches	________________	guesses	________________
reflex	________________	larynx	________________
reflexes	________________	larynxes	________________

Write any troublesome words three times.

________________ ________________ ________________

________________ ________________ ________________

SPELLING
Common misspellings

Please ask your parent or teacher to read to you the spelling words on page 249.
Write the correct spelling of each word in the box.

1 The ______ was unsuitable for my family, so we left.

2 The ______ caused horrific burns to the young girl's face and hands.

3 I confessed to my best friend that I still enjoy listening to nursery ______.

4 Harry, it is of extreme urgency that you turn the ______ down!

5 ______ those two uncontrollable children at once!

6 I was tempted by the ______ cake that sat on the kitchen table.

7 The chair was lovely and ______; nothing could move me.

8 The delicate ______ of the dancers was seamless.

9 I was thoroughly impressed by the ______ of the engineers.

10 The ______ played happily outside whilst Sejong ate lunch.

11 The teacher said to use ______ to create imagery.

12 The ______ for the pizza looked delicious.

13 Twenty large ______ arrived at my house, each containing a surprise.

14 The ______ of the small family made me sad and frustrated.

15 Love is a ______ I never want to catch!

The spelling mistakes in these sentences have been underlined.
Write the correct spelling for each underlined word in the box.

16 The day will be sunny according to the <u>Bureuw</u> of Meteorology.

17 Many <u>organismes</u> aid in the digestion of food.

18 The girl refused to make a <u>comittment</u> to her boyfriend.

19 The playwright tried to create a <u>humourous</u> play but failed.

20 The swift <u>evaparashion</u> of the water on the deck was caused by the sun.

☞ Answers on pages 187-188

SPELLING
Common misspellings

Each sentence has one word that is incorrect.
Write the correct spelling of the word in the box.

21. There are severe consiquenses for breaking the law, Ji's father warned.

22. I don't believe all the government propogander, it's all lies.

23. Frank, with the oily black hair, is my collegue at the bank.

24. Jonny took posesion of the ball and, swerving around the winger, scored!

25. The shop sold missillanious novelties such as pretty fairies sitting on frogs.

☞ Answers on page 188

GRAMMAR AND PUNCTUATION
Types of nouns, adjectives, adverbs, verbs and participles

Key Points

1. There are four main types of **nouns**.
   a **Common nouns** are the names of things.
   Examples: laboratory, cathedral, theatre
   b **Abstract nouns** are the names of concepts.
   Examples: prejudice, commitment, poverty
   c **Proper nouns** are the names of particular people, places or things. Proper nouns begin with a capital letter.
   Examples: Central Park, George Orwell, Wednesday
   d **Collective nouns** are words that define a group of things such as people, animals or emotions. Collective nouns can be general, such as the collective noun 'group' for a 'group of friends', or they can be specific such as the collective noun 'murder' for a 'group of crows'.
   Examples: a <u>parliament</u> of owls, a <u>crowd</u> of onlookers, a <u>wash</u> of emotions
   Note: a collective noun is singular if it refers to just one group.

2. **Adjectives** are words that provide us with more information about nouns or describe them.
   Examples: clever Orwell, unacceptable prejudice, radiant cathedral, the poverty is depressing
   a **Proper adjectives** are formed from proper nouns.
   Examples: Orwell → Orwellian, Shakespeare → Shakespearean
   b Adjectives have three **degrees of comparison**.
   Examples: Keenan is hilarious. (One person is funny.)
   Balin is funnier than Keenan. (Two people are compared.)
   Lee is the cleverest person in the group. (Three or more people are compared.)
   c For longer words the convention is to add '**more**' or '**most**' to show **degree**.
   Examples: glamorous → more glamorous → most glamorous;
   obnoxious → more obnoxious → most obnoxious
   d Many adjectives have **opposites**: words with an opposite meaning.
   Examples: rebellious → conservative, outgoing → reserved, naive → sophisticated

3. **Adverbs** add greater meaning to verbs.
   a They inform us how, when, where or to what extent something happened. It is easy to identify an adverb because most end with the suffix 'ly'.
   Examples: independently, sincerely, generously, insightfully, marginally
   b **Adverbial phrases** often don't use adverbs. However, they function in the same way to provide information about how, when, where or to what extent something happened.
   Examples: I'll be home <u>in an hour</u>, I'll be home <u>next Thursday</u>, I'll be home <u>when I've finished rehearsing with the band</u>

4. **Verbs** are often called 'doing words' as they provide the action of a sentence or clause and present to us a sense of what is happening. 'Doing' verbs include verbs for performing actions, thinking and speaking.
   Examples: contemplate, improvise, narrate, exclaim
   a Some verbs are used to **express a thought or feeling**.
   Examples: engage, embarrass, disappoint, evaluate, concentrate
   b Verbs indicate **tense** by altering their form. There are three basic or simple tenses: **past**, **present** and **future**.

GRAMMAR AND PUNCTUATION
Types of nouns, adjectives, adverbs, verbs and participles

Examples: She divulged the secret (past); She is divulging the secret (present); She will divulge the secret (future)

c There are two types of participles: **present participles** and **past participles**. Participles are forms taken by verbs to indicate their tense. Participle verbs need 'helper verbs' to form complete verbs. 'Helper' verbs include *am, are, is, was, were, has, have* and *had*.
Examples: was manoeuvring, had referenced, is classified, was colonised, is exclaiming

d **Finite verbs** (or complete verbs) are verbs that can form a complete sentence when combined with a subject.
Example: Josie deliberates (verb—deliberates; subject—Josie)
Non-finite verbs are derived from other parts of speech. They cannot stand alone.
Example: to see (It was the film to see.)

Test Your Skills

1 Name the types of nouns for each of the words below.
a erosion ________ b landscape ____________ c choir __________ d instrument ___________
e November ____________ f portfolio ____________ g Tokyo ____________ h virus ___________

2 Underline the verbs in the sentences below.
a She agonised over the decision that she knew could cost her precious time.
b Entering the long, dark hallway he became conscious of the rhythmic beating of his heart.

3 What adjectives can be made from these proper nouns?
a Germany ______________ b Canada __________________ c Tasmania ____________________
d Europe _______________ e Elizabeth _______________ f Victoria ____________________

4 Circle the correct participle in the sentences below.
a Jackson and James (was, were, is) taking their little brother Johnny to the fair.
b Mr Jones (would have, will have, has) delivered the present had he been asked.

5 Underline the adverbial phrase in the sentences below.
a Trisha went to the shops last Thursday.
b David will return home after he visits his grandson.

6 Underline the adverbs in the sentence below.
The young soldier marched steadily and stared expressionlessly as he headed towards the temple.

Answers: 1 a abstract b common c collective d common e proper f common g proper h common 2 a agonised, knew, cost b Entering, became, beating 3 German, Canadian, Tasmanian, European, Elizabethan, Victorian 4 a were b would have 5 a last Thursday b after he visits his grandson 6 steadily, expressionlessly

GRAMMAR AND PUNCTUATION
Types of nouns, adjectives, adverbs, verbs and participles

1. Which of the following sentences has the correct punctuation?
   - A Betty asked, 'Where are you going Jane?'
   - B Betty asked. 'Where are you going Jane?'
   - C Betty asked 'Where are you going Jane?'
   - D Betty asked 'Where are you going Jane.'

2. Waking with a start, Jenny saw a thin mist hovering over her head like a lost cloud.
   The phrase 'like a lost cloud' is an example of
   - A a simile.
   - B a metaphor.
   - C personification.
   - D onomatopoeia.

3. Which of the following words correctly completes this sentence?
   The research team ______ answers to their questions.

has discover	would discover	will discover	discovers
A	B	C	D

4. Which of the following words correctly completes this sentence?
   Long jump was so ______ the children didn't want to participate.

far	long	difficult	longest
A	B	C	D

5. Which of the following words correctly completes this sentence?
   George Orwell ______ both *1984* and *Animal Farm*.

writes	writ	wrode	wrote
A	B	C	D

6. Which sentence has the correct punctuation?
   - A Professor Harvey, the one with the grey hair, is my favourite.
   - B Professor Harvey the one, with the grey hair, is my favourite.
   - C Professor Harvey, the one with the grey hair is my favourite.
   - D Professor Harvey the one with the grey hair is my favourite.

7. Which sentence has the correct punctuation?
   - A 'Get back here!', screamed Mum.
   - B Get back here! Screamed Mum.
   - C 'Get back here!' Screamed Mum.
   - D 'Get back here!' screamed Mum.

8. Which sentence has the correct punctuation?
   - A We need: five roses; six carnations; seven lilies and eight tulips.
   - B We need; five roses; six carnations; seven lilies and eight tulips.
   - C We need five roses six carnations seven lilies and eight tulips.
   - D We need: five roses: six carnations: seven lilies and eight tulips?

☞ **Answers and explanations on pages 188–190**

GRAMMAR AND PUNCTUATION
Types of nouns, adjectives, adverbs, verbs and participles

9 Which sentence has the correct punctuation?
- A Disaster struck at 9.29 pm, the boat hit an iceberg.
- B Disaster struck at 9.29 pm? The boat hit an iceberg.
- C Disaster struck at 9.29 pm; the boat hit an iceberg.
- D Disaster struck at 9.29 pm: the boat hit an iceberg.

10 Which sentence has the correct punctuation?
- A James who happens to be my brother, was the best performer in the play.
- B James, who happens to be my brother, was the best performer in the play.
- C James who happens to be my brother was the best performer in the play.
- D James, who happens to be my brother was the best performer in the play?

11 William Shakespeare is the greatest writer in the English language.

This text is written in the
- A first person.
- B second person.
- C third person.

12 The name Dracula strikes fear in the hearts of many as it conjures images of vampires, blood and violent death.

The phrase 'strikes fear in the hearts of many' is an example of
- A personification.
- B metaphor.
- C alliteration.

13 Then all of a sudden she let out a shrill cry and the mist vanished.

This text has been written in the
- A present tense.
- B past tense.
- C future tense.

Write the word or words in the box to correctly complete the sentences below.

14 Sean ______ if he had any money.

would not gone	will have gone	have gone	would have gone
A	B	C	D

15 The delivery driver made ______ mistake by delivering those dresses to the warehouse.

a	the	an	and
A	B	C	D

16 The worshippers looked at the statue ______.

with loving	lovingly	with lovingly	really lovely
A	B	C	D

☞ Answers and explanations on pages 188–190

GRAMMAR AND PUNCTUATION
Types of nouns, adjectives, adverbs, verbs and participles

Highlight the correct answer in the sentences below.

17 Shade one circle to show where the missing apostrophe (') should go.

Janet(A)s father enjoy(B)s watching the horse race(C)s.

18 Which contraction is used correctly in this sentence?

The dogs <u>we're</u> (A) in trouble with their owners; <u>they'd</u> (B) eaten all of the balls left in <u>they're</u> (C) yard.

19 Which underlined word in this text is an adjective?

Fairy penguins are often difficult to spot as they like <u>hiding</u> inside rocky caves <u>during</u> the day. Sometimes, if you're lucky, you might spot one <u>racing</u> across the sand as they leap into the <u>crashing</u> waves.

hiding	during	racing	crashing
A	B	C	D

20 He would craft his lines so that the most important words were on the heavy beat and this helped his audience hear these words spoken by the unamplified voices of the actors.

In this sentence, the word 'craft' is used as

A a noun. B a verb. C an adjective.

21 Bram Stoker used these myths about Vlad the Impaler to create his enduring and frightening character.

In this sentence, the word *frightening* is used as

A a verb. B an adverb. C an adjective. D a noun

22 In the sentence 'Stoker drew his inspiration for Count Dracula from the infamous historical figure Vlad the Impaler', the word 'inspiration' is

A a collective noun. B an abstract noun. C a verb. D an adjective.

23 Waking with a start, Jenny saw a thin mist hovering over her head like a lost cloud.

In the sentence, the word 'saw' is

A an adjective. B a noun. C a verb. D an adverb.

24 Which two phrases each complete this sentence so that it makes sense?

________________________, you should exercise every day.

A It is always exhausting
B Whether you feel like it or not
C There is not enough time
D If you want to remain fit

25 Which two phrases each complete this sentence so that it makes sense?

________________________, sunrise is a beautiful time of day.

A Whether you are a morning person or not
B Being slow means you miss out
C Even in the middle of winter
D There is nothing more stunning

☞ Answers and explanations on pages 188–190

READING
Understanding narratives

A narrative is a form of prose writing that tells a story. Its main purpose is to entertain.

Writers of narratives create experiences that are shared with the reader. To do this the writer uses literary techniques such as figurative language (similes and metaphors), variety in sentence length and type, variety in paragraph length and direct speech.

Most narratives are in either the first or third person. When a narrative is in the first person, the author is the creator of the story. The character (first person: *I*) telling the story is referred to as the narrator.

Read this extract from *The Lock Out* by Colin Thiele and answer the questions.

The Lock Out

'Not there! Shoo! Ahh, for Pete's sake!' Jim hastily flicked off the light switch to avoid being exposed to public view, swept the animal up in his hands and ducked through the door.

'Out you go, whether you like it or not!' He ran across the veranda with his bare feet and tossed the cat gently into the garden.

'Off you go! Shoo!'

As he turned to slip back inside again the breeze stirred; the hibiscus swayed by the steps, and the shadows moved in the streetlights. Then gently, very gently, the front door swung shut and the latch sprang into the lock with a soft click. Horrified, Jim ran to the door, pushing and heaving. But he was too late. He was locked out. Locked out of his own house, at midnight, without any clothes on.

For a second or two he cowered, appalled, in the corner of the veranda. But what had seemed so dim and secluded at first soon became more and more exposed as his eyes became accustomed to the dark. Luckily, there was nobody about. The street was deserted, the neighbours were all in bed. Although Jim's mind was strangely numb, one thought charged about in it like a bull in a yard. He had to get back inside—this instant, before anyone saw him.

His only hope was an unlatched window. He skirted the hibiscus bush in the corner of the garden and made for the dining room. It looked out over the front lawn and held a long view up the curve of the street, but at least there was an off chance that the window there might be unlocked. As he stepped on to the soft grass of the lawn he was astonished to find himself walking on tip-toe. For a second he was vaguely aware of his own tension, a kind of catching himself by surprise before he plunged off across the grass.

For the first three strides the spring of the lawn under his feet was urgently pleasant, but at the fourth step he trod sharply on the garden hose, not thirty centimetres from the end near the sprinkler, and a squirt of water shot out like an icy shock. He leapt up with a noisy gasp and ran to the window, but it was locked.

From *The Hijacked Bathtub and other funny stories*, compiled by Michael Dugan, Georgian House, 1988

READING
Understanding narratives

1 What did Jim feel when he heard the soft click of the door?
A panic B surprise C hopelessness D confusion

2 Jim's greatest concern was
A not being able to find a key.
B that it was midnight.
C being seen without any clothes on.
D that all the neighbours were in bed.

3 In which order did Jim do these things? Number the events from 1 to 5.
☐ tried to force the door
☐ cowered on the veranda
☐ walked tip-toe across the lawn
☐ tried to open a window
☐ became aware of moving shadows

4 The most likely reason Jim walked across the lawn on tip-toe was because he
A was unconsciously trying not to draw attention to himself.
B didn't like the feel of the grass under his bare feet.
C was aware that he might step on the garden hose.
D didn't want his feet to get cold.

5 The author states that, for Jim, one thought 'charged ... about like a bull in a yard', (paragraph 5). By this the author is suggesting that Jim
A had a wild idea for getting back into the house.
B was preoccupied about being attacked.
C had only one thought—it was for a change of luck.
D was not thinking logically.

6 Jim left the safety of his house because he had
A to retrieve his clothes.
B to check that the kitchen window was locked.
C decided to put the cat out into the garden.
D to see if the neighbours were asleep.

7 What did Jim realise while he was on the veranda?
A He would have to wait until morning to get back inside.
B It wasn't as dark as he first thought.
C There were strange shadows by the hibiscus plant.
D The streetlights lit up the curve of the street.

8 Which word describes the atmosphere built up by the description of Jim's plight? You may circle more than one option.

determination	desperation	resignation	frustration	desolation
A	B	C	D	E

9 What is the most likely reason that Jim wanted the cat outside?
A Jim was ready for bed.
B The cat was not meant to be inside.
C The cat had made a mess in the house.
D It was not Jim's cat.

Answers: 1 A 2 C 3 2, 3, 4, 5, 1 4 A 5 D 6 C 7 B 8 B, D 9 C

☞ Explanations on page 190

READING
Understanding narratives

Read this extract from *Angel's Gate* by Gary Crew and answer the questions.
In this extract the narrator's name is Kim.

We climbed the track for the second time. At the point where it opened into the clearing, Bobby stopped and looked up. He was watching the homecoming bats. They seemed to swoop from the sky directly above us, hover uncertainly, then vanish into the face of the rock.

Bobby turned to me and pointed. 'There,' he whispered.

We circled the clearing under cover of the rocks. All the while I kept my eye on the spot where the bats had disappeared. I knew one thing: if they could fly in, something else could come out.

When we had completed our circuit, Bobby watched the bats at closer range. They vanished beneath a ledge about 5 metres away. One of the fig trees sprouted from the rocks, and somewhere among its roots, deep in the dark shadow of the ledge, was the entrance to a cave.

With one signal only—a finger to his lips—Bobby dropped to his knees and crawled closer. At the clump of the roots he stretched up into the dark. A bat beating down struck him hard on the back; others veered away suddenly to circle the clearing. Then he was gone.

The fear that had come over me the night before began to return. The same dryness in my mouth; the same weakness in my knees. Even though it was almost daylight, I was shivering. I said to myself, over and over, 'Stop it, stupid. Stop it ...'

I was still saying this as I pulled myself up into the clump of roots. The opening to the cave appeared right in front of me: a yawning black hole, splotched white all over with the droppings of the bats. I had to go in, that was all there was to it.

At first, there was a dark tunnel. Pitch black and terrible, but it widened, and a sickly grey light penetrated, growing brighter and brighter the further I went in. I must have crawled 20 metres before I was able to get to my feet and reach up to touch the roof.

The tunnel ended in what seemed to be full daylight. I guessed that this had been a proper cave, and much longer, but years before the roof must have fallen in and now the sun broke through, at least in places.

I saw Bobby when I reached the light. He was standing on the edge of what seemed like a well. Here the floor of the cave must have collapsed at the same time as the roof, leaving a hole that seemed bottomless. Bats flitted in the void.

From *Angel's Gate* by Gary Crew, Wiliam Heinemann Australia, 1993

1 The cave's entrance was

A high above the two boys' position.
B hidden behind the roots of a fig tree.
C blocked by a rock fall.
D just big enough to crawl through.

2 Draw a line between the two words that describe how Kim feels as he enters the cave.

impulsive	wary
hesitant	annoyed
reluctant	relaxed
undaunted	game

READING
Understanding narratives

3 In narratives, events tend to happen in chronological order. When the narrator climbed into the clump of roots he

A started to shiver.
B saw Bobby standing in dim light deep in the cave.
C was hit on the back by a flying bat.
D got down low and began crawling through the cave.

4 The writer describes the hole as a 'yawning black hole' (paragraph 7). By this he means the hole was

A high up the side of the mountain.
B creating a soft windy sound.
C round and wide open at the entrance.
D about the size of a person's mouth.

5 What is the main reason Kim followed Bobby into the cave? Write your answer on the lines.

____

____

6 Kim, the narrator, has this thought about the cave bats: 'I knew one thing: if they could fly in, something else could come out' (paragraph 3). This suggests that Kim

A knew the cave had a dead end.
B expected the entrance to the cave to be much larger.
C feared that something worse than bats lived in the cave.
D had not anticipated that the cave was in use.

7 Why did Kim reprimand himself with the words 'Stop it, stupid' (paragraph 6)?

A He was afraid Bobby would see him shivering.
B He was worried that shivering would make climbing dangerous.
C He was chastising himself for being left behind.
D He was forcing himself to overcome his embarrassing nervousness.

8 Why did the bats appear to vanish into the face of the rock?

A The cave opening was hidden behind a tree.
B The bats flew too fast to see where they actually went.
C It was not yet daylight and the bats were hard to see.
D The opening of the cave was just a slit in the rock.

9 According to the text which statements about the cave are CORRECT and which are INCORRECT? Write CORRECT or INCORRECT in the box next to the statement.

Statement	
A It became darker the further the boys progressed into the cave.	
B Both the roof and the floor had collapsed in parts of the cave.	
C The cave passage got bigger as the boys ventured further in.	
D The bats roosted in a hole in the roof of the cave.	
E The boys were unable to stand upright in the cave.	

☞ **Answers and explanations on pages 190–191**

READING
Understanding poetry

Poetry can take many forms. It can tell a story (narrative verse), paint a word picture, or be the format for a play.

Poets create experiences that are shared with the reader. To do this the poet uses literary techniques such as figurative language (similes and metaphors), rhyme and rhythm. Poetry does not have to rhyme.

Poetry is often described as the most personal form of expression. Poets choose their words carefully and economically. They create images and feelings with words.

Read the untitled poem by Sheryl Persson and answer the questions.

Wisteria
shimmering lavender chandeliers
wilt with the weight of mauve

Jasmine
exhales a chiffon of pink perfume
spring gasps and swoons

Bougainvillea
dressed to dance with summer
drapes verandas with vermilion lace

Jacaranda
pours a torrent of indigo rain
lays down a plush purple carpet

READING
Understanding poetry

1. Which technique does the poet use in the line 'spring gasps and swoons'? You may tick one or more.
   - [ ] simile
   - [ ] onomatopoeia
   - [ ] metaphor
   - [ ] alliteration
   - [ ] personification

2. The poet describes the shape of which flower?
   A Wisteria B Jasmine C Bougainvillea D Jacaranda

3. The allusion created by the poem is one of
   A an all-pervasive scent.
   B a chaotic garden.
   C a profusion of colour.
   D a feeling of tranquillity.

4. Are the following words from the poem defined correctly? Write **YES** or **NO**.

DEFINITIONS	YES/NO
Plush means 'thick and coarse'.	
Chiffon is an almost transparent fabric.	
Vermillion is a similar colour to yellow.	
Swoon means 'sing softly'.	
Wilt means 'limp and drooping'.	

5. The poet uses imagery to create specific effects. Which of the following statements about imagery is INCORRECT?
   A The poet uses imagery in 'Wisteria' to give the impression of movement.
   B In 'Jasmine' the poet uses auditory imagery to mimic sound.
   C In 'Jacaranda' the poet uses imagery to create an impression of colour.
   D The imagery the poet uses in 'Bougainvillea' uses olfactory imagery.

6. The poet has asked you to think of a title for this poem that incorporates its meaning. The best title would be
   A Summer Rains.
   B Fiesta of Flowers.
   C Gaudy Gardens.
   D Shades of Seasons.

7. The flowers had an effect on the poet. Which word best reflects how the poet felt?

celebratory	romantic	invigorated	exultant	contemplative
A	B	C	D	E

☞ Answers and explanations on page 191

READING
Understanding narratives

Read this extract from 'The Drover's Wife' by Henry Lawson (1867–1922) and answer the questions.

The two-roomed house is built of round timber, slabs, and stringy-bark, and floored with split slabs. A big bark kitchen standing at one end is larger than the house itself, veranda included.

Bush all around—bush with no horizon. The country is flat. No ranges in the distance. The bush consists of stunted trees. No undergrowth. Nothing to relieve the eye, save the darker green of a few she-oaks which are sighing above the narrow, almost waterless creek. Nineteen miles to the nearest sign of civilisation—a shanty on the main road.

The drover, an ex-squatter, is away with sheep. His wife and children are left here alone.

Four ragged, dried-up-looking children are playing about the house—mere babies. Suddenly one of them yells: 'Snake! Mother, here's a snake!'

The gaunt, sun-browned bushwoman dashes from the kitchen, snatches her baby from the ground, holds it on her left hip, and reaches for a stick.

'Where is it?'

'Here! Gone in the wood-heap' yells the eldest boy—a sharp-faced urchin of eleven. 'Stop there, mother! I'll have him. Stand back! I'll have the beggar!'

'Tommy, come here, or you'll be bit. Come here at once when I tell you, you little wretch!'

The youngster comes reluctantly, carrying a stick bigger than himself. Then he yells, triumphantly: 'There it goes—under the house!' and darts away with club uplifted. At the same time, Alligator, the big, black, yellow-eyed dog-of-all-breeds, who has shown the wildest interest in the proceedings, breaks his chain and rushes after that snake. He is a moment late. His nose reaches the crack in the slabs just as the end of its tail disappears. After a struggle he is chained up. They cannot afford to lose him.

The drover's wife makes the children stand together near the dog-house while she watches for the snake. She gets two small dishes of milk and sets them down near the wall to tempt it to come out; but an hour goes by and it does not show itself.

It is near sunset. The children must be brought inside. She will not take them into the house. The snake is there, and may at any moment come up through a crack in the rough slab floor; so she carries several armfuls of firewood into the kitchen, and then takes the children there. The kitchen has no floor—or, rather, an earthen one—called a '*ground floor*' in this part of the bush. She brings all four children in, and makes them get on a large, roughly-made table. She gives some supper, and then, before it gets dark, she goes into the house, and snatches up some pillows and bedclothes—expecting to see the snake any minute. She makes a bed on the table for the children, and sits down beside it to watch all night.

She has brought the dog into the room.

From 'The Drover's Wife' by Henry Lawson, 1892

READING
Understanding narratives

1 The description of the location of the drover's home creates feelings of
A desertion. B poverty. C destitution. D isolation.

2 When Tommy gets a stick to kill the snake he is
A not fully aware of his limitations.
B reacting out of fear.
C behaving in a rational manner.
D showing-off.

3 The writer states that the drover's wife 'snatches up pillows and bedclothes' (second-last paragraph). Why did the drover's wife act in such a way? Write your answer on the lines.

____

____

4 Tick the option that best describes the drover's wife and the type of life she leads.

✓	THE DROVER'S WIFE	THE DROVER'S WIFE'S LIFE
	She is miserable.	She lives a life of poverty.
	She accepts her situation.	Her life is one of exploitation.
	She is resourceful.	Her life is one of hardship.
	She is a lonely woman.	Her life is oppressive.
	She faces danger head on.	She lives a squalid life.

5 Which words best describe the behaviour of Tommy?
A disrespectful and violent
B disobedient and surly
C impulsive and supportive
D brash and defiant

6 The mood of this extract is one of
A harshness. B desperation. C adventure. D callousness.

7 According to the text which statements about the drover's home are CORRECT and which are INCORRECT? Draw a line to connect the statement to the option.

CORRECT

INCORRECT

All the floors are made of dirt.

There are two separate buildings.

The veranda surrounded the entire house.

The kitchen was the main sleeping room for the children.

A primary building material was bark.

8 For the drover's wife, the oncoming of night
A removes some of the pressure she is feeling.
B gives her a chance to take control of the situation.
C increases the dangers to the situation.
D provides an opportunity to take the family inside.

☞ Answers and explanations on pages 191-192

GENERAL WRITING TIPS

Writing tests are designed to test your ability to express ideas, feelings and points of view. You will be assessed on:

- the thought and content of your writing
- the structure and organisation of your ideas
- expression, style and appropriate use of language
- the amount you write in the given time.

To get the best test results, follow these steps.

Step 1 – Before you start writing

- Read the question. Be sure you understand the type of writing requested by the assessors. If you are expected to write a description, there is little point in writing a narrative. Read the instructions carefully. Ask yourself if you should be describing, explaining, entertaining, telling a story, expressing a point of view, expressing an emotion or persuading the reader.
- Check the stimulus material carefully. Make sure the stimulus material forms the basis of your writing. You will likely be given a topic, picture, words/phrases, short poem or prose extract as stimulus material.
- What writing style? If you are given a choice of writing styles (text types), pick the style you are most comfortable with.
- Warning: don't try to make a pre-planned response, i.e. something you have already written, fit the stimulus material given.

Step 2 – Jot down points

Give yourself a few minutes before you start to **get your thoughts in order** and jot down points. You won't have time to write a draft. Depending on the style required, jot down points on:

- who (characters), why (reasons for action), where (setting), when (time)
- sequences of events/arguments/points
- any good ideas you suddenly have
- how to include the senses and your feelings.

Remember: You can discard ideas that don't fit into your final approach.

Step 3 – Make a brief outline

List the points or events in order. This will become your framework. It can be modified as you write.

Step 4 – Start writing

- Make your paragraphing work for you. New paragraphs are usually needed for
    - o new incidents in narratives
    - o changes in time or place
    - o descriptions that move from one sense to another (e.g. from sight to sound)
    - o a change in the character using direct speech.
- The quality and extent of your vocabulary is being tested. Don't use unusual or obscure words just to impress the assessor. A mistake here will expose your ignorance.
- It is important that you complete your piece of writing. Unfinished work will lose you marks, as will extremely short responses.

GENERAL WRITING TIPS

- Get as much of the punctuation, spelling and grammar right as you can, but allow yourself a couple of minutes after you finish to proofread your work. You won't have time for detailed editing.
- If you are writing a narrative, know the ending before you start. Your ending should not be trite or clichéd (e.g. *I woke up and found it was just a dream*).
- If you are asked to give a point of view, think through the evidence you can use to support your argument so that you can build to a strong conclusion.
- If you are including descriptions in your writing, think about the importance and relevance of all the senses—sights, smells, tastes, sounds and physical feelings. You may also include an emotional response.
- Have a concluding sentence that 'rounds off' your work.
- Keep your handwriting reasonably neat (i.e. readable).

Step 5 – When you finish

When you finish, **re-read** your work and do a quick check for spelling, punctuation, capital letters and grammar.

Check the Writing section (www.nap.edu.au/naplan/writing) **of the official NAPLAN website for up-to-date and important information on the Writing Test**. Sample Writing Tests and marking guidelines that outline the criteria markers use when assessing your writing are also provided. Please note that, to date in NAPLAN, the types of texts that students have been tested on have been narrative and persuasive writing.

The Australian Curriculum for English requires students to be taught three main types of texts:

- imaginative writing (including narratives and descriptions)
- informative writing (including procedures and reports)
- persuasive writing (expositions).

Informative writing has not yet been tested by NAPLAN. The best preparation for writing is for students to read a range of texts and to get lots of practice in writing different types of texts. We have included information on all types of texts in this book.

TIPS FOR WRITING PERSUASIVE TEXTS

A **persuasive text** is sometimes known as an **exposition** or an **argument**. A persuasive text aims to argue a position and support it with evidence and reasons.

When writing persuasive texts it is best to keep the following points in mind. They will help you get the best possible mark.

Before you start writing

- Read the question carefully. You will probably be asked to **write your reaction** to a particular question or statement, such as *Excessive Internet usage is bad for teenagers.* Most of the topics that you will be asked to comment on are very general. This means you will probably be writing about something you know and can draw upon your experience.
- Give yourself a few minutes before you start writing to **get your thoughts in order** and jot down points.

Structure of persuasive texts

A persuasive text has a specific structure:

- The **introduction** is where you clearly state your ideas about the topic. You must ensure your position is clearly outlined. It is a good idea to list your main points in your introduction—three points is perfect.
- The **body** comprises a series of paragraphs where your opinions are developed. Evidence and/or reasons are given to support your opinions about the topic. Each paragraph usually opens with a sentence that previews what the paragraph will focus on.
- The **conclusion** is a paragraph where the main points of your argument are summarised and where you restate your opinion on the topic. Your conclusion should not include any new information.

Language features of persuasive texts

You can use some or all of the following features:

- **Emotive language:** use words or phrases that express emotion, e.g. *I find it shocking, terrible crime, terrific, heartless, desirable*.
- **Third-person narrative:** avoid using *I* in your argument. The third person is more formal and appropriate to a persuasive text of this kind.
- **Connectives:** these words link your points together, e.g. *firstly, secondly, finally, on the other hand, however, furthermore, moreover* and *in conclusion.*
- **Modality:** use modals to express different levels of certainty. High modal verbs, including *should, must, will not* and *ensure,* are strongly persuasive.
- **Repetition:** repeat key words or phrases to have a dramatic effect on the reader by drawing emphasis to a point or idea.
- **Rhetorical questions:** these questions are designed to make the reader think, e.g. *Have you ever lost a loved one?*
- **Statements of appeal:** these affect the emotions of your readers and encourage action, e.g. *We owe it to our children to act now on climate change.*

Don't forget to:

- plan your argument before you start
- write in correctly formed sentences and take care with paragraphing
- choose your words carefully and pay attention to your spelling and punctuation
- write neatly but don't waste time
- make no more than three different points
- quickly check your argument once you have finished.

You will find a sample annotated persuasive text on the following page. The question is from Sample Test 1 on page 130. Read the persuasive text and notes before you begin your first Writing Test. This piece of writing has been analysed based on the marking criteria used by markers to assess the NAPLAN Writing Test.

Remember: This sample was not written under exam conditions.

Year 9 Sample Persuasive Writing

(a sample answer to the question on page 130)

Excessive Internet usage is bad for teenagers.

We've all heard the saying 'Watching too much television will make your eyes go square', but what about spending too much time looking at web pages? Will this make our eyes oblong, triangular or even hexagonal? Teenagers today spend an average of three hours per day surfing the web. Understandably parents, teachers and health workers are concerned about the impact that prolonged and excessive Internet usage can have on teenagers. <u>While</u> many argue that too much time spent on the web can result in antisocial behaviour, obesity and laziness, what many opponents neglect are the benefits of using the Internet. <u>Due to</u> the advent of the Internet we can now say that we literally have the world at our fingertips. The World Wide Web enables curious young minds to communicate, collaborate and create with a whole world of people.

Communication is central to the lives of all teenagers. <u>Thanks to</u> social networking services like Facebook and Twitter, young people have the opportunity to communicate with a variety of different people from a diverse range of backgrounds. <u>Furthermore</u>, research shows that communication is central to a healthy and active mental life. If the Internet enables young people to express themselves and their concerns about the world, how can this be seen as a bad thing?

Another positive of Internet usage is access to an array of tools that facilitate collaboration between individuals in different locations. Many young people are all too familiar with MMORPGs (or Massively Multiplayer Online Role-playing Game for the oldies), the most popular being World of Warcraft which has approximately 11.5 million players. MMORPGs see people working together online to defeat a common enemy. It isn't just imaginary enemies that can be defeated through online collaboration. A number of protests against human rights abuse have been organised online. It's actually pretty inspiring what young people can do when assisted by the Internet.

Finally if collaboration and communication aren't enough to convince you that excessive Internet usage isn't a bad thing for teenagers, then what about the fact that almost all of human knowledge is now accessible online? Young people today have access to an unimaginable volume of information. Spending time online gives teenagers the opportunity to consume as well as create content.

Life is different now than twenty years ago. The Internet has opened the world up to young people with the click of a button. If you were young and full of wonder, wouldn't you like to spend most of your time communicating, collaborating and creating with a whole world of people?

This text is beyond what would be expected of a typical Year 9 student. It is provided here as a model. The assessment comments are based on the marking criteria used to assess the NAPLAN Writing Test.

Structure

Audience
- The writer's position is clearly stated: excessive Internet usage isn't bad for teenagers.
- Emotive phrases engage the emotions of the reader.

Persuasive techniques
- Rhetorical questions encourage the reader to think.

Text structure
- The correct structure of a persuasive text is followed, including introduction, supporting paragraphs and conclusion. This structure assists in the development of the writer's position.

Paragraphing
- New paragraphs are used for new arguments and the summary.
- <u>Connectives</u> and <u>referring words</u> are used to show connections between ideas and enhance the argument.
- All supporting lines of argument are articulated fully and supported by evidence and/or reasons.

Language and ideas

Vocabulary
- Language choices are appropriate to the purpose: to persuade.
- The writer uses strong verbs and adjectives.

Sentence structure
- All sentences are grammatically correct, well structured and meaningful.

Ideas
- Well-selected and relevant ideas are elaborated in the body of the text to support the persuasive argument.

Punctuation
- Correct complex punctuation is used throughout the argument.
- Difficult and challenging words are included.

Spelling
- All words are correctly spelled.
- Difficult (e.g. *communication*) and challenging (e.g. *unimaginable*) vocabulary is included.

WRITING
Persuasive text 1

The purpose of writing a persuasive text is to influence or change a reader's thoughts or opinions on a particular topic or subject. Your aim is to convince a reader that your opinion is sensible and logical. Successful persuasive writing is always well planned. Persuasive texts may include advertisements, letters to newspapers, speeches and newspaper editorials, as well as arguments in debates.

Before you start, read the General writing tips on pages 35–36 and the Tips for writing persuasive texts on page 37.

Today you are going to write a persuasive text, often called an exposition.

War is necessary.

What do you think about this topic? Do you agree or disagree with this opinion?
Write to convince a reader of your opinions.

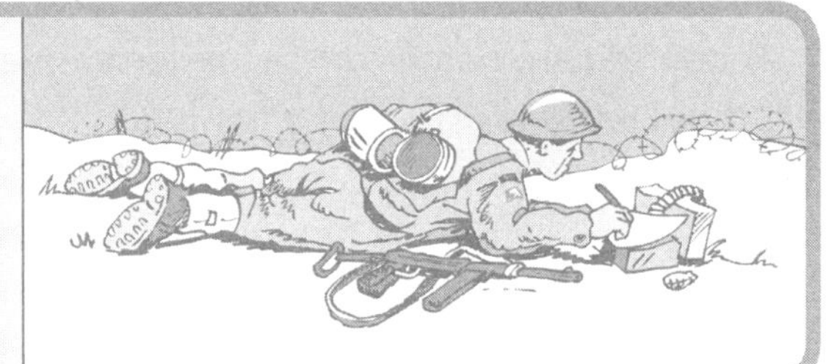

Before you start writing, give some thought to:

- whether you strongly agree or strongly disagree with this opinion
- reasons or evidence for your arguments
- a brief but definite conclusion—list some of your main points and add a personal opinion
- the structure of a persuasive text, which begins with a well-organised introduction, followed by a body of arguments or points, and finally a conclusion that restates the writer's position.

Don't forget to:

- plan your writing before you start—make a list of important points you wish to make
- write in correctly formed sentences and take care with paragraphing
- choose your words carefully, and pay attention to your spelling and punctuation
- write neatly but don't waste time
- quickly check your persuasive text once you have finished—your position must be clear to the reader
- do a quick check for spelling, punctuation, capital letters and grammar.

Remember: The stance taken in a persuasive text is not wrong, as long as the writer has evidence to support his or her opinion. How the opinion is supported is as important as the opinion itself.

Start writing here or type in your answer on a tablet or computer.

☞ Marking guide on pages 192–193

WRITING
Persuasive text 2

The purpose of writing a persuasive text is to influence or change a reader's thoughts or opinions on a particular topic or subject. Your aim is to convince a reader that your opinion is sensible and logical. Successful persuasive writing is always well planned. Persuasive texts may include advertisements, letters to newspapers, speeches and newspaper editorials, as well as arguments in debates.

Before you start, read the General writing tips on pages 35–36 and the Tips for writing persuasive texts on page 37.

Today you are going to write a persuasive text, often called an exposition.

School uniforms should be banned.

What do you think about this idea? Do you support or reject this proposal?
Write to convince a reader of your opinions.

Before you start writing, give some thought to:

- whether you strongly agree or strongly disagree with this opinion
- reasons or evidence for your arguments
- a brief but definite conclusion—list some of your main points and add a personal opinion
- the structure of a persuasive text, which begins with a well-organised introduction, followed by a body of arguments or points, and finally a conclusion that restates the writer's position.

Don't forget to:

- plan your writing before you start—make a list of important points you wish to make
- write in correctly formed sentences and take care with paragraphing
- choose your words carefully, and pay attention to your spelling and punctuation
- write neatly but don't waste time
- quickly check your persuasive text once you have finished—your position must be clear to the reader
- do a quick check for spelling, punctuation, capital letters and grammar.

Remember: The stance taken in a persuasive text is not wrong, as long as the writer has evidence to support his or her opinion. How the opinion is supported is as important as the opinion itself.

Start writing here or type in your answer on a tablet or computer.

☞ Marking guide on page 193

Week 2

This is what we cover this week:

Day 1 **Statistics and Probability:** ◎ Mean, graphs and tables
Number and Algebra: Patterns and algebra
◎ Equations and number plane

Day 2 **Spelling:** ◎ Adding suffixes and prefixes, changing nouns to verbs and verbs to adjectives
◎ Common misspellings
Grammar and Punctuation: ◎ Commas, semicolons and apostrophes

Day 3 **Reading:** ◎ Understanding book reviews
◎ Understanding transactions
◎ Understanding film reviews

Day 4 **Writing:** ◎ Narrative texts

STATISTICS AND PROBABILITY
Mean, graphs and tables

1 What is the mean of the following scores?
12, 18, 4, 6, 10
A 5 B 6 C 10 D 14

2 What is the mode of the following scores?
8, 11, 5, 2, 9, 10, 8
A 2 B 3 C 8 D 11

3 What is the median of the following scores?
10, 3, 4, 11, 50, 18, 5
A 5 B 10 C 11 D 47

4 What is the median of the following scores?
8, 3, 6, 0, 10, 81
A 6 B 7 C 8 D 81

5 What is the range of the following scores?
–4, 19, 25, –1, 0
A 21 B 26 C 28 D 29

Use the stem-and-leaf plot to answer questions 6 to 8:

Stem	Leaf
4	1 5 8 9
5	2 7 7 9
6	3

6 What is the mode of the scores?
A 7 B 57
C 62 D 63

7 What is the median of the scores?
A 2 B 50 C 52 D 54

8 What is the range of the scores?
A 2 B 12 C 18 D 22

The graph relates to questions 9, 10 and 11 and shows the number of laps walked at the school's lap-a-thon by a group of students.

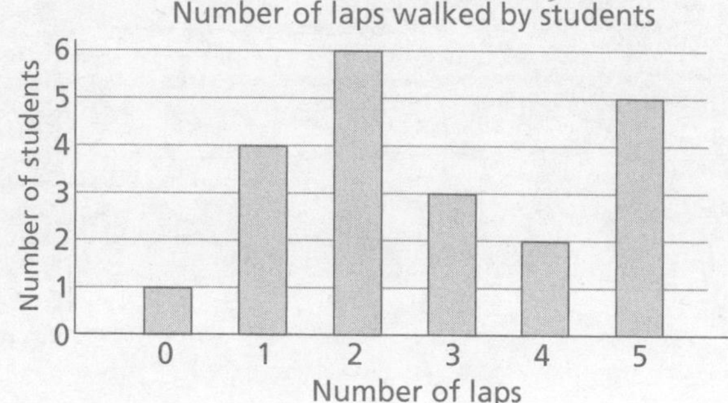

9 What is the mode of the scores?
A 2 B 3 C 5 D 6

10 How many students were in the group?
A 21 B 20 C 16 D 6

11 What was the total number of laps walked by the students?
A 5 B 6 C 58 D 59

12 The average mass of six students is 52 kg. What is the total mass of the six students?
A 58 kg B 302 kg C 312 kg D 322 kg

13 After 5 games, the average of goals scored by a hockey team is 3. How many goals need to be scored in the sixth game to increase the average to 4?
A 15 B 9 C 11 D 24

14 The median of the scores 5, 9, 2, X, 9 and 3 is 6. What is the value of X?
A 6 B 7 C 8 D 9

Use the table to answer questions 15 and 16.

The following scores 32, 45, 28, 25, 34, 41, 36, 31, 26, 46 are placed on an ordered stem-and-leaf plot. One of the numbers is hidden.

Stem	Leaf
2	5 6 8
3	1 2 4 ■
4	1 5 6

15 What is the missing number?
A 6 B 7 C 8 D 9

16 What is the median score?
A 32 B 33 C 34 D 35

17 The average of 3, 6, 9 and X is 5. What is the value of X?
A 18 C 6 C 2 D 1

18 A set of scores has a range of 4 and a median of 4. Which of these could be the scores?
A 2, 4, 6, 6 B 3, 4, 4, 6
C 1, 4, 4, 5 D 10, 14, 14, 14

19 16, 3, 11, 8, 2, P, 12. The range of these scores is 20. What is a possible value of P?
A –4 B –2 C 20 D 40

☞ Explanations on page 194

Answers: 1 C 2 C 3 B 4 B 5 D 6 B 7 C 8 D 9 A 10 A 11 C 12 C 13 B 14 B 15 A 16 B 17 C 18 C 19 A

STATISTICS AND PROBABILITY
Mean, graphs and tables

1 The **mean** is the average and is found by adding the scores and then dividing the sum by the number of scores.

Example: Find the mean of these scores: 12, 18, 2, 6, 22

$$\text{Mean} = \frac{12 + 18 + 2 + 6 + 22}{5} = 12$$

2 The **median** is the middle score when the scores are arranged in ascending order (from smallest to highest).

Example 1: Find the median of 9, 3, 10, 3, 6.
Rearrange scores: 3, 3, 6, 9, 10
The median is 6.

Example 2: Find the median of 21, 4, 9, 3, 8 and 11.
Rearrange the scores: 3, 4, 8, 9, 11, 21
The median is the middle of 8 and 9.
This means the median is 8.5.

3 The **mode** is the most popular, or common, score.
Example: Find the mode of 11, 5, 9, 3, 5, 10.
The mode is 5 as it occurs twice.

4 The **range** is the difference between the highest and lowest score.

Example: Find the range of 15, 9, 12, 2, 18.
The range is 18 – 2 = 16.

5 A **stem-and-leaf plot** is useful for displaying data.

Example: Use a stem-and-leaf plot to display the following data:
18, 31, 26, 18, 25, 10, 33, 27, 22, 59, 39

Range = 59 – 10 = 49
Mode = 18
Median = 26

Outlier = 59 (clearly much higher than other scores)

Stem	Leaf
1	0 8 8
2	2 5 6 7
3	1 3 9
4	
5	9

6 Data can be represented in a **table**.

Example: A survey was conducted to find the number of televisions in the homes of students.

Number of TVs	Students
1	2
2	7
3	4
4	3
5	4

Find the following:
a Range = 5 – 1 = 4 b Mode = 2

7 Data can also be represented in a **graph**.

Example: The graph shows the number of children in the families of students.

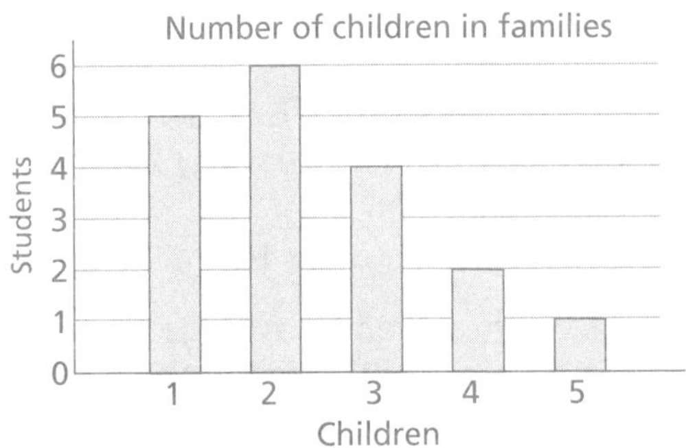

a What is the mode and range?
Mode = 2; Range = 5 – 1 = 4

b How many children in the families?
Number $= 1 \times 5 + 2 \times 6 + 3 \times 4 + 4 \times 2 + 5 \times 1$
$= 42$ ∴ 42 children

8 We often have to find the **impact of including/deleting a score** on a calculated mean, mode, median or range.

Example 1: The mean score in some tests was 6. In a new test the student scores 8. What will happen to the mean?
The mean will increase as the new result is higher than the previous mean.

Example 2: Sam wrote these numbers 2, 7, 9, 9 and 13. If one of the 9s is removed what happens to:

a range? Unchanged: remains 13 – 2 = 11

b median? 2, 7, 9, 10: Median decreases from 9 to middle of 7 and 9 = 8

c mean? Was (2 + 7 + 9 + 9 + 13) ÷ 5 = 8

The removed number is higher than the existing mean, so the mean will decrease.

STATISTICS AND PROBABILITY
Mean, graphs and tables

Here is a list of scores used for questions 1, 2 and 3: 10, 16, 9, 24, 17, 19, 10.

1 What is the difference between the range and the mode of the scores?
A 5 B 6 C 10 D 25

2 What is the median of the scores?
A 10 B 16 C 19 D 21

3 What is the mean of the scores? ☐

4 What is the median of the scores 12, 18, 51, 1, 18, 31, 28, 85?
A 18 B 22 C 23 D 28

5 The mean of six scores is 8. If another score is included, the mean increases by 2. What was the new score? *Hint 1*
A 12 B 16 C 18 D 22

6 A soccer team scored an average of 3 goals in the first 4 games of the competition. After another 6 games the average had been increased to 4 goals. How many goals were scored in the last 6 games?
A 16 B 18 C 24 D 28

For questions 7 and 8, the stem-and-leaf plot shows the mass (in kilograms) of a number of students.

Stem	Leaf
4	3 5 6
5	0 1 8 8
6	3 7 7 7
7	0

7 What is the difference between the mode and the median? ☐

8 The mass of another student is included in the stem-and-leaf plot. If the mass is 44 kg, what effect does it have on the mean and mode? *Hint 2*
A mean decreases and mode decreases
B mean increases and mode is unchanged
C mean decreases and mode is unchanged
D mean decreases and mode increases

9 The range of 3 scores is 10. The smallest score is 4 and the median is 6. What is the mean of the scores?
A 6 B 7 C 8 D 9

10 Ten critics judged a new film as a score out of 10 and the results are listed:
5, 5, 6, 6, 7, 7, 7, 8, 9, 10.
Which of the following is true?
A mean = mode > median
B mean = mode = median
C mean < mode < median
D mean < mode = median

Here is a list of scores that relates to questions 11 and 12: 9, 0, 3, 7, 11, 5, 11, 4.

11 What is the difference between the mode and the median? ☐

12 What is the mean of the scores? ☐

For questions 13 and 14, the graph shows the number of laptops in the homes of students.

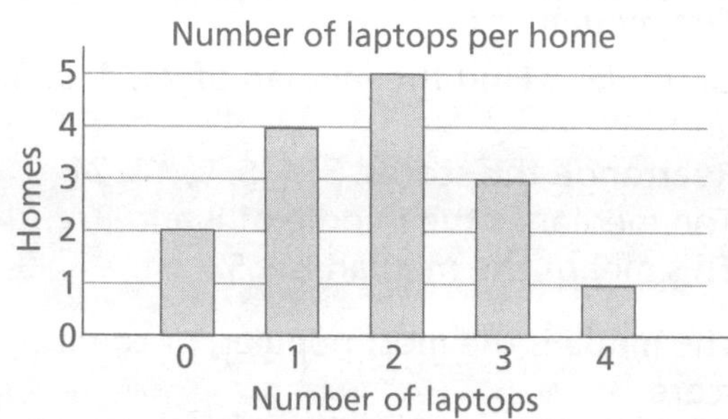

13 If a home is chosen at random, what is the probability that there are 3 laptops?
A $\frac{1}{15}$ B $\frac{1}{5}$ C $\frac{1}{4}$ D $\frac{1}{3}$

14 How many laptops are there in the students' homes? ☐

15 Here is a set of scores: 3, 4, 4, 6, 8, 11. What will change if the score of 6 is removed?
A range B mode C median D mean

16 Here is another set of scores: 2, 6, 8, 12, 12. What will not change if another score of 12 is included? Select **all** correct answers.
A range B mean
C mode D median

Hint 1: *First find the total of the six scores.*
Hint 2: *Notice that 44 is close to the smallest mass in the stem–and–leaf plot and will be less than the existing mean.*

☞ **Answers and explanations on pages 195-196**

NUMBER AND ALGEBRA
Patterns and algebra

1 What is the missing number in the pattern?
12, 19, 26, ___, 40
A 7 B 33 C 34 D 37

2 The rule 'double and add 6' is used to produce this pattern: 2, 10, 26, 58, ___
What is the next number in the pattern?
A 64 B 110 C 116 D 122

3 What is the missing number in the pattern?
94, 80, 66, 52, ___
A 14 B 16 C 36 D 38

4 What is the tenth number in the pattern:
6, 10, 14, 18, ___
A 36 B 42 C 46 D 48

For questions 5 and 6, a pattern of squares is formed using sticks.

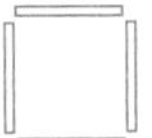 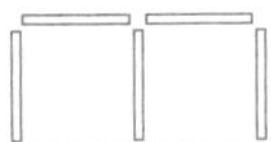 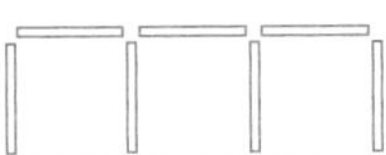

5 How many sticks are needed to make a pattern of four squares?
A 13 B 14 C 5 D 16

6 How many squares could be made using 25 sticks?
A 6 B 7 C 8 D 9

A pattern of triangles is formed using sticks and relates to questions 7 and 8.

  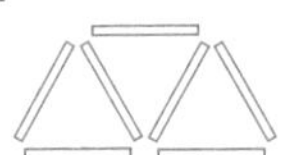

7 How many sticks are needed to make a pattern of six triangles?
A 12 B 13 C 15 D 17

8 How many triangles could be made using 25 sticks?
A 10 B 11 C 12 D 13

For questions 9 and 10, the table has been completed using the rule 'Multiply the top number by 3 and add 2'.

Top number	1	3	6	8	Y
Bottom number	5	11	X	26	32

9 What is the value of *X*?
A 17 B 18 C 19 D 20

10 What is the value of *Y*?
A 10 B 12 C 16 D 35

11 The table shows values for *a* and *b*.

a	0	1	2	3	4
b	3	5	7	9	11

Which of these is a correct rule for *b* in terms of *a*?
A $b = 3a$ B $b = 4a + 1$
C $b = a^2 + 3$ D $b = 2a + 3$

12 The table has been completed using the rule $y = 3x^2 - 4$. What is the value of *P*?

x	−1	1	3	5
y	−1	−1	P	71

A 23 B 28 C 35 D 77

13 The value of $5a + 3b$ when $a = 2$ and $b = 4$ is
A 16. B 13. C 22. D 32.

14 If $a = -3$ and $b = -4$, what is the value of $2ab$?
A −24 B −14 C 14 D 24

15 What is the value of $4x^2$ when $a = -3$?
A −36 B 36 C −144 D 144

16 If $y = 3$, find $5 - 2y$.
A −18 B −9 C −1 D 1

17 Simplify $3x + 2y - x + 5y$.
A $2x - 3y$ B $2x + 7y$ C $3x - 3y$ D $3x + 7y$

18 $3(2a + 5)$ is the same as
A $5a + 5$. B $6a + 5$. C $6a + 15$. D $21a$.

19 What is $8(2 - 7x)$?
A $16 - 56x$ B $16 - x$ C $10 - x$ D $9x$

20 Three consecutive numbers are x, $x + 1$ and $x + 2$. What is the sum of these numbers?
A $6x$ B $9x$ C $3x + 3$ D $3x + 6$

21 A square has a side length of $(x + 3)$ units. The perimeter of the square, in units, is
A $2x + 12$. B $2x + 6$. C $4x + 12$. D $4x + 3$.

☞ Explanations on pages 196–197

Answers: 1 B 2 D 3 D 4 B 5 A 6 C 7 B 8 C 9 D 10 A 11 D 12 A 13 C 14 D 15 B 16 C 17 B 18 C 19 A 20 C 21 C

NUMBER AND ALGEBRA
Patterns and algebra

1 A pattern of numbers can be **described in words.**

Example: Use the rule 'Multiply by 3 and then subtract 6' to find the sixth number in the pattern 4, 6, 12, 30, ___

5th term: $30 \times 3 - 6 = 90 - 6$
$= 84$

6th term: $84 \times 3 - 6 = 252 - 6$
$= 246$

2 A pattern of numbers can be **described as an equation.**

Example: The table has been completed using the rule $y = x^2 + 3$.

x	0	2	5	7
y	3	7		52

What is the missing number?
When $x = 5$, $y = 5^2 + 3$
$= 25 + 3$
$= 28$

3 Algebraic expressions can be evaluated by **substituting the pronumerals** with numbers.

Example 1: Find the value of $2x - 3y$ when $x = 7$ and $y = 3$.
$2x - 3y = 2 \times 7 - 3 \times 3$
$= 14 - 9$
$= 5$

Example 2: Find the value of $pq - 12$ when $p = -5$ and $q = -2$.
$pq - 12 = (-5) \times (-2) - 12$
$= 10 - 12$
$= -2$

Example 3: Find the value of $40 - 2c^2$ when $c = -4$.
$40 - 2c^2 = 40 - 2(-4)^2$
$= 40 - 2 \times 16$
$= 40 - 32$
$= 8$

Example 4: Find the value of $\frac{a+b}{a-b}$ when $a = 12$ and $b = 4$.

$\frac{a+b}{a-b} = \frac{12+4}{12-4}$
$= \frac{16}{8}$
$= 2$

4 In algebraic expressions, **like terms** are $3a$, $6a$, $5a$.

Example: From the list, identify the like terms: $9y$, $2xy$, $5x$, y, $-3y$, y^2.
$9y$, y, $-3y$ are like terms.

5 We can only **add/subtract** like terms.

Example 1: Simplify $8a^2 + 7a^2 - 4a^2$
$8a^2 + 7a^2 - 4a^2 = 11a^2$

Example 2: Simplify $7x - 3y + 2x - 5y$
$7x - 3y + 2x - 5y = 9x - 8y$

Example 3: Simplify $8ab - 3a + 9 - 2ba + 7a$
$8ab - 3a + 9 - 2ba + 7a$
$= 6ab + 4a + 9$

6 We can **multiply/divide** like and unlike terms.

Example 1: Simplify $5 \times a \times b \times c$
$5 \times a \times b \times c = 5abc$

Example 2: Simplify $9x \times 4y$
$9x \times 4y = 36xy$

Example 3: Simplify $-12y \times 3y$
$-12y \times 3y = -36y^2$

Example 4: Simplify $10ab \div 5a$
$10ab \div 5a = 2b$

Example 5: Simplify $\frac{12ab}{6b}$

$\frac{{}^{2}\cancel{12}a\cancel{b}}{{}_{1}\cancel{6}\cancel{b}} = 2a$

7 The number (or term) in front of **grouping symbols** multiplies the expression inside.

Example 1: Expand and simplify $5(2a - 1)$.
$5(2a - 1) = 10a - 5$

Example 2: Expand and simplify $4(5p - 3q + 9)$.
$4(5p - 3q + 9) = 20p - 12q + 36$

8 In **generalised arithmetic** replace the pronumeral with a number and consider the consequences.

Example: Write two consecutive whole numbers after x.
As 7, then $7 + 1 = 8$, then $7 + 2 = 9$, so x, then $x + 1$, then $x + 2$ are consecutive.

NUMBER AND ALGEBRA
Patterns and algebra

1 James wrote this pattern of numbers:
3, 11, 43, 171, ___
What is the rule James used?
A Multiply by 3 then add 4.
B Multiply by 4 then subtract 1.
C Multiply by 5 then subtract 4.
D Square and then add 2.

2 Li used this pattern of numbers: 3, 14, 36, ___
Li's rule is add 4 then multiply by 2.
What is the fifth number in her pattern?
A 160 B 164 C 168 D 328

3

Figure 1

Figure 2

Figure 3

The pattern of dots continues. *Hint 1*
A table summarises the figures and dots

Figure	1	2	3	4	5	6
Dots	1	3	6			X

What is the value of X?
A 15 B 16 C 18 D 21

4 Which of the following is equivalent to $3(6m - 4)$?
A $6m$ B $9m - 4$
C $18m - 4$ D $18m - 12$

5 What is the number 5 less than p? *Hint 2*
A $p + 5$ B $p - 5$ C $5 - p$ D $5p$

6 Which is equivalent to $5 - 2x$? *Hint 3*
A $2x - 5$ B $-2x + 5$
C $2 - 5x$ D $-2x - 5$

7 The diagram shows a rectangle with measurements in units. The area of the rectangle in units^2 is

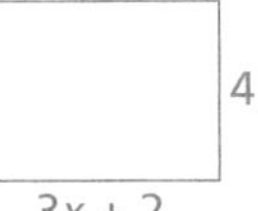

A $12x + 8$. B $3x + 6$.
C $6x + 12$. D $12x + 6$.

8 What is the value of $5x^2$ when $x = -2$?

Write your answer in the box:

9 If $a = 2$ and $b = 4$, which of these is equal to 24? Select **all** correct answers.
A ab B $6a + 3b$ C $(a + b)^2$ D $7b - 2a$

10 If $x = 4$, find $\frac{3x}{x + 2}$.
A 2 B 5 C 6 D 7

11 What is $\frac{2x + y}{3y - 2}$ when $x = 3$ and $y = 4$?
A 8 B 5 C 2 D 1

12 If $p = 3$, what is $(2p)^2 - 2p^2$?

Write your answer in the box:

13

x	0	1	2	3	4
y	–2	0	2	4	6

What rule is used in the table above?
A $y = 2x - 2$ B $y = x - 2$
C $y = 2x - 1$ D $x + y = 0$

14

x	0	0.5	1	1.5	2
y	2	1.5	1	0.5	0

What rule is used in the table above?
A $y = x - 0.5$ B $x + y = 1$
C $x + y = 2$ D $y = x - 1.5$

15 A —— $3x$ —— B *Hint 4*
X —— $2x + 1$ —— Y

The diagram shows the lengths of two intervals. How much longer is AB than XY?
A $x + 1$ B $x - 1$ C $x - 3$ D $5x + 1$

16 If $x = -2$, find the value of $x^2 - 5x + 3$.

Write your answer in the box:

Hint 1: Find the rule from the diagram or table and use it to find the missing number.
Hint 2: Replace the pronumeral with a number and see what happens—then apply the same to the pronumeral.
Hint 3: Consider the signs of the two individual terms in the expression.
Hint 4: When subtracting algebraic expressions, use grouping symbols.

☞ Answers and explanations on pages 197–198

NUMBER AND ALGEBRA
Equations and number plane

1 The table is completed using the rule xy = 12.

x	1	2	3	6	12
y	12	6	4	2	1

Which is the graph showing the information in the table?

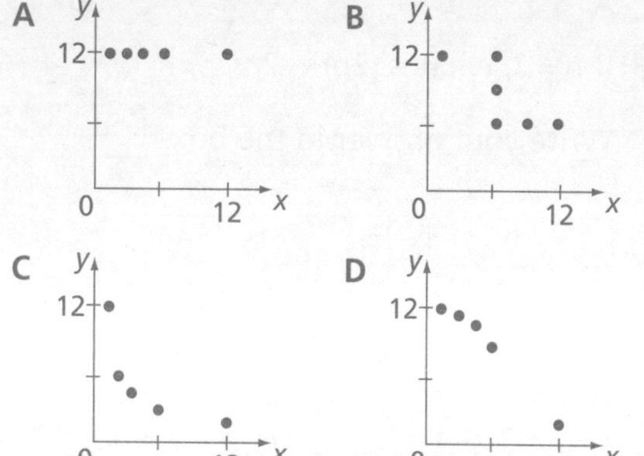

2 Which of these points lie on the line $y = 2x + 1$?
A (0, 1) B (1, 2) C (2, 3) D (3, 4)

3 Which of these points does not lie on the line $y = 3x - 2$?
A (–1, –5) B (0, –2) C (1, 1) D (2, 3)

4 A table is completed using the rule $y = 2x - 2$.

x	0	1	2	3
y	–2	0	2	4

The table is then used to draw the line $y = 2x - 2$. Which of these points is also on the line?
A (–3, –5) B (–1, 2) C (5, 8) D (6, 11)

5 Which of these lines pass through (2, –3)?
A $y = x + 3$ B $y = 2x + 1$
C $y = 2x - 1$ D $y = x - 5$

6 Solve $2x + 5 = 11$.
A $x = 8$ B $x = -8$ C $x = -3$ D $x = 3$

7 Solve $4a - 8 = 4$.
A $a = -1$ B $a = 1$ C $a = 2$ D $a = 3$

8 Solve $3y - 1 = 2y + 4$.
A $y = 3$ B $y = 5$ C $y = -3$ D $y = 2$

9 Solve $2a = a - 6$.
A $a = -6$ B $a = 4$ C $a = -4$ D $a = 6$

10 Solve $5x + 8 = 3x - 4$.
A $x = -6$ B $x = -7$ C $x = 4$ D $x = 6$

11 In the formula $A = 3B - 2$ what values of A and B satisfy the formula?
A $A = 2, B = 4$ B $A = 1, B = 1$
C $A = 3, B = 2$ D $A = 2, B = 0$

12 In the formula $P = \dfrac{24}{Q + 3}$ what values of P and Q satisfy the formula?
A $P = 6, Q = 0$ B $P = 12, Q = 1$
C $P = 2, Q = 9$ D $P = 21, Q = 1$

13 Which value of x satisfies $2x - 1 = x + 5$?
A $x = 3$ B $x = 4$ C $x = 6$ D $x = 2$

14 Which value of x satisfies $3x + 4 = x - 2$?
A $x = -6$ B $x = -2$ C $x = -3$ D $x = 2$

15 If $P = 2a + 2b$, find a if $P = 20$ and $b = 4$.
A 6 B 8 C 12 D 16

16 If A = xy, find x if $A = 48$ and $y = 6$.
A 6 B 8 C 12 D 24

17 Here is a formula: $K = \dfrac{V}{3x^2}$.
If $K = 6$ and $x = 2$, what is the value of V?
A 36 B 72 C 84 D 120

18 Use $M = Pv - L$ to find the value of L if $M = 12$, $P = 1.4$ and $v = 10$.
A 2 B 2.6 C 26 D 26.2

19 Here is a formula: $T = \dfrac{B}{\sqrt{x + y}}$.
If $T = 10$, $x = 11$, $y = 14$, what is the value of B?
A 2 B 20 C 25 D 50

☞ Explanations on pages 198–199

Answers: 1 C 2 A 3 D 4 C 5 D 6 D 7 D 8 B 9 A 10 A 11 B 12 C 13 C 14 C 15 A 16 B 17 B 18 A 19 D

NUMBER AND ALGEBRA
Equations and number plane

1. A **number plane** consists of points which are named as coordinates in terms of (x, y).

2. To **graph a line** on a number plane, first complete a table of values to provide some of the points on the line.

Example: Graph the line $y = 2x - 1$ by first completing the table of values.

x	0	1	2
y			

By substituting values of x into the equation $y = 2x - 1$, the points are $(0, -1)$, $(1, 1)$, $(2, 3)$.

x	0	1	2
y	-1	1	3

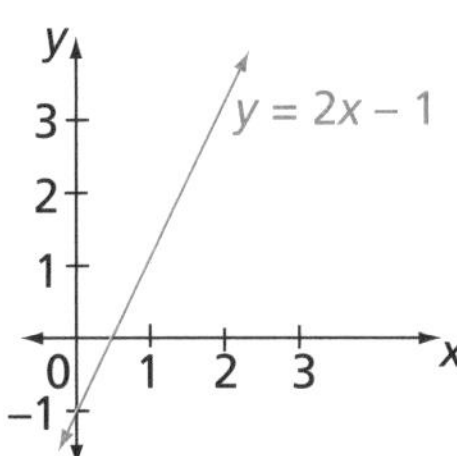

3. When a **line passes through a point** the values of x and y will satisfy the equation of the line.

Example 1: Does $y = 3x - 1$ pass through the point $(2, 5)$?
For $(2, 5)$, $x = 2$ and $y = 5$ are substituted into $y = 3x - 1$; $5 = 3 \times 2 - 1$
The answer is Yes.

Example 2: Determine whether $(2, 3)$ lies on the line $y = 5x - 6$.
For $(2, 3)$, $x = 2$ and $y = 3$ are substituted into $y = 5x - 6$; $3 = 5 \times 2 - 6$
The answer is No.

4. The gradient of a line is the slope. It is expressed in the form $\frac{\text{rise}}{\text{run}}$.

Example: Find the gradient of the line represented on the number plane below.

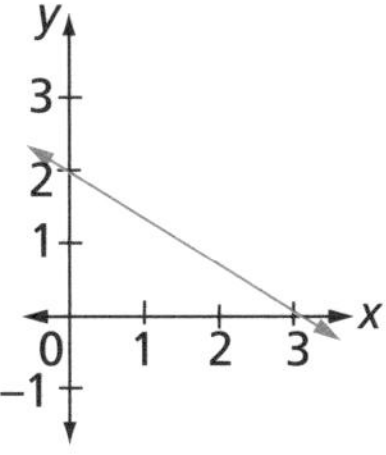

The line drops 2 as it runs across 3 units.

Gradient $= \frac{-2}{3}$

5. An **equation is solved** when the value of the pronumeral has been found (e.g. $x = 3$).

Solve:

Example 1:
$$5a - 2 = 3a + 8$$
$$5a - 3a = 8 + 2$$
$$2a = 10$$
$$a = 5$$

Example 2:
$$4(x - 2) = x - 5$$
$$4x - 8 = x - 5$$
$$4x - x = -5 + 8$$
$$3x = 3$$
$$x = 1$$

6. To check that a number is a **solution of an equation**, substitute the number into the equation.

Example: Determine whether $x = 3$ is a solution to the equation $4x - 2 = 3x + 1$.
Substitute $x = 3$ into the equation:
$4x - 2 = 3x + 1$
The left-hand side: $4 \times 3 - 2 = 12 - 2 = 10$
The right-hand side: $3 \times 3 + 1 = 9 + 1 = 10$
Therefore $x = 3$ is a solution.

7. An **inequality** is like an equation that uses either $<$, $>$, $\leq$ or $\geq$. The solution can be graphed on a number line.

Example: Solve $2x \leq 8$.

$x \leq \frac{8}{2}$

3 4 5

Therefore $x \leq 4$.
[Note: if $<$ or $>$: we use an open circle ○]

8. A **formula** consists of two or more pronumerals and can be solved like an equation.

Example 1: If $A = \pi r^2$, find A when $r = 12.2$. Answer to two decimal places.
$A = \pi \times 12.2^2$
$= 467.59$

Example 2: If $S = \frac{D}{T}$, find D when $S = 80$ and $T = 1.5$.
$$80 = \frac{D}{1.5}$$
$$1.5 \times 80 = D$$
$$D = 120$$

NUMBER AND ALGEBRA
Equations and number plane

1 Two numbers are multiplied together to give 24 and the table shows some of the possible numbers:

x	1	2	6	8	12	24
y	24	12	4	3	2	1

The table is now used to draw a graph. Which of these will be the correct graph?

A
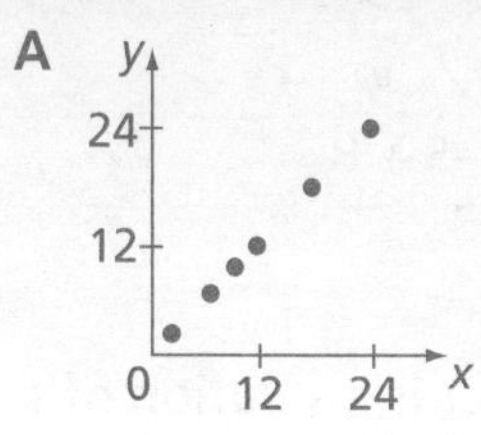

B
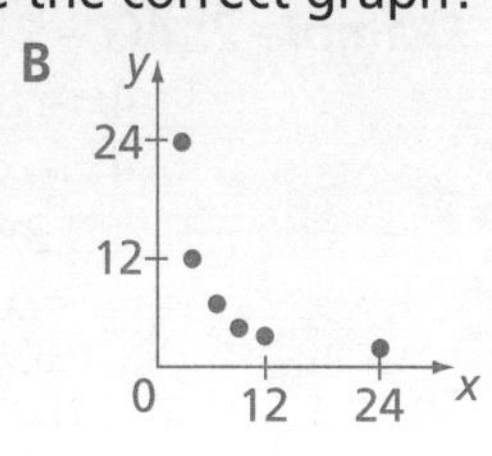

C
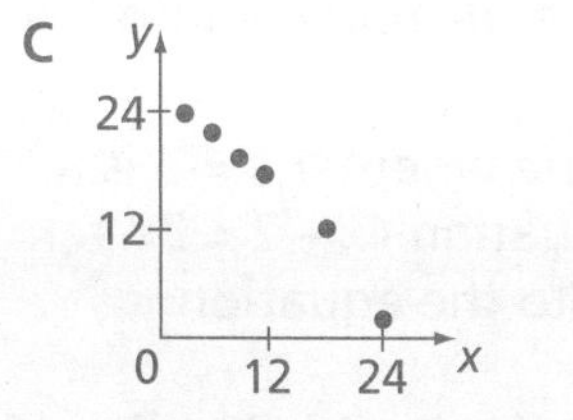

D
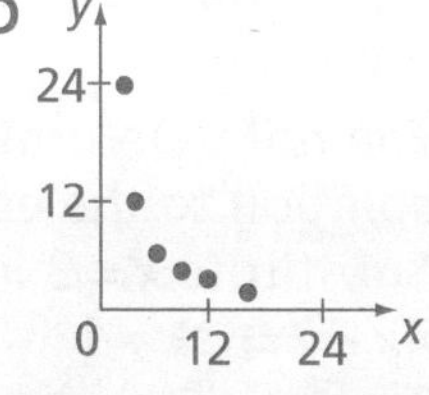

2 The line $y = 3x - 4$ is to be graphed. Which of these points will the line pass through?
A (0, –4) B (1, 1) C (2, 0) D (3, 4)

3 Which of these points lies on the line $y = 2x + 1$?
A (1, 2) B (4, 2) C (0, 3) D (2, 5)

4 What is the value of x in the equation $3x + 8 = 2x - 3$?
A $x = -11$ B $x = -5$ C $x = 5$ D $x = 11$

5 What is the value of b in the equation $4b - 4 = b + 5$? ☐

6 Dhama wrote this inequality $y > 2x - 1$. Which pair of numbers satisfy the inequality?
A $x = 3$ and $y = 1$ B $x = 5$ and $y = 4$
C $x = 2$ and $y = 8$ D $x = 1$ and $y = 0$

7 What is the gradient of the line that passes through (5, 0) and (0, –6)?
A $\frac{5}{6}$ B $\frac{-5}{6}$ C $\frac{6}{5}$ D $\frac{-6}{5}$

8 If $y = 2x + 4$, what is the value of x when $y = 8$? ☐

9 The kinetic energy (E) of an object is found using the formula $E = \frac{1}{2}mv^2$, where m is the mass and v is the velocity of the object. What is the value of m if E is 20 and v is 2?

Write your answer in the box: ☐

10 The diagram shows a rectangle. What is the value of a? *Hint 1*

(3a – 2) cm ☐ (2a + 4) cm

A 6 B 4 C 2 D 8

11 The volume of a cylinder is $V = \pi r^2 h$, where V is the volume, r is the radius in centimetres and h is the height in centimetres. If $r = 4$ and $h = 3$, the volume is closest to
A 113 cm^3. B 150 cm^3. C 452 cm^3. D 1421cm^3.

12 Laura wrote this equation $2x + 3y = 12$. Which of the following is a possible solution?
A $x = 1$ and $y = 2$ B $x = 3$ and $y = 2$
C $x = 6$ and $y = -1$ D $x = 6$ and $y = 4$

13 Here are two equations: $b = 2a - 3$ and $b = a + 4$. Which value of a satisfies both equations?
A $a = 1$ B $a = 2$ C $a = 3$ D $a = 7$

14 Tom wrote this formula: $P = \frac{T^2}{M - 6}$. What is the value of M when $P = 3.6$ and $T = 6$?
A $M = 16$ B $M = 12$ C $M = 26$ D $M = 18$

15 A rule is used to plot points on a number plane. Some of the points are (2, 5), (5, 11) and (6, 13). Which of the following will also be on the line? *Hint 2*
A (10, 19) B (12, 24) C (8, 17) D (15, 35)

16 Which of these lines pass through both (1, 0) and (3, 8)? *Hint 3*
A $y = 3x - 3$ B $y = 4x - 4$
C $y = 2x + 2$ D $y = 5x - 5$

Hint 1: *Opposite sides of a rectangle are equal in length.*
Hint 2: *First find the rule that has been used and then apply that rule to each of the choices to find the correct point.*
Hint 3: *Substitute each point into each of the choices.*

☞ **Answers and explanations on pages 199–201**

SPELLING

Adding suffixes and prefixes, changing nouns to verbs and verbs to adjectives

Key Points

1. **Prefixes** stand **before** a root word.
   Examples: disengage, unhappy, submarine
   Common prefixes are 'un', 'in', 'im', 'ir', 'de' and 'sub'.

2. A prefix **cannot stand on its own**. This should help your spelling, as a prefix is always spelt completely.
   Example: disconnect has only one 's', not two, because the root word connect is combined with the prefix 'dis'.
   Other examples include: disjoint, discover, disempower, deconstruct, devalue, defame, submerge, sublimate, subservient, inappropriate, incapable, inside, irreplaceable, irresponsible, irregular, impossible, immaterial, immobile.

3. **Suffixes** stand **after** a root word. There are many different types of suffixes, and they change both the spelling and the meaning of the word.
   Examples: quickly, darkness, hopeful, terrorism

4. A suffix **cannot stand on its own**. This should help your spelling, as a suffix is always spelt completely.
   Example: quickly is often misspelled 'quickely' or 'quickley', but if you remember that the root word is quick with the added suffix 'ly' then you cannot get it wrong!

5. Suffixes that are used frequently, but that **do not change the meaning of the word**, are often used incorrectly. These suffixes play an important role in grammar as well as spelling, so you need to get them right!
   a Adding the suffix 's' makes a noun a **plural**.
   Example: hazard → hazards
   Adding the suffix 's' can also be used to make a present tense verb **singular**.
   Example: The hazard stops John walking.
   b Adding the suffix 'ed' makes a verb **past tense**.
   Example: play → played
   Adding the suffix 'ed' can also make the verb a **past participle**.
   Example: The boys played football.
   c Adding the suffix 'ing' to a verb makes it a **present participle**.
   Examples: die → dying in the sentence 'The dying woman moaned.'
   d Adding the suffix 'er' to an adjective (strong) or an adverb (fast) shows it to be **comparative**.
   Examples: strong → stronger (adjective), fast → faster (adverb)
   e Adding the suffix 'est' to an adjective (such as strong) or adverb (such as fast) creates a **superlative**.
   Examples: strong → strongest (adjective), fast → fastest (adverb)

   Note: the problem with suffixes is that the adding of a suffix is not as straightforward or easy as adding a prefix: there are a few rules that you need to follow in order to **avoid making simple and repeated spelling errors**. Learn these and not only will you be a great speller, but you'll also be able to understand why words are spelt certain ways!

SPELLING

Adding suffixes and prefixes, changing nouns to verbs and verbs to adjectives

6 If the suffix you wish to add begins with a vowel, e.g. 'ing' or 'ed', use the **doubling rule:** for a root word ending in a single vowel and a consonant, such as shop or tap, the consonant at the end of the word must double before adding the suffix.
Examples: shop → shopping, tap → tapping
Learning this rule will prevent you from misspelling words that drop the 'e' before adding the suffix.
Example: hope → hoping (*not* hopping) as it has an 'e' after the final consonant.

7 Of course, all rules are made to be broken, and this is the case for spelling rules as well. The **main exceptions** are words ending in 'x', 'w' and 'y'. (Note: 'w' and 'y' act as vowels in these words.)
Examples: row → rowing, box → boxing, grey → greyest

8 Also, many common double-syllable words **do not double the last consonant**.
Examples: ticketing, ticketed, entering, towered, widening, tutoring, balloting, sugared, budgeter, budgeting, budgeted

Test Your Skills

Learn the words below. A common method of learning and self-testing is the LOOK, SAY, COVER, WRITE, CHECK method. If you make any mistakes, you should rewrite the word three times correctly, immediately. In this way you will become familiar with the correct spelling. If the word is particularly troublesome, rewrite it several more times or keep a list of words that you can check regularly.

This week's theme word: HISTORY

besiege	______	resource	______
conflicting	______	currently	______
towered	______	republic	______
discover	______	independence	______
invaded	______	deconstruct	______
motivating	______	noblest	______
beginning	______	governments	______
digging	______	hottest	______
rebellion	______	colonisation	______

Write any troublesome words three times.

______ ______ ______

______ ______ ______

SPELLING
Common misspellings

Please ask your parent or teacher to read to you the spelling words on page 249.
Write the correct spelling of each word in the box.

1. The launch will commence at ________ 0800 hours.
2. America was granted ________ from the British Empire in 1776.
3. Some say the ________ was a misunderstood protest.
4. The minister is ________ under investigation.
5. A giant ________ over me as I approached the top of the beanstalk.
6. The family hadn't ________ for meals, so they had to eat plain noodles.
7. The cinematographer ________ the little child in the shot.
8. The behaviour of the young man was ________.
9. The baby's head was out of ________ with its body.
10. George had an allergic ________ to the bee sting.
11. Julie was unsure how to respond to the man's ________.
12. The young child looked ________ as she slept on the lounge.
13. The ________ on the town's foreshore was protested against.
14. Mary and James celebrated their ________ in June.
15. Detailed ________ of the crime scene was necessary.

The spelling mistakes in these sentences have been underlined.
Write the correct spelling for each underlined word in the box.

16. I was required to <u>repproduse</u> a copy of Dali's masterpiece.
17. The radio station had our new single on high <u>rotaishon</u>.
18. Thursday night is when the mall is <u>bombbarrded</u> by an unruly mob.
19. It seeps out of the car park and only <u>disollves</u> again at 9pm.
20. To the <u>uninisheated</u> the scene can be quite daunting as teenagers of all descriptions besiege the previously peaceful shops.

☞ Answers on page 201

SPELLING
Common misspellings

Each sentence has one word that is incorrect.
Write the correct spelling of the word in the box.

21 They lean against walls, loytar in cafes and harass passers-by.

What is Philosophy?

The word 'philosophy' derives from the Greek word *philosophos*

22 which transslates in English to 'a lover of wisdom'.

23 Philosophers are concerned with trying to comprahend the nature of man and the world in which we live.

24 The two most important philosophers orijunated in ancient Greece: their names were Socrates and Plato.
Plato was a student of Socrates until Socrates was sentenced

25 to death by self-poisoning for 'corrupptting the youth of Athens'.

☞ Answers on page 201

GRAMMAR AND PUNCTUATION

Commas, semicolons and apostrophes

Key Points

1. **Commas** are used to:
   a indicate where a reader should **pause**.
   Example: I made a comparison between Josie and Balin, and now KJ is offended.
   b **separate a noun or phrase** from the rest of the sentence.
   Example: Saxon, my nephew, analyses everything I say.
   c **separate** words or phrases **in a list**.
   Example: In Drama we learn about improvisation, play-building, movement and characterisation.
   d separate **words spoken** (quotations) from the rest of the sentence.
   Example: The philosopher declared, 'I think, therefore I am.'
   e **indicate where a main clause begins** if a sentence starts with a subordinate clause or phrase.
   Example: As he edged his way closer, we left the brightly illuminated room.

2. **Semicolons** are used to:
   a **separate pieces of information** that are different, yet related.
   Example: six students began the tournament; the challenges were arduous.
   b **separate lists of items** that are complicated.
   Example: The task will involve: classification of texts; anthologizing shorter texts; editing drafts and indexing all catalogue items.

3. **Apostrophes** have two uses:
   a to **show ownership**: When something belongs to an individual (or thing), ownership is shown with 's.
   Examples: dog's collar, Holden's tyre, doctor's fee, table's leg, team's mascot
   When ownership belongs to **more than one individual (or thing)**, ownership is shown by s'.
   Examples: boys' noses, dogs' tails, teachers' staffroom, babies' playroom
   Note: there is **one exception** to this rule, and it is one that students frequently get wrong. The words *it is* do not use the apostrophe to show ownership. Instead, *it's* is a contraction of *it is*. Imagine that the apostrophe is a tiny letter 'i' and this should help you to remember that *it's* is short for *it is*.
   b to show **a contraction or abbreviation**: when two words are combined to make one shorter word by dropping some letters, the apostrophe is used to illustrate that this contraction has occurred.
   Examples: should not → shouldn't, could not → couldn't, do not → don't
   Note: many students confuse the contractions *could've* and *should've* with the separate words *could of* and *should of*. If you know that *could've* is a contraction of *could have*, this should help you fix this common mistake.

4. **Hyphens** (-) are used to create some **compound words**, specifically adjectives.
   Examples: hand-held, right-wing, third-world

GRAMMAR AND PUNCTUATION
Commas, semicolons and apostrophes

5 **Dashes (—) are used to:**

a replace commas, semicolons, colons and parentheses to **indicate added emphasis, an interruption, or an abrupt change of thought**.
Examples: Lisa—my best friend in the whole world—arrives from Tasmania today.
The cake still needs two things—icing and candles.
It's time for you to—oh, you've done it!

Test Your Skills

1 How many commas (,) should be in this sentence? Put them in the appropriate places.
He informed the judge who was an intimidating individual that he was innocent of all charges even those he knew he had committed.

2 Insert a semicolon (;) in the appropriate place in the following sentence.
The weather was ferocious Kevin was unnerved.

3 Change the following words to their contracted form.

should have	____________	should not	____________
could have	____________	could not	____________
will not	____________	do not	____________

4 Identify if the apostrophe (') in the sentence below is a contraction or shows ownership. Circle your answer.
Jamie's father was a gruff and stubborn man. (ownership, contraction)
Martin, who had raced down the street at full speed, should've caught Harry. (ownership, contraction)

Answers: 1 Three commas (He informed the judge, who was an intimidating individual, that he was innocent of all charges, even those he knew he had committed.) 2 The weather was ferocious; Kevin was unnerved. 3 should've, shouldn't, could've, couldn't, won't, don't 4 ownership, contraction

GRAMMAR AND PUNCTUATION

Commas, semicolons and apostrophes

1 Which of the following sentences has the correct punctuation?

A Yesterday, I went to the promenade for a stroll.
B Yesterday I went to the promenade for a stroll.
C Yesterday, I went to the promenade for a stroll!
D Yesterday I went to the promenade for a stroll?

2 Shade one circle to show where the missing apostrophe (') should go.

Your brother(A)s(B) are crazy. They think it(C)s funny to dance in their underwear.

3 Which sentence uses speech marks (" and ") correctly?

A I envy your "courage during this difficult time," said George.
B "I envy your courage during" this difficult time, said George.
C "I envy your courage during this difficult time, said George."
D "I envy your courage during this difficult time," said George.

4 What does the prefix *un* in the word *unmade* mean?

without	very	not	against
A	B	C	D

5 Which punctuation mark should be used in the spaces in this sentence below?

Jason ordered four items from the catalogue: an encyclopaedia of spiders   a pack of playing cards   a poster of the alphabet and a vegetarian cookbook.

: (colon)	; (semicolon)	... (ellipsis)	— (dash)
A	B	C	D

6 Which sentence has the correct punctuation?

A Florence Nightingale was known as 'The Lady with the Lamp'.
B Florence Nightingale was known as The Lady with the Lamp.
C Florence nightingale was known as 'The Lady with the Lamp'.
D florence Nightingale was known as 'The Lady with the Lamp'.

7 Which of the following words correctly completes the sentence?

The River Nile runs through Egypt, creating ______ fertile green valley across the desert.

some	an	a	those
A	B	C	D

8 Which sentence has the correct punctuation?

A There were no cars in victorian England—People either walked, travelled by boat or used coach horses to move from place to place.
B There were no cars in Victorian England. people either walked; travelled by boat or used coach horses to move from place to place.
C There were no cars in Victorian England people either walked travelled by boat or used coach horses to move from place to place.
D There were no cars in Victorian England. People either walked, travelled by boat or used coach horses to move from place to place.

☞ Answers and explanations on pages 202–203

GRAMMAR AND PUNCTUATION
Commas, semicolons and apostrophes

9 Chocolate is what makes the world go round.

This sentence is an example of

A personification. B oxymoron. C hyperbole. D alliteration.

10 Veganism is becoming increasingly popular for a number of different reasons: ethical, religious or concern for one's health or the environment.

In the third sentence, a colon (:) is used to

A separate two complete ideas.
B introduce a list.
C introduce a new idea.
D separate items in a list.

11 How could this sentence be re-written correctly with the same meaning?

'Can I get your phone number?' asked Jeff.

A Jeff asked for his phone number.
B Jeff asked if "he could have your phone number."
C Jeff asked for your phone number.
D Jeff wanted to know if you asked for his phone number.

12 Which words correctly complete the sentence below?

The caterpillar transformed ______________________.

A slowly into a beautiful butterfly.
B quick into a butterfly.
C slowly of its cocoon.
D quickly into having wings.

13 Which of the following correctly completes the sentence?

Dean is _______ you would call an eccentric character.

A who B that C why D what

Write the word or words in the box to correctly complete the sentences below.

14 Angela [ ] seen her beloved black kitten since yesterday afternoon.

A is B had C hasn't D haven't

15 John changed [ ] mind about going to the disco; [ ] going to go to [ ] friend's house instead.

A he's he his
B his he's his
C his his he's
D he's his he's

16 A longboard [ ] a type of skateboard that has a longer wheel base and larger wheels.

A was B is C are D have

Highlight the correct answer in the sentences below.

17 Climate change activism is becoming increasingly popular amongst teenagers.

In this sentence, the word 'increasingly' is

A an adverb. B an adjective. C an abstract noun. D a verb.

☞ Answers and explanations on pages 202–203

GRAMMAR AND PUNCTUATION
Commas, semicolons and apostrophes

18 More and more people are choosing a vegan diet for environmental reasons because they feel that the production and consumption of meat uses too many precious natural resources.

In this sentence, the word 'vegan' is used as

A a noun. B an adverb. C an adjective. D a pronoun.

19 In the 1700s, with the advent of mechanical mills, chocolate was first made into the solid and sweet product that is consumed today.

The word 'mechanical' in this sentence is

A a pronoun. B a noun. C an adverb. D an adjective.

20 The main ingredients of the chocolate eaten in the largest commercial quantities are cocoa, sugar and milk powder.

The word 'largest' in this sentence is an example of

A a verb. B a noun. C an adjective.

21 Which word in this sentence is a pronoun? Circle your answer.

Having reached (A) the summit (B) of K2 she felt as though she had conquered (C) the world.

22 Shade one circle to show where the missing apostrophe (') should go.

A frog (A) s ability to move quickly is essential if it is to catch it (B) s prey and escape predators (C).

23 Which word in this sentence is a pronoun? Circle your answer.

He (A) was intrigued (B) by the microscopic structures (C) built (D) by aphids.

24 Which of the following words correctly completes the sentence?

There are three different types of clouds ________ that can be seen in our skies.

A … high, middle and low …
B ; high, middle and low ;
C : high, middle and low :
D —high, middle and low—

25 Which sentence correctly combines the information in this table?

BREED	TRAITS
Red Cattle Dog	energetic, big eaters, bounce high
Australian Kelpie	energetic, good natured, slim build

A Red Cattle Dogs and Australian Kelpies are both energetic breeds while they also have slim builds and can bounce high.

B Both Red Cattle Dogs and Australian Kelpies are energetic; they are also good natured and can bounce high.

C Red Cattle Dogs and Australian Kelpies are both energetic breeds; Red Cattle Dogs are also big eaters and can bounce high while Australian Kelpies are good natured and have a slim build.

D Red Cattle Dogs and Australian Kelpies are energetic breeds together; Red Cattle Dogs are big eaters and can bounce high, and Australian Kelpies are good natured and have a slim build.

☞ Answers and explanations on pages 202–203

READING
Understanding book reviews

Book reviews appear in magazines and newspapers. An independent reader gives his or her opinion of the book. Book reviews can be positive (good) or negative (bad).
Read this book review by Sally Murphy of *That's Why I Wrote this Song* and answer the questions.

Young Adult Book Review: *That's Why I Wrote this Song* by Susanne Gervay

Four girls. One dream.

I write because I write. I've always done it. Private, emotions-on-the-page lyrics. Not-to-show-anyone words. Lately it's been spilling out. Flooding me. Sometimes the music screams at me, exploding into my mind. Lyrics and music. I can't stop them.

Pip lives for music. Sometimes it is fun, other times it's an escape from the real world, a world where Mum is scared and her dad is angry. Pip's three friends love music too. Irina plays drums, but her Russian parents don't approve. They want her to play the piano and study hard. Karen's parents are divorced, and Karen has to move between them, left with no home, no space of her own. Without music she might well have nothing. Angie has a perfect life, but she loves music, too. The four girls are very different, but music brings them together.

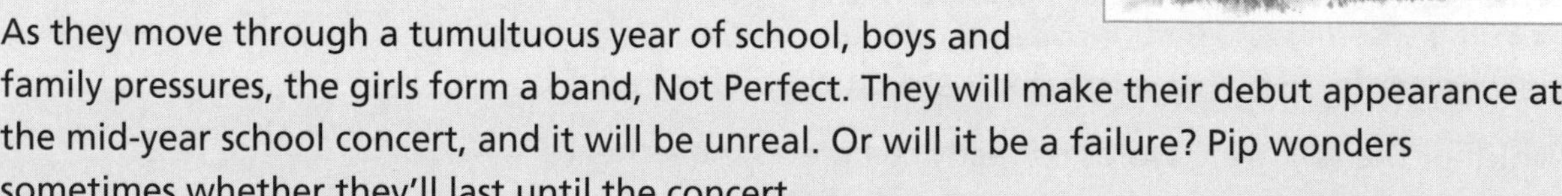

As they move through a tumultuous year of school, boys and family pressures, the girls form a band, Not Perfect. They will make their debut appearance at the mid-year school concert, and it will be unreal. Or will it be a failure? Pip wonders sometimes whether they'll last until the concert.

That's Why I Wrote This Song is an outstanding new young adult read, with the world of music and bands forming an absorbing backdrop for the dramas, big and small, of the four girls' lives. Exploring teen issues including parent-child relationships, family roles, boyfriends, friendships and more, the story is an emotion-filled journey. The lyrics of the girls' songs pepper the book, adding a new dimension to the story and providing an insight into the song-writing process.

That's Why I Wrote This Song is the result of a collaboration between best-selling author Susanne Gervay and her daughter, Tory, who wrote the lyrics. In true family spirit, Susanne's son, Jamie, also had input into the plot. For music fans, there is the added bonus that the two songs featured in the book can be downloaded from the publisher's website, and a film clip viewed at the author's website, www.sgervay.com.

That's Why I Wrote This Song is a brilliant book.

Source: www.aussiereviews.com/page1001.html

That's Why I Wrote This Song by Susanne Gervay, Harper Collins, 2007

READING
Understanding book reviews

1 The reviewer's opinion is that Susanne Gervay's book is

complicated.	insincere.	satisfactory.	exceptional.	unsettling
A	B	C	D	E

2 The text at the top of the review (beginning with: 'I write because ...') is most likely
- A the expectations of the author.
- B the thoughts of a girl in the band.
- C words from a dream.
- D comments from the reviewer.

3 Draw a line between the word 'pepper', Paragraph 5, and the phrase that has the same meaning.

The lyrics of the girls' songs **pepper** the book, adding a new dimension to the story ...'

are scattered throughout   break up the plot of   are examples within   effectively clarify

4 The book is called 'a collaboration' (second-last paragraph). It is a collaboration between
- A the girls in the band.
- B the author and her daughter.
- C Sally Murphy and Susanne Gervay.
- D Tory and Jamie.

5 Which of the girls in the band appears to have the best home life?
- A Pip
- B Irina
- C Angie
- D Karen

6 The song lyrics are called a 'backdrop' (paragraph 5). This implies that
- A action in the book is less important than the girls' interpersonal relationships.
- B relationships are more important than action.
- C the band's success will depend upon the stage settings.
- D all action in the book is seen against the lyrics of songs.

7 According to the review of the book, which statements are TRUE and which are FALSE?
Write T or F in the box.
- ☐ Being in the band helps each of the girls to cope with difficulties in their lives.
- ☐ Each girl believes that the only way to become independent is to join the band.
- ☐ The girls decide to form the band because they are dissatisfied with their home lives.
- ☐ The girls aim to keep the band together so they can play at the mid-year school concert.

8 The story *That's Why I Wrote This Song* is mainly concerned with issues of
- A making a band successful.
- B personal relationships.
- C writing and recording songs.
- D facing failure.

9 What extra bonus can purchasers of the book expect?
- A a chance to join the band
- B a free CD
- C downloads of the songs written by Tory
- D participating in a film clip

Answers: 1 D 2 B 3 are scattered throughout 4 B 5 C 6 D
7 T, F, F, T 8 B 9 C

☞ Explanations on pages 203–204

READING
Understanding transactions

A transactional text is used to sustain relationships and involves simple interactions and negotiations often in the form of letters, invitations and interviews.

Read this interview where Kerri Falls talks with Jon Doust, author of *Boy on a Wire*, and answer the questions.

(Jon Doust's story is about Jack Muir who is sent to boarding school at a young age. He survives because of a quick wit and a fast mouth. Others aren't so lucky.)

What has your previous writing experience been?

I've had two children's books published.

How different was the experience of writing a novel for older readers?

Quite different. The story was very close to me. Yeah, it was draining, a bit emotional. I did a lot of research, because I wanted to reconnect with the time. There were things that I didn't remember happening the way they happened.

Where did the character of Jack emerge from?

The starting point was me. But he became somebody other than me. Some bits are not like me, some bits are worse than me. Jack is an expansion of some of my characteristics and a reflection of others. All the characters are compilations. They just have to fit the story. I didn't start writing knowing what the book was about. The book simply emerged. Everybody was rewritten at least once, Jack more than once. They had to suit the book, and then they had to suit themselves.

How did you treat the autobiographical element?

I simply took an event as I remembered it and wrote it down. Then I blew it apart. Kept rewriting it until it fit the context of the story. For example, the incident where Jack gets beaten by a housemaster with a broomstick is like something that happened to me. But I couldn't remember what I was thinking at the time. I was probably thinking, 'I'll kill them', but I don't know. So I had to inhabit this kid's head. It's Jack's thoughts not mine.

This book has a lot of real pain and some joy too—how do you see the role of humour in telling these kinds of stories?

It's crucial, because it's true. Boys' school life is often quite tense and miserable—but there's also a lot of humour. When people find out I went to boarding school, they often say oh that must have scarred you. And I say, the biggest scar boarding school left on me was the scar it left on others. I survived quite well. But some others didn't.

The book captures a strong sense of injustice really well. Did you consciously create that tone, or did it simply emerge?

It came very early, that sense of justice and injustice. Also, the need for revenge emerged as I wrote. That was unexpected. I was talking to a guy who went to the same school. He went to a party recently and saw this guy who had bullied him at school. So he confronted him. Said, come on, let's take it outside. But this bully just backed off, didn't want anything to do with it. That's ok, but what would have been better was if the bully had said, I'm sorry about the terrible things I did. Some bullies are in denial their whole lives. Others feel deeply guilty about what they did in boarding school.

READING
Understanding transactions

1. Jon Doust's novel is based upon
   - A the life of a boarding school bully.
   - B events in his own life.
   - C fictional characters and events.
   - D events in the life of Kerri Falls.

2. The interviewee, Jon Doust, uses the word 'Yeah' in his response to the second question. What does this suggest?
   - A Jon needed a moment to think before continuing his reply.
   - B Jon finds writing novels for older readers difficult.
   - C Jon was uncertain what the question meant.
   - D Jon was not sure if he wanted to answer the question.

3. Complete the sentence with the correct words. Write one word in each space.
   Jon remembers his school days as ________ but not entirely ________.

   educational stimulating unhappy tedious supportive difficult rewarding

4. According to Jon, what are the two types of bullies that emerged from the boarding school experience? Circle two answers.
   - A bullies who erase past events from their minds
   - B bullies who accept that they were bullies
   - C bullies who are amused by their past behaviour
   - D bullies who are still ready to get into fights
   - E bullies who feel guilty about their past behaviour

5. What aspect of his writing did Jon find unforeseen?
   - A the feeling of revenge that he carried
   - B his inability to remember things that had happened
   - C discovering the amount of bullying that took place at the school
   - D meeting the teacher who had punished him with a broomstick

6. According to the interview, what theme dominates the story?
   - A revenge
   - B betrayal
   - C survival
   - D alienation

7. Jon says that he was scarred by his boarding school experiences. He was scarred
   - A after being hit with a broomstick.
   - B by the feelings of regret he felt for less resilient students
   - C emotionally by his personal trials and experiences.
   - D physically, while being picked on by bullies.

8. Draw one line to the best word to describe the Interviewer's questions and another line to the best word to describe Jon Doust's answers.

Interviewer's questions	terse
	frank
Jon Doust's answers	probing
	inconsiderate
	irrelevant

☞ Answers and explanations on page 204

READING
Understanding transactions

Read this letter of invitation and answer the questions.

23 October 2020
Ms Rayma Mathis
Director, Public Relations
Educational and Career Opportunities Unit
Suite 12, 3 Parkedge St
Westlands 5432

Dear Ms Mathis

The purpose of this letter is to officially invite you, on behalf of the Excel High School Board of Management, to be the Closing Keynote Speaker at the upcoming senior school graduation and awards night. Each year we invite guests to address all the students from senior classes, many of whom are about to either attend a tertiary educational institution or embark upon a career.

The theme of this evening is Life after School. The function will be held at the Brian Trent OAM Auditorium, in the school grounds at 19 Bridge Rd, Mt Warraloo on 9 December 2020. Our function commences at 7 pm.

For your information Simon Makepeace, of the Department of Educational Extension, will be the opening Speaker. The provisional title of his address is Leaving the Nest—Fly or Cry?

Following his address will be a short talk from the President of the school board who will then present the awards. Our School Councillor, Ms Mary Geller, will follow this and address the students and parents on how to interpret external exam marks.

If you are considering accepting our invitation, I will forward a complete draft speaker program to you in a couple of weeks to make you aware of the ideas to be incorporated into the addresses by the other speakers.

Two hundred and seventy-five (275) students are expected to attend and usually about 80% of parents join us on the night. We expect a high attendance rate this year because of the stress families are feeling in these times of global recession and falling employment opportunities. We have extended an invitation to parents from some of the lower grades because of anxieties some feel about the shrinking opportunities for their children. A number of these parents have already responded positively to the invitation.

In closing, the Board would be pleased and honoured if you would consent to be our closing speaker at the 2020 ceremony.

I will call you in a week or so to follow up on this.

Yours sincerely

Dr Wesley Nagle
Principal, Excel High School
Bridge Rd
Mt Warraloo

READING
Understanding transactions

1 How many official speakers are expected to be at the graduation ceremony?
Write the number on the line. ______________

2 The tone of the letter could best be described as
A formal. B confidential. C abrupt. D casual.

3 What could be the reason for inviting Ms Mathis to be the guest speaker?
A She is a friend of the school principal.
B She is a member of the school Board of Management.
C She had been guest speaker at the previous year's awards night.
D She would have had experience in advising career options for students.

4 The words 'Fly or Cry' (paragraph 3) are most likely intended to
A relate to careers in agriculture.
B suggest students resist taking on difficult projects.
C imply that life after school depends on the individual's attitude.
D encourage students to leave home as soon as possible.

5 What reason is suggested for the high attendance anticipated at the awards night?
A deteriorating economic conditions in society
B a higher than average number of successful students
C Ms Geller will address the audience on interpreting exam results
D it is the last opportunity for many students to attend the function

6 If Ms Mathis accepts the offer to speak, the principal will
A inform the school board of management
B advise her of the content of the other guest speakers' addresses
C call Ms Mathis to find out her reaction. D issue a formal invitation to attend.

7 What impression does the letter give of the 'upcoming senior school graduation and awards night'?
You may circle more than one option.

confusing	important	overcrowded	uninspiring	well-planned	lacklustre
A	B	C	D	E	F

8 What reason would the principal have for advising Ms Mathis of the topic and content of the other speakers' addresses?
A to give her the opportunity to prepare a better speech
B to demonstrate his effectiveness as an organiser
C to keep the function flowing smoothly
D to ensure that speakers do not cover the same content

9 Number the boxes from 1 to 5 to show the order in which the events will happen on the awards night.
☐ the President of the board's address
☐ explanation of external exam marks
☐ the Keynote address
☐ presentation of awards
☐ Simon Makepeace's address

☞ Answers and explanations on pages 204–205

READING
Understanding film reviews

Read this film review of *Samson and Delilah* by Sandra Hall and answer the questions.

Backed with the lively sounds of Charley Pride singing Sunshiny Day, the opening scene of the Indigenous filmmaker Warwick Thornton's *Samson and Delilah* has a delicate beauty.

As 15-year-old Samson (Rowan McNamara) wakes, the morning light strikes his bed as if granting a blessing. As he sits up with a groggy air of purpose, he ruins the image by picking up a can from the floor and holding it to his nose to take a long, deep breath. He's a petrol sniffer, and for the next few minutes we're taken through the hazy patterns of his day, which is spent sluggishly kicking the dust around the tiny Aboriginal settlement in the Central Australian desert.

In this place of magnificent skies and endless red plains, Samson and most of the others in his community behave as if trapped in a bell jar and starved of the oxygen necessary to make things happen. Only 16-year-old Delilah (Marissa Gibson) and her grandmother, Nana (Mitjili Gibson), seem content. Nana is the community's painter and her work is spirited away to the city by a dubious character who snaps up each painting as soon as it's finished. And as her grandmother paints, Delilah watches and sometimes helps, rapt both by the media and her grandmother's pleasure in her work. Nana's happiness is infectious. As Samson silently studies the pair from the sidelines, he decides that he wants Delilah for his girlfriend.

Samson's brother has a garage band, which Samson is banned from joining. He resorts to his boom box, while Delilah finds her refuge in the car, where she sits at night, listening to Latin music.

The pace quickens after Nana dies in her sleep. Despite having cared for her, Delilah is accused of neglect and beaten with sticks by the other community women. Deeply stirred by her injuries, Samson steals a van and takes her to Alice Springs, where things inevitably get a lot worse before they get any better.

The few moments of cheerfulness come courtesy of Gonzo (Scott Thornton), a homeless man the teenagers meet while sleeping rough under a bridge on the town's edge.

Like all stories about addiction, this one is dispiriting. Despite the flash of hope that Thornton gives you at the end, he isn't providing the kind of ending you get in more conventional films. He takes you into another world, but finds no obligation to make you comfortable there. He's made a tender film, and an honest one, but it's tough going.

Adapted from Sandra Hall, *Sydney Morning Herald*, 7 May 2009:
www.smh.com.au/news/entertainment/film/film-reviews/samson-and-delilah/2009/05/07/1241289282398.html

READING
Understanding film reviews

1. Which word best describes the reviewer's opinion of the film?
   A optimistic B enjoyable C thrilling D honest

2. Draw a line between an aspect of the film and the word the reviewer would use to describe it.

A Samson's relationship with his community	accepting
B the effect of Nana's paintings on Delilah	apathetic
C Nana's approach to her life	alienated
D the buyer of Nana's paintings	underhanded
E the general mood of people at the settlement	intriguing

3. What is the significance of the song Sunshiny Day?
   A It is the song played by Samson's brother's band.
   B It prepares the audience for an entertaining evening.
   C It contrasts to the lives of the people in the community.
   D It is Samson and Delilah's favourite song.

4. The reviewer states that Samson watches 'from the sidelines' (paragraph 3). By using this phrase the reviewer is suggesting that Samson
   A is on the edge of a sporting field.
   B wishes he was an artist.
   C is not part of the action.
   D has no interest in painting.

5. The film draws a comparison between the harsh restrictions of settlement life and the
   A opportunities available in Alice Springs.
   B way Aboriginal artworks are sought after.
   C traditional ways of Aboriginal life.
   D magnificent skies and endless desert.

6. According to the reviewer, the film *Samson and Delilah* is mainly concerned with issues of
   A homelessness. B addiction. C employment. D family relationships.

7. Why did Samson take Delilah to Alice Springs? Write your answer on the lines.

   ____

   ____

8. Read the statements about the film director, Warwick Thornton. Are the statements FACT or OPINION? Write F or O in the box next to the statement.

   ☐ Warwick Thornton's film is tender, honest and has a few moments of cheerfulness.
   ☐ The ending of Warwick Thornton's film differs from endings in conventional films.
   ☐ Warwick Thornton is an Aboriginal man who made a film about Indigenous issues.
   ☐ In the opening scene Warwick Thornton beautifies the morning and the settlement.
   ☐ Warwick Thornton's tough film suggests there is little hope for the main characters.

☞ Answers and explanations on page 205

TIPS FOR WRITING NARRATIVE TEXTS

A **narrative** is a fiction text and is also known as a **story**. The purpose of a narrative is to entertain, amuse or inform.

Before you start writing

- **Read the question and check the stimulus material carefully. Stimulus material** refers to the topic, title, picture, words, phrases or extract of writing you are given to base your writing on.
- **Decide if you are going to be writing in the first person** (you become a character in your story) or in **the third person** (you are writing about other characters). When writing in the first person be careful not to overuse the pronoun I (e.g. **I did this, I did that**).
- Take a few moments to **plan the structure of your story**. **Remember:** Stories have a beginning, middle and end. It sounds simple but many stories fail because one of these three parts is not well written.

Structure of narrative texts

A narrative has a specific structure, containing:

- Orientation—the introduction of the setting and characters
- Complication—a problem faced by the character(s) that must be overcome
- Climax—a scene of increased tension where the character is faced with some kind of danger
- Resolution—the problem is overcome
- Coda—a lesson is learned and life returns to normal.

Language features of narrative texts

- **Engage the senses** of your reader through description of what can be seen, heard, felt, tasted or smelled. To do this you should include figures of speech such as similes, metaphors and personification.
- **Use strong action verbs** to capture mood and create tension. Instead of The girl took the food you could say The girl lunged for the food.
- **Use emotive words** to engage the emotions of your reader. It is important to consider what emotions you would like your reader to feel for a character in a specific situation. Once you have decided, use emotive words and phrases to evoke these emotions, e.g. Lee sat alone feeling despair descend upon him or Rob's desire for the cookie caused his stomach to tangle.
- **Use dialogue sparingly**. It should be used to develop a character or situation. Remember that dialogue tags should elaborate on the attitude of the speaker. Instead of writing Jane said you should be more specific, such as Jane cried or Jane moaned, flicking her hair over her shoulder.

Don't forget to:

- plan your narrative before you start
- write in correctly formed sentences and take care with paragraphing
- choose your words carefully and pay attention to your spelling and punctuation
- write neatly but don't waste time
- quickly check your narrative once you have finished.

You will find a sample annotated narrative text on the following page. The question is from page 70. Read the narrative text and notes before you begin your second Writing Test. This piece of writing has been analysed based on the marking criteria used by markers to assess the NAPLAN Writing Test. **Remember:** This sample was not written under exam conditions.

Year 9 Sample Narrative Writing

(a sample answer to the question on page 70)

Structure

Audience
- Figurative language is used to create imagery for the reader—simile and personification.

Character and setting
- Personification of the car continues to suggest that it will feature significantly in the narrative.
- Use of parenthesis creates a humorous and personal voice for the main character.

Text structure
- The first paragraph is the story's orientation. The descriptive language early in the story establishes the setting and orients the reader.
- This is the complication of the story—the car didn't work and presents a problem for the main character.
- The resolution is a cliffhanger. The reader is left to consider what the consequences of the accident may be for Miro.

Cohesion
- Appropriate use of connectives enhance the reading. Continuity of ideas is demonstrated throughout the story—the focus on Miro's perspective.

Such is Life

Heavy fat drops fall rhythmically on the windscreen of the groaning car, only to be unceremoniously flicked aside by the overworked wipers. The dance of the blades mesmerise Miro as he stops at the 13th set of red traffic lights. Drop. Flick. Drop. Flick. The rain has been falling for three days.

That morning, Miro's 74 Beetle (toffee-apple red with black racing strips) had refused to start. Turning the key and whispering encouraging words like a mother cajoling a child to swallow bitter medicine, the bug coughed and wheezed then sat silently still. Admitting defeat, and with no other option, Miro ran inside and grabbed the keys for his wife's Getz (fake banana yellow). His wife hadn't driven the car in weeks, having protested loudly that the brakes were as unreliable as Miro himself. She had taken the bus.

So here Miro sits: in a car too small for a child, fighting through three lanes of dense traffic as the sky slowly releases a constant barrage of water. His grey suit pants are tight around his stomach and he begins to regret having eaten the leftover super-supreme for breakfast. Tight black curls on his head turn to spirals of fuzz as the air moistens. Finally, the lights flick to the glory of green and Miro is rewarded for his patience, edging two car lengths forward. Stopped again. Since the rain began Miro has been surprised by what he sees others do in their cars. Most sit with a concentrated look of barely contained rage. Others seem to drift into a trance, hypnotised by the low lullaby of the rain splattering the metal and plastic bubble surrounding them. A bubble that separates these workers—these humans—from nature and from each other.

The next set of lights greets Miro with amber and with a squeeze of the brake he attempts to comply with its command to slow. Unfortunately the brakes are as defiant as bored school children and refuse to oblige. Encased in his own bubble of metal and plastic, Miro races towards the barely contained rage in the car to his left. The crunch of metal on metal and the inaudible splinter of a pricey spray job inform Miro that the cars have met in damage. The next sounds are even less pleasing—the rage that had been so tightly contained has popped and has begun the intimidating (and vocal) approach towards the driver's door of Miro's car. Despite the commotion the rain drives on, throwing sheets of water on the man's body as he glares ominously through Miro's now breath-fogged windows. Hastily fumbling in his pockets Miro retrieves his beaten and bare wallet and removes his driver's licence. A quick fish in the breast pocket of his shirt provides him with a fountain pen and a small piece of paper.

Waving his personal details at the stranger, Miro ventures out into the rain. Such is life.

This text is beyond what would be expected of a typical Year 9 student. It is provided here as a model. The assessment comments are based on the marking criteria used to assess the NAPLAN Writing Test.

Language and ideas

Vocabulary
- Sibilance lengthens the moment of calmness and quiet.
- Imagery created through alliteration and metaphor.
- The writer uses strong verbs to create tension in the scene.
- The word *fish* in this sentence works as a verb, not a noun.

Sentence structure
- A variety of sentence lengths creates interest and shows control of language.
- Short sentences create drama.

Ideas
- The story has sophisticated ideas. The theme is clearly established: it is about the conformity and loss of meaning in modern life. It makes a comment on the isolation of the individual in modern society.

Punctuation
- Correct punctuation is used throughout the story.

Spelling
- All words are correctly spelled.
- Difficult and challenging words (e.g *inaudible*) are included.

© Pascal Press ISBN 978 1 74125 210 1

WRITING
Narrative text 1

There is no way of knowing for certain what type of writing will be included in the NAPLAN Tests in years to come. This is an opportunity for you to practise different types of writing.

Before you start, read the General writing tips on pages 35–36 and the Tips for writing narratives on page 68.

Today you are going to write a narrative or story.

Look at the picture on the right.

The idea that you must base your story on is the famous Ned Kelly phrase SUCH IS LIFE. Your story might be about a day of hard work in a place such as a factory or busy office block, the death of a beloved pet or an individual giving up the fight for freedom. It could be a person's reflection on a failed relationship, an argument with a friend or the loss of a much-loved leather jacket.

Before you start writing, give some thought to:
- where your story takes place
- the characters and what they do in your story
- the events that take place in your story and the problems that have to be resolved
- how your story begins, what happens in your story, and how your story ends.

Don't forget to:
- plan your story before you start writing
- write in correctly formed sentences and take care with paragraphing
- choose your words carefully and pay attention to your spelling and punctuation
- write neatly but don't waste time
- quickly check your story once you have finished.

Start writing here or type in your answer on a tablet or computer.

☞ Marking guide on page 206

WRITING
Narrative text 2

There is no way of knowing for certain what type of writing will be included in the NAPLAN Tests in years to come. This is an opportunity for you to practise different types of writing.

Before you start, read the General writing tips on pages 35–36 and the Tips for writing narratives on page 68.

Today you are going to write a narrative or story.

Look at the picture on the right.

The idea that you must base your story on is THE GIFT. Your story might be about a child receiving a gift of a mud pie from a friend in the playground, an anonymous gift found on a doorstep, or a teenager bribing a teacher with a box of chocolates. It could be about a person making the decision to give the gift of life to a friend in the form of a bone marrow transplant, or about a young man who wakes in the morning to discover he has the gift of mental telepathy.

Before you start writing, give some thought to:

- where your story takes place
- the characters and what they do in your story
- the events that take place in your story and the problems that have to be resolved
- how your story begins, what happens in your story, and how your story ends.

Don't forget to:

- plan your story before you start writing
- write in correctly formed sentences and take care with paragraphing
- choose your words carefully and pay attention to your spelling and punctuation
- write neatly but don't waste time
- quickly check your story once you have finished.

Start writing here or type in your answer on a tablet or computer.

☞ Marking guide on pages 206–207

Week 3

This is what we cover this week:

Day 1 **Measurement and Geometry:** ◎ Time, length, scale and capacity
◎ Area and volume

Day 2 **Spelling:** ◎ 'ice' and 'ise' words, common confusions and irregular plurals
◎ Common misspellings

Grammar and Punctuation: ◎ Pronouns, prepositions, articles and subject/verb agreement

Day 3 **Reading:** ◎ Understanding narratives
◎ Understanding recounts

Day 4 **Writing:** ◎ Descriptions

MEASUREMENT AND GEOMETRY
Time, length, scale and capacity

1 Find the amount of time between 8:30 am and 4:45 pm the same day.
A 7 h 15 min B 7 h 45 min
C 8 h 15 min D 8 h 45 min

2 Each working morning Praena leaves home at 7:22 and travels to the city. She arrives home at 6:08 in the evening. How long has Praena been away from home?
A 10 h 46 min B 10 h 30 min
C 11 h 46 min D 11 h 30 min

3 What time has elapsed between 7:45 pm and 11:40 am the next morning?
A 14 h 5 min B 14 h 55 min
C 15 h 5 min D 15 h 55 min

4 A movie marathon commences at 10:35 pm and lasts nine and a half hours. What is the finishing time?
A 7:35 am B 7:55 am C 8:05 am D 8:55 am

5 Which of these is the same as 2.5 metres?
A 250 cm B 250 mm C 25 cm D 25 mm

6 One hundred and forty millilitres is poured from a container containing 2.6 litres of milk Find the amount remaining in the jug.
A 1.2 litres B 2.46 litres
C 2.54 litres D 2.56 litres

7 A cake mixture has a mass of 940 grams. If 270 grams of sugar is added, what is the mass of the mixture?
A 1.1 kg B 1.21 kg C 1.31 kg D 2.1 kg

8 Find the perimeter of the shape.

4 cm
$(2x - 3)$ cm
$(x + 4)$ cm

A $(6x + 10)$ cm B $(3x + 10)$ cm
C $(3x + 5)$ cm D $(6x + 13)$ cm

9 What is the circumference of a circle with a radius of 10 cm, correct to 2 decimal places?
A 20 cm B 31.42 cm
C 62.83 cm D 125.64 cm

10 The length of rectangle is three times its width. If the perimeter is 24 cm, what is the length?
A 3 cm B 6 cm C 8 cm D 9 cm

11 A map of a playground has a scale of 1:100. The distance from A to B on the map is 35 mm. What is the actual distance from A to B?
A 3.5 m B 35 m C 70 m D 135 m

The table shows the actual distance and the map distance between a number of towns.

From	Map distance	Actual distance
A to B	6 cm	42 km
C to D	5.1 cm	35.7 km
E to F		154 km
G to H	8.9 cm	

12 What is the scale used on the map?
A 7 cm = 1 km B 1 cm = 0.7 km
C 1 cm = 7 km D 1 cm = 70 km

13 How far apart are E and F on the map?
A 7 cm B 18 cm C 22 cm D 32 cm

14 What is the actual distance between G and H?
A 60.3 km B 61.3 km
C 61.4 km D 62.3 km

15 The diagram shows a walking trail where the distance from the car park to the lookout is three times the distance from the picnic tables to the waterfall:

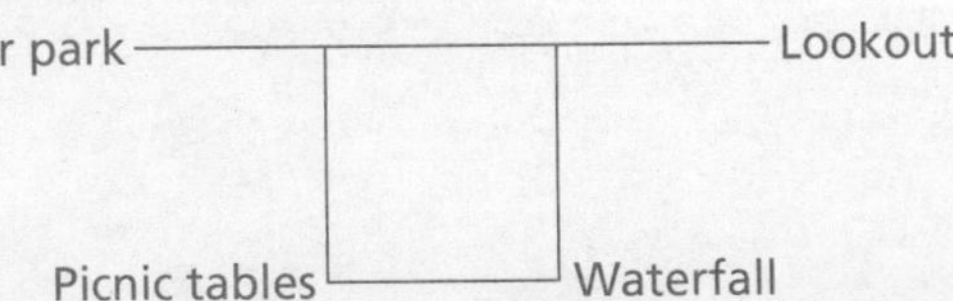

The shortest distance from the picnic tables to the waterfall is 500 metres. What is the best estimate for the shortest distance from the car park to the waterfall?
A 750 metres B 1 kilometre
C 1.2 kilometres D 1.5 kilometres

☞ Explanations on pages 207–208

Answers: 1 C 2 A 3 D 4 C 5 A 6 B 7 B 8 A 9 C 10 D 11 A 12 C 13 C 14 D 15 D

MEASUREMENT AND GEOMETRY
Time, length, scale and capacity

1 **Time elapsed** questions involve subtraction of, or 'counting on', units of time.

Example 1: How much time is between 3:15 pm and 2:10 am the next day?
3:15 to 4:00 is 45 minutes. 4:00 to midnight is 8 hours plus until 2:00 is another 2 hours. Then another 10 minutes until 2:10. This totals 10 hours 55 minutes.

Example 2: A cricket game is being played in South Africa and commences at 7:30 pm Sydney time. The day's play concludes 7 hours 45 minutes later. At what time in Sydney does the game finish for the day?
Adding 7 hours from 7:30 pm makes it 2:30 am. Adding 30 minutes makes it 3:00 am and then another 15 minutes makes it 3:15. The day's play concludes at 3:15 am Sydney time.

2 Some **conversions** between units of measurement:

Time	60 s = 1 min
	60 min = 1 h
	24 h = 1 day
	365 days = 1 yr
	366 days = 1 leap yr
	10 yr = 1 decade
	100 yr = 1 century
	1000 yr = 1 millennium
Length	1000 mm = 1 m
	100 cm = 1 m
	1000 m = 1 km
Mass	1000 mg = 1 g
	1000 g = 1 kg
	1000 kg = 1 t
Capacity	1000 mL = 1 L
	1000 L = 1 kL
	1000 kL = 1 ML
Area	10 000 m^2 = 1 ha

Example: A 1-litre juice container is three-quarters full and a further 360 mL is poured out. How much juice remains in the container?
As 1 litre = 1000 mL,
three-quarters of a litre is 750 mL.

Remaining = 750 – 360
= 750 – 350 – 10
= 390
Therefore 390 mL remains in the container.

3 The **circumference** of a circle is the perimeter, or the distance around the outside of the circle. The formula used is $C = 2\pi r$ or $C = \pi d$, where C is the circumference, π is pi and measures about 3, r is the radius and d is the diameter.

Example 1: What is the approximate circumference of a circle with a diameter of 12 mm?
$C = \pi d$
$= 3 \times 12 = 36 \quad \therefore$ 36 mm

Example 2: Find the perimeter of this shape, writing your answer correct to 2 decimal places.

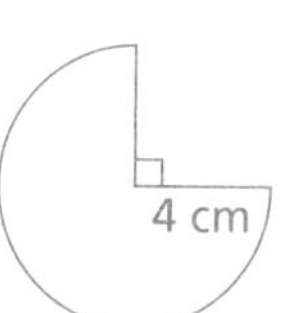

The perimeter is two radii plus $\frac{3}{4}$ of a circle.
Perimeter $= 4 + 4 + \frac{3}{4} \times 2 \times \pi \times 4$
$= 26.85$ (to 2 decimal places)
Therefore perimeter is 26.85 cm.

4 A **scale drawing** is the same as the original but has been reduced or enlarged.

Example 1: A map is drawn using a scale of 1 cm = 40 m. If two places were 7.3 cm apart on the map, what is the actual distance between them?
Distance $= 7.3 \times 40 = 292$
$\therefore$ 292 m

Example 2: The grid shows a map where the distance from A to B is 120 km.

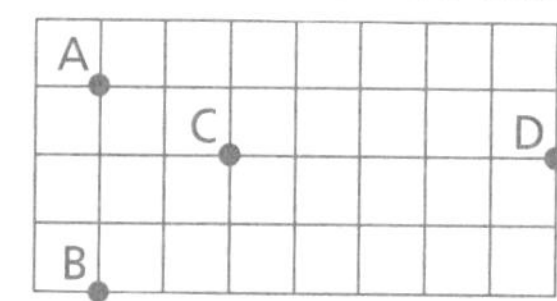

By first finding the scale used on the map, find the distance between C and D.
From A to B: 3 units = 120 km
1 unit = 40 km
From C to D: 5 units $= 40 \times 5 = 200$
$\therefore$ 200 km

MEASUREMENT AND GEOMETRY

Time, length, scale and capacity

1 A multiplex cinema offered four movie marathons.

Cinema	Start	Finish
A	11:30 pm	6:15 am
B	11:45 pm	6:25 am
C	11:55 pm	6:50 am
D	12:00 am	6:35 am

Which marathon lasts for the longest time?

A A B B C C D D

2 A water tank leaks at the rate of 15 mL per minute. How much water will leak in one day?

A 900 mL B 21.6 L C 129.6 L D 200 L

3 A jug contains 1.25 litres of milk. Kelvin needs a total of 2 litres. If he adds 50 mL to the jug, how much more milk is required?

A 25 mL B 250 mL C 70 mL D 700 mL

4 Herman calculates the distance around the outside of a circle with a diameter of 8 cm. Which is closest to his answer? *Hint 1*

A 12 cm B 24 cm C 48 cm D 72 cm

5 The perimeter of the shape is about *Hint 2*

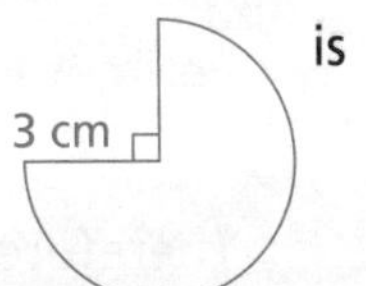

A 12 cm. B 16 cm.
C 20 cm. D 27 cm.

The map shows the homes of four friends: Jake (J), Gil (G), Moni (M), Sam (S). Jake and Gil live 40 km apart.

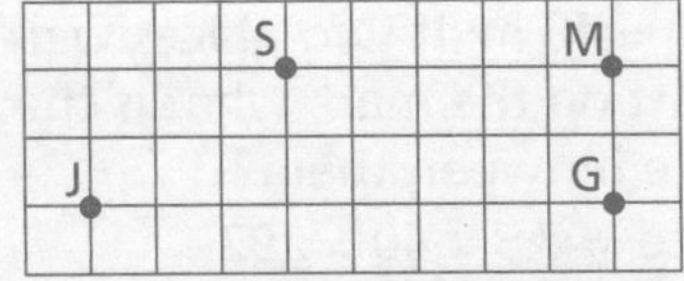

6 How far apart are Moni (M) and Sam (S)?

A 20 km B 25 km C 30 km D 45 km

7 Jake leaves Sam's home and drops Moni and Gil off on his way home. If the journey takes 1 hour, what was his average speed? *Hint 3*

A 100 km/h B 80 km/h
C 75 km/h D 50 km/h

8 Lenfell and Blight are two towns 12 cm apart on a map but the actual distance between the two towns is 54 kilometres. Complete the scale used on the map:

1 cm = ☐ km

9 On the same map, Craven is 8 cm from Blight. What is the actual distance between Craven and Blight?

A 36 km B 40 km C 42 km D 48 km

10 Blight is exactly two-thirds of the distance on the road from Lenfell to Lochneed. How far is it from Blight to Lochneed on the map?

A 6 cm B 8 cm C 12 cm D 16 cm

11 Fiona slept from 10:18 pm to 7:27 am. How many hours and minutes did she sleep?

A 8 h 11 min B 8 h 35 min
C 9 h 9 min D 9 h 11 min

12 The circumference of a circle is about 60 cm. The diameter is closest to

A 10 cm. B 15 cm. C 20 cm. D 30 cm.

While bushwalking Daniel found this sign:

1.5 km Lake	Lookout 2.3 km

13 From this sign Daniel walked to the lake and then back past the sign to the lookout. How far did he walk?

A 3.8 km B 5.3 km C 5.5 km D 7.6 km

14 From the lookout, he jogged back to the sign which took him 10 minutes. At what speed did he jog? ☐ km/h

15 The enlargement of a photo 8 cm by 5 cm has a length of 12 cm. What is the width of the enlargement? ☐ cm

16 If a timber beam is cut into 2 lengths in the ratio of 2:3, the shorter length will be 80 cm. Instead, the beam is to be cut in the ratio 5:3. What will be the longer length?

☐ m

Hint 1: The approximate value of π is 3.
Hint 2: Remember to add the 2 radii when finding the perimeter.
Hint 3: Speed = Distance divided by Time.

☞ **Answers and explanations on pages 208–209**

MEASUREMENT AND GEOMETRY

Area and volume

For questions 1, 2 and 3, the diagram shows a triangle PCD inside a square ABCD. The area of the square is 36 cm².

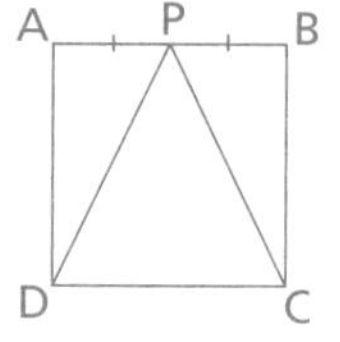

1 What is the perimeter of the square ABCD?

A 9 cm B 18 cm C 24 cm D 81 cm

2 What is the area of the triangle PCD?

A 18 cm² B 24 cm² C 32 cm² D 36 cm²

3 What is the area of the triangle APD?

A 4.5 cm² B 9 cm² C 18 cm² D 36 cm²

For questions 4, 5 and 6, the diagram shows rectangles ABCD and ANEM, where N is the midpoint of AB and M is the midpoint of AD.

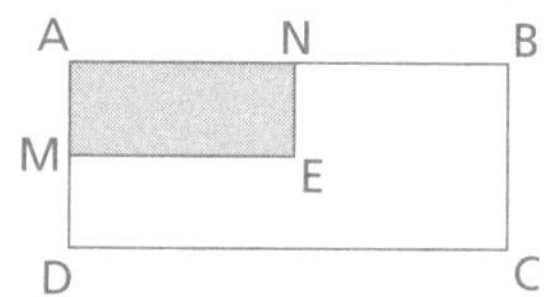

4 What fraction of the area of rectangle ABCD is the area of rectangle ANEM?

A $\frac{1}{4}$ B $\frac{1}{3}$ C $\frac{1}{2}$ D $\frac{3}{4}$

5 If the area of rectangle ANEM is 4 cm², what is the area of the unshaded region?

A 8 cm² B 12 cm² C 16 cm² D 20 cm²

6 If AM = x cm and AN = $(x + 1)$ cm, what is the area of the rectangle ABCD?

A $x(x + 1)$ cm² B $2x(x + 1)$ cm²
C $2x(2x + 2)$ cm² D $4x(x + 4)$ cm²

7 A rectangle has a perimeter of 36 cm and an area of 72 cm². What is the length of the rectangle?

A 9 cm B 8 cm C 10 cm D 12 cm

8 A square has an area of 16 cm². If the dimensions are doubled, what will happen to the area of the square?

A the area will double
B the area will triple
C the area will multiply by 4
D the area will multiply by 16

9 A rectangular prism has a length of 10 cm and a width of 6 cm. If the volume is 300 cm³, what is the height?

A 5 cm B 6 cm C 15 cm D 30 cm

10 A circle has a radius of 5 cm. What is the best estimate for the area of the circle?

A 15 cm² B 30 cm² C 75 cm² D 225 cm²

11 What is the area of the semi-circle with diameter 12 cm, to 2 decimal places?

A 37.70 cm²
B 56.55 cm²
C 113.10 cm²
D 226.19 cm²

For questions 12 and 13, a cube has a volume of 8 cm³.

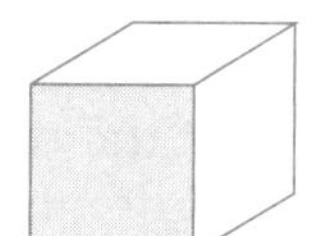

12 What is the area of one of its faces?

A 2 cm² B 3 cm² C 4 cm² D 16 cm²

13 What is the perimeter of each of the faces?

A 2 cm B 4 cm C 8 cm D 12 cm

14 A rectangular prism has dimensions of 4 cm, 3 cm and 2 cm. What is the surface area of the prism?

A 24 cm² B 32 cm² C 48 cm² D 52 cm²

15 A triangular prism is made from equilateral triangles and rectangles. The area of the triangles is 18 cm² and the area of the rectangles is 24 cm². What is the surface area of the prism?

A 42 cm² B 84 cm² C 108 cm² D 126 cm²

16 How many small squares with sides 4 cm can fit in a large square with sides 12 cm?

A 3 B 9 C 16 D 27

17 What is the area of the triangle?

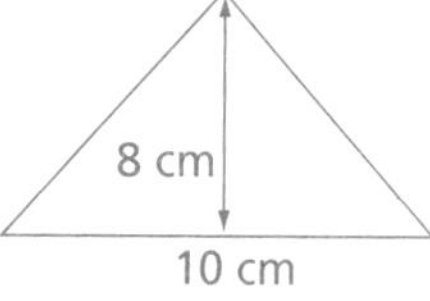

A 18 cm² B 40 cm²
C 80 cm² D 120 cm²

☞ Explanations on pages 209–210

Answers: 1 C 2 A 3 B 4 A 5 B 6 C 7 D 8 C 9 A 10 C 11 B 12 C 13 C 14 D 15 C 16 B 17 B

MEASUREMENT AND GEOMETRY
Area and volume

1 The **area** is a measure of the amount of space contained within a plane shape.

Square	s^2:	side × side
Rectangle	lb:	length × breadth
Triangle	$\frac{1}{2}bh$:	$\frac{1}{2}$ × base × height
Circle	πr^2:	π × radius × radius

Example 1: Find the area of a square which has a perimeter of 24 cm.
Perimeter = 24 cm Length of side = 24 ÷ 4
= 6
Area = 6^2
= 36 ∴ 36 cm^2

Example 2: A rectangle has a length of 12 cm and a perimeter of 36 cm. What is the area of the rectangle?
Perimeter = 2 × (length + breadth)
36 = 2 × (12 + breadth)
18 = 12 + breadth
breadth = 6
The breadth of the rectangle is 6 cm.
Area = 12 × 6
= 72 ∴ 72 cm^2

Example 3: The diagram shows a shaded triangle inside a rectangle. The rectangle has dimensions 12 cm by 8 cm. Find the area that remains unshaded.

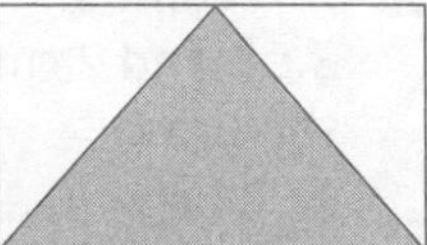

Area of rectangle = 12 × 8
= 96
Area of triangle = $\frac{1}{2}$ × 12 × 8
= 48
Area unshaded = 96 – 48
= 48
The unshaded section has an area of 48 cm^2.

Example 4: What is the area of a circle of diameter 10 cm? Give your answer correct to 2 decimal places.
Radius = 10 ÷ 2 = 5 cm
Area = πr^2
= $\pi \times 5^2$
= 78.54 (2 decimal places)
= 78.54 cm^2

2 The **volume** is a measure of space contained within a solid shape.

Cube	s^3:	side × side × side
Rectangular prism	lbh:	length × breadth × height
Any prism	Ah:	Area of base × height

Example 1: What is the volume of a cube if it has a face with an area of 9 cm^2?
Area of square face = 9 cm^2
Length of side = 3 cm
Volume of cube = 3^3
= 27 ∴ 27 cm^3

Example 2: A rectangular prism has dimensions of 4 cm, 3 cm and 6 cm. What is the volume?
Volume = 4 × 3 × 6
= 72 ∴ 72 cm^3

Example 3: Find the volume of the triangular prism.

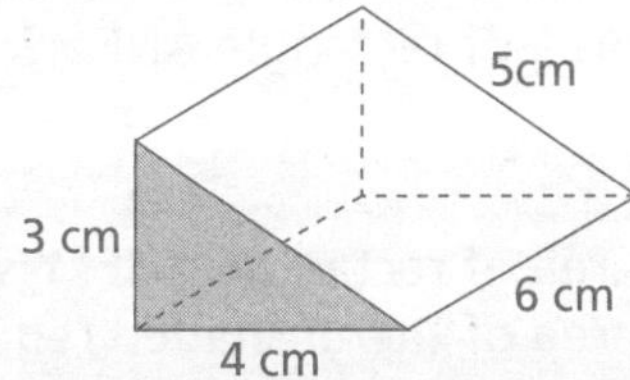

Volume = Area of triangular base × height
= $\frac{1}{2}$ × 4 × 3 × 6
= 36 ∴ 36 cm^3

3 The **surface area** of a solid is found by adding the areas of each of the faces.
Example: Find the surface area.

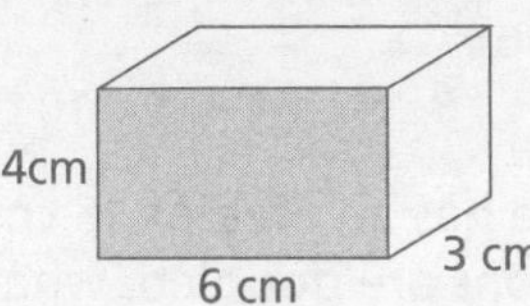

The prism has 6 rectangular faces:
2 rectangles with sides 6 × 3;
2 rectangles with sides 6 × 4; and
2 rectangles with sides 4 × 3.
Surface area = 2 × 6 × 3 + 2 × 6 × 4 + 2 × 4 × 3
= 108 ∴ 108 cm^2

MEASUREMENT AND GEOMETRY
Area and volume

1. Find the area of a square with sides 2.7 cm.

   Write your answer in the box: ☐ cm^2

2. What is the area of a rectangle whose length is twice the size of its width and the perimeter is 24 cm? *Hint 1*

   A $32\ cm^2$ B $18\ cm^2$ C $16\ cm^2$ D $64\ cm^2$

3. The diagram shows a rectangle with two identical shaded triangles. If the area of the rectangle is $16\ cm^2$, what is the area of one of the triangles?

   A $4\ cm^2$ B $6\ cm^2$ C $7\ cm^2$ D $8\ cm^2$

4. A rectangle measures 4 cm by 3 cm. It is to be enlarged so that its dimensions are multiplied by 2. What will happen to its area?

   A same area as the original
   B 2 times the area of the original
   C 4 times the area of the original
   D 8 times the area of the original

5. A square is drawn on a grid. The area of the square is $8\ cm^2$. What is the area of the grid that is unshaded?

   A $5\ cm^2$ B $30\ cm^2$
   C $40\ cm^2$ D $48\ cm^2$

6. From a rectangle measuring 6 cm by 4 cm, a square of side x cm is removed. What is the area of the remaining shape?

   A $(10 - x^2)\ cm^2$ B $(24 - x^2)\ cm^2$
   C $24x^2\ cm^2$ D $(x^2 - 24)\ cm^2$

7. What is the area of a circle with diameter 12 cm, to the nearest cm^2?

   A $38\ cm^2$ B $76\ cm^2$
   C $113\ cm^2$ D $123\ cm^2$

8. A square has a perimeter of 48 cm. If the dimensions are halved, what is the area of the new square?

   A $16\ cm^2$ B $36\ cm^2$ C $48\ cm^2$ D $64\ cm^2$

9. Shannon makes a rectangular prism. She measures the areas of three faces as $12\ cm^2$, $8\ cm^2$ and $6\ cm^2$.

   What is the surface area of the prism?

   A $26\ cm^2$ B $36\ cm^2$ C $52\ cm^2$ D $60\ cm^2$

10. When a square is enlarged the area has changed from $16\ cm^2$ to $36\ cm^2$. The perimeter of the old square is increased by

    A 2 cm. B 4 cm. C 8 cm. D 12 cm.

11. The surface area of a cube is $600\ cm^2$. What is the volume? *Hint 2*

    A $10\ cm^3$ B $100\ cm^3$
    C $360\ cm^3$ D $1000\ cm^3$

12. Which of the following rectangular prisms has a volume of $1000\ m^3$?

    A 10 m × 10 m × 5 m B 25 m × 50 m × 25 m
    C 20 m × 20 m × 4 m D 40 m × 5 m × 5 m

13. What is the area of this shape? *Hint 3*

    2a cm
    2a cm
    3a cm

    A $4a\ cm^2$
    B $4a^2\ cm^2$
    C $5a^2\ cm^2$
    D $6a^2\ cm^2$

14. A hexagonal prism is made from hexagons and rectangles. Each hexagon has an area of $16\ cm^2$ and each rectangle has an area of $20\ cm^2$. What is the surface area of the prism? ☐ cm^2

15. What is the best estimate of the area of a circle with radius 7 cm? *Hint 4*

    A $150\ cm^2$ B $220\ cm^2$
    C $490\ cm^2$ D $560\ cm^2$

16. The diagram shows the diagonals of a regular hexagon. The area of the hexagon is $73.2\ cm^2$. What is the area of the shaded rhombus?

    ☐ cm^2

Hint 1: As perimeter is twice the sum of length and breadth, first find length + breadth.
Hint 2: First find the length of each side of the cube.
Hint 3: The shape is made from a rectangle and a triangle.
Hint 4: The approximate value of π is 3.

☞ **Answers and explanations on pages 210–211**

SPELLING
'ice' and 'ise' words, common confusions and irregular plurals

Key Points

1. In Week Two you learned how to create plural nouns by adding the suffix 's' or 'es'. These can be referred to as **regular plurals**. There are also **irregular plurals** that you also need to know how to spell. Irregular plurals use a variety of different suffixes to create the plural form of a noun. You will come across many of these as you progress into senior school.
2. Some nouns that **end in 'us'** replace the 'us' ending with the suffix 'i' to create the plural.
   Examples: radius → radii, nucleus → nuclei, stimulus → stimuli
3. Some nouns that **end in 'is'** replace the 'is' with the suffix 'es' to create the plural.
   Examples: hypothesis → hypotheses, synthesis → syntheses, oasis → oases
4. Some nouns that **end in 'ix'** replace the 'ix' with the suffix 'ices' to create the plural.
   Examples: appendix → appendices, matrix → matrices
5. Some nouns that **end in 'eau'** add the suffix 'x' to create the plural.
   Examples: bureau → bureaux, tableau → tableaux
6. Some nouns that **end in 'a'** add the suffix 'e' to create the plural.
   Examples: formula → formulae, antenna → antennae, vertebra → vertebrae
7. Many nouns that **end in 'um'** drop the 'um' and add the suffix 'a' to create the plural.
   Examples: bacterium → bacteria, medium → media, datum → data
8. Some nouns make no changes at all; their **singular and plural forms are the same**.
   Examples: species, series, offspring
9. Longer, common words that **end in 'ice'** and 'ise' can cause problems. Many words ending in 'ice' are **nouns**.
   Examples: prejudice, apprentice, armistice, accomplice, justice, liquorice, novice, sacrifice
   Many words that **end in 'ise'** are **verbs**.
   Examples: synchronise, dramatise, improvise, exercise, advertise, prioritise, surprise
   In Australian English a number of verbs can take 'ise' or 'ize'. Some words must take 'ise'. When in doubt, use 'ise'. However, a few words are always 'ize'.
   Examples: capsize, prize, size
10. There are some words that are easily confused. These words can become 'demon' words for both teachers and students. Unfortunately there isn't one simple rule to help you to overcome this problem—you simply need to practise them so you can remember them. Some **commonly confused words** include:
    advise—advice, conscience—conscious, affect—effect, breath—breathe, cloth—clothe
    For each of the above examples you should consider whether the word you wish to use is a verb or a noun. Learn the correct form and you will spell it correctly in your chosen context.
    Examples: 'conscience' is a noun and 'conscious' is a verb. Therefore you would use the noun 'conscience' in the following sentence:
    The young boy had a guilty conscience after stealing his brother's cookie.
    You would use the verb 'conscious' in the following sentence:
    The boy was conscious of the fact that stealing his brother's cookie was wrong.

SPELLING
'ice' and 'ise' words, common confusions and irregular plurals

11 A trick you can use to tell if a word is a verb or a noun is the **a—to** test. To check if a word is a noun, simply put the preposition 'a' before the word and if it makes sense the word is a noun. *Examples:* 'a vehicle' makes sense whereas 'to vehicle' doesn't make sense, so 'vehicle' must be a noun and not a verb. To check if a word is a verb, simply put the preposition 'to' before the word and if it makes sense the word is a verb.

Examples: 'to choose' makes sense whereas 'a choose' doesn't make sense, so 'choose' must be a verb.

Some other commonly confused words include:
quiet—quite, bought—brought, loose—lose—loss

Test Your Skills

Learn the words below. A common method of learning and self-testing is the LOOK, SAY, COVER, WRITE, CHECK method. If you make any mistakes, you should rewrite the word three times correctly, immediately. In this way you will become familiar with the correct spelling. If the word is particularly troublesome, rewrite it several more times or keep a list of words that you can check regularly.

This week's theme word: THEATRE

dramatise	______________	improvise	______________
exercise	______________	advertise	______________
advise	______________	advice	______________
affect	______________	effect	______________
allusion	______________	illusion	______________
quiet	______________	quite	______________
surprise	______________	liquorice	______________
media	______________	medium	______________
theses	______________	thesis	______________
tableaux	______________	tableau	______________

Write any troublesome words three times.

______________ ______________ ______________

______________ ______________ ______________

SPELLING
Common misspellings

Please ask your parent or teacher to read to you the spelling words on page 250.
Write the correct spelling of each word in the box.

1. We were ______ residents of Elwood Beach, but now we reside in Bondi.
2. The ______ swimming titles were marred by controversy.
3. The scientist's ______ was that too much sunlight killed the plants.
4. Our ______ of an event is altered by our life experiences.
5. The numerous ______ confused Jane on her first day of Extension Science.
6. I struggled to ______ after choking on a boiled lolly.
7. Barry became John Turtle's painting ______.
8. To his horror, the boy realised he would be ______ during his surgery.
9. We demand ______ for this heinous crime!
10. The ______ of goods in sweat shops should be illegal worldwide.
11. I enjoyed the ______ swimming at the Olympic Games.
12. It is important to ______ your study schedule.
13. The Prime Minister will abolish ______ in his nation.
14. What is your ______, chocolate or strawberry?
15. The parents ______ their child's future with the principal.

The spelling mistakes in these sentences have been underlined.
Write the correct spelling for each underlined word in the box.

16. The boy exhaled his <u>breathe</u> loudly after the 600-metre race.
17. Claudia's tenacious <u>acumplise</u> back-flipped over the fence to escape.
18. I suppose you could say I'm a <u>novise</u> at skiing, as today is my first time.
19. I covered the old chair with some new red <u>clothe</u>.
20. Jamie was overjoyed to be selected to play <u>percushen</u> in the school band.

☞ Answers on page 211

SPELLING
Common misspellings

Each sentence has one word that is incorrect.
Write the correct spelling of the word in the box.

21 It is only through sacrafyse and hard work that people succeed in life.

22 The accident played on the boy's conschense.

23 What is the radii of the circle?

24 The young family were forced to immigrate from China to Australia.

25 The warring parties agreed to an armistiss.

☞ Answers on page 211

GRAMMAR AND PUNCTUATION
Pronouns, prepositions, articles and subject/verb agreement

Key Points

1 **Pronouns** are words that take the place of nouns.
Examples: Mackenzie drew an equilateral triangle for Tia-Lynne. He drew an equilateral triangle for her. ('he' and 'she' are pronouns)
Some common pronouns include: I, we, me, us, you, they, them, he, she, him, her, it.

2 **Prepositions** show the relationship between a noun, pronoun or other word. They show the position of something.
Some common prepositions include: at, in, above, under, off, until, up, upon, beside, between.

3 There are only three **articles** in English. These are the small words 'a', 'an' and 'the'.

a The word 'the' is referred to as the **definite article**. This is because when used it refers to a specific object or person as in it is definitely this object or person and not another one. You use the definite article when you can confidently assume that the reader or listener can determine the thing or person you are talking about.
Example: The teacher taught the students how to correctly calculate the circumference of the circle.

b The words 'a' and 'an' are referred to as **indefinite articles**. This is because when used they refer to objects or people in general rather than specific ones. You use the indefinite article when referring to something that the reader or listener does not know.
Example: A vegetarian will often consider the feelings of an animal before deciding what to eat.
Note: the word 'a' is used before words that start with consonants.
Examples: a republic, a politician, a settlement
The word 'an' is used before words that start with vowels.
Examples: an immigrant, an invasion, an organism

4 It is essential to ensure that the **subject and the verb agree**, that is, they are both plural or both singular.
Examples: the girls go—the girl goes, the bomb explodes—the bombs explode, Jack walks—Jack and Jill walk, the price is—the prices are

Note: many mistakes occur when the subject is a pronoun.
Examples: you was late (wrong)—you were late (correct); she don't agree (wrong)—she doesn't agree (correct)

Note: these pronouns are examples of words that always take a singular verb: each, every, everyone, someone, nobody, no-one, everybody, anybody, anyone, somebody.
Subjects that name quantities take a singular verb.
Examples: five dollars is too much for that; two metres of string is enough.

GRAMMAR AND PUNCTUATION
Pronouns, prepositions, articles and subject/verb agreement

Test Your Skills

1 Write 'a', 'an' or 'the' in spaces to complete the sentences below.

The devastated mother picked up ____ novel her son had been reading before he disappeared. It had been ____ unusually hot day and the boy had gone to buy ____ bottle of soft drink from the store. He never returned.

2 Underline the pronouns in the following sentence.

The consequences of his misbehaviour would be severe, so she talked him out of going through with his plan.

3 Choose the correct verb to use in the sentences below.

The panther (prowl/prowls) the enclosure.
The speckled leaves of the trees (flutters/flutter) in the breeze.
I couldn't believe it when the teacher told me I (were/was) wrong!

4 Circle the prepositions in the sentence below.

Looking deep into the cave, Anderson could see a faint light gleaming from under what seemed to be a small door made of stone.

Answers: 1 the, an, a 2 his, she, him, his 3 prowls, flutter, was 4 into, from, under, of

GRAMMAR AND PUNCTUATION

Pronouns, prepositions, articles and subject/verb agreement

1. Which sentence tells the reader who performed the action?
   - A The fathers played football in the backyard all day.
   - B The football game was intended for children.
   - C In 2011 $90 million was spent on sport in Australia.
   - D The most popular football team was decided in an online poll.

2. Which sentence is correct?
   - A Thinking, only of himself Peter began eating the wrapped chocolates in the box.
   - B Thinking only of himself, Peter began eating the wrapped chocolates in the box.
   - C Thinking, only of himself, Peter began eating the wrapped chocolates in the box.
   - D Thinking only of himself Peter began eating the wrapped chocolates, in the box.

3. Which words correctly complete this sentence?

   Even though it was tired, ______ old dog scamprered down the alley in search of ______ bed for the night.

the the	the an	an the	the a
A	B	C	D

4. Ron and Judy have nothing but admiration for ______: 'We're just so proud of her. She really is a super dog.'
   - A their dogs Juju the star
   - B their dog, Juju the star
   - C their, dog, Juju the star
   - D their dog Juju, the star

5. Which sentence is correct?
   - A Terry felt that has he performed better at school then he would not be feeling so unsatisfied with his career.
   - B Terry felt that had he performed better at school then he would not be feeling so unsatisfied with his career.
   - C Terry felt that had he performed better at school then he won't be feeling so unsatisfied with his career.
   - D Terry felt that hadn't he performed better at school then he would not be feeling so unsatisfied with his career.

6. Which sentence has the correct punctuation?
   - A Ellen said that 'working in the hospital was the best experience she had ever had.'
   - B Ellen said that working in the hospital was the best experience she had ever had.
   - C Ellen said 'that working in the hospital' was the best experience she had ever had.
   - D Ellen said that working in the hospital was the best experience she had ever had?

7. Which sentence has the correct punctuation?
   - A Running swiftly like a gazelle, the young boy caught up to Jamie, his younger brother.
   - B Running swiftly like a gazelle; the young Boy caught up to Jamie his younger brother.
   - C Running swiftly like a gazelle the young boy caught up to jamie his younger brother.
   - D Running swiftly like a gazelle, the young boy caught up to jamie his younger brother.

☞ **Answers and explanations on pages 212–214**

GRAMMAR AND PUNCTUATION
Pronouns, prepositions, articles and subject/verb agreement

8 Which sentence has the correct punctuation?

A 'Don't worry about coming in to work tomorrow,' her boss said, 'the office is flooded.'
B 'Don't worry about coming in to work tomorrow', her boss said, 'The office is flooded.'
C Don't worry about coming in to work tomorrow, her boss said, 'the office is flooded.'
D 'Don't worry about coming in to work tomorrow.' her Boss said, 'the office is flooded.'

9 In which sentence is the underlined contraction **incorrect**?

A On Friday <u>he'll</u> be packing to go on his holiday.
B For the last two days <u>we'd</u> been trying hard to win the car.
C The parents knew <u>they'd</u> been lied to by their children.
D Last July was the worst month ever because <u>you're</u> away.

10 Which sentence has the correct punctuation?

A I certainly wouldn't trust a surgeon who wasn't registered as a professional?
B I certainly wouldn't trust a surgeon who wasnt registered as a professional.
C I certainly wouldn't trust a surgeon who wasn't registered as a professional.
D I certainly wouldnt trust a surgeon who wasnt registered as a professional.

Write the word or words in the box to correctly complete the sentences below.

11 Two days ago, Juju Jones, pet Labrador of Ron and Judy Jones, saved her two-year-old neighbour, Madison Reynolds, ________ by an out of control bicycle.

being hit	from being hit	by being hit	of being hit
A	B	C	

12 Juju ________ enjoying one of her favourite hobbies—lying under the balcony watching the cars whizz by the family home on Palm Drive.

was	were being	had been	have been
A	B	C	D

13 'It's just unbelievable that Maddie ________ badly hurt.'

isn't being	hasn't been	wasn't got	didn't get
A	B	C	D

14 Which of the following correctly completes this sentence?

Doug ________ beaten Gigi but he fell over the tree root.

could of	couldn't	could've	could has
A	B	C	D

15 The ________ were happy to have visited the famous Ned Kelly suit of armour at the Old Melbourne Gaol.

tourist	all tourists	tourists will	tourists
A	B	C	D

16 ________ are the onions going to grow in that tiny garden?

Where's	Were	We're	Where
A	B	C	D

☞ Answers and explanations on pages 212–214

GRAMMAR AND PUNCTUATION

Pronouns, prepositions, articles and subject/verb agreement

Highlight the correct answer in the sentences below.

17 Which of the following correctly completes this sentence?

Last night the weather ______ the worst I've ever seen.

am	is	were	was
A	B	C	D

18 The girls ______ from ploughing the field.

were tired	is tired	has tired	tyring
A	B	C	D

19 He ______ happy that his mother switched the cartoons off.

weren't	were	wasn't	am
A	B	C	D

20 The largest of the birds ______ enclosed within the zoo's aviary.

were	was	is	where
A	B	C	D

21 Put a circle around the adjective and proper noun in the sentence below.

Despite finding the roller-coaster thrilling, Balin did not wish to repeat the thrill.

22 Shade **three** circles to show where the missing apostrophes (') should go.

Don(A)t you dare eat that pie, it(B)s Ari(C)s (D).

23 Shade **two** circles to show where the missing quotation marks (' ') should go.

'It's absolutely unbelievable! (A) exclaimed (B) Heather. (C) Where did you find it?'

24 Madison had woken from her daily nap early and had stealthily escaped ______ of their home.

A out of the front door

B into the front door

C around the front door

D over the front door

25 Which of the following correctly completes this sentence?

External hard drives, ______, are the most reliable way to store your data.

A expensive though

B even though they are expensive

C very expensive they is

D are very much money

☞ Answers and explanations on pages 212–214

READING
Understanding explanations

The purpose of an explanation is to tell how or why something happens. Explanations can be about natural or scientific phenomena, how things work or events.

Read *Lucid dreams* and answer the questions.

Lucid dreams

1 The most basic definition of lucid dreaming is 'being aware you are dreaming while dreaming'. Lucid dreams usually occur while a person is in the middle of a regular dream and suddenly realises that she or he is asleep and must be dreaming.

2 A lucid dream is also described as a conscious dream. During lucid dreams, it is possible to exert conscious control over the dream characters and environment and have them perform feats which would be physically impossible in the waking world. Lucid dreams can be extremely vivid and real depending on the dreamer's level of self-awareness throughout the dream.

3 A dreamscape is the realm where dreams take place. It can be shaped and changed by skilled dreamers. Artists would see it as a blank canvas on which scenes are created.

4 Lucid dreaming transforms the dreamscape into a vivid alternate reality, where everything the dreamer perceives (sees, hears, feels, tastes and smells) is as authentic as being awake. The person is said to be lucid and may enter one of many various levels of lucidity. At the lowest level, the dreamer may be dimly aware that he or she is dreaming, but not think rationally enough to realise that events, people and actions in the dream are not real—and pose no threat. At the highest level, the dreamer is fully aware that she or he is asleep, and can have complete control over his or her actions in the dream.

5 A lucid dream can begin in one of two ways. A dream-initiated lucid dream (DILD) starts as a normal dream, and the dreamer eventually concludes that he or she is dreaming, while a wake-initiated lucid dream (WILD) occurs when the dreamer goes from a normal waking state directly into a dream state with no apparent lapse in consciousness.

6 Wake-initiated lucid dreams are used to rehearse real-life events, re-live memories, meet up with friends, fulfil wild fantasies or simply explore the unconscious dream world. It is very possible to dream what you want to dream. Lucid dreaming is the ability, while dreaming, to have the thought process 'I am dreaming' or 'This is a dream'.

7 Lucid dreaming has been researched scientifically, and its existence is well established.

Sources: www.luciddreaming.com/information/lucid-dreams.php
http://selfawareness.suite101.com/article.cfm/wake_initiated_lucid_dreams#ixzz0ljqsrXS4&D

READING
Understanding explanations

1 A feature of lucid dreams is their
- A short duration.
- B vividness.
- C regular occurrence.
- D uncontrolled revelation.

2 The difference between DILD and WILD is in the
- A manner in which they commence.
- B effect each has upon the dream.
- C level of fantasy experienced.
- D variety of sensations that can be experienced.

3 The writer, in his conclusion, maintains that the present understanding of lucid dreaming can best be regarded as
- A unsustained.
- B speculative.
- C emerging.
- D accepted.

4 While in a lucid dream, the performance of unrealistic feats
- A indicates that the dream is becoming a nightmare.
- B exaggerates incidents from daily events.
- C is taken for granted.
- D causes the dreamer to wake up.

5 According to the text, which statement is correct?
- A During lucid dreams the dreamer is aware that he or she is dreaming.
- B A DILD is easier to manipulate than a WILD.
- C It is possible to slide into a WILD from a DILD.
- D Research into lucid dreams has found no difference between DILD and WILD.

6 A feature of having a lucid dream at the highest level is that the dreamer
- A doesn't know that he or she is asleep.
- B can take complete control of the dream.
- C can become unconscious.
- D may have no control over the ability to wake up.

7 Each paragraph in the text has a main idea. Write the number of the paragraph next to the correct main idea for paragraphs 2 to 6.

Paragraph ____	the purpose of dreams that start in a normal waking state
Paragraph ____	the level of control the dreamer has in lucid dreams
Paragraph ____	a definition of the setting of dreams
Paragraph ____	the specific ways in which lucid dreams start
Paragraph ____	awareness of dream experiences at differing levels of lucidity

8 Overall, the purpose of the explanation is to advise those who experience lucid dreams that such dreams are

dangerous.	stimulating.	suspect.	liberating.	stressful.
A	B	C	D	E

Answers: 1 B 2 A 3 D 4 C 5 A 6 B 7 6, 2, 3, 5, 4 8 B

☞ Explanations on page 214

READING
Understanding explanations

Read *Urban legends* and answer the questions.

Urban legends

Urban legends (sometimes called urban myths) are popular stories alleged to be true which are repeatedly retold and passed on. Typically, such stories concern outlandish, humiliating, humorous, terrifying or supernatural events which always happened to someone else, most likely a distant associate. Horror and bizarre humour are characteristic of urban legends. The victims are usually innocent.

In lieu of evidence, the teller of an urban legend relies on narrative skill and reference to allegedly trustworthy sources, such as a relative or a friend of a friend to boost its credibility. Sometimes, there's an implied lesson to be learnt: be careful, this could happen to you!

Urban legends are a type of folklore. They are the beliefs, stories and traditions of ordinary people. The one crucial way of differentiating between urban legends and other kinds of popular fiction is by examining where they come from and how they are disseminated. Legends tend to arise spontaneously and are rarely traceable to a single point of origin. They spread from individual to individual through interpersonal communication, and only in rare instances through mass media.

Like viruses, urban legends spread avidly, **3** as they pass from carrier to carrier—stories change over time. No two versions of an urban legend are ever exactly the same. There can be as many variants as there are taletellers.

An urban legend example

A teenager drove his girlfriend to a dark and deserted Lovers' Lane. The car was warm and after tuning the radio for mood music, he leaned over and began kissing the girl.

Suddenly the music stopped. An announcer's voice came on warning that a convicted murderer had just escaped from a nearby asylum for the criminally insane. He advised anyone seeing a strange man lurking about, with a hook instead of a right hand, should immediately report his whereabouts to the police.

The girl became frightened and asked to be taken home. The boy, feeling bold, locked all the doors instead, and assuring his date they would be safe, attempted to kiss her again.

She became frantic and pushed him away, insisting that they leave the remote spot. Relenting, the boy started the car, pulled it quickly into gear and left the parking site in a spray of gravel.

When they arrived at the girl's home she sullenly got out of the car. As she closed the door, she gasped and began to scream uncontrollably. The boy ran to her side to see what was wrong.

There, dangling from the door handle was a bloody hook.

Sources: www.urbanlegends.about.com/od/errata/a/urban_legends.htm
Good Weekend, Sydney Morning Herald, 3/10/1994, p. 38

READING
Understanding explanations

1 Urban legends are considered true because
A people think they come from a reliable source.
B they have been reported in the mass media.
C of the number of people who retell them.
D their origin is easily traced.

2 The intent of many urban legends, such as the one provided, is to
A pass on factual information.
B illustrate how wrong information is circulated.
C provide detailed information for storytelling.
D be the means of issuing a subtle warning.

3 In paragraph 4 a word is missing from the text. Circle the word that would correctly complete the paragraph.

motivating	expanding	mutating	comparing	deviating
A	B	C	D	E

4 After hearing the warning on the radio the teenage boy
A ignored the warning.
B locked all the car doors.
C immediately left Lovers' Lane.
D switched off the radio.

5 Complete the sentence to correctly identify the way the passage has been written.
Write your answers in the spaces.
The structure of the text, *Urban legends*, is ____________ followed by ____________.
A a description
B an explanation
C a narrative
D a factual report
E a summary
F an essay

6 One reason 'no two versions of an urban legend are ever exactly the same' (paragraph 4) lies in the fact
A that re-tellers of the story have access to additional information.
B that urban legends are rarely written down.
C that the story was poorly reported after the event took place.
D that the event happened in another place, some time ago.

7 What likely reason could there be for the teenage boy driving off 'in a spray of gravel'?
A the couple had heard the murderer approaching
B a bloody hook was found in the door handle
C the boy was annoyed that his plans had been thwarted
D in a hurry to escape, the teenager accelerated too quickly

8 Can the following statements about the writer be concluded from the text?
Write **YES** or **NO** next to the statement.

CONCLUSION	YES / NO
The writer is a skilled storyteller.	
The writer is sceptical of urban legends.	
The writer prefers popular fiction to urban legends.	
The writer is scornful of teenagers.	
The writer thinks some urban legends contain humour.	

☞ Answers and explanations on pages 214–215

READING
Understanding recounts

A recount is a record of events that happened in sequence. A recount has several forms. It can be personal or historical. It may also contain opinions or personal comments on the events. Many newspaper articles are recounts.

Read *A trip to The Tip* by Elaine Horsfield and answer the questions.

A trip to The Tip

To most people the idea of a trip to the tip conjures up images of the trailer loaded up with old furniture and garden waste, heading off to the council dump. So on a recent holiday to Thursday Island, when we were offered 'A trip to the tip', we were at first unimpressed. What was on offer, we discovered, was actually something quite different.

Setting off from the Thursday Island wharf in a fast boat at 6.30 am, we headed directly towards the mainland of Australia. As the sun rose over the eastern horizon, we settled back to enjoy the hour-long trip.

On arrival at the wharf at Seisia, on the west coast of Cape York, we were met by our guide in a four-wheel-drive, who took our small tour group for a beach breakfast before the drive north to 'The Tip'. Many people do not realise that 'The Tip' is almost level with Port Moresby, capital of Papua New Guinea (Latitude: 9° South).

The narrow, **1** road wound between patches of savannah scrub with **2** pockets of monsoon rain forest, across **3** rutted creek beds and through deep **4** streams. Our driver regaled us with tales of early explorers' adventures and follies. We passed an abandoned cattle station and the remnants of an Eco Lodge, rapidly being reclaimed by the forest.

Quite suddenly we burst out of the bush and were confronted by the sea. Here we were directed towards the rocky climb, which led to the northernmost tip of mainland Australia. The climb was not arduous and we passed other tourists, many of them 'grey nomads'.

At the summit the view was breathtaking. The glittering sea scattered with islands and white sailing yachts was picture postcard perfect. A quick, but careful, descent and we were standing on the rocky point, admiring the view while waiting our turn to have the obligatory photos taken under a somewhat predictable sign to prove we'd made it: 'You are standing on the northernmost point of the Australian continent'.

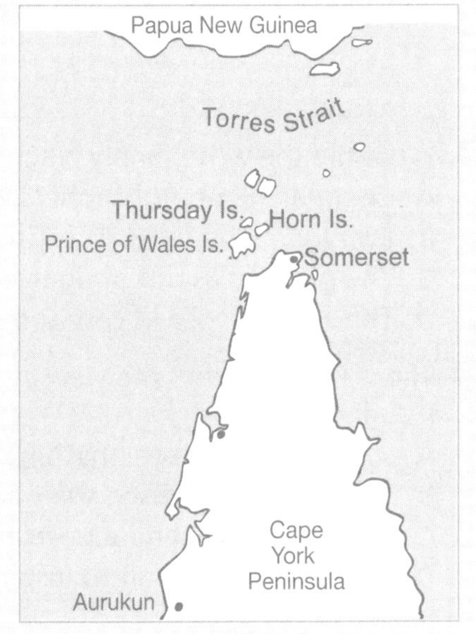

Reluctant as we were to leave, the steady stream of arrivals meant we had to make way for others to enjoy the experience in this remote part of Australia. After lunch we headed back to Seisia, detouring to visit some places of interest including air wrecks from World War II and local villages under the administration of Aborigines or Torres Strait Islanders.

Back at the wharf we watched the boat arrive that would take us across the Torres Strait, back to Thursday Island. 'A trip to the tip' is something we'll never forget.

READING
Understanding recounts

1. Initially, the writer found the idea of going on 'a trip to The Tip'
   A innovative but unacceptable.
   B objectionable and disrespectful.
   C interesting and not tempting.
   D perplexing but amusing.

2. Correctly complete the sentence. Write your answers in the spaces.

   Two stylistic features included in the text are ______________ and ______________.

scientific jargon	a sincere tone	a journalistic style
academic detail	geographical facts	a suspenseful atmosphere

3. The sign at 'The Tip' was described as 'predictable'. This implies that
   A there was nothing original about the sign or its message.
   B the sign had been well advertised before arrival at 'The Tip'.
   C everyone knew in advance what to expect.
   D the sign was an elaborate structure on an isolated peninsula.

4. To go directly from Thursday Island to Seisia, the writer passed by
   A Horn Island.
   B Port Moresby.
   C Hammond Island.
   D Cape York.

5. In which order did the writer do these things? Number them from 1 to 5.
   - [ ] watched yachts sailing in Torres Strait
   - [ ] visited the wrecks of old aeroplanes
   - [ ] drove by a derelict Eco Lodge
   - [ ] stopped to have lunch
   - [ ] walked past some elderly tourists

6. Four adjectives in the first sentence in paragraph 4 have been hidden by numbered boxes.
   The words are: sudden; bumpy; gushing; dry.
   Write one word in each box to correctly complete the sentence.

1	2	3	4

7. What did the writer imply when she stated the 'obligatory photo' (paragraph 6) was taken?
   A Commercial photographers were required to take photographs.
   B Everyone who visits 'The Tip' has to have a record of the experience.
   C The photo was not obligatory but everyone does it, so it felt that way.
   D There is a record in case someone fails to return.

8. The writer describes the view at the tip as 'picture postcard perfect' (paragraph 6). The writer is suggesting
   A she had never seen anything like it before.
   B she was so impressed she had to take a picture.
   C visitors should send a postcard featuring the view.
   D it was good enough to inspire a professional photographer.

☞ Answers and explanations on page 215

READING
Understanding recounts

Read the extract from *The rise and fall of Concorde* by Bruce Harris and answer the questions.

The rise and fall of Concorde

Christian Marty was a top-gun pilot. He had been flying Air France aeroplanes for more than thirty years. He was 54, fit and courageous, with a confident personality. In 1982, to test his own mental strength, he spent 37 days sailboarding more than 4500 kilometres across the Atlantic Ocean from South America to Senegal on the west coast of Africa,

In 1999, after years as a pilot of Boeing 747s and Airbus aircraft, he had been promoted to one of Air France's top captains. For nearly a year he had been chief pilot flying Concordes.

Friends report he was meticulous in everything he did. On Tuesday 25 July 2000 he had held back his Concorde flight departure for an hour to have a minor problem corrected with the thrust-reverser—the device that slows the aircraft's speed on landing. Now ready to go, he finalised cockpit checks with co-pilot Jean Marcot and taxied Air France Flight 4590 onto runway 24 of Charles de Gaulle Airport. Time: 4.30 pm. Destination: New York.

Concorde's take-off speed is 380 km/h. Once the plane has reached that speed, aborting the take-off is not an option. With Concorde's nose up, its main wheels about to leave the tarmac, Marty was given chilling information from the control tower: 'Concorde zero ... 4590, you have flames ... You have flames behind you!'

As the Concorde climbed away, flames and black smoke spiralled out in the slipstream. It is reported that terse messages to the tower advised that there was trouble with first one, then both, port-side engines. The co-pilot was heard to call that they would try to land at Le Bourget airport, close by.

The gleaming white bird, starkly underlined with black and crimson smoke, rose into the air, slewed to the left, stalled and crashed into a small 72-room hotel, the Hotelissimo.

An explosive firestorm engulfed the hotel and plane. Captain Christian Marty, eight other crew members and all 100 passengers—mainly German tourists flying to join an ocean liner in New York to sail to Sydney for the Olympic Games—were killed. Four more people died in the hotel.

This was the first and only destruction of one of these supersonic airlines in 31 years of flying, 27 of them commercially. It was an ugly exclamation mark in the romantic, adventurous and politics-laden story of the Anglo–French icon.

From 'Good Weekend', *Sydney Morning Herald*, 4/10/2000

READING
Understanding recounts

1. What is implied by the term 'top-gun pilot' (paragraph 1)?
   A a gunner on a transport plane
   B a man with a strong belief in firm discipline
   C the very best in his field
   D a fighter with exceptional shooting skills

2. Following their Concorde flight, most passengers were intending to
   A sail to Australia for the Olympics.
   B land at Charles De Gaulle Airport.
   C take a room at the Hotelissimo.
   D holiday in Germany.

3. According to the text which statements are CORRECT and which are INCORRECT? Draw a line to connect the statement to the option.

   CORRECT

   INCORRECT

   Marty was expected to take off for New York on 25 July 2000.
   On his last flight, Marty took off from runway 24 after a delay.
   Marty began flying for Air France in 1982 when he was 54.
   At 36, Marty went sailboarding in Senegal to test his abilities.
   In 1999 Marty was the pilot on doomed Air France flight 4590.

4. As the Concorde left the ground the
   A plane began to slew to the left.
   B captain was advised to head for Le Bourget airport.
   C two engines on the port-side failed.
   D control tower reported a fire.

5. At what point is it NOT possible to abort a take-off? Write your answer on the line.

   ____

6. Circle the word that best describes how the writer feels about Christian Marty. You may choose more than one.

resentment	admiration	anger	regret	displeasure	adoration
A	B	C	D	E	F

7. What is implied by the term 'an ugly exclamation mark' (last paragraph)?
   A The history of the aircraft ended in a shocking manner.
   B The crash was made worse by hitting a hotel.
   C The flight could have been stopped and lives saved.
   D The victims of the crash were on an important journey.

8. The writer uses the description 'the gleaming white bird, starkly underlined with black and crimson smoke' to
   A downplay the tragic nature of the disaster.
   B highlight the fallibility of men and machines.
   C distract the reader from the gruesome reality of the event.
   D draw a ghastly contrast.

9. The writer considers the Concorde era to be one of
   A accomplishment.
   B frustration.
   C turbulence.
   D misfortune.

☞ **Answers and explanations on pages 215–216**

TIPS FOR WRITING DESCRIPTIONS

Descriptions function as pictures in words of people, places or things. In a description you aim to give the reader a clear and vivid picture of what you are describing. After reading your description the reader should be able to close his or her eyes and picture the subject.

Descriptions are seldom written to stand alone in the same way as, say, narratives or recounts. Descriptions are often part of another kind of writing; they help to make other text types interesting.

When writing descriptions, it is best to keep the following points in mind. They will help you get the best possible mark.

Before you start writing

- **Read the question and check the stimulus material carefully**. *Stimulus material* means the topic, title, picture, words, phrases or extract of writing you are given to base your writing on.
- **Decide how you are going to present your description**. It could be in the first person or third person. Take care when using the first person not to overuse the pronoun *I*.
- **Decide on the tense you are going to use**. Descriptions are usually written in the present tense but feel free to use past or future tenses if this suits your purpose.

The introduction

- **Introduce the subject early** in your writing. The title should put the subject in focus.

The body

- **Always include some facts**. Descriptions in an information report may consist entirely of facts.
- **Don't just focus on what can be seen**. Enhance your writing by adding 'imagined' sounds and smells—you can even describe how something feels.
- **Make full use of adjectives and adverbs**. Use a short series of adjectives to paint a vivid picture.
- **Use action verbs to describe behaviour**. This adds interest to your description.
- **Use figurative language such as similes and metaphors** to make your description clear and interesting. Avoid clichés.

The conclusion

- The final paragraph may **include some brief personal opinions** in your description—the best place for this is often in the form of a concluding comment.

When you have finished writing give yourself a few minutes to read through your description. Quickly check spelling and punctuation, and insert any words that have been accidentally left out.

You will find a sample annotated description **on the following page**. The question is from page 99. Read the description and notes before you begin your third Writing Test. This piece of writing has been analysed based on the marking criteria used by markers to assess the NAPLAN Writing Test. **Remember:** This sample was not written under exam conditions.

Year 9 Sample Description Writing

(a sample answer to the question on page 99)

The Fight

As the garbage truck wearily whirred along the eerie moonlit street and the awaking birds drowsily rustled the frigid dew from their tired feathers, Iggy's alarm clock sounded out with ironic vigour. He reluctantly rolled over and pressed the snooze button, partly out of defiance to the day ahead, partly due to lethargy, but mostly out of sheer apathy. Meanwhile, Agnes fumbled with her keys in the dark somewhat hopelessly trying to make her way into the door after a long night's work. 'I should really devise some sort of system to differentiate these keys,' she thought to herself.

The sound of the P-plater's thumping car stereo could faintly be heard through the unit block's cracked and dilapidated walls.

As she sat there with her indicators on, signifying her intention to reverse into the vacant car space behind her, she gazed into her rear-view mirror in disbelief as her hallowed patch of bitumen was arrogantly replaced by a neighbour's pieced-together car.

Agnes fumbled.

The dump truck dropped a bin in the gutter and shook Iggy out of his hazy subconscious stirrings, setting him en route to a sharp, kettle-fuelled caffeine hit. 'Just get me through the day, without head-butting my supervisor,' he meandered. The minor birds shook on as the sun slowly rose, illuminating the day and all of its possibilities. Possibilities far and beyond, possibilities obscure yet near. This had the three wondering …

Iggy contemplated quitting his job.

The P-plater considered slapping her audacious neighbour.

Agnes ruminated and recited the local locksmith's contact details inside her mind.

'I could just phone and tell him that I've been recruited for some charity work in the Sudan,' Iggy thought. Iggy despised his job as personal trainer at the local gym; especially the lazy and opinionated clients who he was charged with rescuing from a life of severe and excessive inactivity. Most mornings for Iggy began with a mental and philosophical battle regarding whether to continue with his dissatisfying employment or whether to throw the towel in on it all and begin forging a new career path.

Agnes had her conflicts too. She loved her work as a registered nurse but the night shifts were long and at times lonely. Over the last few years she had noticed that her eyesight and memory were progressively diminishing. She'd often lose track of important patient records; at times even forgetting in which ward some patients were and directing visiting family members in the wrong direction. Now, as she struggled to perform the relatively simple task of opening her front door, she wondered where her life was heading. Was she to wind up in the nursing home with her patients? To lie alongside them in the beds and wards she had been maintaining for all these years? It required considerable fortitude for her to play down the possibility. 'I'll be fine,' she thought. 'As soon as I find this damn key I'll put it on a separate key ring. Then I'll always know where it is'.

The P-plater was at her wit's end with the parking situation in her busy street. She aggressively got out of her vehicle and slammed a folder on her neighbour's bonnet. The neighbour confronted her and an argument ensued. The sun rose higher and glistened on the silver trim of the neighbour's car.

As the day ambled on, the fight continued for them all.

This text is beyond what would be expected of a typical Year 9 student. It is provided here as a model.
The assessment comments are based on the marking criteria used to assess the NAPLAN Writing Test.

Structure

Character and setting
- A metaphor is used to create humour and add to the characterisation of the P-plater.

Text structure
- Descriptive language is used to describe the setting and orient the reader.
- This is an effective ending to a short story. The simple final sentence concludes with tension and does not resolve the situation for the characters, adding to the theme of fighting one's way through life in modern society.

Cohesion
- Correct use of connectives indicates a continuity of ideas and cohesion in the narrative.

Language and ideas

Vocabulary
- Sophisticated vocabulary (e.g. *defiance*) is included.
- Strong verbs are used to describe the sounds of the setting.

Sentence structure
- Short sentences engage the audience.
- There is a sophisticated narrative structure that intertwines the stories of three distinct characters, yet all are related to the concept: The Fight.

Ideas
- Humour is used to make an insightful comment about the image obsession that many suffer from in Western cultures.
- An insightful thematic comment is made about the connection between employment and personal satisfaction with life.

Punctuation
- Punctuation is used correctly for dialogue.
- Ellipsis is used to establish suspense and engage the reader.
- Effective use of rhetorical questions engages the reader in the conflict of the character.
- Selective use of direct speech to develop characters.

Spelling
- All words are correctly spelled.
- Difficult (e.g. *aggressively*) and challenging (e.g. *fortitude*) vocabulary is included.

WRITING
Description 1

There is no way of knowing for certain what type of writing will be included in the NAPLAN Tests in years to come. This is an opportunity for you to practise different types of writing.

The aim of a description is to give the reader a clear and vivid word picture of a person, thing, place or scene. Descriptions of scenes are often important in narratives. They can help create different moods and atmosphere.

Before you start, read the General writing tips on pages 35–36 and the Tips for writing descriptions on page 97.

Today you are going to write a description.

Look at the picture on the right.

The idea that you must base your description on is THE FIGHT. Your description might be of a young boy's fight for life after being hit by a car, a worker's fight with the photocopier or a prey's fight against its predator. Your description could be of a physical, mental or emotional fight.

Before you start writing, give some thought to:

- the setting—what you are describing
- what kind of fight you will write about
- specific details of the situation.

Don't forget to:

- plan your description before you start writing.
- write in correctly formed sentences and take care with paragraphing
- choose your words carefully and pay attention to your spelling and punctuation
- write neatly but don't waste time
- quickly check your description once you have finished.

Start writing here or type in your answer on a tablet or computer.

☞ Marking guide on page 216

WRITING
Description 2

There is no way of knowing for certain what type of writing will be included in the NAPLAN Tests in years to come. This is an opportunity for you to practise different types of writing.

The aim of a description is to give the reader a clear and vivid word picture of a person, thing, place or scene. Descriptions of scenes are often important in narratives. They can help create different moods and atmosphere.

Before you start, read the General writing tips on pages 35–36 and the Tips for writing descriptions on page 97.

Today you are going to write a description.

Look at the picture on the right.

The idea that you must base your description on is THE CAVE. You might write a description of a climber attempting to grip the sides of a cave's overhang, the contents of an abandoned cave or an unknown species discovered in the depths of a cave. It could be a description of a person found hiding themselves in a cave having been wrongly accused of a crime, or of a secret society meeting weekly in a cave on the outskirts of a small town.

Before you start writing, give some thought to:

- the setting—what you are describing
- the special features of the cave
- specific details of the situation.

Don't forget to:

- plan your description before you start writing.
- write in correctly formed sentences and take care with paragraphing
- choose your words carefully and pay attention to your spelling and punctuation
- write neatly but don't waste time
- quickly check your description once you have finished.

Start writing here or type in your answer on a tablet or computer.

☞ **Marking guide on page 217**

Week 4

This is what we cover this week:

Day 1 **Measurement and Geometry:** ◎ Angles, lines and polygons
◎ 3D shapes, scale and position

Day 2 **Spelling:** ◎ Words ending with 'y', homophones, and technical, complex and scientific vocabulary
◎ Common misspellings

Grammar and Punctuation: ◎ Narrative, direct and indirect speech, and clauses

Day 3 **Reading:** ◎ Understanding visual texts
◎ Understanding procedures
◎ Understanding essays

Day 4 **Writing:** ◎ Recounts

MEASUREMENT AND GEOMETRY
Angles, lines and polygons

1 Two angles in a triangle are 45° and 65°. What is the size of the other angle?
A 60° B 70° C 75° D 90°

For questions 2, 3 and 4, the diagram shows a pair of parallel lines with missing angles *x*, *y*, *z*.

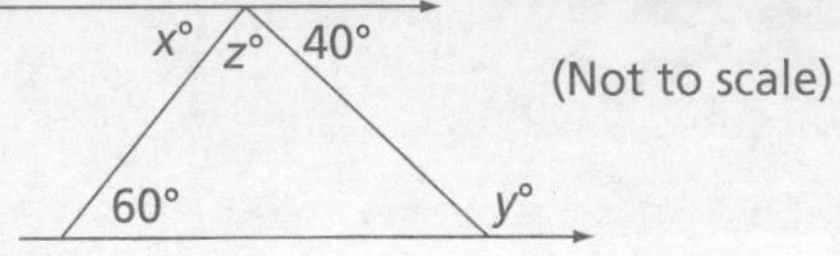

(Not to scale)

2 What is the value of *x*?
A 30 B 60 C 120 D 140

3 What is the value of *y*?
A 40 B 70 C 140 D 160

4 What is the value of *z*?
A 90 B 80 C 70 D 60

5 Two angles in a certain triangle are 40° and 70°. The triangle is
A isosceles. B right-angled.
C obtuse-angled. D scalene.

The diagram shows a triangle and missing angles *x* and *y*.

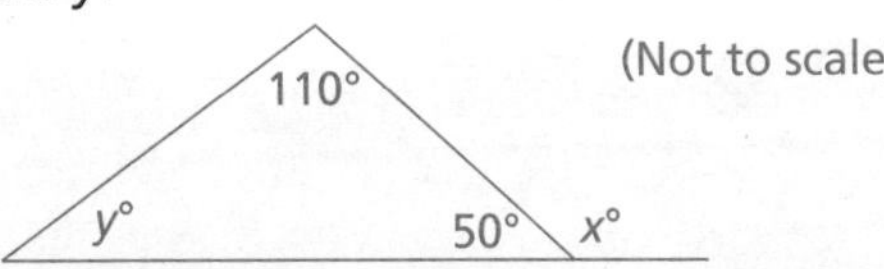

(Not to scale)

6 What is the value of *x*?
A 50 B 100 C 130 D 150

7 What is the value of *y*?
A 20 B 40 C 50 D 60

8 One angle in an isosceles triangle is 100°. Find another angle in the triangle.
A 40° B 50° C 80° D 100

9 What is the value of *y*?

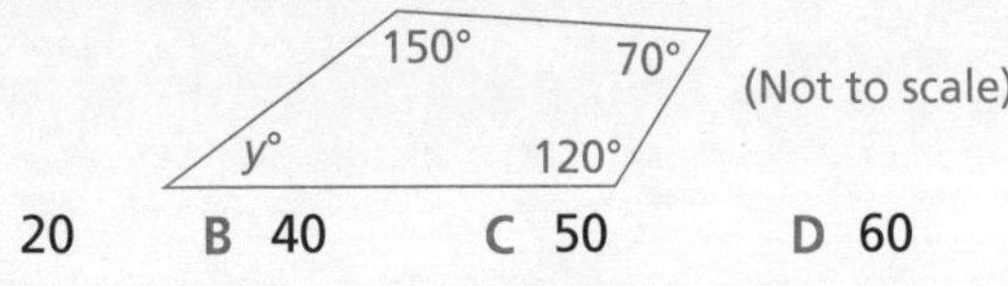

(Not to scale)

A 20 B 40 C 50 D 60

10 What is the sum of the angles in a hexagon?
A 360° B 450° C 540° D 720°

For questions 11 and 12, the diagram shows a triangle and some missing angles.

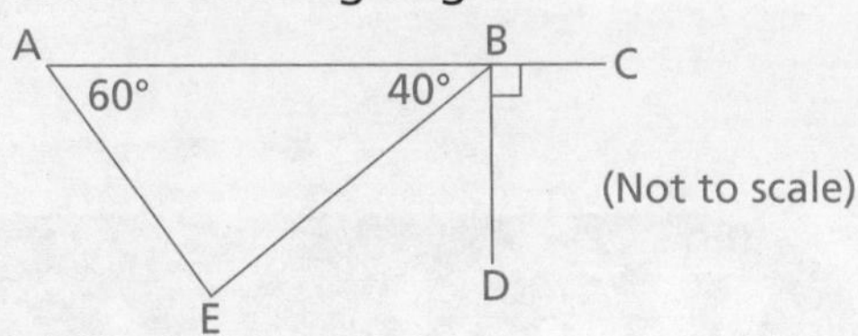

(Not to scale)

11 What is the size of angle DBE?
A 40° B 50° C 80° D 90°

12 What is the size of angle AEB?
A 30° B 40° C 80° D 100°

13 How many axes of symmetry has an isosceles triangle?
A 1 B 2 C 3 D 4

14 Which one of these flags has more than one axis of symmetry?

A 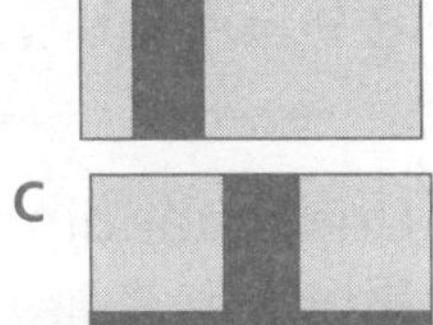
B 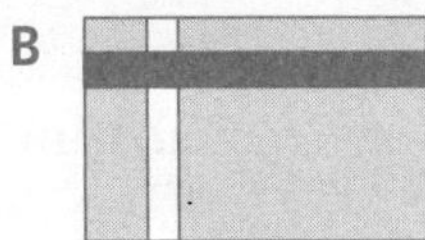
C 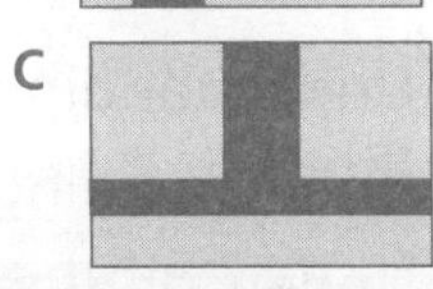
D 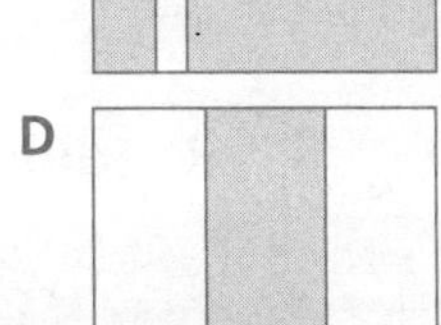

15 What is the size of one of the angles in a right-angled isosceles triangle?
A 40° B 45° C 50° D 60°

16 Find the size of each angle in a regular pentagon.
A 50° B 55° C 72° D 108°

17 The diagram shows a triangle and missing angles *x* and *y*. What is the value of *x*?
A 61 B 76
C 116 D 122

58°
x° y°
(Not to scale)

18 The value of *y* can be found using what equation?
A $y = x + 58$ B $y = 180 - (x + 58)$
C $y = 180 - (58 - x)$ D $y = 58 - (180 - x)$

☞ Explanations on pages 217–218

Answers: 1 B 2 B 3 C 4 B 5 A 6 C 7 A 8 A 9 A 10 D 11 B 12 C 13 A 14 D 15 B 16 D 17 A 18 A

MEASUREMENT AND GEOMETRY
Angles, lines and polygons

1. A **protractor** measures angles.

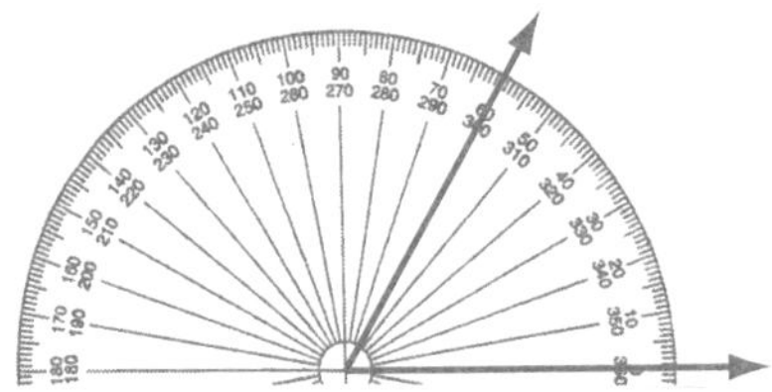

The angle measures 60°.

2. **Angle types**: acute—less than 90°; right—90°; obtuse—between 90° and 180°; straight—180°; reflex—between 180° and 360°; revolution—360°

3. The **angle in a straight line** is 180° and the **angles in a triangle** add to 180°.

Example: Find the values of x and y.

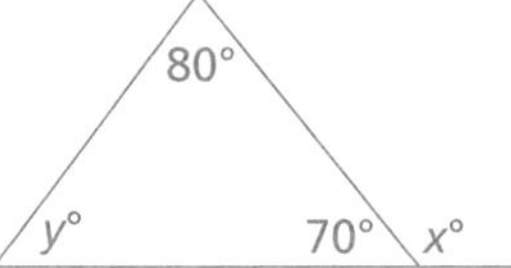

$x = 110$ as there is 180° in a straight line.
$y = 30$ as there is 180° in a triangle.

4. When a line (transversal) cuts across **parallel lines**, the angles formed have the following properties:
   - **Corresponding angles** are equal.

   - **Alternate angles** are equal.

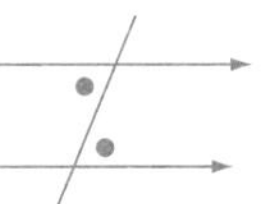

   - **Co-interior angles** are supplementary (add to 180°).

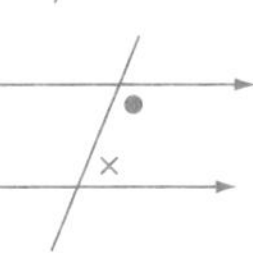

Example: Find the value of the pronumerals.

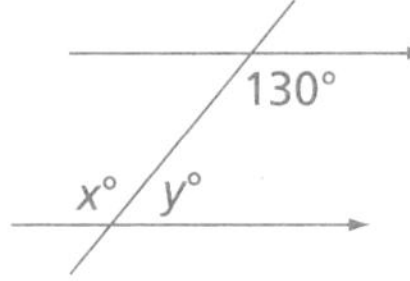

$x = 130$ (alternate angles, ll lines)
$y = 50$ (co-interior angles, ll lines)

5. Triangles can be classified:
   Scalene: angles and sides different sizes
   Isosceles: 2 angles and 2 sides equal
   Equilateral: 3 angles and 3 sides equal
   Right-angled: 1 right angle
   Obtuse-angled: 1 angle greater than 90°

6. Some quadrilaterals can be classified as:
   Square: 4 equal sides, diagonals equal and at right angles
   Rectangle: opposite sides equal and parallel, diagonals equal
   Parallelogram: opposite sides equal and parallel
   Rhombus: 4 equal sides, opposite sides parallel

7. The **angle sum of a quadrilateral** is 360°.

8. Polygons are named according to the number of sides (and angles): pentagon (5 sides), hexagon (6), octagon (8) and decagon (10). A **regular polygon** has all sides (and angles) equal in size.

9. The **angle sum of a polygon** can be found using the rule 180 × (sides – 2). Each **angle in a regular polygon** is then found by dividing the angle sum by the number of sides.

   Example 1: What is the sum of the angles in a pentagon?

   As a pentagon has 5 sides, then
   Angle sum = 180 × (sides – 2)
   = 180 × 3
   = 540 ∴ 540°

   Example 2: Find the size of each angle in a regular octagon.

   As an octagon has 8 sides, then
   Angle sum = 180 × (sides – 2)
   = 180 × 6
   = 1080 ∴ 1080°
   Angle in regular octagon = 1080 ÷ 8
   = 135 ∴ 135°

10. An object has a **line of symmetry** (or axis of symmetry) when half the object can be reflected on to the other half of the object.

MEASUREMENT AND GEOMETRY
Angles, lines and polygons

The diagrams are not drawn to scale.

1 What is the value of x?

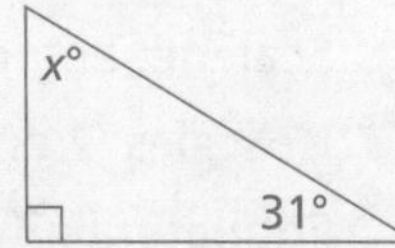

A 59° B 62°
C 69° D 79°

2 What is the size of angle *CBA*?

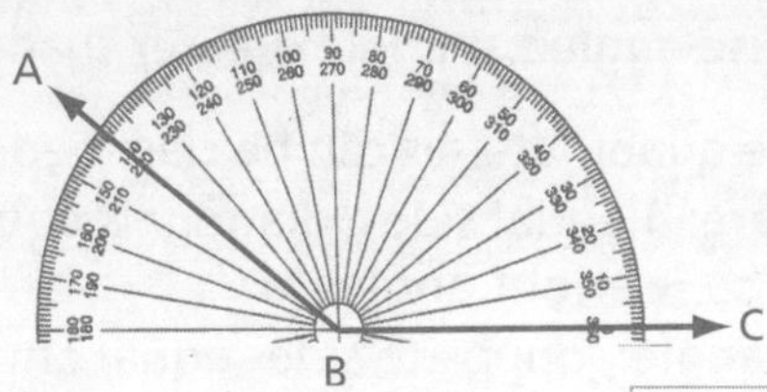

Write your answer in the box: ☐

3 What is the value of x?

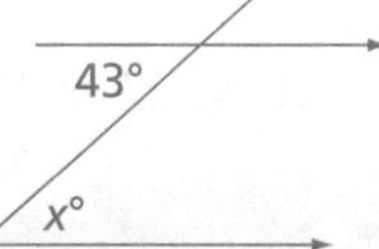

A 43° B 47°
C 57° D 137°

4 A triangle has angles of 80° and 25°. What is the size of the other angle? *Hint 1*

A 55° B 60° C 65° D 75°

5 What is the sum of the angles inside a hexagon? *Hint 2*

A 720° B 800° C 880° D 1080°

6 What is the value of x?

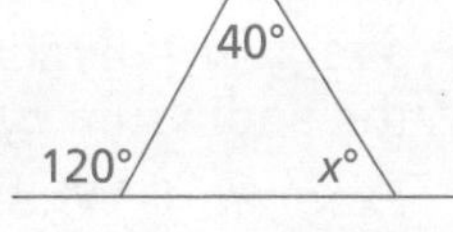

A 20° B 40°
c 60° D 80°

7 What is the value of y?

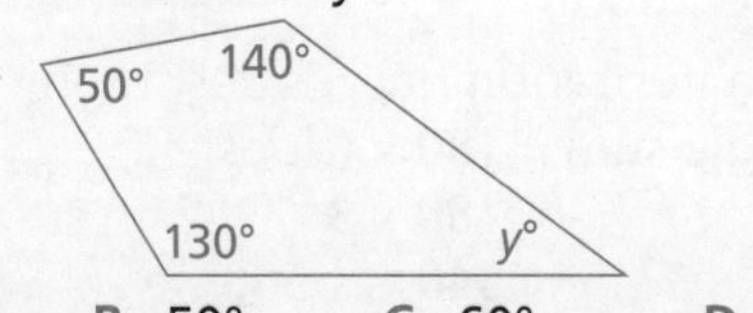

A 40° B 50° C 60° D 70°

8 The angles in a triangle are in the ratio of 1:2:3. What is the size of the largest angle?

A 60° B 70° C 75° D 90°

9 An isosceles triangle has an angle of 120°. What is the size of another angle?

A 20° B 30° C 40° D 120°

10 What is the size of x? *Hint 3*

Write your answer in the box: ☐

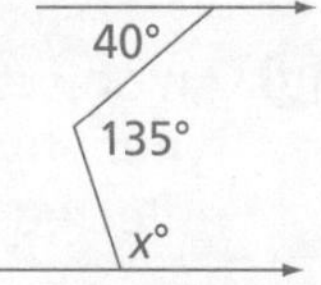

11 What is the size of each angle in a regular 10-sided polygon? *Hint 4*

A 60° B 66° C 120° D 144°

12 What is the size of x?

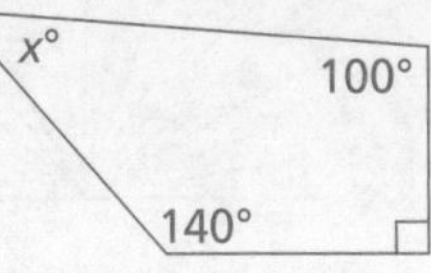

A 30° B 40°
C 50° D 60°

13 AC and DB are parallel.
Triangle ABC is isosceles. What is the size of angle ABD?

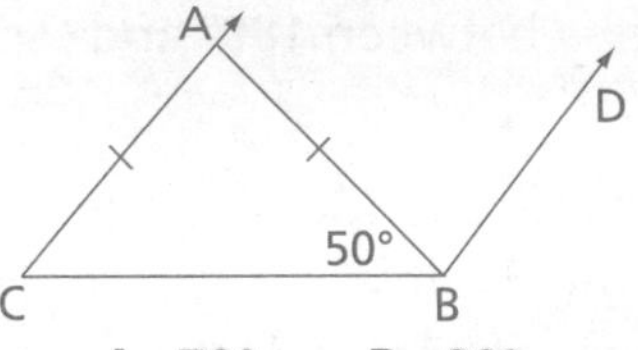

A 70° B 80° C 100° D 130°

14 ABCDE is a regular pentagon.
What is the value of x?

☐ degrees

15 How many axes of symmetry does a rhombus have?

☐

16 The diagram shows a square and an equilateral triangle. AC is a straight line. What is the size of angle DBE?

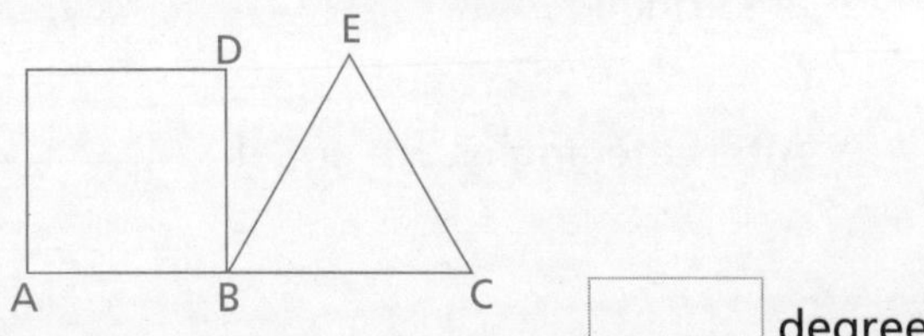

☐ degrees

Hint 1: *Angle sum of a triangle is 180 degrees.*
Hint 2: *Angle sum of a polygon is 180 x (number of sides – 2).*
Hint 3: *Pretend there is a third parallel line and use alternate angles.*
Hint 4: *After finding the angle sum, each angle in a regular polygon is found by dividing by the number of sides.*

☞ Answers and explanations on pages 218–219

MEASUREMENT AND GEOMETRY
3D shapes, scale and position

1 How many more small cubes are needed to make the solid into a larger cube?

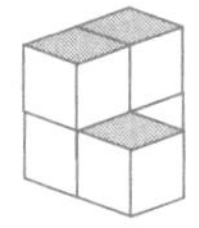

A 1 B 2
C 3 D 4

2 The diagram shows the net of a cube. What is the letter on the face that is opposite F?

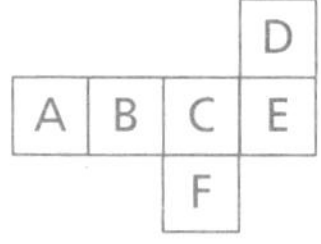

A A B B
C C D D

3 A large cube is made from 27 small cubes. If the large cube is painted and then broken up into its small cubes, how many of the small cubes have three painted surfaces?

A 4 B 6 C 8 D 9

4 A net of a solid is made up of two triangles and three rectangles. What is the name of the solid?

A triangular prism
B triangular pyramid
C rectangular prism
D rectangular pyramid

5 Which of these solids has the same number of faces as a square pyramid?

A pentagonal prism
B pentagonal pyramid
C triangular prism
D rectangular prism

For questions 6 and 7 use the map below showing the location of places in a small town. The post office is south-west of the school.

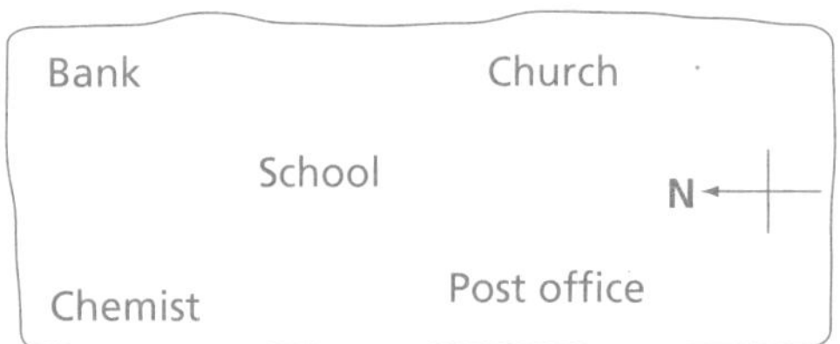

6 What direction is the church from the post office?

A north B south C east D west

7 What direction is the chemist from the school?

A south-east B south-west
C north-east D north-west

8 A cylinder is cut with a knife. What is the shape of the cross-section?

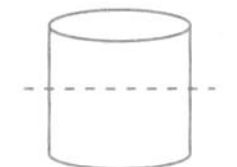

A B C D

9 This object is made from 9 cubes. What is the top view of the cubes?

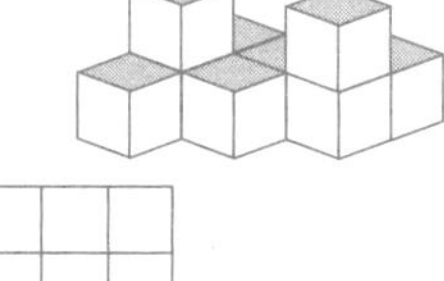

A
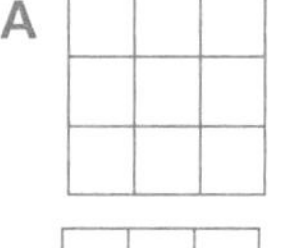

B
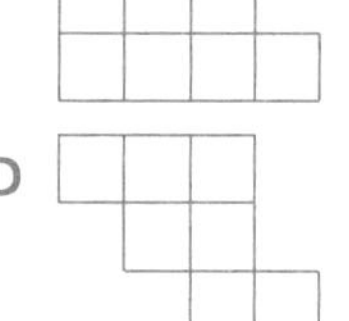

C

D

10 What is the enlargement factor used in the diagram of similar triangles below?

A $\frac{2}{3}$ B 1
C $\frac{3}{2}$ D 2

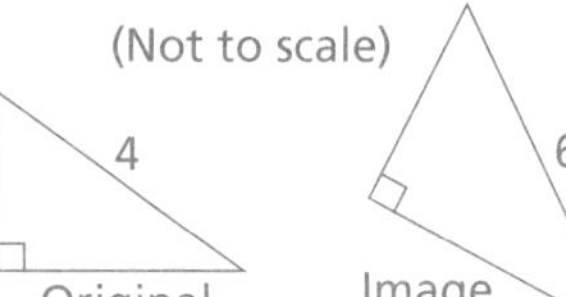

For questions 11 and 12, the diagram shows triangles ABC and ADE which are similar where ABC is enlarged to produce ADE.

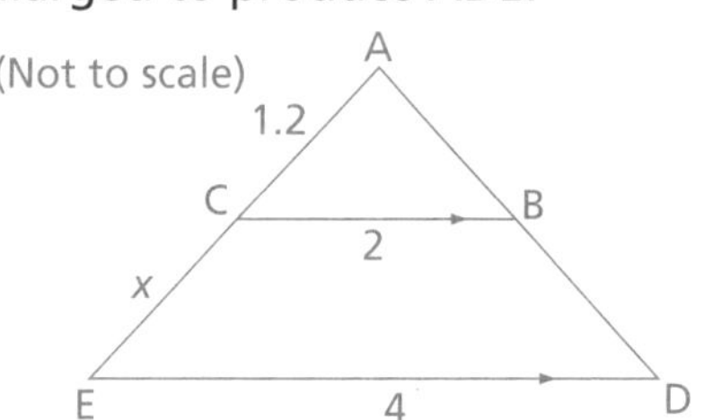

11 What is the enlargement factor used?

A $\frac{1}{2}$ B 1 C 2 D 3

12 What is the value of x?

A 1.2 B 2.4 C 3.6 D 4

☞ Explanations on pages 219–220

Answers: 1 C 2 D 3 C 4 A 5 C 6 C 7 D 8 D 9 D 10 C 11 C 12 A

MEASUREMENT AND GEOMETRY
3D shapes, scale and position

1 When an object is made from small cubes it can be **viewed** from different directions.

Example: What is the top view of this object?

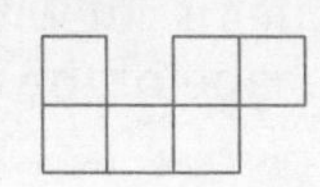

2 Small **cubes** are glued together to form two objects.

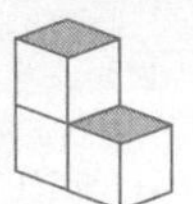

The two objects are now joined together. Here are two possible results:

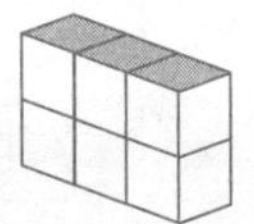

or

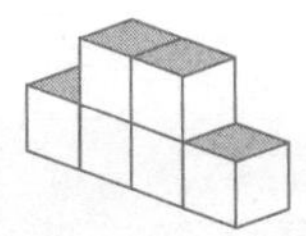

3 A **net** can be used to form a solid.

Example: The diagram shows the net of a cube.

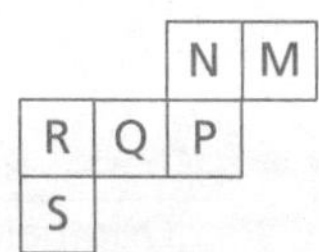

When the cube is formed, what is on the face opposite the letter M?

The letter is Q.

4 When a solid is cut with a knife the shape of the **cross-section** is dependent on the direction of the cut.

Example: The cylinder is cut and the shape of the cross-section is .

Which of the following is the direction of the cut?

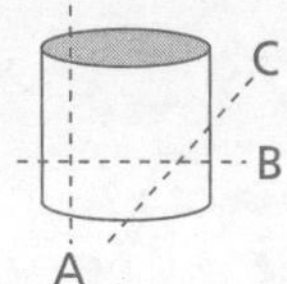

The direction of the cut is C.

5 Directions are based on the **compass** rose.

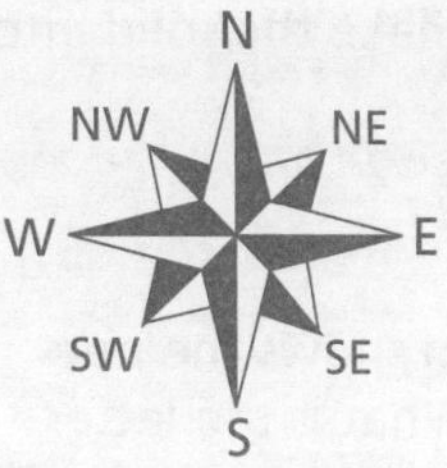

Example: Jelena is facing west and turns 135° in a clockwise direction. What direction is she facing?

From west to north is 90°, so adding another 45° makes it NE.

6 Two shapes are **similar** if they have matching angles and their sides are in proportion. One shape is an enlargement of the other.

Example 1: What is the enlargement factor if the shape on the left is used to form the image on the right?

(Not to scale)

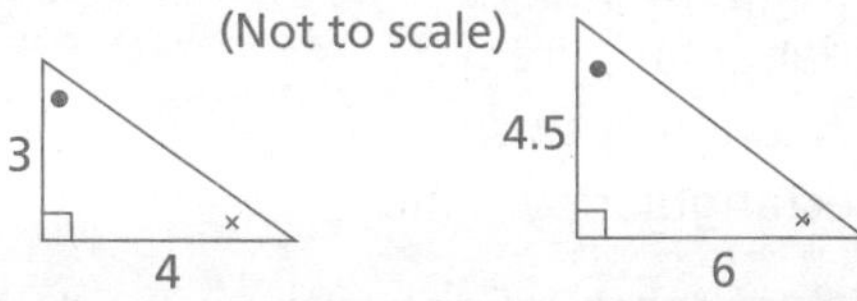

Consider the sides that are opposite the same angles in the triangles:

4.5 and 3 are opposite matching angles.

6 and 4 are sides opposite matching angles.

Enlargement factor = $\frac{4.5}{3} = \frac{6}{4} = 1.5$

Example 2: Find the value of x.

(Not to scale)

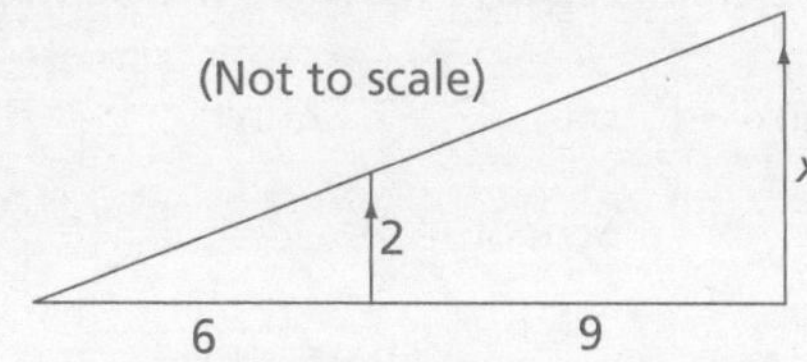

Two triangles have heights x and 2.

Two triangles have base lengths 15 and 6.

Match up the sides: $\frac{x}{2} = \frac{15}{6}$

Therefore $x = 5$.

MEASUREMENT AND GEOMETRY
3D shapes, scale and position

1. This object is made from 10 small cubes.

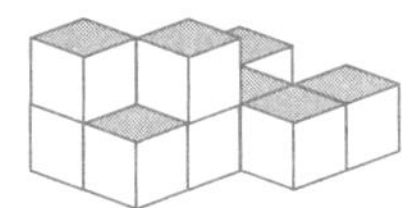

What is the view from the top?

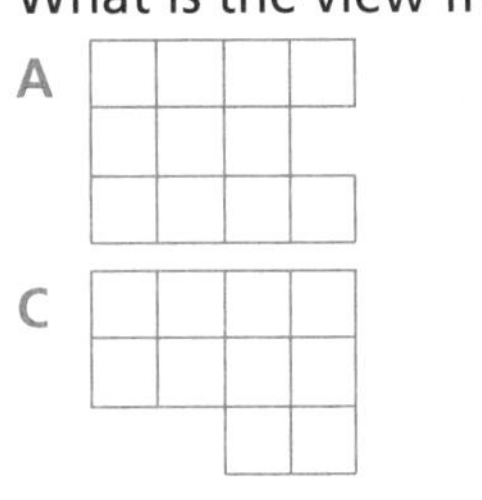

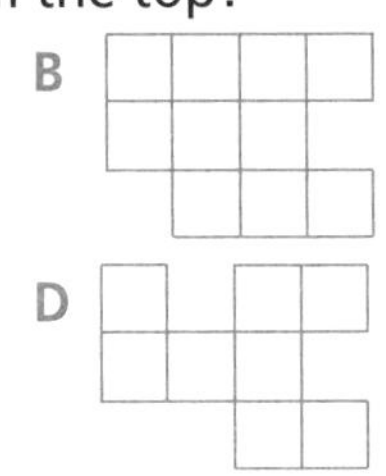

2. How many rectangles are in the net of a pentagonal prism?

A 4 B 5 C 6 D 7

3. Jack glues small cubes together to make these 2 objects:

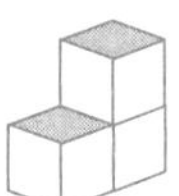 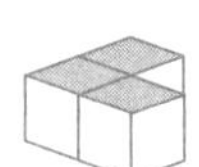

He then glues the two objects together. Which object below could **not** be made?

A 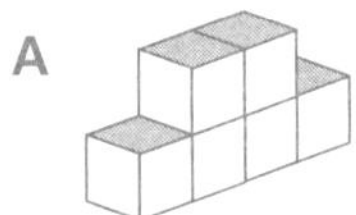

B 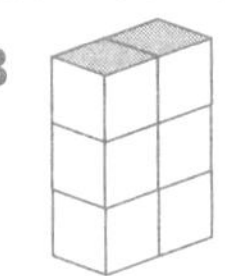

C 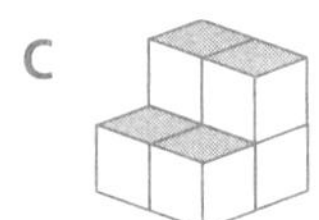

D 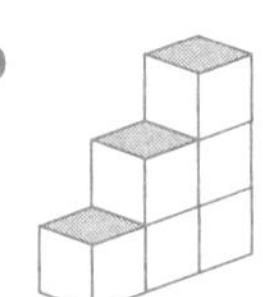

4. A solid shape is cut with a knife. The shape of the cross-section is always a circle. What is the solid shape?

Write your answer in the box: 

For questions 5, 6, 7 and 8, use this map of Boa Island.

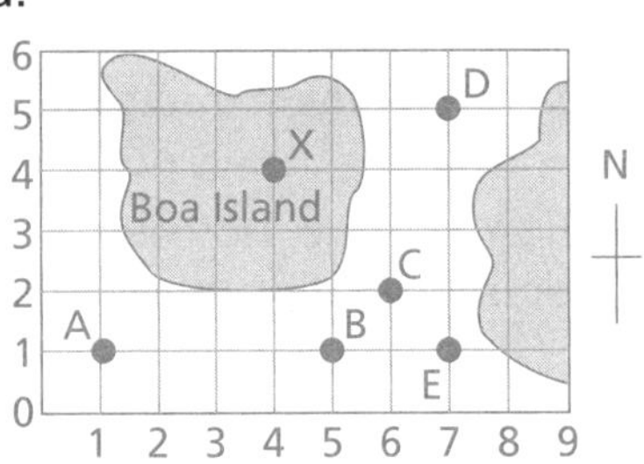

5. Which one of these points is located on Boa Island?

A $(5, \frac{1}{2})$ B $(3\frac{1}{2}, 4)$

C (8, 1) D (7, 5)

6. Adam is standing at X and is facing towards A. He turns to face E. Through how many degrees does Adam turn in a **clockwise** direction?

45°	90°	180°	225°	270°
A	B	C	D	E

7. Jannah is at B and Alysha is at C. What direction is Jannah from Alysha?

A north-west B south-west

C south-east D north-east

8. If the scale used on the map is 1 unit = 6 km, how long would it take a boat to travel from A to E and then E to D if the boat travels at an average speed of 25 km/h? *Hint 1*

☐ hours

Triangle ABC has been enlarged as triangle ADE. *Hint 2*

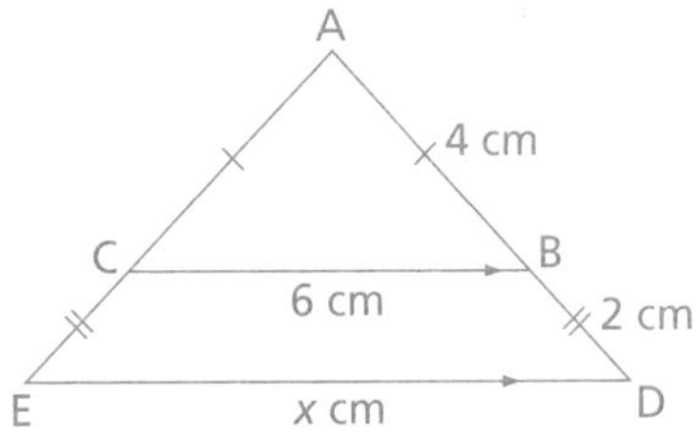

9. What is the enlargement factor used?

☐

10. What is the value of x?

☐

Hint 1: Estimate the distance in units before changing to kilometres. Then use Time = Distance divided by Speed.

Hint 2: Remember to compare side of small triangle to side of big triangle to find enlargement factor.

☞ Answers and explanations on page 220

SPELLING

Words ending with 'y', homophones, and technical, complex and scientific vocabulary

Key Points

1. When adding a **suffix that begins with a vowel**, such as 'able', 'ing' or 'ed', to a word ending with an 'e', the final 'e' is dropped before adding the suffix.
   Example: hate → hating

   Once again there are a couple of exceptions to this rule. Don't drop the 'e' if the letter before the 'e' is a vowel.
   Example: see → seeing.

   Also, the 'e' is not dropped if the first letter of the suffix is a consonant.
   Example: definite → definitely

   However, words that end in 'ue' drop the 'e' even if the first letter of the suffix is a consonant.
   Example: blue → bluest

2. When adding a suffix to a **word that ends with a 'y' that follows a consonant**, such as 'bury', you need to drop the 'y' and add 'i' before the suffix.
   Examples: bury → buries, marry → married

   However, when adding a suffix to a **word that ends with a 'y' that follows a vowel**, keep the 'y' and simply add the suffix.
   Examples: convoy → convoys, deploy → deploying.
   There is one exception to this rule: when adding the suffix 'ing', you keep the 'y'.
   Example: worry → worrying

   Also, when adding a suffix to a **word that ends with 'ie'**, you need to change the end to 'y' before adding 'ing'.
   Examples: die →dying (not 'dieing'), lie → lying (not 'lieing')—this is a common mistake made by Year 9 students.

3. People often misspell **words that sound the same but are spelt differently and have different meanings**. These words are referred to as **homophones** and you may remember learning about them earlier in your schooling. To know how to spell these words simply requires practice, as there isn't any spelling pattern or rule to help you. The ones that are most frequently misspelt and which probably cause you and your teachers the most annoyance are *you're—your*, *it's—its* and *their—there—they're*. Others that you may come across are:

sites—sights	source—sauce	allowed—aloud
braking—breaking	practise—practice	to—too—two
course—coarse	incidence—incidents	threw—through
principal—principle	boarder—border	intense—intents

   It's really important that you learn the difference between these words because spellchecker will not identify them for you, since the spelling of the word is correct—it's just being used incorrectly!

4. As you move into your senior years of schooling you will notice that words become more complex, especially technical and scientific words that are subject specific. Many of these will be **multi-syllable words**, so you should use the same rule when trying to spell them: break them into sound chunks, e.g. ver—te—brate.

   Examples: decimal, quadrilateral, apparatus, laboratory, circulation, particle, isosceles, immigrant, constitution, invasion, longitude, erosion, prejudice, harmony, lyric, syncopation, playwright, illusion

SPELLING

Words ending with 'y', homophones, and technical, complex and scientific vocabulary

Test Your Skills

Learn the words below. A common method of learning and self-testing is the LOOK, SAY, COVER, WRITE, CHECK method. If you make any mistakes, you should rewrite the word three times correctly, immediately. In this way you will become familiar with the correct spelling. If the word is particularly troublesome, rewrite it several more times or keep a list of words that you can check regularly.

This week's theme word: MUSIC

harmony	__________	harmonies	__________
lyric	__________	crotchet	__________
practice	__________	practise	__________
braking	__________	breaking	__________
course	__________	coarse	__________
melody	__________	melodies	__________
allowed	__________	aloud	__________
dynamics	__________	musician	__________
rhythm	__________	quaver	__________
syncopation	__________		

Write any troublesome words three times.

__________ __________ __________

__________ __________ __________

SPELLING
Common misspellings

Please ask your parent or teacher to read to you the spelling words on page 250. Write the correct spelling of each word in the box.

1. Severe wind storms have resulted in the ________ of the sand dunes.
2. Amendments can be made to a ________ if enough people support them.
3. The life of a new ________ is often lonely and stressful.
4. The city's ________ was meticulously planned by skilled engineers.
5. Aazim was excited to make the ________ to the holy land.
6. The ________ had an impressive vision for the future of his new school.
7. We noticed the ________ lines on the road that indicated no overtaking.
8. The shop owner tried to ________ the cost of the water damage.
9. The new product did not meet the company's ________, causing turmoil.
10. What you believe happened, Harry, is ________.
11. The footballer's ________ gained him a spot in the Australian team.
12. What ________ will you use to defeat the ferocious gargoyle Gongala?
13. The ________ of the lasagne was thick and gelatinous; no-one wanted to eat it.
14. Combine the ________ in the bowl, and add into the food processor.
15. The ________ of Cyprus by the Turks was inevitable.

The spelling mistakes in these sentences have been underlined. Write the correct spelling for each underlined word in each box.

16. In this <u>sceneario</u>, Martha reveals her deepest emotions to Ashley.
17. Working in the <u>labatry</u> can be hazardous if you are not careful.

The Rat

18. A dark grey, matted ball crouched <u>suspishusly</u> in the corner of the box.
19. Its tiny <u>insessint</u> breath streamed from its filthy mouth.
20. With each <u>exhalashion</u> the dirty black lips parted to reveal a row of tightly bunched teeth.

☞ Answers on pages 220–221

SPELLING
Common misspellings

Each sentence has one word that is incorrect.
Write the correct spelling of the word in the box.

21 The rat's unappealing appearance meant that it eliseted no sympathy from its tormentor—a pipette-wielding scientist.

Visions of the Future

22 Throughout history, a number of indvidduials have attempted to

23 predict the future of humanity. One of the most illusstrius people to undertake this task was the French seer, Nostradamus. He published

24 a number of books in his lifetime, with the most reknownned being The Prophecies in which, it has been claimed, he prophesised the rise of Napoleon, Adolf Hitler and other significant historical events. Despite his many admirers, most people believe that it is impossible

25 to envissige the future and prefer to see what life brings them. What do you believe?

☞ Answers on pages 220-221

GRAMMAR AND PUNCTUATION
Narrative, direct and indirect speech, and clauses

Key Points

1 The point of view in which a piece of writing is presented is determined by the **narrative voice** chosen by the writer.

a **First-person narrative** refers to a piece of writing written from the point of view of the character or persona. First-person narrative is indicated by the use of 'I', 'me', 'my' and 'myself'.
Example: I couldn't bring myself to walk down that alley again. The memories of the accident last week were still too raw in my mind.

b **Second-person narrative** refers to a piece of writing that is explicitly directed at the reader and is often used in commands. Second-person narrative is indicated by the use of 'you', 'you're' and 'your'.
Example: If you're ever lost in the wilderness, the best thing to do is keep hydrated and stay calm.

c **Third-person narrative** refers to a piece of writing that is written from the omniscient point of view. This means that the story is being told from the perspective of a narrator who cannot be seen and who has complete control over the elements of the narrative that the reader is presented with. Third-person narrative is indicated by the use of 'he', 'she' and 'they', and also the names of characters.
Example: Maynard walked over to Jeff and shook his hand.

2 **Direct speech** refers to the actual words spoken by a person or character. Direct speech is signified by the use of quotation marks. Students often use incorrect punctuation to indicate direct speech.

a Often it is the use of the **comma** that confuses students. If opening with an introductory clause before the direct speech, such as 'He said', then the comma must follow this clause.
Example: He said, 'I require your signature.'
If the direct speech comes first, then the comma must be placed before the final quotation mark.
Example: 'I require your signature,' he said.

b A **comma** is not used if the direct speech ends with a question mark or an exclamation mark.
Example: 'May I have your signature?' he asked.

c **Capital letters** in direct speech often cause confusion as well. Just like in all sentences, capital letters must only be used in direct speech at the beginning of a sentence or for the beginning of a proper noun. You need to pay close attention to where a sentence begins and ends.
Example: 'We need to begin rehearsal now, Keenan,' said Mrs Richards, 'so get your drum sticks.'
The above example is one sentence only and only uses a capital letter for the beginning of the sentence and for the names of the people. A capital letter is not required for the beginning of the second half of the direct speech as it is still part of the one sentence.
If the direct speech includes two separate sentences, then a capital must be used.
Example: 'Where's my tea?' shouted John. 'I ordered it five minutes ago!'

3 **Indirect speech** refers to the inclusion of words spoken by a person or character. However, these are not written word for word and don't use quotation marks.
Example: Sienna said she wasn't coming to saxophone rehearsal today.

GRAMMAR AND PUNCTUATION

Narrative, direct and indirect speech, and clauses

4 A **clause** is a group of related words that include a subject and a verb.
Example: It is cold, yet Addison is playing outside. (This includes two separate clauses linked by the connective 'yet'.)
There are two important types of clauses with which you must be familiar.

a An **adjectival clause** functions just like an adjective in that it gives extra information to a noun or a noun group.
Example: The boy, who was feverish and hungry, accepted the stranger's hospitality.
(The underlined clause is the adjectival clause.)

b An **adverbial clause** works like an adverb in that its purpose is to add greater meaning to an action. It adds information to an existing clause.
Example: Addison went inside to escape from the cold. (The underlined clause is the adverbial clause.)

Test Your Skills

1 Identify what narrative voice the following sentences use.

From the tense atmosphere Ashley could perceive that the meeting was not going according to plan.

It will take sustained moral effort for me to change my unhealthy lifestyle.

You should have seen it! Those kids you trained were amazing!

2 Underline the adjectival clause in the sentence below.

William sank to his knees, exhausted and delirious, waiting for the final blow.

3 Underline the adverbial clause in the sentence below.

Running from the dogs, Joe sprinted past the safe house.

4 State whether the following are examples of direct or indirect speech.

'Sorry I couldn't come to your graduation,' apologised Maree, 'my mother was hospitalised that day.'

Maree apologised for not coming to my graduation. She claimed her mother was put in hospital on that day.

5 Insert the correct punctuation in the direct speech below.

It's impossible to get good service these days complained Judy because all the good waiters have moved to the city.

Answers: third person, first person, second person 2 William sank to his knees, exhausted and delirious, waiting for the final blow. 3 Running from the dogs, Joe sprinted past the safe house. 4 direct, indirect 5 'It's impossible to get good service these days,' complained Judy, 'because all the good waiters have moved to the city.'

GRAMMAR AND PUNCTUATION
Narrative, direct and indirect speech, and clauses

1 Which of the following correctly completes this sentence?

John couldn't comprehend the enormity of the situation; ______ too overcome with grief.

we is	he were	he was	he am
A	B	C	D

2 This is my city and I breathe its breath into my core every day.

In this sentence, the word 'core' is used as

an adjective.	a verb.	an adverb.	a noun.
A	B	C	D

3 Which of the following correctly completes this sentence?

Navigating the continent with little more than a hand-drawn sketch, the explorer ______ frustrated and isolated.

felted	felt	feeling	are feeling
A	B	C	D

4 Having spied Sally from across the department store floor, Kane, choosing his moment carefully, asked her whether she preferred strawberry or lavender scented drawer liners.

This text is written in the

present tense	past tense.	future tense.
A	B	C

5 Which part of this sentence is an adjectival clause?

The woman who was older than my mum screamed at me and made me jump.

The woman	who was older than my mum	screamed at me	and made me jump
A	B	C	D

6 Which sentence is correct?

A Although entirely true, people are often surprised when they discover that elephants have no natural predators.

B Although, entirely true people are often surprised when they discover that elephants have no natural predators.

C Although entirely true, people are often surprised, when they discover that elephants have no natural predators.

D Although entirely true people are often surprised when they discover that elephants have no natural predators?

7 Which sentence is correct?

A I went to the local supermarket and collected all of the ingredients required for my ANZAC biscuits; sugar—bicarbonate soda—oats—coconut and butter.

B i went to the local supermarket and collected all of the ingredients required for my ANZAC biscuits—sugar bicarbonate soda oats coconut and butter.

C I went to the local supermarket and collected all of the ingredients required for my Anzac biscuits: sugar, bicarbonate soda, oats, coconut and butter.

D I went to the local supermarket and collected all of the ingredients; required for my ANZAC biscuits sugar: bicarbonate soda, oats, coconut and butter.

☞ Answers and explanations on pages 221-223

GRAMMAR AND PUNCTUATION

Narrative, direct and indirect speech, and clauses

8 Brackets ( ) are needed in this sentence. Which part of the sentence needs brackets?

Eager to fill his empty stomach, Martin made himself a triple-decker sandwich three pieces of bread with three toppings and sat down in front of the television.

A sat down in front
B three pieces
C three pieces of bread with three toppings
D his empty stomach

9 Which sentence has the correct punctuation?

A 'I am thoroughly impressed by the food preparation in this kitchen? exclaimed Darrel.'
B I am thoroughly impressed by the food preparation in this kitchen! exclaimed Darrel.
C 'I am thoroughly impressed by the food preparation in this kitchen!' exclaimed Darrel.
D 'I am thoroughly impressed by the food preparation in this kitchen!,' exclaimed Darrel.

10 Which of the following correctly completes this sentence?

Charlie firmly believes that ________ unlucky to put shoes on the table.

A i'ts
B it's
C its
D it are

11 Which sentence has the correct punctuation?

A On the night of 14 April 1912, the rms Titanic collided with a submerged iceberg.
B On the night of 14 April 1912, the RMS Titanic collided with a submerged iceberg.
C On the night of 14 April 1912 the RMS Titanic collided with a submerged iceberg?
D On the night of 14 April 1912, the RMS titanic collided with a submerged iceberg.

12 Jill asked Julie if she wanted to go on a date.

The above is an example of

A direct speech.
B indirect speech.
C an oxymoron.

13 Reading philosophy books and watching YouTube videos are my passions.

This text is written in

A first-person narrative.
B second-person narrative.
C third-person narrative.

Write the word or words in the box to correctly complete the sentences below.

14 The detectives ________ with the progress of the investigation.

was pleased	were pleased	is pleased	am pleased
A	B	C	D

15 Instead of watching the DVD, Mary ________ assisted Juan with his homework.

shouldn't	shouldv'e	should of	should have
A	B	C	D

16 The pie ________ delicious; I could've eaten a dozen or more.

were	were so	wasn't	was
A	B	C	D

☞ Answers and explanations on pages 221–223

GRAMMAR AND PUNCTUATION
Narrative, direct and indirect speech, and clauses

Highlight the correct answer in the sentences below.

17 Which sentence is correct?

A Despite the sign warning against it Amir continued, on towards the abandoned house.
B Despite the sign warning against it, Amir continued on towards the abandoned house.
C Despite the sign warning against it, Amir continued on towards the abandoned house?
D Despite the sign warning against it, Amir continued on towards the abandoned house!

18 What type of word is *inspire* in this sentence?

The captain of the team was finding it difficult to inspire his team to try harder during the game.

verb	adverb	noun	adjective
A	B	C	D

19 Which sentence has the correct punctuation?

A Your assignment is extremely untidy; you're going to have to complete the task again.
B your assignment, is extremely untidy; you're going to have to complete the task again.
C Your assignment is extremely untidy, you're going to have to complete the task again.
D Your assignment is extremely untidy; You're going to have to complete the task again.

20 Shade a circle to show where the missing apostrophe (') should go.

Phineas (A) danced as the sun (B) s (C) rays rose over the green mountains (D).

21 Shade **two** circles to show where the missing commas (,) should go.

Marco (A) lost his balance when (B) Morgan (C) an inconsiderate and selfish child (D) pushed (E) his way to the front of the canteen line.

22 Understandably the question resulted in a wry grin from Kane and a confused, yet amused, grin from Sally.

In this sentence, the word 'amused' is used as

an adverb.	an adjective.	a verb.	a noun.
A	B	C	D

23 Which of the following correctly completes this sentence?

During the 19th Century, children ______ expected to work more than ten hours per day.

were	is	where	are
A	B	C	D

24 Which of the following correctly completes this sentence?

Every week in America ______ people who protest against injustice.

A they're are B there is C they're is D there are

25 I enjoy looking out at the vast ocean of vehicles that swim towards me as I make my way through the city.

In the second sentence, 'vast ocean of vehicles' is an example of

A a metaphor. B a simile. C imagery. D alliteration.

☞ Answers and explanations on pages 221–223

Resuscitation of Children

DANGER 1.

ASSESS THE SITUATION

For your own safety and that of the child, consider:

- **Falling debris**
- **Traffic**
- **Violence**
- **Fumes/Gases**
- **Electricity**
- **Fire**

NB If fire is present, activate the fire alarm immediately.

If any hazards are present, consider neutralising or containing them. Only consider removing the child if you cannot neutralise any hazard(s).

RESPONSE 2.

CHECK WHETHER THE CHILD IS CONSCIOUS

- **Call out the child's name or ask for name.**
- **Ask them to open their eyes.**
- **Pinch an ear lobe or squeeze the shoulders.**
- **Shout for HELP!**
- **DO NOT move the child unless the environment or situation is dangerous.**

"Are you alright?"
"Can you hear me?"

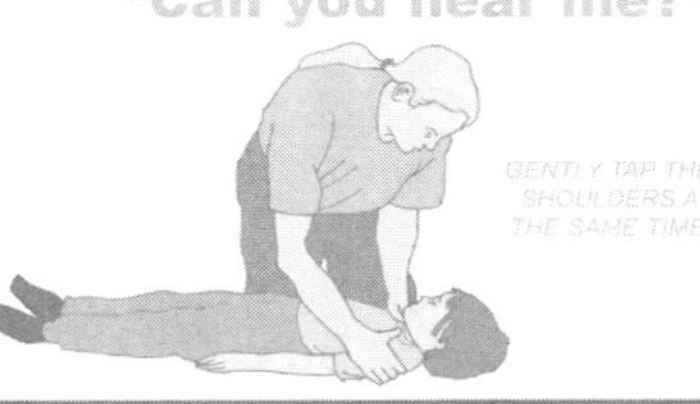

GENTLY TAP THE SHOULDERS AT THE SAME TIME

SHOUT 3.

CALL FOR HELP

If alone call for help. If someone responds to your call ask them to stay with you whilst you assess the Airway and Breathing. One of you should wait with the child whilst the other calls the emergency medical services (EMS).

NB If no-one responds, do not leave the child but go on to assess the airway and breathing.

CALLING THE EMERGENCY MEDICAL SERVICES

Lift the receiver and wait for a dialling tone. DIAL 000 in Australia.

The operator will ask you which service you require. Once you have stated 'Ambulance' you will be connected to ambulance control. The operator will ask you a set of questions. Do not hang up at any stage of the conversation. The operator will terminate the call when appropriate.

AIRWAY 4.

OPEN THE AIRWAY

FOR AN UNRESPONSIVE CHILD

- **Look into the mouth to see if any obvious foreign objects are present. If there are, gently remove with your finger tips. DO NOT USE A FINGER SWEEP.**
- **Open the airway by lifting the chin and tilting the head back slightly.**

NB If any neck injuries are suspected; lift the chin by placing forefingers under the jaw and pushing up. DO NOT MOVE THE NECK.

BREATHING 5.

IS THE CHILD BREATHING?

Check for breathing. Look for chest movement, listen for breathing and feel for airflow.

IF CHILD IS BREATHING NORMALLY

- **Check for any life threatening injuries such as severe bleeding and treat accordingly.**
- **Turn the child on to their side into the recovery position.**
- **Check for continued breathing.**
- **Get help: send someone to call for an ambulance. Remain with the child and continue to monitor their breathing. If you are on your own, you may have to do this yourself.**

The recovery position is used when a casualty is unconscious and breathing. The recovery position allows the head to be placed tilted back and down. This stops the tongue from blocking the airway and will allow any vomit and fluid to drain from the mouth.

UNDER 1 YEAR OLD

Tilt the baby's head downwards whilst cradling him in your arms, ensuring that the airway is open.

CIRCULATION 6.

IF THE CHILD IS NOT BREATHING NORMALLY

Commence Cardio Pulmonary Resuscitation (CPR)

- **Ensure the casualty is on a firm, flat surface.**
- **Place hands in the centre of the casualty's chest.**
- **Compress the chest approxiamtely one third of the chest depth. Compress 30 times at a rate of 100 compressions per minute using 1 or 2 hands to achieve adequate depth of compression. (2 fingers to be used on an infant).** ***A child is between the ages of 1 year to puberty. An infant is below the age of 1 year.***
- **The compressions and releases should take an equal amount of time.**
- **After 30 compressions, open the airway again using head tilt/chin lift.**
- **Seal the nostrils with your thumb and forefinger.**
- **Blow steadily into the mouth until you see the chest rise.**
- **Remove your mouth to the side and inhale some fresh air. When breathing for the casualty, take about a second to make the chest rise.**
- **Repeat so you have given 2 effective rescue breaths in total.**
- **Return your hand(s) to the correct position on the chest and give a further 30 chest compressions.**

USE A FACESHIELD IF ONE IS AVAILABLE.

CONTINUE WITH CPR

- **Untill the casualty shows signs of recovery.**
- **Emergency services arrive.**
- **You become exhausted and unable to continue.**

The following modifications as recommended by the resuscitation council (UK) will make it more suitable for use on children:

- **Give 5 initial rescue breaths before starting chest compressions.**
- **If you are on your own, perform 1 minute of CPR before going for help.**

SFAP??? Version 8

Images supplied by Seton Australia: www.seton.net.au

READING
Understanding visual texts

You may often see a poster like the one on the previous page. It is important that you can interpret graphics as well as read text. Posters can take many forms. They can be a form of persuasive text (advertising) or an explanation or procedure. Read *Resuscitation of children* and answer the questions.

1 The frames on this display are arranged
- A from most important to least important.
- B in order of difficulty.
- C to enhance the look of the page.
- D in the order in which they should be conducted.

2 The symbol [skull and crossbones] is meant to warn
- A of a situation that may be dangerous or deadly.
- B of a possible violent attack.
- C that the location has a history of disasters.
- D children to play in patrolled areas.

3 A suggestion for checking if a child is unconscious is to
- A lift the child.
- B pinch the child's earlobe.
- C tilt the child's head backwards.
- D look for chest movements.

4 Each frame on the poster has a title. Which title is a command? Write your answer on the line.

Frame number ______________

5 If you dial 000 you will be
- A asked for your name and location.
- B talked through any medical procedures.
- C put straight through to an ambulance service.
- D asked which service you require.

6 Draw a line to match this illustration to the correct instruction.
- A Remove foreign matter from the mouth with the fingertips.
- B Lift the chin gently with the forefingers if there is a neck injury.
- C Use a finger sweep to check for unresponsiveness.
- D Lift the chin and tilt the head back slightly to open the airway.
- E Look into the mouth to check for foreign objects.

7 When should an unconscious child be moved?
- A when someone responds to your shouts and can be of assistance
- B when there is an immediate threat to the child's safety
- C before phoning 000
- D as soon as possible

8 The child's breathing recovery position is intended to
- A stop the tongue from blocking the airways.
- B make the breathing easier to monitor.
- C prevent the child from vomiting.
- D help the child to sleep.

9 Who has initial responsibility for attending to an unconscious child? Tick one box.
- ☐ either of the child's parents
- ☐ the first medical officer to arrive
- ☐ the first adult on the scene
- ☐ anyone trained in resuscitation
- ☐ someone with first-aid qualifications

Answers: 1 D 2 A 3 B 4 3 5 D 6 D 7 B 8 A 9 the first adult on the scene

☞ Explanations on pages 223–224

READING
Understanding visual texts

Read the cartoon strips and answer the questions.

Comics and cartoons are often broken up into sections called frames.

Example 1: Magic Trick

Most magic tricks succeed if they are accompanied by an engaging, running spiel. It helps to distract the audience or volunteer.

How's it done?

It's a quick-switch gambit.

When you turn your back you change the cards. Examine closely the cards in frame 3. You will see that none of the three cards shown the second time were in the first frame. This works because your 'victim' will concentrate so hard on his card that he'll completely forget to take note of what the other cards are!

Example 2: Comic Strip

READING
Understanding visual texts

Example 1: Magic Trick

1. The intention of the series of illustrations and text in *Magic Trick* is to
   A amuse the reader. B provide instructions. C expose a fraud. D explore an issue.

2. Artists use a variety of common strategies to 'get their message across'. What does the magic trick artist do to show puzzlement?
   A uses a thought bubble with a question mark
   B creates characters that have unnatural features
   C fills the speech bubbles with unnecessary text
   D uses a thought bubble with an exclamation mark

3. According to the text which statements are CORRECT and which are INCORRECT? Write CORRECT or INCORRECT in the box next to the statement.

A The card trick is based on the performer creating an illusion.	
B Performing a quick-switch gambit requires good speaking skills.	
C Only one of the original cards is shown at the end of the trick.	
D The word 'victim' suggests the volunteer believes in magic	
E A running spiel is necessary to distract the watcher's attention.	

4. Draw a line between the expression 'ham up' and the phrase that has the same meaning.
   'It's a good ploy to really **ham up** this part.'
   perform in a showy style   act confidently   speak loudly   learn your script by heart

Example 2: Comic Strip

5. The intention of the series of frames in the cartoon is to
   A reveal unusual practices. B simplify instructions.
   C entertain the reader. D warn farm workers.

6. The humour in the comic strip depends upon
   A drawing unfair comparisons. B sickening possibilities.
   C a play on words. D an unexpected ending.

7. A good title for the comic strip would be
   A Sick Sheep B Meatballs C The Master Chef D Not Spaghetti Again!

8. Compare the two cartoon strips, Example 1 and Example 2. Tick ✓ the box to show if the following textual features are in both cartoons.

	YES	NO
caricatures of famous people		
stereotypical character types		
a resolution in the last frame		
dialogue between two characters		
a conflict between characters		

☞ Answers and explanations on page 224

READING
Understanding procedures

A procedure is a set of instructions on how to do something. These are often called steps. Read *How to change a car tyre* and answer the questions.

How to change a car tyre

A flat tyre can happen anywhere—back street, highway, home garage or remote country road. It may be the result of bad road conditions, a faulty tyre or poor owner maintenance. Whatever the reason it is always inconvenient. The driver may be in an isolated area (without mobile phone service), experiencing extreme weather conditions, running late or simply physically unable to carry out the operation. Whatever and wherever, it is an inconvenience. Some drivers call upon friends or family to help, others rely on a motoring organisation.

Some motoring experts suggest that changing a tyre need not cause undue delay if these steps are followed.

Step 1 When you realise you have a 'flat', pull off the road as far as possible, onto a hard and flat surface. Switch on the car's hazard lights regardless of the time of day. Ensure that automatic cars are in Park and the hand brake is on. All passengers alight from the vehicle.

Step 2 Remove the jack, wheel brace and spare tyre from their storage well. As a safety measure, place a chock (a rock will do) under the wheel diagonally opposite the 'flat'.

Step 3 Locate the notch or groove (jacking point) above where the jack is to be positioned to lift the car. One will be located close to the 'flat' tyre. Place the jack under this point and slowly turn the jack handle until it just takes the car's weight off the flat tyre. The tyre should not be able to spin.

Step 4 Now loosen the wheel nuts—there are usually five. Place the brace on one of the wheel nuts and using a straight arm and back, snap loose each nut in turn in an anti-clockwise direction. Foot leverage (force) may be more effective although body weight is usually sufficient to loosen the nuts.

Step 5 Use the jack to elevate the car's 'flat' wheel right off the ground.

Step 6 Remove all nuts—usually finger pressure is enough. Slide the 'flat' off the studs and drop it to the ground to one side.

Step 7 Place the spare against the wheel's assembly unit, lining the holes up with the studs. You may need to lift the spare a couple of centimetres. Tighten all the wheel nuts by hand starting with the bottom nut. A little extra twist may be given by the brace.

Step 8 Lower the jack slowly until the spare takes the weight of the car. Remove the jack when it frees itself from its connection point. Use body weight to give a final tightening of all the wheel nuts.

Step 9 Place the 'flat', jack and wheel brace in the car's boot well.

Remember to have the 'flat' repaired at the first opportunity. You never know when you will get your next 'flat'. Check your spare tyre regularly for correct tyre pressure.

Sources: Mitsubishi Magna Owner's Manual, 2003
NRMA *Open Road Get a Grip* 2009, p. 26

READING
Understanding procedures

1. These instructions could be most useful when the
   - A driver is late for an appointment.
   - B road conditions have deteriorated.
   - C driver is in an isolated situation.
   - D weather is not unpleasant.

2. Regardless of when the driver gets a flat, the driver is advised to
   - A immediately call their motoring organisation.
   - B drive slowly to a service centre.
   - C check the state of the spare tyre.
   - D turn on the hazard lights.

3. It is recommended that once getting a flat tyre, the driver should move the car to a hard flat surface (Step 1). The main reason for this is because it will
   - A ensure greater safety from passing traffic.
   - B enable other drivers to get a clear view of the hazard.
   - C provide a safer and more stable location for the jack.
   - D allow easy access to the car's boot well.

4. After replacing the flat tyre with the spare tyre, the driver should not forget to
   - A advise the motoring organization of the new situation.
   - B get the flat tyre repaired as soon as possible.
   - C continue the journey without delay.
   - D report the incident to the appropriate traffic authority.

5. It is important not to jack the car right off the ground before starting to change the tyre because
   - A the wheel will spin and the nuts will be difficult to loosen.
   - B the equipment needed will still be in the boot well.
   - C the chock under the wheel may not hold the car from running forward.
   - D it makes foot leverage of the wheel brace difficult.

6. In which order should the following things be done when changing a car tyre? Number them from 1 to 5.
   - ☐ Line up the holes on the spare with the studs.
   - ☐ Use the brace to help tighten the nuts.
   - ☐ Place an object under one of the wheels.
   - ☐ Ensure the wheel to be changed is elevated.
   - ☐ Look for the position of the jacking point.

7. These instructions are most likely intended for
   - A drivers wishing to become skilled in changing tyres.
   - B city drivers who have time to spare.
   - C drivers wishing to demonstrate their independence.
   - D situations where help is not readily available.

8. According to the instructions what part of changing a tyre could prove difficult and why? Write your answer on the lines. ______________________________

   ____

9. If the spare tyre is not checked regularly the driver may find that
   - A it needs to be replaced.
   - B it has become flat and unusable.
   - C it has moved about in the boot well.
   - D it is covered in dirt and dust.

☞ Answers and explanations on pages 224–225

READING
Understanding essays

Expositions and discussions are used to explore an issue. They may be a response to a subject that has become contentious. They are often in essay format. Expositions are used to argue a case for or against a particular position or point of view. They may concede that there are opposing arguments.

Discussions are used to look at more than one side of an issue. They provide an opportunity to explore an issue before coming to an informed decision.

Read *The silent epidemic* and answer the questions.

The silent epidemic

It is claimed many people are the victims of 'calcuholism'. This is an over-dependence on calculators, resulting in a diminished ability to do the simplest mental calculations. Technological advances in schools, business and homes has resulted in an over-dependence on modern devices, especially the mobile phone and calculator. It is the calculator that concerns me most.

Calcuholism starts in schools. It can be avoided in schools if schools introduced a policy where students were required to use brains to do mathematics rather than relying on calculators for basic mathematical operations.

Obviously the term *calcuholism* has been **7** with the intent to compare it with other addictions such as alcoholism. Of course, it is not nearly as serious as alcoholism. However, dependence on the calculator can be just as harmful. Abuse of something normally beneficial may lead to harmful dependence. Sugar and salt come to mind. It is not that calculators are harmful, but their overuse may be harmful, causing people to abandon their memory for basic combinations, as well as being unable to complete simple mathematical tasks.

The problem arises in schools because students must be prepared to graduate into a world dependent upon electronic gadgetry. Calculators are permitted, even essential, in many advanced mathematics and science classes because they increase speed and efficiency—both of which are necessary in today's businesses and industries.

However, offices and shop employees spend hours working with numbers but rarely calculate mentally. They have lost the skill to do simple estimations! Sensible estimates give the calculator users a quick indication that they have used their calculators correctly. Some banking errors have resulted in not noticing an incorrectly positioned decimal point. The calculator's solution was trusted unquestioningly: 'I can't have got it wrong. I used a calculator!'

To alleviate the problem, schools should discourage students from using calculators too early, especially in primary and junior secondary classes. Teachers should plan classwork that is not subject to calculator use. At home, parents should restrict the child's use of these devices and insist that mathematics be done as brain exercise so that the child grows up with some mathematical competency.

Calcuholism has increased recently. There are calculators on the computer desktop and they are built into mobile phones. And it's only going to get worse. To avoid total dependency we all must do mathematics with our brains from time to time rather than with a machine.

Adapted from *Cliffs TOEFL Guide* by Michael A Pyle and Mary Ellen Munoz, John Wiley & Sons USA, 1987

READING
Understanding essays

1. The writer objects most to
   A calculators built into mobile phones.
   B the use of calculators for work in primary schools.
   C using calculators in business and industry.
   D calculators without decimal points.

2. Who uses the excuse: 'I can't have got it wrong. I used a calculator!' (paragraph 5)?
   A the writer of the essay
   B the writer's family
   C students
   D many calculator-reliant people

3. The writer would like to see calculators
   A completely banned.
   B banned only in schools.
   C used only when doing complex calculations.
   D removed from shops and offices.

4. The title, *The silent epidemic*, implies that calculator use
   A is spreading quickly and extensively, and causing unsuspected harm.
   B causes people to lose their ability to communicate.
   C is responsible for an increase in brain damage.
   D prevents people from becoming fully mathematical.

5. What is the writer's point in mentioning the ingredients 'sugar and salt' (paragraph 3)?
   A They are as readily available as calculators.
   B They can be beneficial if used appropriately.
   C They can affect the mind adversely.
   D They are used in the treatment of an addiction.

6. What is the most important skill needed when using a calculator? Write your answer on the lines.

   ____

   ____

7. A word is missing from the text in paragraph 3. Circle the word that would correctly complete the sentence.

changed	coined	minted	printed	raised
A	B	C	D	E

8. The tone of the essay suggests that the writer
   A views the overuse of calculators as unavoidable.
   B has grave fears for the mental ability of the next generation.
   C is poking fun at people who are not concerned about mathematics.
   D is making his point lightly but is concerned.

9. Draw lines to show which statements are FACTS and which are OPINIONS.

FACT	Parents are responsible for children being unable to estimate.
	Calculators are available on computer desktops and phones.
OPINION	Too much work prepared by teachers is reliant on calculators.
	In some careers, advanced calculator skills are essential.

☞ **Answers and explanations on page 225**

TIPS FOR WRITING RECOUNTS

A **recount** tells about events that have happened to you or other people. It is usually a record of events in the order they happened. If it is a personal recount you will use the personal pronoun *I*. You could also write a recount of an event in the third person. A recount can conclude with a personal opinion of the event. Recounts are always written in the past tense.

Before you start writing

- **Read the question and check the stimulus material carefully**. Stimulus material means the topic, title, picture, words, phrases or extract of writing you are given to base your writing on.
- Give some thought to:
  - where your recount takes place
  - the characters and what they do in your recount
  - the events that take place in your recount
  - the problems that have to be resolved
  - how you and others reacted to the event. You may make brief personal comments on events as you write about them.
- Remember that a recount is usually told **in the past tense** because the events have already happened.
- When you have chosen your topic it might be helpful to **jot a few ideas** quickly on paper so you don't forget them. Decide if you will write a first-person recount (using I as the main character) or a third-person recount.

Structure of recounts

The introduction

- The first paragraph of a recount is important as it must provide the reader with a **brief overview** of the event being recounted. It must inform the reader about who, what, when and where.
- The introduction may feature **proper nouns** such as the names of places and people—this helps orient the reader.

The body

- Recounts recall events **in the order in which they happened**. The body of a recount is a series of chronological paragraphs detailing important aspects of the event being recounted.
- **Conjunctions** and **connectives** must be used to indicate when events occur. These include *firstly, then, next, later and finally.*
- **Correctly paragraph your writing**. You need a new paragraph when there is a change in time or place or a new idea.
- **Include personal comments**, e.g. about your feelings, your opinions and your reactions, but only include comments that add to your recount.

The conclusion

- A conclusion is necessary as it **informs the reader of how the event ended**. It is also a good idea to include a final comment on the events or experiences. This may be as simple as reflecting on the impact that the event had on the individuals involved.

Language features of recounts

- **Engage the senses** of your reader through description of what can be seen, heard, felt, tasted or smelled. To do this you should include figures of speech such as similes, metaphors and personification.
- **Use strong action verbs** to capture mood and create tension. Instead of *The girl took the food* you could say *The girl lunged for the food.*
- **Use emotive words** to engage the emotions of your reader. It is important to consider what emotions you would like your reader to feel in a specific situation. Once you have decided, use emotive words and phrases to evoke these emotions, e.g. *Lee felt anxious having lost his wallet.*

You will find a sample annotated recount **on the following page**. The question is from page 128. Read the recount and notes before you begin your fourth Writing Test. This piece of writing has been analysed based on the marking criteria used by markers to assess the NAPLAN Writing Test.

Remember: This sample was not written under exam conditions.

Year 9 Sample Recount Writing

(a sample answer to the question on page 128)

Celebration

The air was thick with sweat and stale beer. Beside me I could see dull plumes of grey smoke spiralling from the thin-lipped smile of a young punter. He laughed as he exhaled and continued staring ahead of him. Following his gaze to the bare stage, I had become conscious of the first pangs of pain as the weight of my youngest son on my shoulders began to wear on me. It was almost half past 12 and my small family and I were waiting for a family favourite—The Drones—to take the stage.

The crowd was smaller than I expected. Standing directly in front of the stage I could see a handful of die-hard fans, each layered with the appropriate 'indie-rock' attire—skinny jeans, moth-eaten tee and scuffed Chucks. Behind this row we stood—about 10 metres from the far-too-small stage. I noticed the amps were precariously perched on the hand-painted black plywood while the drum kit seemed to sprawl too far upstage. It surprised me that such an intensely talented and highly revered band would be forced to play in such a space, and to such a motley crowd.

After ten minutes of waiting, Balin began to jiggle around; evidently his seat (my bony shoulders) was not as comfortable as he had hoped, not nearly the royal box seat he was anticipating. His bare feet, chubby and coated in dirt, bumped against my sunburnt flesh in a driving rhythm. He was keen to see 'his' band, to sing along to his favourite songs and watch the angst and passion on the face of his favourite singer.

In a vain attempt to stop his movements, I grabbed hold of his wiggling piggies and turned to my left to see my eldest son, Keenan, being lifted onto his dad's shoulders. I remember Keenan's shoulder-length blonde hair. It was so dirty that it hung limply over his face. It hadn't been washed for over five days—in fact, no-one's had. The car trip from Devonport to Marion Bay had taken us to places wild, free and unimaginably beautiful. It had not, however, taken us to warm showers or shampoo. Not that it mattered—those around us were similarly unkempt, adding to the feeling of being removed from the mainstream, away from suburbia and the banality it breeds.

The thump of the bass drum broke my reverie and my attention was given fully to the stage and the four musicians cramped onto it. As the tempo of the opening track *Nail it Down* increased, we had shuffled towards the stage to join the throng of fellow music lovers. As one, (small shoulder-sitting boys included) the crowd had chanted the chorus: 'Listen here, listen here, tomorrow is the first day of the year'. And it was. This is how my small, music-loving, Kombi-travelling family celebrated the New Year in 2008—a celebration of music and freedom. And it's how we'll be celebrating it every year.

This text is beyond what would be expected of a typical Year 9 student. It is provided here as a model.
The assessment comments are based on the marking criteria used to assess the NAPLAN Writing Test.

Structure

Text structure
- The first paragraph is the orientation of the recount.

Sentence structure
- A variety of sentence lengths creates interest and shows control of language. Short sentences direct the reader's attention more effectively to a particular person or thing.

Character and setting
- Use of descriptive language creates a clear image of the characters within the recount.

Cohesion
- Appropriate use of connectives enhances reading. These indicate changes in time or location and help guide the reader through the events in the recount.

Language and ideas

Vocabulary
- The writer uses strong verbs (e.g. *perched, sprawl*) to create imagery.

Audience
- Figurative language is used to create humour and atmosphere.
- Descriptive language also orients the reader to the people and places described in the recount.

Ideas
- The recount is sophisticated as it includes an opinion and observation about life. In this case, the observation is about the need to celebrate difference and freedom from the constraints of society.

Punctuation
- Correct punctuation is used throughout the recount.

Spelling
- All words are correctly spelled.
- Difficult and challenging vocabulary is included (e.g. *reverie, banality*).

WRITING
Recount 1

There is no way of knowing for certain what type of writing will be included in the NAPLAN Tests in years to come. This is an opportunity for you to practise different types of writing.

A recount is a retelling of an event. It usually retells an event in the order the incidents happened.

Before you start, read the General writing tips on pages 35–36 and the Tips for writing informative texts: recounts on page 125.

Today you are going to write a recount.

Look at the picture on the right.

The event that you must base your recount on is THE MEETING. Your recount might be about the meeting between a first-time surfer and a great white shark, a meeting between two boys in a pie-eating competition or a meeting between an adopted child and his or her birth mother. It could be about a meeting at the United Nations to discuss the end of the world or meeting yourself for the first time after suffering from amnesia for fifteen years.

Before you start writing, give some thought to:

- where your recount takes place
- the characters and what they do in your recount
- the events that take place in your recount and the problems that have to be resolved
- how you, and others, felt about the event—you may comment on events as you write about them.

Don't forget to:

- plan your recount before you start writing
- write in correctly formed sentences and take care with paragraphing
- choose your words carefully and pay attention to your spelling and punctuation
- write neatly but don't waste time
- quickly check your recount once you have finished.

Start writing here or type in your answer on a tablet or computer.

☞ Marking guide on pages 225–226

WRITING
Recount 2

There is no way of knowing for certain what type of writing will be included in the NAPLAN Tests in years to come. This is an opportunity for you to practise different types of writing.
A recount is a retelling of an event. It usually retells an event in the order the incidents happened.
Before you start, read the General writing tips on pages 35–36 and the Tips for writing informative texts: recounts on page 125.

Today you are going to write a recount.

Look at the picture on the right.

The idea that you must base your recount on is CELEBRATION. Your recount might be about celebrating something simple and everyday, such as passing a test or turning thirteen. It could be about something more significant such as graduating from university or celebrating an event such as Christmas or Easter.

Before you start writing, give some thought to:

- where your recount takes place
- the characters and what they do in your recount
- the events that take place in your recount and the problems that have to be resolved
- how you, and others, felt about the event—you may comment on events as you write about them.

Don't forget to:

- plan your recount before you start writing
- write in correctly formed sentences and take care with paragraphing
- choose your words carefully and pay attention to your spelling and punctuation
- write neatly but don't waste time
- quickly check your recount once you have finished.

Start writing here or type in your answer on a tablet or computer.

☞ Marking guide on page 226

Sample NAPLAN Online-style tests

Different test levels

- There are eight tests for students to complete in this section. These sample tests have been classified as either Intermediate or Advanced according to the level of the majority of questions. This will broadly reflect the NAPLAN Online tailored testing experience where students are guided into answering questions that match their ability.
- The following tests are included in this section:
  - one Intermediate-level Test for each of Reading, Conventions of Language and Numeracy
  - one Advanced-level Test for each of Reading, Conventions of Language and Numeracy
  - two Writing Tests.

Checks

- The NAPLAN Online Reading, Conventions of Language and Numeracy tests will be divided into different sections.
- Students will have one last opportunity to check their answers in each section when they have reached the end of that section.
- Once they have moved onto a new section, they will not be able to go back and check their work again.
- We have included reminders for students to check their work at specific points in the Sample Tests so they become familiar with this process before they take the NAPLAN Online tests.

Excel Test Zone

- After students have consolidated their topic knowledge by completing this book, we recommend they practise NAPLAN Online–style questions on our website at www.exceltestzone.com.au.
- Students will be able to gain valuable practice in digital skills such as dragging text across a screen, using an onscreen ruler, protractor and calculator to answer questions, or listening to audio recording of a spelling word which they then type into a box.
- Students will also become confident in using a computer or tablet to complete NAPLAN Online–style tests so they will be fully prepared for the actual NAPLAN Online tests.

WRITING TEST 1

Today you are going to write a persuasive text, often called an exposition.
Excessive Internet usage is bad for teenagers.
What do you think about this topic? Do you agree or disagree with this opinion?
Write to convince a reader of your opinions.

Before you start writing, give some thought to:

- whether you strongly agree or strongly disagree with this opinion
- reasons or evidence for your arguments
- a brief but definite conclusion—list some of your main points and add a personal opinion
- the structure of a persuasive text, which begins with a well-organised introduction, followed by a body of arguments or points, and finally a conclusion that restates the writer's position.

Don't forget to:

- plan your writing before you start—make a list of important points you wish to make
- write in correctly formed sentences and take care with paragraphing
- choose your words carefully, and pay attention to your spelling and punctuation
- write neatly but don't waste time
- quickly check your persuasive text once you have finished—your position must be clear to the reader.

Remember: The stance taken in a persuasive text is not wrong, as long as the writer has evidence to support his or her opinion. How the opinion is supported is as important as the opinion itself.

Start writing here or type in your answer on a tablet or computer.

☞ Marking guide on page 227

READING TEST 1
Intermediate Level

Read *Minimum-water gardens* and answer questions 1 to 9.

Minimum-water gardens

Cacti garden—Lightning Ridge
Photo by A Horsfield

We usually think of gardens as lush, well-planned, well-watered areas with rich loamy soil. This is not always so. There is a growing interest in another type of garden—the 'dry' garden. The Japanese have always had their seki tei—sand and stone gardens. These walled gardens are often used for prayer by Buddhist monks. Sand and rocks symbolically arranged are the key elements in these gardens.

Cactus gardens in the more arid regions require little maintenance. The biggest killer is too much love, too much water or too much fertilizer. Cacti (plural of cactus) are succulents with spine cushions called areoles that can bear spines and/or flowers but the plants do not have branches or leaves. A succulent is a juice- or sap-storing plant. Succulents have evolved to grow in harsh conditions. They store water for future use.

The soil of a cacti garden is about one-third sand, one-third 'dirt' and one-third gravel. Using rocks in these gardens is in keeping with how cacti would look in the desert where rocks may be common. A cacti garden has to be well drained.

The Royal Botanic Gardens in Cranbourne, Victoria, has developed a series of dry-garden environments to demonstrate not only the diversity of Australian flora but to put Australian plants into a cultural context.

Visitors can walk through the Red Sand Garden where the expanse of red sand contrasts with grey foliage. On the northern hill of this garden, mass plantings of *Acacia binervia* and the *Spinifex sericeus* are used to stabilise the sandhills. The lower slopes are covered with a carpet of shrubs (*Kunzea pomifera*), producing edible berries used for food by the Aborigines.

A second garden is the Dry River Bed, which relates to the fleeting nature of water within the Australian landscape, and the power of water to shape the land into riverbeds, on a seasonal basis. The central landscape of Australia is characterised by large river systems that can be located beneath the land surface, as part of the artesian water supply. On the surface, the plants respond by growing in the bars of sand that are shaped into curved lines along often-dry riverbeds.

A third garden is the Arid Garden. It has trees used sparingly, yet accurately representing the whole continent. Beneath are the lower species, such as Hedge Salt-bush, Sword-sedge, Fan-flowers, Bluebush, Poverty Bush and many types of daisies. The seasonal flower displays bring colours to this desert landscape.

Population growth has increased demands on water in times of lower rainfall and dwindling supplies. It is time for gardeners to consider drier gardens rather than gardens dependent upon a high water consumption. A dry garden can be just as attractive and interesting, and more environmentally friendly.

Source: Royal Botanic Gardens Cranbourne, www.rbg.vic.gov.au

READING TEST 1
Intermediate Level

1 The writer is
- **A** encouraging gardeners to think about gardens that are drought tolerant.
- **B** advising gardeners in arid regions on what to grow.
- **C** imploring gardeners to plant more succulent-type plants.
- **D** asking gardeners to reduce the size of their gardens.

2 What would be an important reason for having the cacti (as shown in the photograph) in a raised bed?
- **A** It allows for comfortable maintenance.
- **B** It adds to the visual appeal of the garden.
- **C** It assists in drainage.
- **D** It prevents the growth of lush weeds.

3 Complete the sentence. Write your answer on the line.

The ______________ garden is often subjected to irregular water supplies.

4 'Dry gardens' are becoming increasingly relevant, not only because of climate change, but because of
- **A** increased population.
- **B** households using more water per capita.
- **C** people making larger gardens.
- **D** less people living on suburban blocks.

5 An important purpose of the Royal Botanic Gardens (Cranbourne) is to
- **A** provide visitors with a fun day out.
- **B** show people who live in arid areas how to have a garden.
- **C** convince residents from Cranbourne (Vic.) area to change their gardening attitudes.
- **D** display the wide range of Australian plants and their habitats.

6 The 'seki tei'-type of garden is designed to
- **A** maximise water use.
- **B** create a feeling of peace.
- **C** improve the look of temples.
- **D** make use of available stones.

7 Draw a line to match the garden with the word that best describes it according to the text.

A The Dry River Bed	seasonal
B The Japanese seki tei	self-sustaining
C The Arid Garden	vivid
D The Cacti Garden	food-producing
E The Red Sand Garden	traditional

8 What is a major problem faced by some cacti garden owners? Write your answer on the lines.

____

____

9 The Dry River Bed Garden is designed with curved lines to
- **A** minimise the need for watering.
- **B** add an attractive feature to the garden.
- **C** replicate the shape of inland rivers.
- **D** take full advantage of any rainfall.

☞ **Answers and explanations on pages 227–228**

Read *So you want to be an actor?* by John Andrews and answer questions 10 to 17.

So you want to be an actor?

Many aspiring actors want to be on television or in a film. The truth is, a lot of the work is in commercials and corporate films (company training films) and these actually pay better.

As an actor, I started out as a 'fifty-worder'. This means that you may say anything from one to fifty words in the role. This is a step up from being an extra. Later I became a featured extra—which means you get to say a few words and a credit: your name, at the end of the television show. From there you can be given a guest appearance or even become a regular on the show.

There are few Australian actors that make a lifetime's living from acting. A few will make a living for several years from working on a soapie such as *Home and Away* or *Neighbours*, etc. Some will work as a major character in a long-running series, for example, *Homicide* and *Underbelly*. Others will concentrate on straight theatre (plays) or musical theatre.

Many young actors create their own work: writing plays or television shows, acting in them and producing them. Producing can mean anything from finding the money to put on a play or television show to finding the actors, directors, venues (places to perform) and getting anything required for the production.

In one low-budget film I was in, the producer found a backer (someone who was prepared to risk their money having the film made); wrote the film; directed it; found someone to feed the cast and crew; found assistant directors; make-up people; found locations—including a hospital that was being demolished the very next day; and an explosives expert to set the actors up to be 'shot'. After shooting the film, he helped edit it (decide which parts to use and throw out) and then market (sell) it.

Paid work for actors is mainly centred on Sydney, Melbourne and the Gold Coast. This means that although there are greater opportunities, there is also more competition. So, what does the aspiring professional do to get noticed?

Be professional. Turn up on time; know what you have to do; listen to what you are told; take direction, i.e. try to do what you are told by the director; be polite to everyone—you don't know how much influence they may have; remember that you may be the centre of attention one day and almost ignored the next—it's the nature of the business; remember that it is a business and treat it as such; be friendly to everyone; watch, listen and learn.

I once read that the difference between an amateur and a professional is that an amateur learns their lines until they remember them whilst a professional learns them until they can't forget them. Partly true, but re-read the previous paragraph.

From *Cygnet*, Tasmania

10 Complete the sentence. Write your answer on the line.

For aspiring actors, the best immediate money to be made is in commercials and ____________.

11 Any person who backs a low-budget film could best be described as a

A film critic. B failed actor. C shrewd investor. D gambler.

12 To make a success of acting, John Andrews recommends that actors should

A concentrate on straight theatre.
B treat acting as a business.
C enjoy acting as an interest and a pastime.
D attend professional acting classes.

13 What is the typical career path for many actors, from beginner to established actor? Number the steps from 1 to 5.

☐ regular
☐ 'fifty worder'
☐ guest appearance
☐ extra
☐ featured extra

14 Being a successful actor is not only knowing lines, but also

A being prepared to write plays and scripts.
B helping out with editing films.
C being polite to the people in the industry.
D ignoring much of what you are told.

15 A feature of low-budget films is

A their high instant success rate.
B the number of roles the producer undertakes.
C the number of parts for aspiring actors.
D their good box-office returns.

16 The general impression of professional acting implied by John Andrews is that it provides a lifestyle that is

A precarious but interesting.
B financially rewarding and glamorous.
C glamorous but poorly paid.
D difficult and demeaning.

17 You have read 'Minimum-water gardens' and 'So you want to be an actor?'. Tick the box to show which techniques the writers use in their texts.

The writer	'Minimum-water gardens'	'So you want to be an actor?'
includes personal experiences.		
provides definitions in parentheses.		
sustains a formal tone.		
gives a suggestion regarding future action.		
combines past and present tense.		

It would be a good idea to check your answers to questions 1 to 17 before moving on to the other questions.

☞ **Answers and explanations on pages 228–229**

Read the poem *Desert Dweller* by Sheryl Persson and answer questions 18 to 23.

Desert Dweller

A lizard torpedoes the knotted terrain
its toes, webbed finely, splay
divining rock and searing sand.
It has a repertoire, dances with the land
a flamenco first and then the tango.
Sharp agate eyes reflect a flaming sun
and dressed in armour; waxed leather mail,
this jousting knight charges foes
a pre-determined destiny
its weaponry an arsenal of muscle, sinew, instinct.

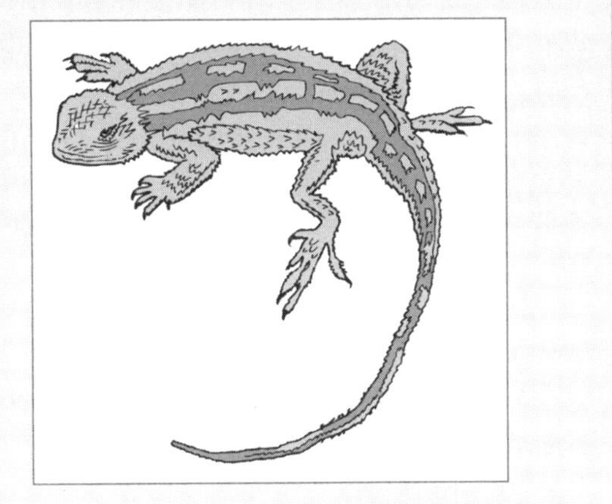

18 The poet uses the word 'torpedoes' to describe
- A how strong the lizard is.
- B the size of the lizard.
- C how the lizard moves.
- D the length of the lizard.

19 The word 'splay' is closest in meaning to
- A spread apart.
- B curve outwards.
- C supports weight.
- D sway gently.
- E bend easily

20 The poet's description of the lizard's eyes as 'agate eyes reflect a flaming sun' suggests that the lizard is
- A agile.
- B alert.
- C afraid.
- D able.

21 Tick ✓ the correct box to show which words from the poem describe aspects of the lizard and which words describe aspects of the environment.

	Lizard	Environment
knotted		
webbed		
searing		
sharp		
waxed		

22 Which of the following conclusions can be drawn from the poem? You may choose one or more.
- A The poet is fascinated by the features of the desert landscape.
- B The poet is worried that the lizard is vulnerable to its enemies.
- C The poet admires the agility of the lizard as it negotiates difficult terrain.
- D The poet wonders how long the lizard can survive the harsh conditions.
- E The poet marvels at how the lizard has adapted to its environment.

23 Which technique does the poet employ most in the poem to create visual images of the lizard?
- A alliteration
- B symbolism
- C personification
- D simile

☞ Answers and explanations on page 229

Read *Cadaver Dog* by Alan Horsfield and answer questions 24 to 30.

Shane and his father (an ex-policeman) are sleeping in a caravan in the yard of an abandoned school that Shane's father has just bought. Now read on.

Cadaver Dog

When Shane woke up during the night, he was vaguely aware that he had been woken up by an alien noise. The dog growling? Someone calling? As his eyes became accustomed to the light he realised there was a faint glow coming in the window. At first he thought it was dawn. But there were no magpies warbling. There was a soft, indistinct crackling sound.

He thought he heard a muffled shout, or a cry.

Sleepily he turned over. It was then he noticed that the glow was not the steady glow of dawn but a flickering glow. It didn't make sense. When he looked out of his window he realised why.

The school was on fire!

The dog barked.

Grotesque shadows danced in the trees.

It took him a moment to react.

'Dad! The school's burning down!' he cried out, suddenly fully awake.

He became aware of the roar of the flames as they turned from a bonfire into an inferno.

In a moment his father was blundering around the caravan. A light went on. His father was fumbling with his mobile phone and swearing impatiently.

Caddy's barking grew angry, urgent.

From then on the action became a blur.

By the time the local bushfire brigade arrived the old school house was little more than a large smouldering heap of burning timber and twisted corrugated iron.

Leaves in the nearby trees were scorched.

A nagging worry troubled Shane, as he and his father watched the firefighters complete the clean-up operations. Then they all stopped and congregated near a corner of the building. They had found something.

Caddy sat on her haunches near Shane's feet. She was whining nervously.

'Steady, girl,' said Shane's father softly.

One fireman left the group and dashed for the truck. Within moments he was on the CB radio talking softly and urgently.

Then Shane suddenly realised why he was feeling uneasy. It wasn't the loss of the school—after all, it was on the 'get rid of' list. He gasped at the enormity of his realisation.

A person had died in the fire!

His father was looking at him. 'You right?'

'Dad, I think ...' For a moment Shane was lost for words. Then he blurted out his fears. With a deep sinking feeling he remembered the cry he had vaguely heard when he first woke up.

Shane's father was silent for a moment. Shane could almost imagine his father's detective mind putting pieces together. Looking for bits that would fit.

Another fireman was talking on a mobile phone.

From *Cadaver Dog* by Alan Horsfield, Lothian Books (Crime Wave series), 2000

24 Shane was aroused from his sleep. What is the most likely reason for this?

A the dog growling
B a flickering light
C magpies warbling
D a crackling sound

25 The school building was on fire. Write the numbers 1 to 4 in the boxes to show the sequence of events around the outbreak of fire.

☐ the dog barks
☐ Shane's father finds a light
☐ Shane becomes aware of a strange sound
☐ Shane's father calls the fire brigade

26 Shane complains of a 'nagging worry'. A 'nagging worry' is one that

A irritates persistently because there is no obvious reason for the worry.
B has nothing to do with the present situation.
C is not as important as it first seemed.
D causes irrational thoughts that seem to race about in the brain.

27 Which words best describe the speed and effect of the fire? Circle two words.

predictable   rapid   impressive   destructive   fierce   menacing   expected

28 The writer states 'Grotesque shadows danced in the trees'.

What does he mean by this?

A The shadows created by the fire flickered erratically in a disturbing way.
B The bush around the caravan was lit by the flames.
C The light caused moving shadows in the trees.
D People close to the fire had to move away quickly.

29 Shane's father swore because

A he couldn't find the light or his phone.
B he was being clumsy when he had to respond quickly.
C he didn't want the school to burn down.
D his mobile phone wasn't operating.

30 According to the text which statements are CORRECT and which are INCORRECT?
Write CORRECT or INCORRECT in the box next to the statement.

A The firefighters gathered at the spot where Caddy was whining. ☐
B Shane remembered hearing a cry and knew someone was dead. ☐
C Shane was very upset about what had happened to his school. ☐
D It was Shane's father who worked out what had caused the fire. ☐
E The dog stayed with Shane and his father while the fire burned. ☐

☞ Answers and explanations on pages 229–230

READING TEST 1
Intermediate Level

Read the book review of *Facetime* by Sally Murphy and answer questions 31 to 38.

Book review: Facetime by Winnie Salamon
by Sally Murphy

Chat rooms, geeks, gnomes, b-grade movies—oh, and inflatable underwear.

When Esmerelda moves in with Charlotte, she's not sure if she's done the right thing. The two don't have much in common. Charlotte takes herself way too seriously and Esmerelda finds her intimidating and aloof.

Charlotte doesn't hit it off with Esmerelda's best friend Ned, either. Ned is a hardcore geek who wears flannies and Linux T-shirts and has no sense of style. He loves bad movies and trashy music. Esmerelda thinks he's great.

When Ned suggests Esmerelda try Internet chat rooms, she meets and falls for Jack, an American geek who is both charming and mysterious, and who seems to like all the things Esmerelda likes. They share secrets, even passion— so much so that Jack decides to fly to Australia so they can meet.

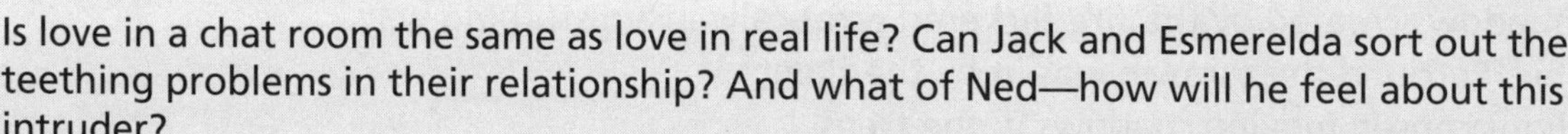

Is love in a chat room the same as love in real life? Can Jack and Esmerelda sort out the teething problems in their relationship? And what of Ned—how will he feel about this intruder?

If you have ever sung along to '99 Luftballons' or 'Electric Dreams' or lip-synched with B-grade horror films, then *Facetime* is for you. If you haven't, you will probably find yourself somewhere in this book anyway. Full of geeks and gnomes, and young people finding their way through life, along with inflatable underwear and loads of other weird stuff, this is a fun read for the 16-plus young person (of any age).

Author Winnie Salamon is a writer and freelance journalist who has written about everything from amputee fetishes to Posh Spice. This is her first novel.

This closet geek hopes it won't be her last.

Facetime by Winnie Salamon (Allen & Unwin, 2002)
Cover design by ... oid design
Source: www.aussiereviews.com/article1093.html

31 The story, *Facetime*, is mainly aimed at
A a teenage audience.
B readers of romance.
C parents of teenagers.
D readers interested in technology.

32 From the information in the review, the main theme of the book is
A using chat rooms responsibly.
B coping with people with no taste.
C surviving living with friends.
D the search for true love.

33 The heavy use of jargon and slang suggests that the book
A is of low literary quality.
B is intended to have movie potential.
C is well researched.
D has a shallow plotline.

34 Draw a line between the word 'intimidating' and the phrase that is closest in meaning.
'Charlotte takes herself way too seriously and Esmerelda finds her **intimidating** and aloof.'

very conceited	overly self-assured	generally unfriendly	somewhat frightening

35 The cover graphic suggests that *Facetime* is actually
A an adventure program.
B a successful dating program.
C a DVD movie.
D an advertisement for a dance studio.

36 The book cover is pixelated (made up of dots) suggesting it represents a
A grainy photo.
B crude animation.
C computer screen.
D newspaper reproduction enlargement.

37 What is the result of Esmerelda's chat-room experience?
A Ned decides to leave the flat.
B Charlotte has an argument with Esmerelda.
C Ned moves into the flat with Charlotte and Esmerelda.
D Jack decides to fly from America to meet Esmerelda.

38 What does the last sentence in the review suggest about the reviewer? Tick one box or more.
- [ ] The reviewer often works in a small office.
- [ ] The reviewer has kept her love of technology a secret.
- [ ] The reviewer has used *Facetime* to find romance.
- [ ] The reviewer is opposed to the use of *Facetime*.
- [ ] The reviewer positively endorses the novel *Facetime*.

It would be a good idea to check your answers to questions 18 to 38 before moving on to the other questions.

☞ Answers and explanations on page 230

READING TEST 1
Intermediate Level

Read the instructions for *Tying a knot* and answer questions 39 to 44.

Tying a knot

There are a number of ways to tie a tie. To many of us there seems to be little difference (except for the bow tie!). For the expert the differences are important.

Types of tie knots

Windsor, Half Windsor, Small knot, Four-in-hand, Prince Albert and Bow tie are the names of some of the common tie knots.

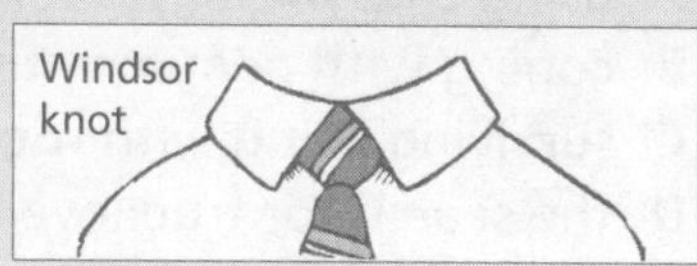

The Windsor knot, incorrectly named after the Duke of Windsor, is a wide triangular knot that is preferred by business executives. This knot looks smartest worn with a shirt collar that is considerably cut-away. Most students prefer the Small Knot.

For the best results

1 Drape the tie around your raised collar with the wider end extending about 30 cm below the narrow end; cross it over.

2 Wrap the wide end around, and bring it up over and through the loop between the collar and the tie. Gently pull it down toward the front.

3 Curl the wide end that is left behind the narrow end.

4 Bring the wide end back up again through the loop.

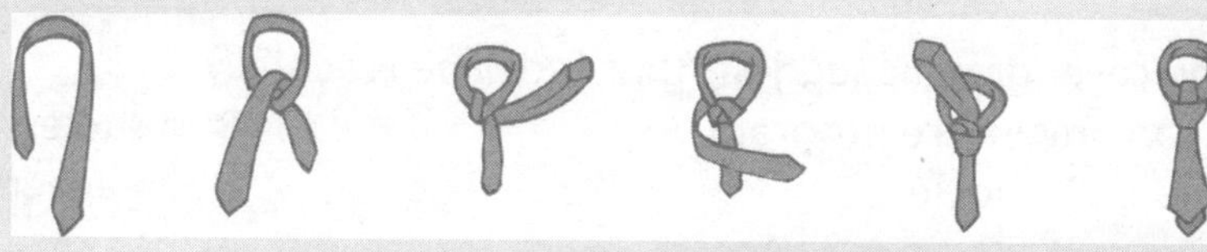

5 Put down through the loop and pull around across the narrow end as shown.

6 Bring the wide end up and tuck it through the loop a third time, and bring it back down to the front.

7 Finally, pull down on the wide end carefully to tighten and draw up the knot snugly into your collar.

8 If both ends don't meet perfectly, simply start over and adjust the length of the tie accordingly. Make sure your collar sits nicely and centre the knot precisely.

A very common mistake many school students make once they get the first knot done correctly is that they are reluctant to untie the tie at the end of the school day. They prefer to make the loop just big enough to pull their head out and hang the tied tie on the back of a chair. Unfortunately, that is the most damaging (and disrespectful) thing to do to a tie.

There is a second end-of-the-day student mistake. It is to simply rip the tie off the moment the student gets out the school gate!

The clip-on tie is one which is permanently tied. It is fixed to the front of the shirt collar by a metal clip. The clip-on tie was reportedly invented in 1928. Maybe this is the best solution for school students!

Sources: http://www.brooksbrothers.com/tieknots/smallknot.tem
http://www.tieanecktie.com/WindsorKnot.php

39 The instructions for tying a tie using a Windsor knot would be used most often by
A school students.
B professional people.
C descendants of the Duke of Windsor.
D the British peerage.

40 Choose the word that best completes the sentence. Write your answer on the line.

The instructions suggest that the writer is extremely careful and ____________________.

A accurate B showy C sophisticated
D flippant E adaptable F insolent

41 Which line best suggests that the writer despises sloppy tie tiers?
A Make sure your collar sits nicely.
B The Windsor knot is a wide triangular knot that is preferred for formal occasions.
C Maybe this is the best solution for school students!
D There are a number of ways to tie a tie.

42 After looping the tie the second time, the next step is to
A adjust the length of the narrow end.
B pull the wide end across the narrow end.
C open the loop to let the narrow end slip through.
D tighten this section of the knot before proceeding.

43 Draw lines to show which statements are TRUE and which statements are FALSE according to the information in the text.

TRUE	Most of the action in tying a tie is based on manipulating the wide end of the tie.
	When tying a Windsor knot, the narrow end of the tie is left longer.
	The knot is tightened after tucking the wide end through the loop three times.
FALSE	The Four-in-hand knot is as popular with business executives as the Bow tie.
	If the two ends of the tie end up exactly the same length, the tie is not correct.

44 Based on his knowledge and attitude towards school children, the writer suggests
A they shouldn't have to wear ties.
B removing the school tie by looping it over the head.
C it would be better if they had clip-on ties.
D using a Windsor knot rather than a Small knot.

Answers and explanations on pages 230–231

READING TEST 1
Intermediate Level

Read the newspaper editorial *Euthanasia—what do you think?* and answer questions 45 to 50.

Euthanasia—what do you think?

What do you think about euthanasia?

You don't get topics hotter than this one and the *Advocate* letters page is the place where you can express your opinion on such issues.

Some people believe euthanasia is one of those slippery slopes just too steep to consider. Where do you draw the line? How can you be sure that the person is of 'sound mind'? And so the questions go.

Churches have traditionally been against it, saying life is a precious gift and must be preserved.

Others, like the vocal advocate, Dr Phillip Nitschke, believe people should be able to die with dignity when they are ready.

Great Lakes resident Lesley Archer is also of that opinion. 'A peaceful death is everyone's right,' she said.

She will convene a public meeting on the issue next Wednesday at 10:30 am at the Coastal Patrol Headquarters, Forster Breakwater.

If there is enough interest at the meeting, Dr Nitschke himself has said he will visit Forster to conduct a workshop sometime later in the year.

There is no doubt he is dicing with the law but he's no stranger to that.

So what do you think?

Why not write us a letter to share your views? This page is for you.

Janine Watson

From *The Great Lakes Advocate*, 14/05/08

45 According to the editorial, the paper is
A supporting euthanasia.
B supporting euthanasia in special circumstances.
C encouraging debate on the issue of euthanasia.
D opposed to euthanasia.

46 What argument does the paper put forward against euthanasia?
A It is a much too difficult subject to consider.
B No-one can be sure a person accepting euthanasia is of 'sound mind'.
C The churches are opposed to euthanasia.
D Dr Phillip Nitschke has a criminal record.

47 The editor says that Dr Phillip Nitschke is 'dicing with the law'. By this, she is implying Dr Nitschke is
A challenging the law on euthanasia issues.
B treating the matter as a game of life and death.
C taking a gamble on not getting caught.
D breaking the law by attending the meeting.

48 Tick the statement if it is correct. You may tick more than one statement.
☐ Referring to euthanasia as a 'hot topic' means the topic creates heated public debate.
☐ People who refer to euthanasia as a 'slippery slope' think it can only have bad outcomes.
☐ The expression 'draw the line' is used to suggest that debate should be controlled.
☐ The phrase 'sound mind' refers to people who put forward arguments that are irrational.
☐ By saying 'he's no stranger' the editor implies Dr Nitschke is a very experienced doctor.

49 What argument is implied in the editorial for attending the euthanasia meeting? By attending the meeting people will
A be able to show their support for Dr Phillip Nitschke.
B write informed letters to *The Great Lakes Advocate*.
C learn how to have a peaceful death, as is their right.
D be better informed on the euthanasia issue.

50 You have read 'Tying a knot' and 'Euthanasia—what do you think?'. For which primary purposes were these texts written? Tick two purposes for each text.

Purpose	'Tying a knot'	'Euthanasia—what do you think?'
to inform		
to describe		
to persuade		
to recount		
to explain		

☞ Answers and explanations on page 231

CONVENTIONS OF LANGUAGE TEST 1
Intermediate Level

1. In which sentence is the word *tan* used as a noun?
   A Tan is not a suitable colour for hospitals.
   B We used tan polish to shine our shoes.
   C Early settlers used to tan the hides of kangaroos.
   D Some people lie on the beach to tan their skin.

2. Which sentence has the correct punctuation?
   A Jane told Jenny that the committee has ceased to exist.
   B Jane told Jenny that the, 'committee has ceased to exist.'
   C Jane told Jenny 'that the committee has ceased to exist.'
   D Jane told Jenny that the committee 'has ceased to exist.'

3. Which of the following correctly completes this sentence?

   The rebellion occurred ______ April, 1916.

at	for	in	about
A	B	C	D

4. Which of the following correctly completes this sentence?

   The young boy ran as swiftly ______ a gazelle.

is	are	if	as
A	B	C	D

5. Which sentence has the correct punctuation?
   A The, charismatic ms P, the nicest teacher in school, was taking our class.
   B The charismatic Ms p, the nicest teacher in school, was taking our class.
   C The charismatic Ms P the nicest teacher in school, was taking, our class.
   D The charismatic Ms P, the nicest teacher in school, was taking our class.

6. Which of the following words correctly completes this sentence?

   The ______ I have ever been was when I was accepted into university.

happy	happier	happiness	happiest
A	B	C	D

7. Which of the following correctly completes this sentence?

   It was a widely regarded fact that Alli was the ______ member of the class.

clever	cleverer	most clever	cleverest
A	B	C	D

8. Which of the following correctly completes this sentence?

   Sally quietly paced back and forth as she ______ nervously for news of her missing sister.

waits	waiting	weight	waited
A	B	C	D

☞ **Answers and explanations on pages 231–233**

CONVENTIONS OF LANGUAGE TEST 1
Intermediate Level

9 Which sentence tells the reader who performed the action?
- A More was done in previous decades to help those in need.
- B The prosperity of the Western World has never been shared with developing nations.
- C More money was invested last year in education.
- D Last year Médecins Sans Frontières sent 27 000 trained medical personnel to help people in need.

10 Which of the following correctly completes this sentence?

______ Maddie was only three, she wasn't allowed to attend the concert.

Although	Unless	However	Because
A	B	C	D

11 Choose the correct word fo fill the gap.

To me it ______ that I'd go to uni to complete a Bachelor of Science in agriculture so I can learn how to best manage our farms out here.
- A just made sense
- B would make sense
- C would made sense
- D wouldn't makes sense

12 Growing up on a 4000-acre farm just north of Dubbo in New South Wales, Samantha ______ a girl devoted to the country.
- A was always
- B has always been
- C have always been
- D is always been

13 Samantha ______ her degree in two years time and hopes to use her experience to help her family.
- A wouldn't complete
- B was completing
- C is completing
- D will complete

Write the word or words in the box to correctly complete the sentences below.

14 The T-shirt design created by Anne was similar ______ the one created by Jess.

to	at	of	from
A	B	C	D

15 Each individual ______ their role in the kitchen.

know	knowing	knows	knew
A	B	C	D

16 We were concerned when we saw ______ person it was who had been evacuated.

when	who	what	which
A	B	C	D

☞ Answers and explanations on pages 231–233

CONVENTIONS OF LANGUAGE TEST 1
Intermediate Level

Highlight the correct answer in the sentences below.

17 Shade **two** circles to show where the missing question marks (?) should go.

You haven't heard, have you (A) The most important words are in blue (B) Is that too hard to remember (C)

18 Put a circle around the adjective in the sentence below.

The novel was unbearable so I refused to finish reading it.

19 Shade a circle to show where the missing comma (,) should go.

Jackson (A) do you (B) believe in (C) supernatural (D) beings?

20 Shade a circle to show where the missing comma (,) should go.

'Nothing (A) is worse than a rainy day (B) ' (C) lamented (D) Todd.

21 Which apostrophe is used correctly in this sentence?

Don't (A) you dare eat that pie, it belong's (B) to Janie and she like's (C) it best when it sit's (D) there to cool down.

22 Shade a circle to show where the missing comma (,) should go.

'I do not believe (A) that the countries (B) will reconcile,' admitted the academic (C) 'because the hatred is too strong.' (D)

23 Circle the words that 'it' refers to in the sentences below:

Diving into rock pools can be dangerous. It may lead to severe injuries or even death.

24 What is the subject of the main clause in this sentence?

Ghost stories are a lot of fun if you tell them late at night with the lights off.

A Ghost stories
B a lot of fun
C late at night
D with the lights off

25 Which of the following correctly completes this sentence?

It was difficult to express my ______ at the continual interruption of the film.

frustrate	frustrating	frustrated	frustration
A	B	C	D

It would be a good idea to check your answers to questions 1 to 25 before moving on to the other questions.

☞ Answers and explanations on pages 231–233

CONVENTIONS OF LANGUAGE TEST 1
Intermediate Level

To the student
Ask your teacher or parent to read the spelling words for you. The words are listed on page 251. Write the spelling words on the lines below.

26 ____________________

27 ____________________

28 ____________________

29 ____________________

30 ____________________

31 ____________________

32 ____________________

33 ____________________

34 ____________________

35 ____________________

36 ____________________

37 ____________________

38 ____________________

39 ____________________

40 ____________________

The spelling mistakes in these sentences have been underlined. Write the correct spelling for each underlined word in each box.

41 The <u>comitie</u> worked long and hard on the latest proposal. ☐

42 This <u>acomodation</u> is far below our expectations. ☐

43 Please give your full <u>attenshion</u> to our guest speakers. ☐

44 Samantha had the most <u>buewtiful</u> dress at the formal. ☐

45 Biology is a <u>fasinating</u> subject. ☐

Each sentence has one word that is incorrect. Write the correct spelling of the word in the box.

46 I defanatly think we should have gone the other way. ☐

47 In Australia the parlyment sits in Canberra. ☐

48 Lurking in the shadows, he seemed weerd to the other children. ☐

49 Decomposed organic matter derrived from household scraps, also known as compost, is an effective fertiliser for gardens. ☐

50 Commpossting household scraps also helps the environment by reducing landfill and greenhouse gases. ☐

☞ Answers and explanations on page 231

NUMERACY TEST 1
Intermediate Level

Section 1: Non-calculator questions

1. There are 10 red cars in a carpark containing 50 cars. Which of these is the percentage of the cars that are red in colour?
   A 0.2% B 0.5% C 2%
   D 5% E 20% F 50%

2. There are 86 400 seconds in a day. Which of these shows 86 400 written in scientific notation?
   A 8.64×10^2 B 8.64×10^3
   C 8.64×10^4 D 8.64×10^5

3. Lara's grandfather is celebrating his 85th birthday. Lara needs to buy 85 birthday candles. The candles are sold in packets of 12. What is the smallest number of packets Lara needs to buy?
   [ ]

4. To make a certain shade of green paint, Kate mixes 2.5 L of blue paint with 1 L of yellow paint. How many millilitres of yellow paint is needed to mix with 800 mL of blue paint to make the shade of green?
   200 mL (A) 300 mL (B) 320 mL (C) 400 mL (D) 480 mL (E)

5. On a Saturday morning a real estate agency sold two properties at auction. An apartment was sold for $978 000 and a house for $1.25 million. What is the difference between the two prices?
   $ [ ]

6. $4 + 3 \times (12 - 4 \div 2) =$ [?]

   What number does [?] represent?
   16 (A) 28 (B) 34 (C) 38 (D) 70 (E)

7. Zoe baked 48 muffins. Two-thirds of the muffins were blueberry and one-quarter were choc-chip. How many of the muffins were not blueberry or choc-chip?
   [ ]

8. Cedar wrote this pattern of numbers.

   $1^2 \quad 2^2 \quad 3^2 \quad 4^2 \quad 5^2 \quad 6^2 \quad 7^2$

   What is the sum of the first five terms in Cedar's pattern?
   [ ]

This is the end of the part where you are not allowed to use a calculator. It would be a good idea to check your answers to the questions in this section before moving on to the other questions.

Section 2: Calculator Allowed questions

9. The table shows the time and average speed taken by a vehicle over a 240 km-section of highway.

Time (h)	2	3	4	8	10
Average speed (km/h)	120	80	60	30	24

   Which graph shows the information in the table for time and average speed?

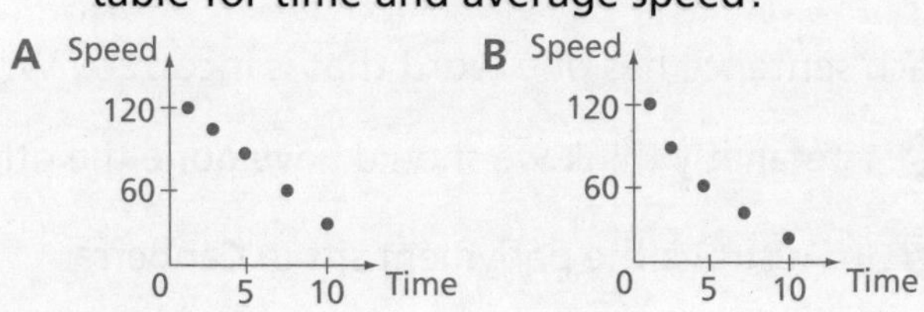

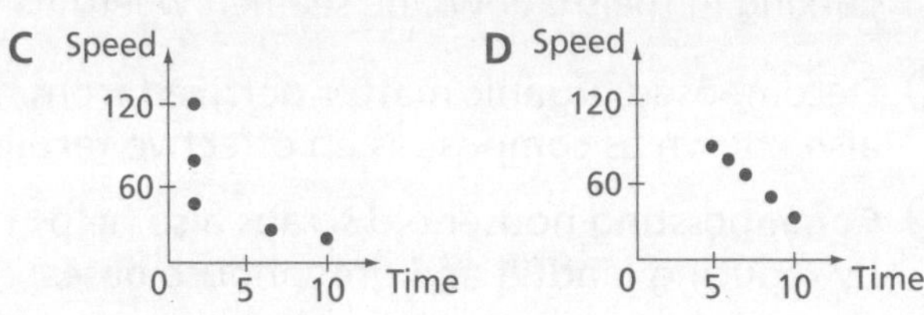

☞ Answers and explanations on pages 234–237

10 The ratio of the length of AB to the length of BC is 3:2.

If the length of AC is 35 cm, what is the length of BC?

A 14 cm B 21 cm C 27 cm D 30 cm

11 The diagram shows a regular polygon. The diagonals of the shape have been drawn.

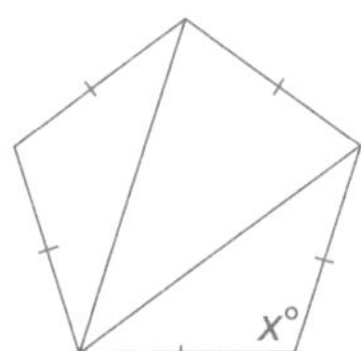

What is the size of x?

Write your answer in the box: 

12 The coordinates of P are (6, 2). The length of PQ is 5 units and RQ is 9 units.

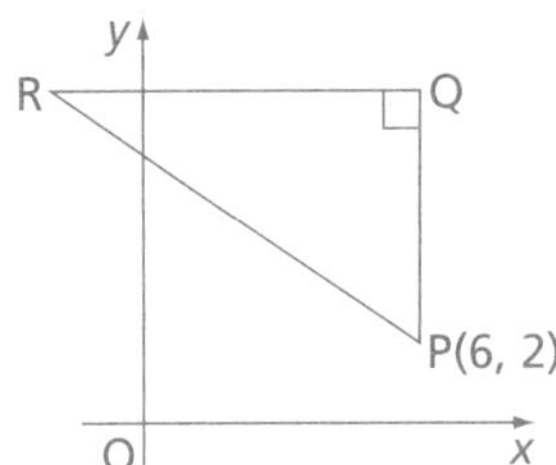

What are the coordinates of point R?

A (5, 9) B (–3, 7)
C (–3, 5) D (–2, 7)

13 The table shows the minimum temperatures on a June morning in some Australian cities.

City	Minimum temperature (°C)
Brisbane	8
Sydney	10
Canberra	–3
Melbourne	6
Hobart	2
Adelaide	8
Perth	3
Darwin	19

What is the range of temperatures in the table?

A 8 B 16 C 19 D 22

14 The table shows the increase in height of four plants in a science experiment over a 24-hour period.

Plant height	Tuesday height	Wednesday increase	%
A	61 cm	61.5 cm	0.8%
B	42 cm	42.3 cm	0.7%
C	80 cm	?	0.5%
D	38 cm	38.6 cm	1.6%

What was the height of Plant C on Wednesday?

Write your answer in the box: ______ cm

15 The diameter of a circle is 28 cm. What is the area of the circle to the nearest square centimetre?

A 88 cm^2 B 616 cm^2
C 1231 cm^2 D 2463 cm^2

16 At a school dance the ratio of boys to girls was 2:3. There were 480 girls at the dance. What was the total number of students who attended the dance?

A 320 B 700 C 740 D 800

It would be a good idea to check your answers to questions 9 to 16 before moving on to the other questions.

17 A survey was conducted to find the favourite holiday activity for a group of students.

Activity	Students
Movies	6
Shopping	5
Beach	4
Bushwalking	1
Other	4
Total	20

If a student was chosen at random, what is the chance that their favourite activity was going to the beach?

A 0.2 B 0.3 C 0.4 D 0.5

☞ Answers and explanations on pages 234–237

18 Expand the expression $2(3x + 5)$.

A $5x + 7$　　B $6x + 5$
C $6x + 7$　　D $6x + 10$

19 At recess today Miriam drank 60% of her bottle of water. At lunch time she drank 75% of the remaining water. What percentage of the water remains in the bottle?

A 5%　　B 10%
C 15%　　D 85%

20 Mitchell drove his car at an average speed of 60 km/h for 3 hours. He then drove for 100 kilometres in 2 hours. What is his average speed for the entire journey?

A 52 km/h　　B 54 km/h
C 55 km/h　　D 56 km/h

21 There are usually *c* students in Mrs Jackson's Mathematics class. On the last day of the school year *d* students are absent. She buys each student present a bottle of juice which costs $*y*. What will be the total cost of the bottles in dollars?

A cdy　　B $y(c + d)$
C $y(c - d)$　　D $y(d - c)$

22 ❁ ❁ ❂ = 12　　❂ ❂ ❂ = 24　　❂ ❁ ❄ = 17

What is the value of ❄ ❄ ❁?

Write your answer in the box. ☐

23 If $x = -2$, what is the value of $(3x)^2 - 3x^2$?

☐

24 The line $y = 3x - 4$ is drawn on a number plane. Which of the points does the line pass through? Select **all** correct answers.

(–4, 0)	(0, –4)	(1, 1)	(2, 2)	(3, 4)
A	B	C	D	E

25 The perimeter of a square is 12 cm. If the sides of the square are doubled, what is the area of the new square?

A 24 cm²　　B 36 cm²
C 48 cm²　　D 64 cm²

26 The large square is to be covered in identical triangles of the same size ◺.

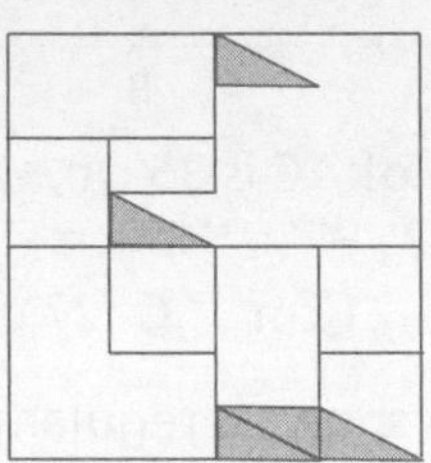

Altogether, how many triangles will be needed to cover the square?

A 16　　B 32　　C 48　　D 64

27 Students in Mr Hamilton's class were graded from 1 to 6 on the basis of their end-of-term test. The graph below shows the results.

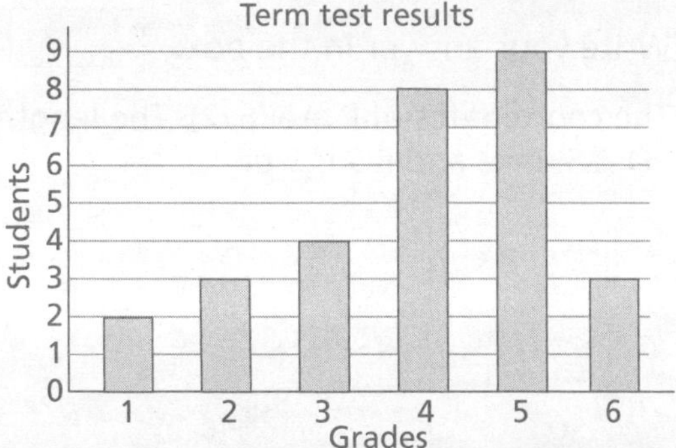

Jacqueline was absent on the day of the test and completed the test later. If she gained a grade of 6, what effect will Jacqueline's result have on the data?

A The mean and the mode will remain unchanged.
B The range will increase.
C The mode will remain unchanged but the mean will increase.
D The mode will increase but the mean will remain unchanged.

28 Jono wrote this equation for *y* in terms of *x*:

$$y = 12 - \frac{3x}{4}$$

What is the value of *y* if $x = 1.6$?

☐

☞ **Answers and explanations on pages 234–237**

29 Here is a plan of a small farm.

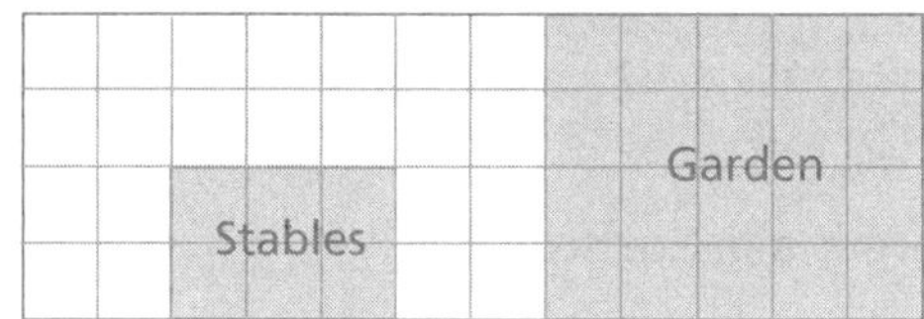

The area of the stables is 24 m^2.
What is the area of the garden?

A 64 m^2 B 72 m^2 C 80 m^2 D 94 m^2

30 A movie marathon commenced at 11:45 pm and finished at 6:10 am the next day.
How long did the marathon take?

A 5 hours 55 minutes B 6 hours 15 minutes
C 6 hours 25 minutes D 6 hours 55 minutes

31 One morning Rose drives her car to the car park at a national park. From the car park she walks to this signpost.

From the sign Rose walks to the lookout, then back past the sign to the waterfall and back again to the sign. She then walks back to her car. In total Rose walks 8 kilometres.
What is the distance from the car park to the sign?

Write your answer in the box: ☐ km

32 In the diagram, AB is parallel to CD.

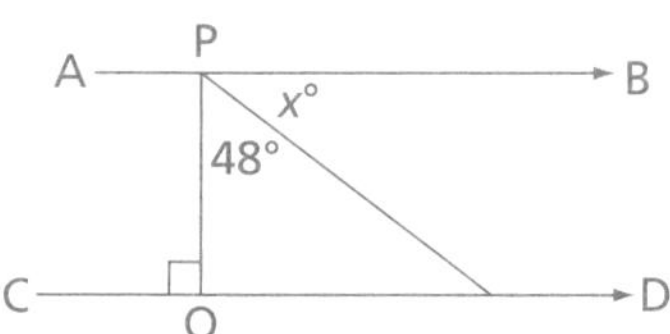

What is the size of x?

A 24° B 42° C 52° D 62°

It would be a good idea to check your answers to questions 17 to 32 before moving on to the other questions.

---

33 Sunyin builds a pattern of towers using small cubes.

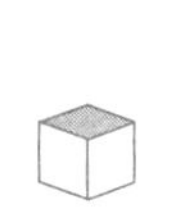
Tower 1

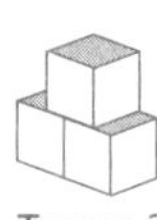
Tower 2

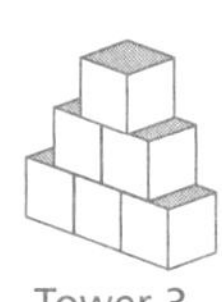
Tower 3

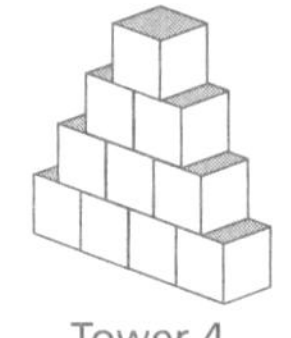
Tower 4

The table shows the cubes she uses for each tower.

Tower	1	2	3	4	5
Cubes	1	3	6	10	?

If she continued the pattern, how many cubes will she need for Tower 5?

A 14 B 15 C 16 D 25

34 The diagram shows a pair of parallel lines.

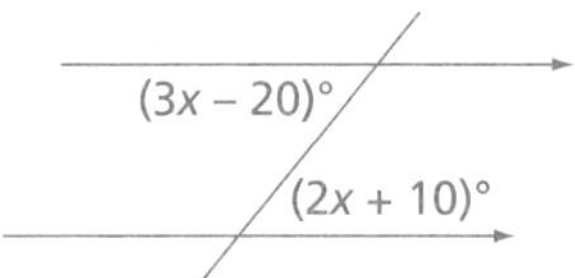

What is the value of x?

A 10 B 20 C 30 D 70

35 What number is halfway between 1.004 and 1.4?

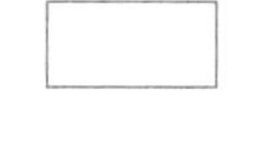

36 A survey was conducted to find how many students in the Mandarin class at school were born in China. The results are shown in the table.

	Students	Percentage born in China
Males	8	25%
Females	16	50%

What fraction of all students were **not** born in China?

A $\frac{5}{12}$ B $\frac{3}{4}$ C $\frac{7}{12}$ D $\frac{2}{3}$

☞ Answers and explanations on pages 234–237

NUMERACY TEST 1
Intermediate Level

37 If $T = a + (n - 1)d$, what is the value of n if $T = 32$, $a = 8$ and $d = 6$.

A 3 B 4
C 5 D 8

38 In the diagram, ABCD is a square, CED is an equilateral triangle and BFC is an isosceles triangle where angle BFC = 40°.

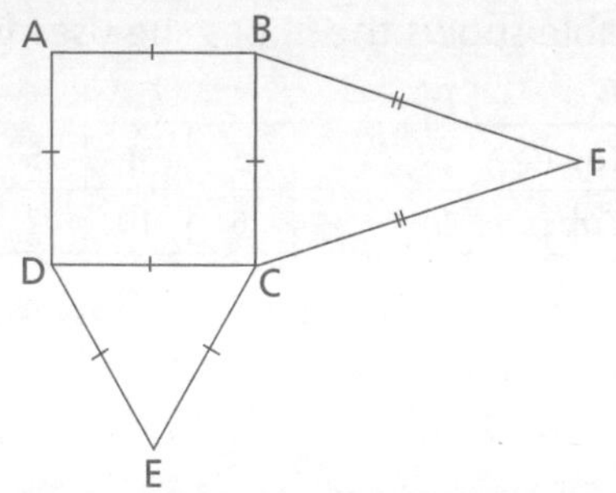

What is the size of obtuse angle ECF?

A 120° B 130° C 140° D 150°

39 Larissa listed some of her favourite download videos in the table below:

Video	Time
Having a Ball	1 h 15 min
Crying Man	1 h 35 min
Skateboard Heaven	48 min
Trouble at Kenny's	1 h 12 min
Break at Snapper R	30 min

What is the average (mean) time for these five videos?

A 64 minutes B 72 minutes
C 106 minutes D 306 minutes

40 Carmel is making this pattern of squares using matches.

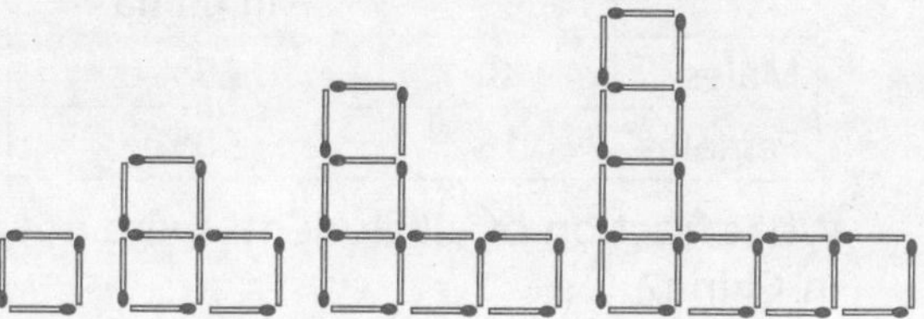

She summarised the information in the table:

Number of squares	1	3	5	7
Number of matches	4	10	16	22

Which rule can be used to work out the number of matches needed to make n squares?

A $n + 3$ B $2n + 3$
C $2n + 6$ D $3n + 1$

41 Here is a list of scores:

2 4 4 5 7 10 18 46

Which of the following is true?
Select **all** the correct answers.

A Mean > Range
B Median > Mode
C Mean < Median
D Range < Mean
E Mode < Median

42 Omar uses this rule to find the next number in a pattern: *add 3 and then double.*

He uses the rule to develop this pattern from 1: 1, 8, 22, 50, ___

What is the sixth number in the pattern?

A 106 B 212 C 215 D 218

43 Penelope writes down these two equations:

$A = 3x - 3$

$A = x + 7$

What value of x satisfies both of these equations?

[ ]

44 Charlotte takes piano lessons which last for $\frac{3}{4}$ of an hour each. This week she had three lessons in preparation for her eisteddfod. What was the total time she spent in lessons this week?

A $2\frac{1}{4}$ hours B $2\frac{1}{2}$ hours
C $2\frac{3}{4}$ hours D $3\frac{1}{4}$ hours

☞ **Answers and explanations on pages 234–237**

45 The sun casts a shadow of 1.5 metres for a metre ruler. At the same time a tree casts a shadow which is 24 metres long.

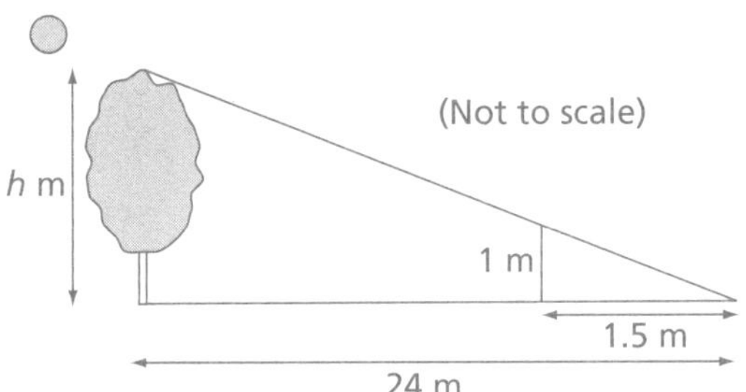

What would be the height (h) of the tree?

46 Ross deposits $650 into a savings account. He earns simple interest of 3.5% per annum. How much interest does Ross earn after 4 years?

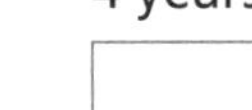

47 A class of 30 students were surveyed to find out whether they had seen a movie or gone to the beach over the weekend.

- 16 had seen a movie.
- 6 had not seen a movie or gone to the beach.

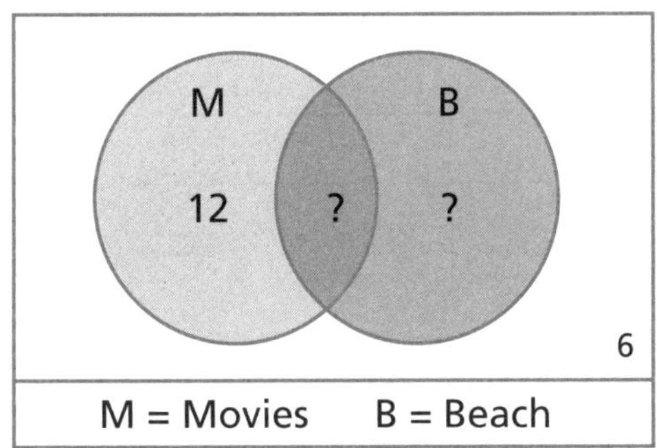

The diagram is missing some information. How many students had gone to the beach over the weekend?

48 Harvey plotted the points (0, 2) and (3, −3) on a number plane and drew a line that passed through both points.

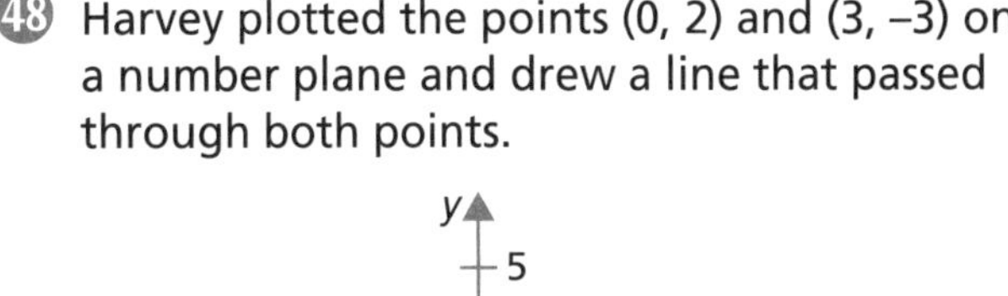

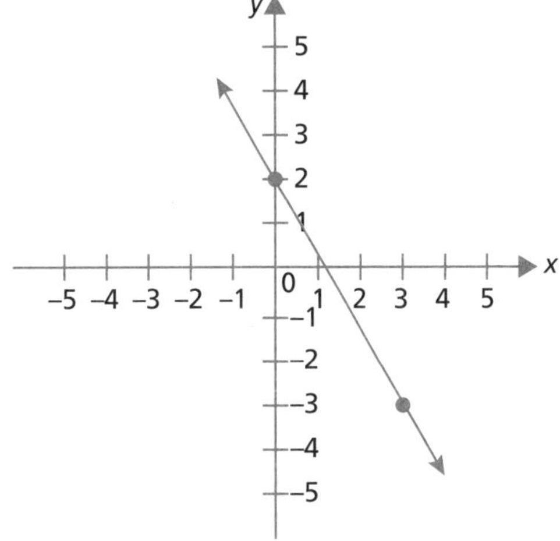

What is the gradient of the line that Harvey drew?

A $-\frac{5}{3}$ B $-\frac{3}{5}$ C $\frac{3}{5}$ D $\frac{5}{3}$

Answers and explanations on pages 234–237

WRITING TEST 2

Today you are going to write a narrative or story.
Look at the picture on the right.
The idea you must base your narrative on is DISASTER.
Your narrative might be about something simple and everyday such as making your breakfast and the toast landing on the ground spread-side down, you turn up to a party and your best friend is wearing the same dress as you or your laptop dies half-way through your assignment.
It could be about a large-scale disaster such as a tsunami, a bushfire or a volcanic eruption.

Before you start writing, give some thought to:

- where your narrative takes place
- the characters and what they do in your narrative
- the events that take place in your narrative and the problems that have to be resolved
- how your narrative begins, what happens in your narrative, and how your narrative ends.

Don't forget to:

- plan your narrative before you start writing
- write in correctly formed sentences and take care with paragraphing
- choose your words carefully and pay attention to your spelling and punctuation
- write neatly but don't waste time
- quickly check your narrative once you have finished.

Start writing here or type in your answer on a tablet or computer.

Marking guide on pages 237–238

READING TEST 2
Advanced Level

65 MIN

Read *Flying foxes* by Vivien Jones and answer questions 1 to 9.

Flying foxes

1 These flying mammals are often called bats, megabats, fruit bats and flying foxes—they're all the same animal. This is confusing because they are no relation to foxes, fruit is not usually their main food and they are very different from other members of the bat family.

2 The bat family can be divided approximately into two groups: the megabats (flying foxes are megabats) and microbats (the little ones that are talked about in stories from Europe and the USA). Flying foxes do not occur naturally in Europe or the USA, so all those spooky bat stories have nothing to do with Australia's flying foxes.

3 In many ways, flying foxes are more biologically similar to monkeys and humans than they are to the microbats. They do not use sound or echolocation to 'see' but have excellent eyesight like ours in daylight and they see better than we do at night. They do not hibernate in winter, as is common with microbats. Most of them prefer to roost in trees and avoid caves and buildings, so will not come into your house, as do micros. They are principally vegetarian, whereas microbats commonly eat insects. They certainly do not suck blood like the 'vampire' bats that are found in Central America. There are more differences but these are some of the obvious ones.

4 Maybe they are called fruit bats because they look like dark fruit hanging in trees. Unfortunately, this name gives the impression that they are big fruit eaters, but in fact these on Bellingen Island concentrate more on nectar and pollen. People are just more likely to notice what they are eating when it is fruit, because we like to eat fruit, too.

5 Most of the flying foxes on Bellingen Island are the species called Greyheaded Flying Fox, and these are found only in Australia. However, the numbers of Black Flying Foxes is increasing. Ten years ago Black Flying Foxes were rare summer visitors from their more northerly range but now you can always find some of them roosting on Bellingen Island. This is part of a general pattern of the Black species spreading southwards.

6 Little Red Flying Foxes visit occasionally in summer when food supplies are short in their inland range. Australia's fourth main type, the Spectacled Flying Fox, is never found naturally this far south of its North Queensland range.

Courtesy of Vivien Jones
Source: www.bellingen.com/flyingfoxes/bats_or_flying_foxes.htm

1. The most likely intention of this article is to
   A assist readers in understanding flying foxes.
   B encourage readers to do more to protect flying foxes.
   C warn readers of the damage flying foxes do to fruit trees.
   D educate readers on how to care for flying foxes.

2. The names of the bat groups, megabats and microbats, is based upon
   A food preferences.
   B habitat.
   C size.
   D colour.

3. The writer finds the common names applied to flying foxes generally are
   A appropriate.
   B misinformed.
   C unfortunate.
   D prejudicial.

4. Which is the most common flying fox in the Bellingen Island area? Write your answer on the lines.

   ____

   ____

5. Which fact is the writer most emphatic about?
   A Flying foxes look like dark fruit hanging in trees.
   B Flying foxes do not suck blood.
   C Flying foxes are closely related to monkeys.
   D Flying foxes roost in trees.

6. In which paragraph does the writer cover the following topics? Write the number of the paragraph next to the topic that the paragraph covers.

Paragraph ____	speculation about why people misname flying foxes
Paragraph ____	a species of flying fox that is found only in Australia
Paragraph ____	an explanation of why the name flying fox is ironic
Paragraph ____	behavioural traits of flying foxes compared to microbats
Paragraph ____	the origin of supernatural tales about flying foxes

7. According to the passage, which statement is correct?
   A Flying foxes are known for attacks on people and other animals.
   B Flying foxes prefer to roost in caves or sheltered places.
   C Flying foxes depend upon echolocation to navigate at night.
   D Flying foxes have an unfair reputation of being big fruit eaters.

8. Generally, Australian flying foxes
   A suck blood from warm-blooded animals.
   B avoid entering houses.
   C 'see' in the dark by relying on echos, a form of radar.
   D hibernate in winter.

☞ **Answers and explanations on pages 238–239**

READING TEST 2
Advanced Level

Read the information on the *Thursday Island timeline* and answer questions 9 to 16.

Thursday Island (Torres Strait) timeline

It is interesting to see the comparisons between the various 'discoveries' of Australia. Captain Cook's discovery of the East coast in 1770 was centuries after other discoveries of the 'southern continent'. The settlement at Sydney Cove was established in 1788.

Torres Strait (Thursday Is.)

? BC Torres Strait Islanders develop a maritime trading lifestyle with links to Papua New Guinea to the north and the Aborigines to the south.

1606 Luis Vaez de Torres, a Spaniard, sails through the Torres Strait.

1606 William Janszoon, a Dutchman, in *The Duyfkun* reaches Cape York near present-day Aurukun.

1644 The Dutchman, Abel Tasman, explores the area.

1770 James Cook sails through the area. Cook notices that the islanders use bows and arrows, whereas the mainland people use lances (spears).

1789 William Bligh sails through Torres Strait after being cast adrift by mutineers on *The Bounty*.

1803 Matthew Flinders maps the coastline.

1843 The cutter, *America*, is wrecked. A 16-year-old girl survives on Prince of Wales Island until rescued in 1879.

1848 Edmund Kennedy speared while exploring the Cape.

1864 Somerset is established as a colonial settlement. Hostilities break out between Europeans and local inhabitants.

Tasmania

1642 Abel Tasman sailed from Batavia and was among the first Europeans to sight Tasmania.

1772 The first French voyage to Van Diemen's Land was led by Captain Nicholas Marion du Fresne.

1792 Bruni d'Entrecasteaux, in *The Recherche*, was sent to search for French explorer Comte de la Perouse, overdue from the Pacific since 1788. He explored parts of southern Tasmania.

1803 The first European settlement was made at Risdon when Lieutenant John Bowen landed with about 50 settlers, crew, soldiers and convicts.

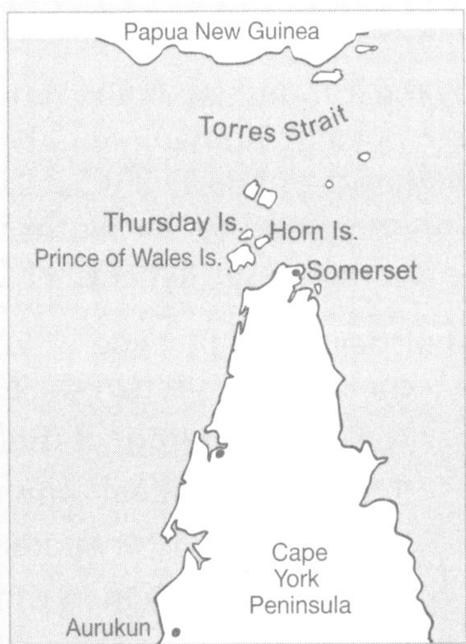

West Coast (Australia)

1616 Dirk Hartog, a Dutchman, discovers the west coast of Australia. He is the first European to set foot on Western Australia. He leaves behind an inscribed pewter plate.

1627 François Thijssen in *The Gulden Zeepaert* sailed along a lengthy section of the Great Australian Bight.

1679 Willem de Vlamingh removed Hartog's plate and replaced it with another.

1827 Western Australia was established as a small British settlement at King Georges Sound.

1829 The new Swan River Colony was officially proclaimed. The colony was proclaimed a British penal settlement in 1849.

1850 Convicts arrive.

Thursday Island Township
Photo by A Horsfield

9 It can be concluded from the timeline that the European discovery and settlement of Australia was

A a competitive race.
B an unrelated progression.
C a determined effort.
D an organised invasion.
E a methodical occupation.

10 The layout of information in columns
- **A** provides a quick cross-reference to dates of exploration.
- **B** demonstrates the importance of naval exploration.
- **C** shows evidence of the difficulties of establishing settlements in Australia.
- **D** shows clearly the differences between northern and southern Australia.

11 What is intended by the ? BC at the top of the Torres Strait column?
- **A** Recorded history has been lost.
- **B** There is no recorded history.
- **C** The area was uninhabited.
- **D** Nothing of importance happened.

12 In what order did the following events take place? Number them from 1 to 5.
- ☐ Captain Cook sailed through the islands of the Torres Strait.
- ☐ A European settlement was established on Cape York Peninsula.
- ☐ A Frenchman voyaged as far as southern areas of Tasmania.
- ☐ Part of the Great Australian Bight was explored by a European sailor.
- ☐ Lieutenant Bowen established the first settlement in Van Diemen's Land.

13 What proof exists that Dirk Hartog actually reached the Western Australian coast?
- **A** He drew maps of the coast.
- **B** He was observed by a fellow explorer, Willem de Vlamingh.
- **C** He left behind a pewter dish that was retrieved by a later sea explorer.
- **D** He collected spears and bows and arrows.

14 Which statement is correct?
- **A** There was no opposition to early European settlement in Cape York.
- **B** A European settlement was established in Somerset before one was established in Tasmania.
- **C** By the early 1800s most of Australia was settled.
- **D** William Bligh's time in the Torres Strait was not for exploration or settlement reasons.

15 The overall impression suggested by the information in the three columns is that
- **A** the Torres Strait has been slow to develop human habitation.
- **B** the Torres Strait has been better known by Europeans for longer than other parts of Australia.
- **C** most European sea explorers were attracted to the southern regions of Australia.
- **D** the east coast of Australia was a flourishing settlement before other regions had been explored.

16 You have read 'Flying foxes' and 'Thursday Island timeline'. They may have some techniques in common. Draw lines to show if the techniques are used in the texts.

'Flying foxes'

'Thursday Island timeline'

- **A** Scientific jargon is used to support the writer's purpose.
- **B** An unemotional tone is predominant in the text.
- **C** The introductory paragraph raises a contradiction.
- **D** The information in the text is presented impartially.
- **E** The writer suggests what the purpose of their text is.

It would be a good idea to check your answers to questions 1 to 16 before moving on to the other questions.

☞ **Answers and explanations on page 239**

Read the poem *A Smuggler's Song* by Rudyard Kipling and answer questions 17 to 23.

A Smuggler's Song
If you wake at midnight, and hear a horse's feet,
Don't go drawing back the blind, or looking in the street,
Them that ask no questions isn't told a lie.
Watch the wall my darling while the Gentlemen go by.

Five and twenty ponies,
Trotting through the dark—
Brandy for the Parson, 'Baccy for the Clerk.
Laces for a lady; letters for a spy,
Watch the wall my darling while the Gentlemen go by!

Running round the woodheap if you chance to find
Little barrels, roped and tarred, all full of brandy-wine,
Don't you shout to come and look, nor use 'em for your play.
Put the brushwood back again—and they'll be gone next day!
If you see the stable-door setting open wide;
If you see a tired horse lying down inside;

If your mother mends a coat cut about and tore;
If the lining's wet and warm—don't you ask no more!
If you meet King George's men, dressed in blue and red,
You be careful what you say, and mindful what is said.

If they call you "Pretty maid," and chuck* you 'neath the chin, (*tap gently)
Don't you tell where no one is, nor yet where no one's been!
Knocks and footsteps round the house—whistles after dark—
You've no call for running out till the house-dogs bark.

Trusty's here, and *Pincher's* here, and see how dumb they lie
They don't fret to follow when the Gentlemen go by!
If you do as you've been told, likely there's a chance,
You'll be give a dainty doll, all the way from France,

With a cap of Valenciennes**, and a velvet hood— (**fine lace)
A present from the Gentlemen, along 'o being good!
Five and twenty ponies,
Trotting through the dark—
Brandy for the Parson, 'Baccy for the Clerk.
Them that asks no questions isn't told a lie—
Watch the wall my darling while the Gentlemen go by!

17 The narrator is directing his words to
A a young girl. B a smuggler. C a dog owner. D soldiers.

18 Choose an adjective and a noun to correctly complete the sentence. Write your answer on the lines.
In the location in which the poem is set, people consider smuggling to be a ________ (adjective) ________ (noun).

Adjective	**Noun**
surprising	intrusion
despised	upheaval
common	tradition
feared	practice

19 The narrator refers to the people going by as gentlemen. The word is being used
A nervously. B disparagingly. C facetiously. D euphemistically.

20 When referring to the dogs, the narrator says, see how dumb they lie. This, most likely, is intended to
A suggest that the dogs are completely useless as watchdogs.
B highlight the point that the dogs are well behaved.
C reassure people that there is nothing to worry about.
D advise everyone that the safest thing to do is to watch the wall.

21 The language used in the poem is
A abrasive and threatening
B cheering and confiding.
C formal and educated.
D friendly and reassuring.

22 The men refer to one female as 'Pretty maid', and 'chuck' her '[be]neath the chin'. This, most likely, is intended to
A compliment her on her behaviour and looks.
B be a ruse to win her confidence and persuade her to disclose information.
C be a cruel comment and to act as a veiled threat.
D let her know that they know who she is if there are problems.

23 What conclusion can be drawn about the family which is involved in the action described in the poem? You may tick one box or more.
☐ They are spies for the French.
☐ Stolen goods are stored on their property.
☐ They are owners of an English inn.
☐ Smugglers can rely on them for assistance.
☐ Secretly they support King George's soldiers.
☐ They supply brandy and tobacco to the village.

☞ **Answers and explanations on pages 239–240**

Read the passage *The freak show* and answer questions 24 to 31.

The freak show

For over one hundred years freak shows were popular in travelling circuses and carnivals. The freak-show era began about 1840, but interest in 'freaks' goes back centuries. Mary Shelley (1797–1851) wrote her best-known novel, *Frankenstein*, in 1818.

A freak show is an exhibition of rarities, 'freaks of nature'—such as unusually tall, very short, very fat and deformed people. Some were too mentally retarded to have a judgement of their own. Though many 'freaks' signed their contracts and displayed themselves willingly, many others were sold or drafted by their parents or guardians into the freak show, virtually as slaves. These people were ogled at regardless of their feelings. They were put on show along with performances that were intended to shock audiences.

Heavily tattooed or excessively pierced people have sometimes been seen in freak shows, along with fire-breathing and sword-swallowing acts. Such acts eventually lost their thrill as they were exposed as clever stunts.

Although many examples were widely referred to as freaks, a distinction must be made between self-made freaks and born freaks.

With the rise of the Internet, morbid freak-show fascination has had a revival of interest on some dubious sites, allowing people to see 'freakish' abnormalities that would not have been permitted during the free-to-air television era, due to concepts of acceptable good taste and political correctness.

Some shows also exhibited deformed animals such as two-headed cows, one-eyed pigs, and four-horned goats and famous hoaxes, or simply as 'science gone wrong' exhibits. The Venice Beach Freakshow in Venice (California) housed a large collection of two-headed animals including a live two-headed snake and the only living three-headed turtle ever found. Visitors may have been sceptical, but there was also a morbid attraction.

Advances in medicine and political changes all sounded the death knell for the freak show. As mysterious deformities were scientifically explained as genetic mutations or the result of diseases, freaks became the objects of pity then compassion, rather than fear or disdain.

Freak shows are the exploitation of those who are powerless to protect themselves against **30** operators.

The term 'freak show' has become archaic. Freak shows (with animals or humans) are outlawed in most countries. Many of the shows that appear to have an element of freakishness about them are often cleverly contrived illusions.

Source: www.en.wikipedia.org/wiki/Freak_show

24 The end of the era for freak shows came about
- A when parents could no longer sell deformed children to show operators.
- B when extreme acts were exposed as frauds or their stunts explained.
- C when deformities were explained as genetic or disease-related conditions.
- D with the advent of free-to-air television.

25 A word that has become 'archaic' (last paragraph) is one that
- A has become offensive to many people.
- B belongs to another period and is no longer in use.
- C is politically incorrect in present times.
- D describes unpleasant attitudes from an earlier period.

26 The writer distinguishes between two basic types of exhibits in freak shows. There were the shows that had self-made freaks and those
- A using animals.
- B with ones that were sold to shows as children.
- C whose acts were illusions.
- D with ones who were born with or developed abnormalities.

27 Draw lines to show which conclusions drawn from the text are FACTS and which are OPINIONS.

FACT	The internet has provided a platform for renewed interest in 'freaks'.
	'Freaks of nature' sadly lacked the ability to make sound judgments.
OPINION	Audiences at the Venice Beach Freakshow were mostly sceptical.
	Fire-breathing and sword-swallowing acts were exposed as stunts.

28 The attitude to travelling freak shows has changed over the centuries. Which line best reflects the change from earliest to latest?
- A disdain, compassion, pity, fascination
- B fascination, pity, compassion, disdain
- C disdain, fascination, compassion, pity
- D fascination, disdain, pity, compassion

29 The word 'ogled' (paragraph 2) suggests that the audiences at freak shows
- A are shocked by what they see.
- B stare in a manner that gives personal pleasure.
- C become spellbound by the spectacle.
- D watch in fear.

30 In paragraph 7 a word has been omitted from the last sentence. Circle the **two** words that could correctly complete the sentence.

unsociable unscrupulous irresponsible unprincipled irredeemable irreverent

31 The word 'freaks' is in inverted commas (paragraph 1). This is because the writer is
- A aware that the word is offensive to the operators of sideshows.
- B preparing the reader for a word that may offend some people.
- C indicating the word may carry some additional or unusual meaning.
- D attempting to downplay any hidden meaning in the word.

☞ **Answers and explanations on page 240**

READING TEST 2
Advanced Level

Read the extract from *Great Expectations* by Charles Dickens and answer questions 32 to 39.

My sister, Mrs Joe Gargery, was more than twenty years older than I, and had established a great reputation with herself and the neighbours because she had brought me up 'by hand'. Having at that time to find out for myself what the expression meant, and knowing her to have a hard and heavy hand, and to be much in the habit of laying it upon her husband as well as upon me, I supposed that Joe Gargery and I were both brought up by hand.

She was not a good-looking woman, my sister; and I had a general impression that she must have made Joe Gargery marry her by hand. Joe was a fair man, with curls of flaxen hair on each side of his smooth face, and with eyes of such a very undecided blue that they seemed to have somehow got mixed with their own whites. He was a mild, good-natured, sweet-tempered, easy-going, foolish, dear fellow—a sort of Hercules in strength, and also in weakness.

My sister, Mrs Joe, with black hair and eyes, had such a prevailing redness of skin that I sometimes used to wonder whether it was possible she washed herself with a nutmeg-grater instead of soap. She was tall and bony, and almost always wore a coarse apron, fastened over her figure behind with two loops, and having a square impregnable bib in front, that was stuck full of pins and needles. She made it a powerful merit in herself, and a strong reproach against Joe, that she wore this apron so much. Though I really see no reason why she should have worn it at all: or why, if she did wear it at all, she should not have taken it off, every day of her life.

Joe's forge adjoined our house, which was a wooden house, as many of the dwellings in our country were—most of them, at that time. When I ran home from the churchyard, the forge was shut up, and Joe was sitting alone in the kitchen. Joe and I being fellow-sufferers, and having confidences as such, Joe imparted a confidence to me, the moment I raised the latch of the door and peeped in at him opposite to it, sitting in the chimney corner.

'Mrs Joe has been out a dozen times, looking for you, Pip. And she's out now, making it a baker's dozen.'

'Is she?'

'Yes, Pip,' said Joe; 'and what's worse, she's got Tickler with her.'

At this dismal intelligence, I twisted the only button on my waistcoat round and round, and looked in great depression at the fire. Tickler was a wax-ended piece of cane, worn smooth by collision with my tickled frame.

From *Great Expectations* (1860–1861) by Charles Dickens

32 Mrs Gargery left the house to
- A buy bread from the baker.
- B return Tickler to the church.
- C check her husband's work on the forge
- D find what Pip was doing.

33 The main impression that Charles Dickens creates of Pip's sister is that she is
- A domineering.
- B compassionate.
- C resourceful.
- D sturdy.
- E indecisive.
- F fickle.

34 Tickler was used by Mrs Gargery
- A for protection when she left the house.
- B as a means of physical coercion.
- C as a walking stick.
- D to provide amusement for Pip and Joe.

35 Pip is said to be raised by hand: 'she [Mrs Gargery] had brought me up "by hand" ' (paragraph 1). When Pip says this he
- A is conscious of the amount of work he created as a small child.
- B understands that his carers are of a working-class background.
- C knows it carries a second meaning, that of being smacked.
- D is admiring the way Mrs Gargery worked to raise him.

36 The mood created by the description of the Gargerys is one of
- A mounting despair.
- B working-class simplicity.
- C abject poverty.
- D desperate survival.

37 What does Pip insinuate when he describes Joe as a 'fellow sufferer'? (paragraph 4).
- A They are both waiting for Mrs Gargery to return with bread.
- B They have both come indoors to get warm.
- C They are both tired after a day's activity.
- D They have both experienced Mrs Gargery's displeasure.

38 Pip states he 'twisted the only button on (his) waistcoat round and round' (last paragraph). What does this action indicate about Pip? Write your answer on the lines.

____

____

39 Joe Gargery could best be described as
- A submissive and friendly.
- B considerate but ineffectual.
- C lazy but well meaning.
- D submissive and sullen.

It would be a good idea to check your answers to questions 18 to 39 before moving on to the other questions.

☞ **Answers and explanations on pages 240–241**

Read the information about *Share market returns* and answer questions 40 to 45.

Average yearly returns from share-market investments
109 years of the Australian share market

Shares are a small part of a company's capital stock. Most people in Australia own some shares either directly or through investment companies or superannuation funds. Returns from shares can supplement income from other sources.

Annual average return: 13%

Number of negative performance years: 21 (or 19%)

Other information:
World War I: 1914–1918
World War II: 1939–1945

Number of positive performance years: 88 (or 81%)

Return	Years
–50% to –40%	2008
–40% to –30%	
–30% to –20%	1974, 1937, 1930
–20% to –10%	1990, 1982, 1981, 1970, 1952
–10% to 0%	2002, 1994, 1987, 1984, 1965, 1960, 1951, 1941, 1929, 1916, 1915, 1901
0% to 10%	2000, 1998, 1992, 1976, 1971, 1964, 1962, 1949, 1948, 1944, 1940, 1939, 1938, 1937, 1910, 1904
10% to 20%	2007, 2003, 2001, 1999, 1997, 1996, 1989, 1983, 1969, 1966, 1961, 1957, 1956, 1955, 1953, 1947, 1946, 1945, 1943, 1936, 1935, 1931, 1928, 1927, 1926, 1925, 1924, 1923, 1920, 1919, 1918, 1917, 1914, 1913, 1912, 1911, 1909, 1908, 1907, 1906, 1905, 1902, 1900
20% to 30%	2006, 2005, 2004, 1995, 1978, 1977, 1972, 1963, 1958, 1954, 1942, 1934, 1933, 1932, 1922, 1921, 1903
30% to 40%	1991, 1950
40% to 50%	1993, 1985, 1980, 1979, 1968, 1967, 1959
50% to 60%	1996
60% to 70%	1983, 1975

Source: JP Morgan/Summit Services

40 For long-term shareholders the information in the graph would be
- **A** reassuring.
- **B** controversial.
- **C** mundane.
- **D** shocking.

41 The space separating the two sides of the graph is
- **A** intended to make information more readily readable.
- **B** designed to separate the years of profit from the years of loss.
- **C** to provide balance in the layout of the graph.
- **D** included to make obvious differences in returns between recent years and earlier years.

42 What is particularly unusual about the year 2008?
- **A** It was the last year in which information was available at the time of publication.
- **B** It had a very similar result to 1966 (second-last column).
- **C** It indicated that 2009 could be an even worse year for shareholders.
- **D** It was the worst single year for shareholders.

43 The difference in share return between 2007 (tall column) and 2008 (first column) could be described as a
- **A** result of a world war.
- **B** dramatic fall.
- **C** predicable fall.
- **D** not unusual variation.

44 The advantage of setting out this information in graph form
- **A** makes it immediately obvious what the long-term situation is.
- **B** warns of the pitfalls in owning shares.
- **C** shows the years in which to purchase shares.
- **D** provides information on the returns that can be expected from shares.

45 According to the graph, which statements are TRUE and which are FALSE? Write T or F in the box.

☐ There were no years in which shares lost between 30% and 40% of their value.

☐ As a generalisation, shareholders received average returns during World War II.

☐ The returns on share-market investments were better in 1901 than a century later.

☐ The majority of Australians earn money from shares either directly or indirectly.

☐ Over the 109 years, the average return on investments on the stock market was 19%.

☞ **Answers and explanations on page 241**

Read *Teenage drivers* and answer questions 46 to 50.

Teenage Drivers

New learner drivers (mostly teenagers) need 120 hours of compulsory training. This is a critical issue for most learner drivers and their parents either in hours in a car or the cost of a driving instructor. However frustrating it is for both parents and learners, young drivers have tens of thousands of accidents each year due to inexperience.

46 What is Kevin implying in the way he uses the term 'teen years'?

- **A** He is still a teenager, but not for much longer.
- **B** He will no longer be a teenager when he gets his driver's licence.
- **C** His teenage years are his best years and they are being wasted.
- **D** Time goes very slowly for teenagers who can't do what they want to do.

47 This cartoon would most likely be appreciated fully by

- **A** parents of teenagers generally.
- **B** learner drivers of all ages.
- **C** teenage P-platers.
- **D** driving instructors.

48 The cartoon gains much of its impact because

- **A** it sends up driving requirements for learner drivers.
- **B** it is a familiar situation for many families of younger learner drivers.
- **C** parents don't understand how difficult it is to get a driving permit.
- **D** it makes fun of over-concerned mothers.

49 Draw a line to match the technique used by the cartoonist with the effect the cartoonist intends to convey.

TECHNIQUE	EFFECT CONVEYED
A exclamation mark after 'Any infringement!'	puzzlement
B question mark in speech bubble '?'	disbelief
C the use of bold in 'forever!'	anguish
D Kevin's hands covering his eyes	overreaction
E exclamation mark after '...speeding!'	assertiveness

50 You have read 'Share market returns' and 'Teenage Drivers'. What purpose do both texts have in common?

to instruct	to warn	to influence	to prove	to inform
A	B	C	D	E

☞ **Answers and explanations on pages 241–242**

CONVENTIONS OF LANGUAGE TEST 2
Advanced Level

1 How does the suffix *er* change the word *preach* in this sentence?
Little Jane liked to hear the pastor preach and hoped that when she grew up she could be a preacher too.
It changes
A an adverb into a noun.
B a verb into a noun.
C a noun into an adverb.
D an adjective into an adverb.

2 What does the prefix *un* in the word *unwritten* mean?

without	very	not	against
A	B	C	D

3 Read these three sentences.
Joe began playing guitar. Three years went by. Then Joe started at Davidson High School.
Which option accurately combines the information about Joe into a single sentence?
A Joe started at Davidson High School after he began playing guitar.
B Three years after Joe began playing guitar, he started at Davidson High School.
C Three years later, Joe began playing guitar and started at Davidson High School.
D Joe began playing guitar and three years later started at Davidson High School.

4 Which sentence tells the reader who performed the action?
A The club was founded to benefit disadvantaged kids.
B Playgrounds have been built in every suburb.
C The shopping centre has been closed down.
D Sergeant Anderson escorted the children home to their parents.

5 Which of the following correctly completes this sentence?

Jasmine wanted to carry on with her job ______ Harry had other plans.

but	so	although	instead
A	B	C	D

6 Which of the following correctly completes this sentence?

Reports into childhood obesity suggest that young children fail to ______ enough exercise.

doing	does	do	don't
A	B	C	D

7 Choose the correct words to fill the gap.

'I'm so excited about this project, but ______ to put down the books and get onto the land to make a real difference,' stated Samantha.
A I could wait
B I wasn't waiting
C I can't wait
D I can waited

8 Which of the following correctly completes this sentence?

______ vegetarians are small in number, they are big in heart.

Although	Unless	However	Because
A	B	C	D

☞ Answers and explanations on pages 242–244

CONVENTIONS OF LANGUAGE TEST 2
Advanced Level

9 Which of the following correctly completes this sentence?

Joni was positive she was outside when she ______ the gun go off.

had heard	has heard	will hear	hears
A	B	C	D

10 Which sentence has the correct punctuation?

A Keenan said, 'I love playing the drums'.
B Keenan, said 'I love playing the drums'.
C Keenan said: 'I love playing the drums.'
D Keenan said, 'I love playing the drums.'

11 Which word correctly completes this sentence?

The mother wrapped the fish ______ two sheets of newspaper.

A on B beside C in D near

12 Green tree frogs are an endangered species according to the World Wildlife Fund.
The sentence above is written in the

A past tense. B present tense. C future tense.

13 Which option best combines this information into one sentence?
Ryo pulled the door open. His heart was beating fast.

A With his heart beating fast, Ryo pulled open the door.
B The door was pulled open by Ryo, whose heart was beating fast.
C Ryo, whose heart was beating fast, pulled open the door.
D Ryo pulled open the door whilst his heart was beating fast.

For questions 14–16, write the word or words in the box to correctly complete the sentences below.

14 Wollongong's beaches are ______ than Sydney's.

more clean	cleanest	cleaner	more neatest
A	B	C	D

15 We discovered that the cupcakes could be made ______ if others were prepared to help.

more easy	really easy	more easily	easy
A	B	C	D

16 It's important to ______ the correct shoes when operating heavy machinery.

where	wear	we're	wore
A	B	C	D

☞ Answers and explanations on pages 242–243

CONVENTIONS OF LANGUAGE TEST 2
Advanced Level

Highlight the correct answer in the sentences below.

17 What is the main clause in this sentence?
I first met my great aunt in Paris when I lived in France as a young boy.
A my great aunt
B in Paris
C I first met my great aunt in Paris
D I lived in France as a young boy

18 Which group of words in this sentence is an adverbial phrase?
Without thinking, the tractor driver turned across the road.
A Without thinking
B the tractor driver
C across the road
D Without thinking, the tractor driver turned

19 Shade a circle to show where the missing comma (,) should go.
Deep in (A) the cave (B) the young boy cried (C) for help. (D)

20 Even though Evelyn thought the film was interesting, it did not sustain her daughter's interest for very long.
In this sentence, *interesting* and *interest* are:

	interesting	interest
A	noun	verb
B	noun	adjective
C	adjective	noun
D	verb	noun

21 In which sentence is the word *back* used as a noun?
A Rita turned back toward the unusual sound.
B Dad will back the car out of the garage before we clean it.
C The cat climbed up and over the back fence.
D His back was covered in mosquito bites.

22 In which sentence is the word *hoop* used as a verb?
A The girl wore thick hoop earrings.
B It was dangerous to stand near the hoop of fire.
C The dog catcher tried to hoop the stray around the neck with his rope.
D At recess the boy used the garbage bin as a basketball hoop.

23 Which group of words in this sentence is an adverbial phrase?
For answers to all your questions, just do a Google search.
A For answers
B to all your questions
C For answers to all your questions
D just do a Google search

☞ Answers and explanations on pages 242–243

CONVENTIONS OF LANGUAGE TEST 2
Advanced Level

24 Which two clauses can both complete the sentence so it makes sense?

Smaug, ________, swiftly and softly flew over the mountains.

A even though he was angry with Bilbo
B angry at having been cheated by Bilbo
C the ugly dragon who
D eager to wreck destruction on the town of Dale

25 Which two clauses each complete the sentence so it makes sense?

Mr Anderson, ________, is my fourth-grade teacher.

A he isn't very friendly to me
B who is the funniest person I know
C the one with the bushy eyebrows
D hurt his hand whilst playing soccer

It would be a good idea to check your answers to questions 1 to 25 before moving on to the other questions.

To the student
Ask your teacher or parent to read the spelling words for you. The words are listed on page 251. Write the spelling words on the lines below.

26 ________
27 ________
28 ________
29 ________
30 ________
31 ________
32 ________
33 ________
34 ________
35 ________
36 ________
37 ________
38 ________
39 ________
40 ________

☞ **Answers and explanations on pages 242–243**

CONVENTIONS OF LANGUAGE TEST 2
Advanced Level

The spelling mistakes in these sentences have been underlined. Write the correct spelling for each underlined word in each box.

41 He was proud to be made a member of the squadrin.

42 Grafiti should be legalised if it constitutes art.

43 Silently the burgular crept out of the sleeping home.

44 The family discovered asbestus in their ceiling.

45 Salvador Dali was well known for his etsentric behaviour and unusual moustache.

Each sentence has one word that is incorrect. Write the correct spelling of the word in the box.

46 The siloute of the trees resembled a scarecrow.

47 The holiday house overlooked the platoe.

48 An impressive manuvar secured first place for the driver.

49 She feared an asteroid could anialate mankind.

50 A deep and warm bath can be very therapyoutic.

☞ Answers and explanations on pages 242–243

NUMERACY TEST 2
Advanced Level

Section 1: Non-calculator questions

1 At the school's swimming carnival Heath broke the record for the 50-metres freestyle by 17 hundredths of a second. If the previous record was 27.14 seconds, which of these is the new record?

A 25.44 seconds B 26.7 seconds
C 26.93 seconds D 26.97 seconds
E 27.31 seconds

2 12 13 5 10 20

What is the mean of these five scores?

5	12	13	14	47
A	B	C	D	E

3 The mass of a dust particle is 0.007 68 milligrams. Which of these shows the mass in milligrams in scientific notation?

A 7.68×10^{-3} B 7.68×10^{-2}
C 7.68×10^{2} D 7.68×10^{3}

4 A bag contains red balls, blue balls and green balls in the ratio of 5 : 4 : 3. It is known that there are 12 green balls in the bag. If four balls of each colour are removed from the bag which of these is the new ratio of red to blue to green balls?

A 3 : 2 : 1 B 4 : 3 : 2
C 3 : 3 : 2 D 5 : 4 : 3

5 Which of these is arranged in order from smallest to largest?

A $\sqrt{0.25}$, $(0.3)^2$, 0.4 B 0.4, $(0.3)^2$, $\sqrt{0.25}$

C 0.4, $\sqrt{0.25}$, $(0.3)^2$ D $(0.3)^2$, 0.4, $\sqrt{0.25}$

6 Raymond purchased 4.8 kg of flour to make bread. He used three-quarters of the flour to make 5 loaves of bread. What mass of flour was used to make each loaf of bread?

☐ kg

7 Steve had 60 golf balls. He gave two-fifths of the balls to Kate. Steve then gave half of his remaining balls to Daniel.
How many more balls did Kate receive than Daniel?

8 It is given that 1! = 1, 2! = 2 × 1 = 2, 3! = 3 × 2 × 1 = 6, and so on.
What is the value of 8! ÷ 5!? ☐

This is the end of the part where you are not allowed to use a calculator. It would be a good idea to check your answers to the questions in this section before moving on to the other questions.

Section 2: Calculator Allowed questions

9 What is the area of the shape?

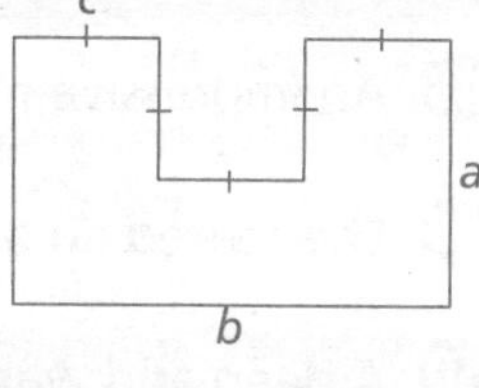

A $(a - c) \times (b - 2c)$
B $(a \times c) - (5 \times c)$
C $(a \times b) - (c \times c)$
D $(a + c) \times (b + 2c)$

10 A household's water bill showed that the household uses an average of 590 litres of water per day. If there are three people living in the home, what calculation is used to find the number of kilolitres used per week by each person?

A 590 ÷ 3 × 7 ÷ 1000 B 590 × 3 × 7 ÷ 1000
C 590 ÷ 3 ÷ 7 × 1000 D 590 ÷ 3 × 7 × 1000

11 ? multiplied by 6 plus 8 equals 32.
What is the number? ☐

12 A straight line can be drawn through the points (6, 2) and (14, 6). What is the equation of the line?

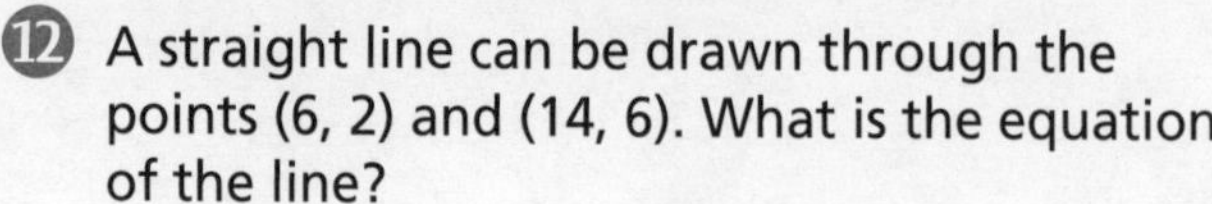

A $y = x - 4$ B $y = x - 8$
C $y = \frac{1}{2}x + 1$ D $y = \frac{1}{2}x - 1$

☞ Answers and explanations on pages 244–248

NUMERACY TEST 2
Advanced Level

13 Scott spins the arrow 120 times and records the results in a table. Which of the following tables is most likely to show his results?

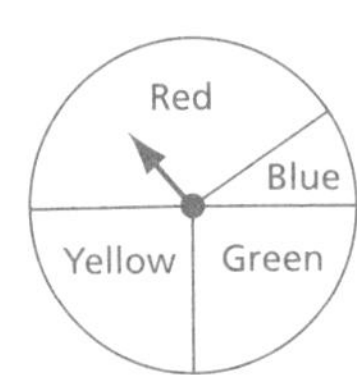

A

Colour	Number of spins
Yellow	30
Red	50
Blue	10
Green	30

B

Colour	Number of spins
Yellow	30
Red	10
Blue	50
Green	30

C

Colour	Number of spins
Yellow	30
Red	30
Blue	30
Green	30

D

Colour	Number of spins
Yellow	20
Red	60
Blue	20
Green	20

14 A family consists of three children. There are 8 possible combinations of boys and girls. What is the probability of a family consisting of 2 boys and a girl in any order?

A $\frac{1}{3}$ B $\frac{2}{3}$ C $\frac{3}{8}$ D $\frac{1}{8}$

15 The co-ordinates of point P are (–2, –1). PQ is parallel to the *y*-axis.

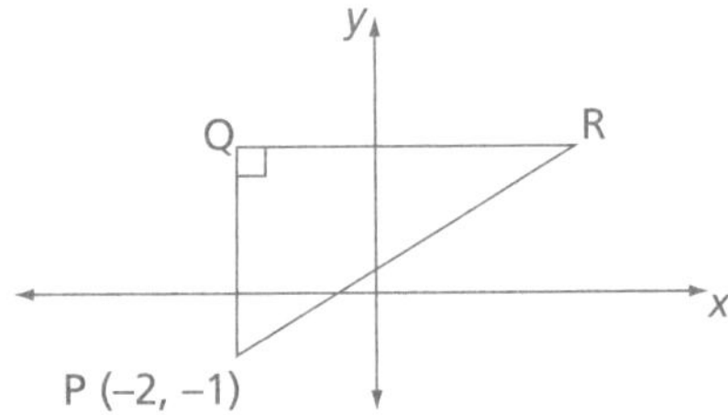

If PQ = 3 units, QR = 4 units and PR = 5 units, what are the co-ordinates of point R?

A (3, 3) B (2, 2) C (2, 3) D (3, 2)

16 Julia has some wooden blocks like the one shown.

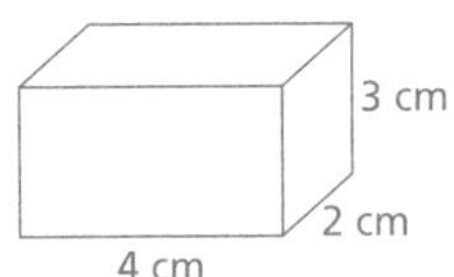

She uses some of the blocks to make a cube. What is the smallest number of blocks that can form a cube?

Write your answer in the box. ☐

It would be a good idea to check your answers to questions 9 to 16 before moving on to the other questions.

---

17 A vertical cut is made with a knife all the way through a sphere, as shown. Which shape shows the cross-section?

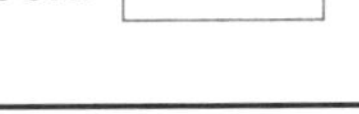

A ▭ B ⬭ C ○ D △

18 Michael wrote the following number sentences, where

☐ is greater than △,

☐ times △ equals 6, and

☐ plus △ equals –5.

What are the values of the shapes?

☐ = _______ and △ = _______

19 

The diagram shows the points at which equally spaced fence posts A, B C, D, E and F are placed on a fence. The length of AD is 12 m. What is the length of BF?

A 10 m B 12 m C 16 m D 18 m

☞ Answers and explanations on pages 244–248

NUMERACY TEST 2
Advanced Level

20 A square is to be covered with black tiles. One tile is already placed. How many more tiles are needed to fill the square?

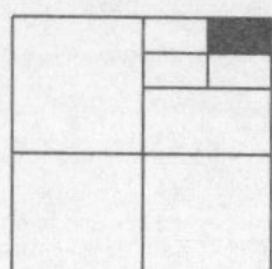

☐ more tiles

21 $3(2x + 3) - x + 1 =$

A $5x + 10$ B $5x + 4$
C $5x + 8$ D 13

22 The diameter of a one-dollar coin is 25 mm. Class 9R4 is fundraising and gets donations to make a line of one-dollar coins. Which calculation is used to find the total number of one-dollar coins in a 10-metre line?

A 10×0.025 B $10\,000 \times 0.25$
C $10 \div 0.025$ D $10\,000 \div 0.25$

23 What is the value of $x°$?

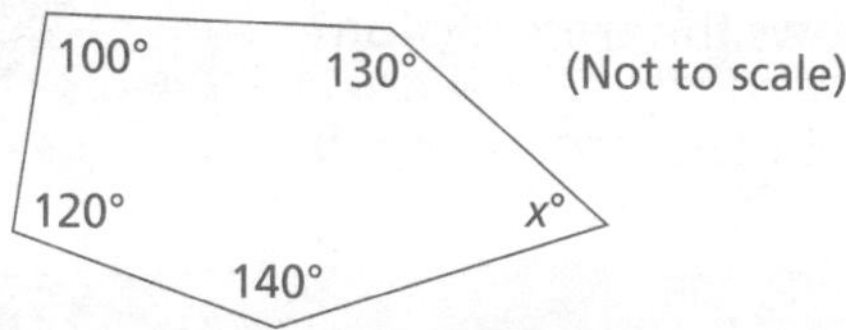

A 50 B 60 C 70 D 80

24 Lim made this pattern of rectangles using matches.

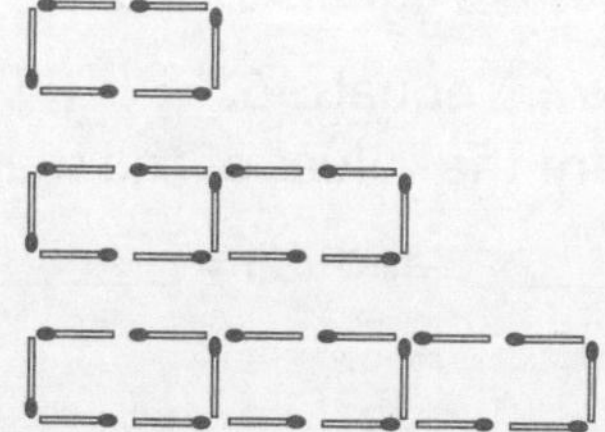

What is the rule used for the number of rectangles and the number of matches?

A number of matches = 6 × number of rectangles
B number of matches = 5 × number of rectangles – 1
C number of matches = 5 × number of rectangles + 1
D number of matches = 6 × number of rectangles – 1

25 A bag contains yellow, pink and purple counters. It is known that

- $\frac{1}{3}$ of the counters are pink; and
- $\frac{1}{6}$ of the counters are purple.

If there are 12 yellow counters, how many of the counters are pink?

3	4	6	8	12
A	B	C	D	E

26 Cans of soft drink can be purchased in packs of 4 and 6.

Packs of 4
$2.40

Packs of 6
$3.20

Imran and Kate went to the shop to buy 24 cans of the soft drink each. Imran buys packs of 4 while Kate buys packs of 6. What is the difference in the amounts paid?

A $1.20 B $1.60 C $2.40 D $3.20

27 The surface area, S, of a cylinder is given by $S = 2\pi r(r + h)$, where r is the radius and h is the height in centimetres. When $r = 5$ and $h = 15$, the surface area of the cylinder is closest to

A 51 cm^2. B 172 cm^2.
C 486 cm^2. D 628 cm^2.

28 Renai wrote these two equations.

$b = 2a - 3$
$b = 3a + 1$

Which value of a satisfies both of Renai's equations?

A $a = -4$ B $a = -1$
C $a = 1$ D $a = 4$

29 Craig is a fireman and uses a formula relating water pressure, force and an area.

The formula is $P = \frac{F}{A}$, where P = pressure, F = force and A = area. What is the area if the pressure is 24 and the force is 6?

A 4 B 0.25 C 144 D 18

☞ **Answers and explanations on pages 244–248**

30 The map shows a cycle path through a Botanical Garden.

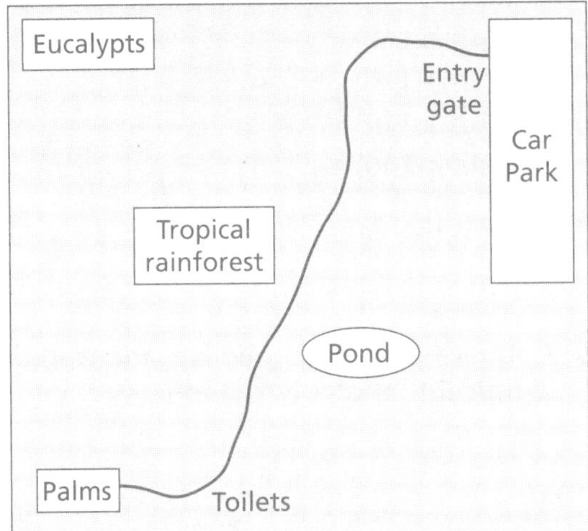

The scale used on the map is 1 cm = 400 m. Phil rides his bike from the Entry Gate to the Palms. If he rides at an average speed of 12 kilometres per hour, what is the best estimate of the time the journey will take Phil?

A 2 minutes B 10 minutes
C 15 minutes D 45 minutes

31 Max wrote this formula $P = 8m - 8500$.

What is the value of m if P is 1500?

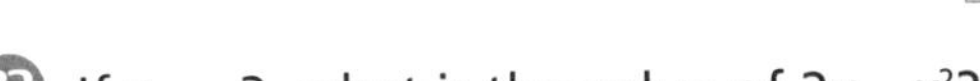

32 If $x = -3$, what is the value of $2x - x^2$?

A −15 B −10
C 3 D 12

It would be a good idea to check your answers to questions 17 to 32 before moving on to the other questions.

---

33 The rectangle has an area of 12 square units.

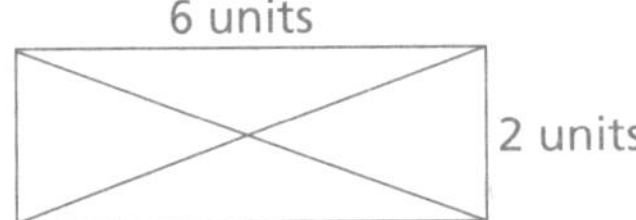

The shaded triangle is removed. What is the area of the remaining shape?

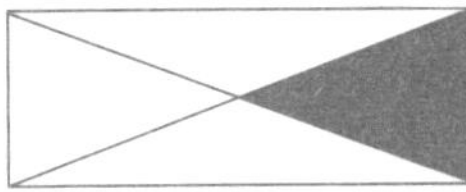

square units

34 A school yard has 4 trees. Tree A is

- 6 times the height of tree B
- 2 times the height of tree C
- 12 times the height of tree D.

How many times taller is tree C than tree D?

35 Neville made up this series of formulae.

$$B = A + \frac{A}{10} \qquad C = B + \frac{B}{10} \qquad D = C + \frac{C}{10}$$

If $A = 2000$, what is the value of D?

Write your answer in the box.

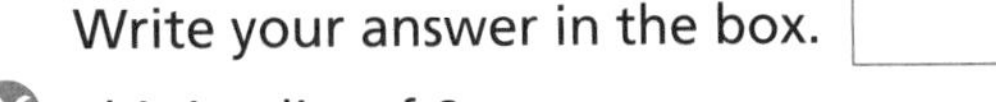

36 This is a list of 6 scores.

2 7 7 7 8 9

If the score of 2 is removed from the list what will change?

A the mode and the range
B the mean and the median
C the range and the mean
D the mode and the median

37 ABGH, BCFG and CDEF are identical squares.

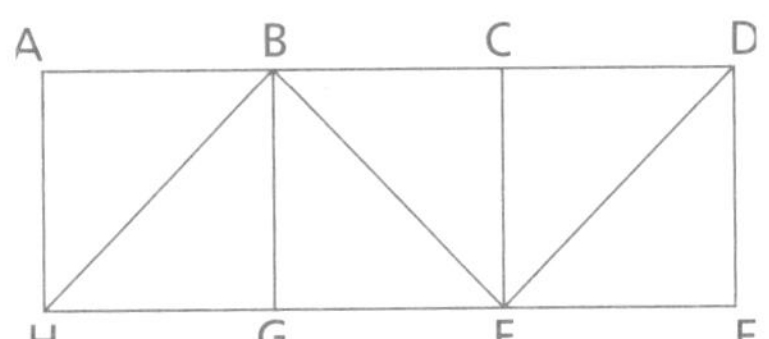

The area of triangle BFH is:

A one-half the area of rectangle ADEH
B one-third the area of rectangle ADEH
C two-thirds the area of rectangle ADEH
D one-sixth the area of rectangle ADEH

38 Tran drew a semi-circle. The diameter of the semi-circle is 10 cm. The perimeter of Tran's semi-circle is closest to

A 16 cm. B 20 cm. C 26 cm. D 36 cm.

39 There were 24 people at a party. The ratio of girls to boys at a party was 3:5. Later 3 girls arrived and 3 boys left the party. What is the new ratio of girls to boys?

☞ Answers and explanations on pages 244–248

40 The diagram shows a rectangle measuring 8 cm by 4 cm.

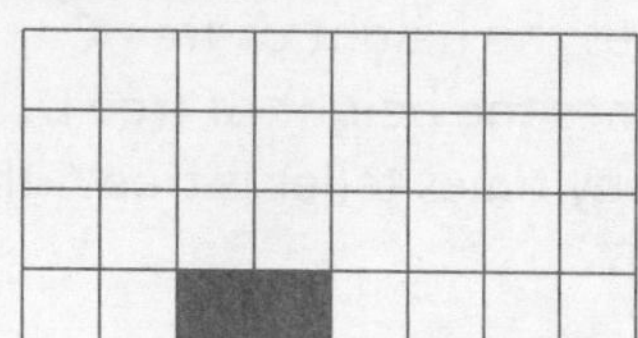

Aaron enlarges the rectangle as much as possible so that the image still fits on the grid. What are the dimensions of the image?

☐ cm by ☐ cm

41 It costs \$1.50 to park in a car park. Each driver pays the exact amount to park. The ticket machine accepts only \$1.00 and 50 cent coins. The table shows the coins that were put into the coin in one day.

\$1 coins	50 cent coins
200	350

What percentage of the drivers paid with three 50-cent coins?

A 20% B 25% C 30% D 40%

42 A rectangle is drawn inside a regular hexagon.

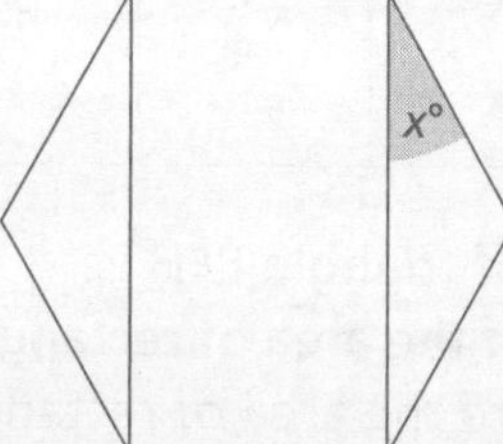

Find the value of x.

Write your answer in the box. ☐

43 Lilley plays basketball for the school. After p games, Lilley's average number of points per game is q. After another t games her average increases to w. How many points does Lilley score throughout the entire season?

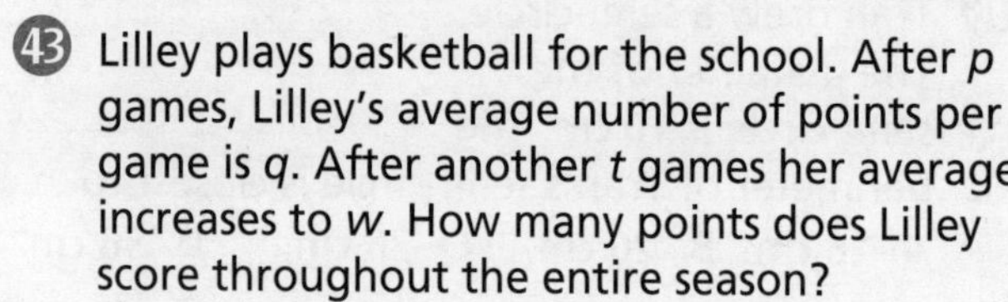

Write your answer in the box. ☐

44 Four friends earned money by picking strawberries. Olivia earned \$$n$, Cooper earned \$20 more than twice as much as Olivia earned. Jack earned \$60 more than Cooper. Mia earned half as much as Jack.

Which expression represents the total amount of money earned by the four friends?

A \$$4n$
B \$$(4n + 140)$
C \$$(5n + 110)$
D \$$(6n + 110)$
E \$$(6n + 140)$

45 What is the value of x if $\frac{2x}{3} + 1 = x + 3$?

$x =$ ☐

46 A square-based pyramid is made from four identical triangles and a square.

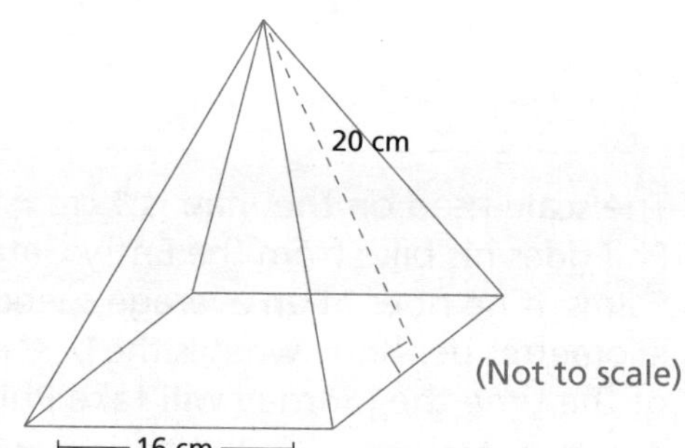

What is the total surface area of the five faces of the pyramid in total?

☐ cm^2

47 An electrical store has a set of headphones priced at \$240.
Ella buys the headphones at a 20% discount sale. She uses a \$50 gift voucher as well as cash to purchase the headphones. What percentage of the original price did Ella pay in cash? Give your answer correct to one decimal place.

☐

48 There are twice as many children as adults at an end-of-year concert for the local dance studio. A child ticket costs \$20 and an adult ticket costs \$30. If ticket sales totalled \$5250, how many tickets in total were sold?

☐

☞ **Answers and explanations on pages 244–248**

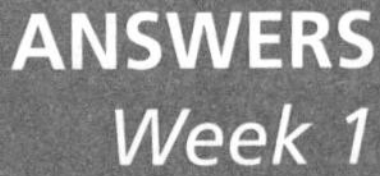

WEEK 1

NUMBER AND ALGEBRA (Test Your Skills)
Whole numbers Page 2

1. $141 \div 4 = 35$ and the remainder is 1.
2. Factors of 18: 1, 2, 3, 6, 9, 18
   Factors of 28: 1, 2, 4, 7, 14, 28
   The highest common factor is 2.
3. Primes: 2, 3, 5, 7, 11, 13, 17, 19
   This means 8 primes less than 20.
4. A multiple of 3 has a sum of digits that is a multiple of 3: For 75, $7 + 5 = 12$
   This means 75 is multiple of 3.
5. As $2 \times 2 \times 2 \times 2 \times 2 \times 2 = 64$
   $= 2^6$
6. $2^3 \times 3^2 = 8 \times 9$
   $= 72$
7. As $4^2 = 16$ and $5^2 = 25$, then $(4\frac{1}{2})^2$ is between 16 and 25.
8. $2^5 = 2 \times 2 \times 2 \times 2 \times 2$
   $= 32$
9. $\sqrt{100} + \sqrt{121} = 10 + 11$
   $= 21$
10. $4 \times 3^2 = 4 \times 9$
    $= 36$
11. $\sqrt{3^2 + 4^2} = \sqrt{9 + 16}$
    $= \sqrt{25}$
    $= 25$
12. As 48 is close to 49 and $\sqrt{49} = 7$, then $\sqrt{48}$ is closest to 7.
13. $-5 - 3 + 8 = -8 + 8$
    $= 0$
14. As $-7 + 17 = 10$, missing number is 17.
15. $-4 + (-2) + 8 = -4 - 2 + 8$
    $= -6 + 8$
    $= 2$
16. $(-4)^2 = -4 \times -4$
    $= 16$
17. As $-24 \div (-4) = 6$, missing number is -24.
18. $(-1) \times (-1) \times (-1) \times (-1) \times (-1) = -1$
19. $15 - 6 \times 2 = 15 - 12$
    $= 3$
20. $3 - (2 - 4) = 3 - (-2)$
    $= 3 + 2$
    $= 5$
21. $9 + 2 \times 0 \times 5 = 9 + 0$
    $= 9$
22. $24 \div (4 \times 2) = 24 \div 8$
    $= 3$
23. $(1 + 1) \times (1 + 1) = 2 \times 2$
    $= 4$
24. $\dfrac{4 + 6}{2 + 3} = \dfrac{10}{5}$
    $= 2$
25. $3\,450\,000 = 3.45 \times 1\,000\,000$
    $= 3.45 \times 10^6$
26. Halfway $= \dfrac{56 + 74}{2}$
    $= \dfrac{130}{2}$
    $= 65$
27. Average $= \dfrac{7 + 23 + 30}{3}$
    $= \dfrac{60}{3}$
    $= 20$
28. The middle number = 4
    The total of 2 numbers = 8
    This means 1 plus 'a number' = 8
    The missing number is 7.

NUMBER AND ALGEBRA (Real Test)
Whole numbers Page 5

1 C 2 C 3 29 4 A 5 D, C, E, A, B 6 A 7 D 8 A 9 C 10 B 11 D 12 C 13 B 14 D 15 B 16 C

EXPLANATIONS

1. $52 \div 6 = 8$ and the remainder is 4.
2. Light A flashes after 3, 6, 9, 12, 15, …
   Light B flashes after 4, 8, 12, 16, …
   This means they flashed together after 12 seconds, which means that A flashed at 3 sec, 6 sec, 9 sec: this means 3 times.
3. The next prime is 29.

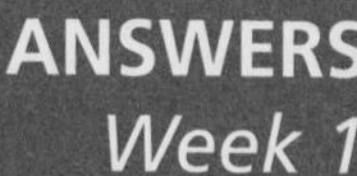

4 $4^2 = 16$ and $2^4 = 16$

5 $3^3 = 3 \times 3 \times 3 = 27$
$2^5 = 2 \times 2 \times 2 \times 2 \times 2 = 32$
$3^2 = 3 \times 3 = 9$
$2^3 = 2 \times 2 \times 2 = 8$
$4^2 = 4 \times 4 = 16$

6 $3^2 + 2^4 = 9 + 16$
$= 25$
$= 5^2$

7 As $9^2 = 81$ and $10^2 = 100$, Bridgett's number is between 9 and 10.

8 $4 + 5 \times 6 = 4 + 30$
$= 34$

9 $4 \times 2 - 12 \div 6$

10 $\sqrt{1 + 3 + 5} = \sqrt{9}$
$= 3$

11 The number was 60.

12 $4^2 - 4^0 = 16 - 1$
$= 15$

13 $-3 + 8 - 4 = 1$. This means 1°.

14 Middle $= \dfrac{-8 + 6}{2}$
$= \dfrac{-2}{2}$
$= -1$

15 Arrow points to -2.
$-2 + 6 - 4 - 1 + 2 = 1$

16 270 million $= 270 \times 1\,000\,000$
$= 2.7 \times 100\,000\,000$
$= 2.7 \times 10^8$

NUMBER AND ALGEBRA (Test Your Skills)
Fractions and decimals — Page 6

1 $\dfrac{29}{4} = 7\dfrac{1}{4}$

2 $2\dfrac{5}{9} = \dfrac{23}{9}$

3 $2\dfrac{4}{6} = 2\dfrac{2}{3}$

4 Change each to the same denominator:
$\dfrac{3}{4} = \dfrac{9}{12}$; $\dfrac{5}{6} = \dfrac{10}{12}$; $\dfrac{2}{3} = \dfrac{8}{12}$; $\dfrac{7}{12}$

the largest fraction is $\dfrac{5}{6}$.

5 As $1\dfrac{2}{5} = \dfrac{7}{5}$, the reciprocal is $\dfrac{5}{7}$.

6 First, change 2 hours = 120 minutes
$\dfrac{20}{120} = \dfrac{1}{6}$

7 As $\dfrac{1}{2} = \dfrac{3}{6}$ and $\dfrac{1}{3} = \dfrac{2}{6}$, then
$\dfrac{1}{2} + \dfrac{1}{3} = \dfrac{3}{6} + \dfrac{2}{6}$
$= \dfrac{5}{6}$

8 As $\dfrac{1}{4} = \dfrac{3}{12}$ and $\dfrac{2}{3} = \dfrac{8}{12}$, then
$2\dfrac{1}{4} + 3\dfrac{2}{3} = 2\dfrac{3}{12} + 3\dfrac{8}{12}$
$= 5\dfrac{11}{12}$

9 As $\dfrac{1}{2} = \dfrac{5}{10}$ and $\dfrac{2}{5} = \dfrac{4}{10}$, then
$\dfrac{1}{2} - \dfrac{2}{5} = \dfrac{5}{10} - \dfrac{4}{10}$
$= \dfrac{1}{10}$

10 $\dfrac{3}{4}$ of $36 = 36 \div 4 \times 3$
$= 27$

11 $2\dfrac{1}{2}^2 = 2\dfrac{1}{2} \times 2\dfrac{1}{2}$
$= \dfrac{5}{2} \times \dfrac{5}{2}$
$= \dfrac{25}{4}$
$= 6\dfrac{1}{4}$

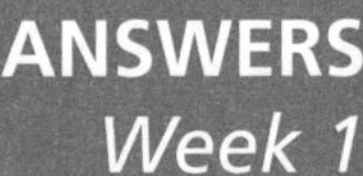

12 $\frac{2}{3}$ of $24 = 24 \div 3 \times 2$
$= 16$
Now as $16 + 2 = 18$,
Number with blonde hair $= 24 - 18$
$= 6$

Fraction with blonde hair $= \frac{6}{24} = \frac{1}{4}$

13 $\frac{10}{21} \div \frac{5}{6} = \frac{{}^{2}\cancel{10}}{{}^{7}\cancel{21}} \times \frac{\cancel{6}^{2}}{\cancel{5}^{1}}$
$= \frac{4}{7}$

14 Number of quarters in $8 = 8 \div \frac{1}{4}$
$= 8 \times 4$
$= 32$

15 As $\frac{2}{3} = 0.666...$, $4\frac{2}{3} \approx 4.667$

16 Smallest is the negative number –0.4.

17 $0.63 + 1.20 = 1.83$

18 $4.00 - 1.07 = 3.00 - 0.07$
$= 2.93$

19 $0.11 \times 0.11 = 0.0121$
$= 0.01$ (2 decimal places)

20 $4 - 0.3 \times 0.4 = 4 - 0.12$
$= 4.00 - 0.12$
$= 3.88$

21 Average $= \frac{0.3 + 0.6 + 1.5}{3}$
$= \frac{2.4}{3}$
$= 0.8$

NUMBER AND ALGEBRA (Real Test)
Fractions and decimals Page 8

1 A 2 C 3 B 4 D 5 C 6 D 7 C 8 A 9 B 10 B
11 D 12 B 13 A 14 D 15 1.4 16 A, D, B, C

EXPLANATIONS

1 $3\frac{4}{5} = \frac{19}{5}$

2 $\frac{23}{3} = 7\frac{2}{3}$

3 As 8 times 6 is 48, then 3 times 6 is 18.
The triangle is 18.

4 $\frac{3}{5} + \frac{1}{3} = \frac{9}{15} + \frac{5}{15}$
$= \frac{14}{15}$

5 $3\frac{3}{4} + \frac{1}{3} = 3 + \frac{9}{12} + \frac{4}{12}$
$= 3 + \frac{13}{12}$
$= 3 + 1 + \frac{1}{12}$
$= 4\frac{1}{12}$

6 $2 - \left(\frac{1}{2} - \frac{1}{4}\right) = 2 - \left(\frac{2}{4} - \frac{1}{4}\right)$
$= 2 - \frac{1}{4}$
$= 1\frac{3}{4}$

7 As $4 \times 60 = 240$,
then 4 hours = 240 minutes.
$\frac{2}{3}$ of $240 = 240 \div 3 \times 2$
$= 160$
Now 160 minutes = 2 hours 40 minutes.

8 Missing number $= \frac{1}{2} \div \frac{3}{4}$
$= \frac{1}{{}_{1}\cancel{2}} \times \frac{\cancel{4}^{2}}{3}$
$= \frac{2}{3}$

9 As $30 - 24 = 6$,
Fraction $= \frac{6}{30} = \frac{1}{5}$

10 As $\frac{1}{4} = \frac{6}{24}$ and $\frac{1}{3} = \frac{8}{24}$,
then the middle is $\frac{7}{24}$.

11 As $\frac{11}{8} = 1\frac{3}{8}$, the error is in Line 4.

12 Firstly, $\frac{3}{5} = 0.6$ and $\frac{1}{2} = 0.5$,
then $\frac{3}{5} + \frac{1}{2} = 0.6 + 0.5$
$= 1.1$

13 As $23 \times 8 = 184$, then
$2.3 \times 0.08 = 0.184$

14 $\frac{3 - 1.4}{0.2} = \frac{3.0 - 1.4}{0.2}$
$= \frac{1.6}{0.2}$
$= 16 \div 2$
$= 8$

15 $5.2 - 3.8 = 5.2 - 3 - 0.8$
$= 2.2 - 0.8$
$= 1.4$

16 $2.4 \div 0.3 = 24 \div 3$
$= 8$
$2.4 - 0.3 = 2.1$
$2.4 \times 0.3 = 0.72$
$2.4 + 0.3 = 2.7$
From largest to smallest the order is A, D, B, C.

NUMBER AND ALGEBRA (Test Your Skills)
Percentages Page 9

1 $\frac{4}{5} = \frac{80}{100}$ $\therefore$ 80%

2 As $\frac{18}{24} = \frac{3}{4}$, then $\frac{3}{4} \times \frac{100}{1} = 75$ $\therefore$ 75%

3 First \$2 = 200 cents.
Now, $\frac{50}{200} = \frac{1}{4}$, then $\frac{1}{4} \times \frac{100}{1} = 25$ $\therefore$ 25%

4 6 out of 8 unshaded.
Now, $\frac{6}{8} = \frac{3}{4}$, then $\frac{3}{4} \times \frac{100}{1} = 75$ $\therefore$ 75%

5 As 2 = 200% and
$\frac{4}{5} = \frac{80}{100} = 80\%$, then $2\frac{4}{5} = 280\%$

6 $\frac{3}{4}$ of the circle is shaded.
This means 75% of the circle is shaded.

7 $\frac{18}{40} = \frac{9}{20}$, $\frac{9}{20} \times \frac{100}{1} = 45\%$
$\frac{45}{100} = 45\%$
$\frac{9}{20} = 45\%$
$\frac{4}{5} = 80\%$
This means $\frac{4}{5}$ is not 45%.

8 Total $= 4 + 9 + 5 + 2$
$= 20$
Fraction read 2 books $= \frac{5}{20} = \frac{1}{4}$
Percentage $= \frac{1}{4} \times \frac{100}{1}$
$= 25$ $\therefore$ 25%

9 Fraction $= \frac{8}{40} = \frac{1}{5}$
Percentage $= \frac{1}{5} \times 100$
$= 20$ $\therefore$ 20%

10 Change each to decimals:
$\frac{2}{5} = 0.40$, 0.30, 31% = 0.31, 0.08
The largest is 0.40, or $\frac{2}{5}$.

11 As 1 hour = 60 minutes,
Fraction $= \frac{15}{60} = \frac{1}{4}$
Percentage $= \frac{1}{4} \times 100$
$= 25$ $\therefore$ 25%

12 As 20% is $\frac{1}{5}$, $\frac{1}{5} \times 50 = 10$

13 As 10% is $\frac{1}{10}$, $\frac{1}{10} \times 200 = 20$ $\therefore$ \$20

14 As 15% is 0.15, $0.15 \times 200 = 30$

15 As 50% is $\frac{1}{2}$, $\frac{1}{2} \times 150 = 75$ $\therefore$ \$75

16 As there are 10 squares, 60% is 6 out of 10. Wendy needs to shade another 4 squares.

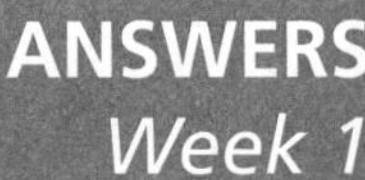

17 As 10% is $\frac{1}{10}$, $\frac{1}{10} \times 80 = 8$

New amount $= \$80 + \$8$
$= \$88$

18 By counting, there are 20 squares.

$80\% = \frac{4}{5} = \frac{16}{20}$

This means that 16 squares are shaded, and 4 squares remain unshaded.

19 As 10% is $\frac{1}{10}$, $\frac{1}{10} \times 70 = 7$, and 20% = 14

New amount $= \$70 + \$14$
$= \$84$

NUMBER AND ALGEBRA (Real Test)

Percentages Page 11

1 15 2 D 3 A 4 C 5 B 6 C 7 A 8 B 9 A 10 C
11 18 12 D 13 B 14 B 15 60 16 72

EXPLANATIONS

1 As 20 – 17 = 3, there are 3 oak trees.

Percentage $= \frac{3}{20} \times 100$
$= 15$ ∴ 15%

2 Percentage $= \frac{12}{25} \times 100$
$= 48$ ∴ 48%

3 As $20\% = \frac{1}{5}$, an estimate is:

60 000 ÷ 5 = 12 000
This means $12 000 is an estimate.

4 As 10% is $\frac{1}{10}$, $\frac{1}{10} \times 140 = 14$

Now, add: 140 + 14 = 154
Height = 154 cm

5 Savings = 80 – 72
= 8

Percentage $= \frac{8}{80} = \frac{1}{10}$ ∴ 10%

6 The water is 1 metre deep on the 4 metre post.

As $\frac{1}{4} = 25\%$, then 75% of the post is out of water.

7 As 40% replied,

$40\% = \frac{40}{100} = \frac{2}{5}$

Number of replies $= \frac{2}{5} \times 15$
$= 6$

As replied to 6, Dorothy did not reply to 9.

8 Simple interest $= 2000 \times 0.04 \times 3$
$= 240$

This means Logan earns interest of $240.

9 Finding 5% and then adding on to the original is the same as 5% + 100% = 105%
As 105% = 1.05, then the calculation is 45 × 1.05.

10 New height = 120% of 30
$= 1.20 \times 30$
$= 36$ ∴ 36 cm

Or, as $20\% = \frac{1}{5}$,

Growth $= \frac{1}{5}$ of 30
$= 6$

New height is 30 + 6 = 36 cm

11 Fraction $= \frac{180}{1000} = \frac{18}{100}$, or 18%

12 As 8 + 3 + 4 + 6 = 21,
Number of blue = 24 – 21
= 3

After eating 4 pink, there are 20 left.

Percentage that are blue $= \frac{3}{20} \times 100$
$= 15$

∴ this means 15% are blue.

13 Games not won = 16 – 12
= 4

Percentage not won $= \frac{4}{16} \times 100$ ∴ 25%

14 The cost will be found by subtracting 15% of \$9.90 from \$9.90.
Using 15% as 0.15, the calculation is
$9.9 - 0.15 \times 9.9$.

15 As 20% = $\frac{20}{100} = \frac{1}{5}$,

Pages read night 1 = $\frac{1}{5} \times 100$
$= 20$

This leaves 80 pages.

As 25% = $\frac{25}{100} = \frac{1}{4}$,

Pages read night 2 = $\frac{1}{4} \times 80$
$= 20$

This leaves 60 pages.

16 As 25% = $\frac{25}{100} = \frac{1}{4}$,

Discount $= \frac{1}{4} \times 96$
$= 24$

New price $= 96 - 24$
$= 72 \therefore \$72$

NUMBER AND ALGEBRA (Test Your Skills)
Chance, rates and ratio Page 12

1 There are 5 numbers less than 6.
P(less than 6) = $\frac{5}{6}$

2 Odd numbers = 1, 3, 5, 7, 9

P(odd) = $\frac{5}{9}$

3 As 25% = $\frac{1}{4}$, then $\frac{3}{4}$ are not rotten.
This means P(not rotten) = $\frac{3}{4}$, or 3 in 4.

4 As P(red) = $\frac{2}{3}$, then
Number of red balls $= \frac{2}{3} \times 24$
$= 24 \div 3 \times 2$
$= 16$

$\therefore$ 16 red balls.

5 There are 6 lots of 10 seconds in a minute.
Number of drips $= 6 \times 3$
$= 18 \therefore 18$ drips

6 Distance = Speed × Time
$= 63 \times 3$
$= 189 \quad \therefore 189$ km

7 Speed = Distance ÷ Time
$= 108 \div 4$
$= 27 \quad \therefore 27$ km/h

8 Time = Distance ÷ Speed
$= 60 \div 15$
$= 4 \quad \therefore 4$ hours

9 Time = Distance ÷ Speed
$= 200 \div 40$
$= 5$
Therefore X = 5.

10 Speed = Distance ÷ Time
$= 180 \div 2$
$= 90$
$\therefore Y = 90$.

11 Distance = Speed × Time
$= 10 \times 45$
$= 450$
$\therefore Z = 450$.

12 Total pay for 4 weeks $= 15 \times 4$
$= 60$

Casey is paid a total of \$60.
This means she saves \$30.

13 As $350 \div 100 = 3.5$, then there are 3.5 lots of 100 km.
Number of litres $= 3.5 \times 8$
$= 28 \quad \therefore 28$ litres

14 Cost $= 0.60 \times 40$
$= 24.00$
This means the cost is \$24.

15 As 2 + 3 = 5, Paul receives $\frac{3}{5}$ of \$200

Amount = $\frac{3}{5} \times 200$
$= 200 \div 5 \times 3$
$= 120$

$\therefore$ Paul receives \$120.

16 3 parts = 36
1 part = 36 ÷ 3
= 12
4 parts = 12 × 4
= 48
∴ there are 48 cats.

17 Total mass = 400 × 300
= 120 000
As 120 000 grams = 120 kg, the baker needs 120 kg of flour.

18 8 boys and 16 girls
Total number of students = 8 + 16
= 24
Ratio boys to total = 8:24
= 1:3
∴ the ratio is 1:3.

19 10:15 = 2:3 by dividing through by 5.

20 6 shaded and 6 unshaded
Ratio = 6:6
= 1:1

NUMBER AND ALGEBRA (Real Test)
Chance, rates and ratio Page 14

1 A 2 D 3 D 4 C 5 C 6 A 7 C 8 360 9 B 10 A
11 D 12 225 13 D 14 C 15 A 16 D

EXPLANATIONS

1 Number of green marbles = 40 – (8 + 12)
= 20

P(green marble) = $\frac{20}{40} = \frac{1}{2}$, or 1 in 2

2 There are 2 Es out of 9 letters.

P(E) = $\frac{2}{9}$, or 2 in 9

3 As 12 + 4 + 2 + 6 = 24, and there are 20 balls that are not blue, then

P(not blue)= $\frac{20}{24} = \frac{5}{6}$, or 5 in 6

4 As 12 + 18 = 30, then

P(boy) = $\frac{12}{30}$

= $\frac{2}{5}$

5 As 3 + 2 = 5, then

P(blue) = $\frac{2}{5}$

= 0.4

6 Total = 14 + 7 + 8 + 11
= 40

P(green) = $\frac{8}{40}$

= $\frac{1}{5}$

7 Using boy (B) and girl (G), the possible outcomes are BBB, BBG, BGB, BGG, GBB, GBG, GGB, GGG. There are 3 ways of having a girl and 2 boys. This means:

P(girl and 2 boys) = $\frac{3}{8}$, or 3 in 8.

8 Distance = Speed × Time

= $80 \times 4\frac{1}{2}$

= $80 \times 4 + 80 \times \frac{1}{2}$

= 320 + 40

= 360 ∴ 360 km

9 Distance in first 2 hours = 80 × 2
= 160
Distance in last 4 hours = 360 – 160
= 200
Bintang has to travel 200 km in 4 hours.
Speed in last 4 hours = 200 ÷ 4
= 50
Bintang travels at 50 km/h to complete journey.

10 Firstly, as 200 ÷ 100 = 2, Jack travels 2 lots of 100 km.
Also 129.9 cents = $1.299
Cost = 9 × 2 × 1.299

11 As 10 Litres = 10 × 1000 mL
= 10 000 mL,
Ratio of LawnKleen:Water = 10:10 000
= 1:1000

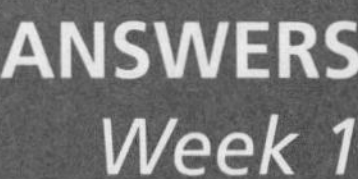

12 Firstly, $5 + 3 = 8$,

then $\frac{3}{8}$ of the population are children.

$$\begin{aligned}\text{Number of children} &= \frac{3}{8} \times 600 \\ &= 600 \div 8 \times 3 \\ &= 75 \times 3 \\ &= 225\end{aligned}$$

There are 225 children living in the town.

13
$$\begin{aligned}5 \text{ parts} &= 70 \\ 1 \text{ part} &= 70 \div 5 \\ &= 14 \\ 2 \text{ parts} &= 14 \times 2 \\ &= 28\end{aligned}$$

$\therefore$ there are 28 girls.

14 As $3 + 1 + 4 = 8$, then

$$\begin{aligned}\text{Mass of oranges} &= \frac{3}{8} \times 120 \\ &= 120 \div 8 \times 3 \\ &= 15 \times 3 \\ &= 45\end{aligned}$$

45 kg of oranges sold.

15 RU = 3 units, PS = 3 units

$$\begin{aligned}RU : PS &= 3:3 \\ &= 1:1\end{aligned}$$

16 As $3 + 2 = 5$, then

$$\begin{aligned}\text{Red balls} &= \frac{3}{5} \times 20 \\ &= 12\end{aligned}$$

This means there are 12 red balls and 8 blue balls. There needs to be 5 blue balls added to the bag so that there are more blue balls than red balls.

NUMBER AND ALGEBRA (Test Your Skills)
Using the calculator Page 15

1 $(12 - 6) \times (2 + 2) = 24$

2 $11 - 9 \div (6 - 3) = 8$

3
$$\begin{aligned}\frac{10 + 6}{2 + 2} &= (10 + 6) \div (2 + 2) \\ &= 4\end{aligned}$$

4
$$\begin{aligned}\frac{24}{4 + 2} &= 24 \div (4 + 2) \\ &= 4\end{aligned}$$

5
$$\begin{aligned}\frac{12 - 8}{2 + 6} &= (12 - 8) \div (2 + 6) \\ &= 0.5\end{aligned}$$

6
$$\begin{aligned}\sqrt{9 + 16} &= \sqrt{25} \\ &= 5\end{aligned}$$

7
$$\begin{aligned}\text{Average} &= (2 + 8 + 11 + 7) \div 4 \\ &= 7\end{aligned}$$

8
$$\begin{aligned}\text{Average} &= (0.3 + 4.5) \div 2 \\ &= 2.4\end{aligned}$$

9 $5 \div 8 \times 100 = 62.5$

$\therefore$ 62.5%

10 $\sqrt{441} = 21$

11 $\sqrt{12.96} = 3.6$

12
$$\begin{aligned}\text{Missing number} &= 85.2 \div 12 \\ &= 7.1\end{aligned}$$

13
$$\begin{aligned}\text{Missing number} &= 28 \div 11.2 \\ &= 2.5\end{aligned}$$

14 $2.3^2 = 5.29$

15
$$\begin{aligned}\sqrt{5^2 + 12^2} &= \sqrt{(5^2 + 12^2)} \\ &= 13\end{aligned}$$

16
$$\begin{aligned}3 - (-8) &= 3 + 8 \\ &= 11\end{aligned}$$

17 $\frac{18}{48} = \frac{3}{8}$

18 $\frac{23}{5} = 4\frac{3}{5}$

19 $\frac{4}{5} + \frac{3}{10} = 1.1$ [using $4 \div 5 + 3 \div 10 =$]

20 Middle = Average

$$\begin{aligned}&= \left(1\frac{1}{4} + 2\frac{3}{4}\right) \div 2 \\ &= 2\end{aligned}$$

[using $(1 + 1 \div 4 + 2 + 3 \div 4) \div 2$]

21 Average

$$\begin{aligned}&= \left(\frac{2}{5} + \frac{1}{4} + \frac{3}{4} + \frac{1}{2}\right) \div 4 \\ &= 0.475\end{aligned}$$

[using $(2 \div 5 + 1 \div 4 + 3 \div 4 + 1 \div 2) \div 4$]

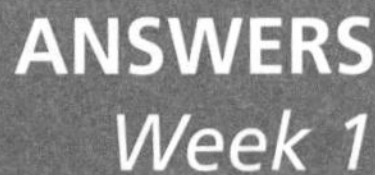

22 $4 \div \frac{2}{3} = 6$ [using $4 \div (2 \div 3) =$]

23 $2 \times \pi \times 6 = 37.699\ 111\ 84\ldots$
$= 37.70$ (2 decimal places)

24 $\pi \times 4^2 = 50.265\ 482\ 46\ldots$
$= 50.27$ (2 decimal places)

25 $\pi \times 5^2 \times 8 = 628.318\ 5307\ldots$
$= 628$ (nearest whole)

NUMBER AND ALGEBRA (Real Test)
Using the calculator Page 17

1 B 2 C 3 C 4 B 5 A 6 B 7 130 8 C 9 A 10 B
11 D 12 D 13 B 14 C 15 C, D 16 B

EXPLANATIONS

1 Population of Voss = 13 876 − 2941
= 10 935

2 Total distance $= 1\frac{3}{4} + 1\frac{3}{4}$
$= 3.5 = 3\frac{1}{2}$

3 Missing number $= 8 \div 18$
$= 0.\dot{4}$

4 Bottom number = Top number ÷ 4
$= 14 \div 4$
$= 3.5$

5 $260 - (160 + 50 + 25) = 25$

6 Answer $= 48 \times 0.93$
$= 44.64$

7 $180 - (25 + 25) = 130$

8 $\frac{\pi \times 3^2 \times 8}{5} = (\pi \times 32 \times 8) \div 5$
$= 45.238\ 934\ 21$
$= 45$ (nearest whole)

9 $\frac{6^2}{9 \times 4} = 6^2 \div (9 \times 4)$
$= 1$

10 Average $= (-6 + (-3) + 3) \div 3$
$= -2 \quad \therefore -2°$

11 Product $= (-4) \times (-5)$
$= 20$

12 As there are 3 lots of 4 in 12,
Mass of pumpkin $= 1\frac{3}{4} \times 3$
$= 5.25$
Fiona requires 5.25 kilograms.

13 As 27 − 12 is 15, then percentage not flown
$= \frac{15}{27} \times 100$
$= 55.555\ \ldots$
$= 56$ (nearest whole)
$\therefore$ 56% of people have not flown overseas.

14 Consider each of the choices:
$2^4 \times 5^2 \times 3 = 1200$
$2^4 \times 10^2 \times 5 = 8000$
$3^4 \times 5^2 \times 2 = 4050$
This is correct.

15 $x = 2$: As $\frac{2}{2} = 1$, then $1 < \frac{3}{5}$? No!
$x = 3$: As $\frac{2}{3} = \frac{10}{15}$ and $\frac{3}{5} = \frac{9}{15}$, then $\frac{2}{3} < \frac{3}{5}$? No!
$x = 4$: As $\frac{2}{4} = \frac{1}{2} = \frac{15}{30}$ and $\frac{3}{5} = \frac{18}{30}$, then $\frac{2}{4} < \frac{3}{5}$? Yes!
$x = 5$: $\frac{2}{5} < \frac{3}{5}$? Yes!
The possible values of x are 4 and 5.

16 As diameter is 6 metres, radius is 3 metres.
Area $= \pi r^2$
$= \pi \times 3^2$
$= 28.274\ 333\ 88\ldots$
which is close to 28 m^2.

SPELLING (REAL TEST)
Common misspellings Pages 20–21

1 accommodation

2 chemical

3 rhymes

4 temperature

ANSWERS
Week 1

5 Separate
6 chocolate
7 comfortable
8 movement
9 innovation
10 puppies
11 metaphors
12 ingredients
13 boxes
14 poverty
15 disease
16 Bureau
17 organisms
18 commitment
19 humorous
20 evaporation
21 consequences
22 propaganda
23 colleague
24 possession
25 miscellaneous

GRAMMAR AND PUNCTUATION (Real Test)
Types of nouns, adjectives, adverbs, verbs and participles Pages 24–26

1 A **2** A **3** C **4** C **5** D **6** A **7** D **8** A **9** C **10** B **11** C **12** B **13** B **14** D **15** A **16** B **17** A **18** B **19** D **20** B **21** C **22** B **23** C **24** B, D **25** A, C

EXPLANATIONS

1 This is a punctuation question. The correct sentence is: *Betty asked, 'Where are you going Jane?'*
Tip: Only the actual words spoken are enclosed in the quotation marks (inverted commas). The comma comes before the quotation marks and after the introductory clause.

2 This question is asking about language devices. The correct answer is *a simile*.
Tip: A simile is a figure of speech that compares two things using *like* or *as*.

3 This is a grammar question. The correct answer is *will discover*.
Tip: The future tense verb *will* suggests that an event is likely to occur. In this instance it is a discovery that will occur.

4 This is a grammar question. The correct word is the adjective *difficult*.
Tip: *Difficult* implies an activity that is too hard like the jump is for the children. *Far* and *long* suggest a distance to be covered which is incorrect in the context of this sentence. *Longest* is a degree of the adjective *long* and suggests that three or more things are being compared.

5 This is a grammar question. The correct word is the verb *wrote*.
Tip: *Wrote* is an irregular verb. Most verbs in English form their past tenses by adding *ed*. There are a number of irregular verbs when this doesn't happen. We say *wrote* instead of 'writed'.

6 This is a punctuation question. The correct sentence is: *Professor Harvey, the one with the grey hair, is my favourite*.
Tip: Commas are added to show a pause. The clause *the one with the grey hair* provides more information about Professor Harvey. This is an example of an adjectival clause.

7 This is a punctuation question. The correct sentence is: *'Get back here!' screamed Mum*.
Tip: Only the actual words spoken are enclosed in the quotation marks (inverted commas). There is no comma needed after the spoken words as an exclamation mark is used to complete the statement. A capital letter is not used at the start of the dialogue tag.

8 This is a punctuation question. The correct sentence is: *We need: five roses; six carnations; seven lilies and eight tulips.*
Tip: A colon (:) is used to indicate the introduction of a list. Semicolons are used to divide complex lists of items.

9 This is a punctuation question. The correct sentence is: *Disaster struck at 9.29 pm; the boat hit an iceberg.*
Tip: A semicolon is used to divide this sentence as it contains two separate and complete sentences that are closely related. A comma should not be used in this instance.

10 This is a grammar question. The correct sentence is: *James, who happens to be my brother, was the best performer in the play.*
Tip: The commas in this sentence come before and after the adjectival clause *who happens to be my brother*. An adjectival clause acts like an adjective as it adds more information to a noun.

11 This is a question asking about narrative voice. The correct answer is *third person*.
Tip: Third-person narrative is indicated by the use of *he*, *she*, *they* and also the names of characters. It does not include the pronouns *I* or *your*.

12 This is a question about figurative language. The correct answer is *a metaphor*.
Tip: A metaphor creates a direct comparison between two unlike things to create an effect. In this case, the writer is comparing the fear the responder feels to the impact of being physically struck in the heart.

13 This is a grammar question. The correct answer is *past tense*.
Tip: The tense of a text is indicated by the form that the verbs take. Look at the form of the verbs *saw* (past participle of *see*), *held* (past participle of *hold*) and *vanished* (past participle of *vanish*).

14 This is a grammar question. The correct answer is *would have gone*.
Tip: With the irregular verb *would* (past participle of *will*) you need a 'helper'—another verb to 'help' it. *Have*, *has* and *had* can be helping verbs. *Gone* is the past participle of *go*.

15 This is a grammar question. The correct word is the article *a*.
Tip: *A* is an article and precedes words beginning with consonant sounds.

16 This is a grammar question. The correct word is the adverb *lovingly*.
Tip: *Lovingly* is an adverb and adds meaning to the verb *looked* (*looked at the statue lovingly*). *Lovely* is an adjective.

17 This is a punctuation question. The correct sentence is: *Janet's father enjoys watching the horse races.*
Tip: *Janet* is a proper noun and has direct ownership of her father and this is shown through the use of the possessive apostrophe. *Enjoys* is the present tense form of the verb *enjoy* and *races* is the plural form of the noun *race*.

18 This is a grammar question. The correct contraction is *they'd*.
Tip: *They'd* requires an apostrophe because it is a contraction of *they had*.

19 This is a grammar question. The correct answer is *crashing.*
Tip: An adjective is a word used to describe nouns and pronouns. In this example the adjective *crashing* describes the waves.

20 This is a grammar question. The correct answer is *a verb*.
Tip: A verb is a word that indicates an action such as *deliberate*, *discuss* and *conspire*. The text suggests that Shakespeare undertakes the action of *crafting* his plays and poems.

21 This is a grammar question. The correct answer is *an adjective*.
Tip: An adjective is a word used to describe a place, person, event or thing. Here the adjective *frightening* is used to describe the character of Dracula.

22 This is a grammar question. The correct answer is *an abstract noun*.
Tip: An abstract noun is a thing that can be identified or felt but cannot be touched or held. Examples: *happiness*, *freedom*, *safety*. In the extract the word *inspiration* is a thing that Stoker experiences but cannot be held or touched.

23 This is a grammar question. The correct answer is *a verb*.
Tip: A verb is a word that indicates an action such as *deliberate*, *discuss* and *conspire*. In the text the verb *saw* indicates the main action of the sentence.

24 This is a grammar question. The correct answers are *Whether you feel like it or not* and *If you want to remain fit*.
Tip: These are dependent clauses and rely on the following independent clause to make sense.

25 This is a grammar question. The correct answers are *Whether you are a morning person or not* and *Even in the middle of winter*.
Tip: These are dependent clauses and rely on the following independent clause to make sense.

READING (Test Your Skills)
Understanding narratives Pages 27–28

The Lock Out

EXPLANATIONS

1 Jim began to panic. He was horrified—he had no clothes on.

2 Jim's greatest fear was being seen on his front veranda with no clothes on.

3 In paragraph 4, 'shadows moved in the streetlights' and Jim 'ran to the door, pushing and heaving'. At the beginning of paragraph 5 he 'cowered…'. In paragraph 6 Jim found 'himself walking on tip-toe' as he stepped on the lawn. In the last paragraph Jim finds the window 'locked'.

4 Jim is not being entirely logical—he was trying to be quiet. The grass was soft under his feet.

5 The image the author is creating is one of uncontrolled, ineffectual activity. Jim's thoughts were jumping all over the place.

6 The animal Jim swept up into his arms was his cat, which he hurriedly took outside.

7 As 'his eyes became accustomed to the dark' Jim realised the night wasn't as dark as he first supposed. He could quite easily be seen naked.

8 The description builds up an atmosphere of desperation and frustration because after the door shuts, Jim does not think clearly and tries unsuccessfully to get back into the house. He is astonished and tense and becomes frustrated and desperate. There is no sense of resignation nor has the situation escalated to an atmosphere of desolation.

9 The words Jim uses, especially 'Not there!', suggest the cat was about to make a mess of some sort and it would be better if it happened outside.

READING (Real Test)
Understanding narratives Pages 29–30

Angel's Gate extract

1 B **2** hesitant—game **3** D **4** C **5** written response **6** C **7** D **8** A **9** B, C: correct; A, D, E: incorrect

EXPLANATIONS

1 The cave's entrance was 'somewhere among its [fig tree's] roots, deep in the dark shadow of the ledge'.

2 Kim is hesitant about entering the cave, but still game enough to follow Bobby. He feels he 'had to go in, that was all there was to it'.

3 Bobby had gone in before Kim. To follow him, Kim had to crawl for about 20 metres.

4 When someone yawns their mouth is open wide. The author uses this as a metaphor to describe the entrance to the cave.

5 The main reason Kim went into the cave was because he felt an obligation to stick with Bobby because they had come this far together. (Even though he felt some fear, Kim felt compelled to go with Bobby, there was no other choice and 'that was all there was to it'.)

6 Kim had been feeling afraid for some time. Under such conditions it is a small step to fearing the worst. It is fairly clear that the boys hadn't been in the cave previously.

7 Kim spoke harshly to himself as a means of controlling his embarrassing fear and to give himself courage to carry on. Bobby had already entered the cave.

8 The bats appeared to vanish into the rock because the actual entrance to the cave was hidden.

9 The cave became 'brighter and brighter', not darker, and got bigger the further into the cave the boys went. After he 'crawled 20 metres', Kim was able to get to his feet and 'reach up to touch the roof'. Therefore, the boys were able to stand. The boys discovered the roof and floor 'must have collapsed at the same time'. The bats 'flitted in the void'. They were flying not roosting.

READING (Test Your Skills)
Understanding poetry Pages 31–32

Poem by Sheryl Persson

1 onomatopoeia, alliteration, personification 2 A 3 C 4 NO, YES, NO, NO, YES 5 D 6 B 7 A

EXPLANATIONS

1 Personification is attributing human qualities to non-human animals, objects or ideas. The poet personifies spring, giving it the human behaviour of gasping and swooning. Alliteration is the repetition of sounds to create an auditory effect. The alliteration of the soft 's' sound and the use of onomatopoeia in the words 'gasps' and 'swoons' mimic the sounds of a person gasping and fainting. Therefore, spring is personified.

2 In the metaphor 'shimmering lavender chandeliers', the poet compares the shape of the wisteria to hanging chandeliers.

3 The imagery created by the poem is one of a profusion of colour. Each couplet contains at least one colour.

4 'Chiffon' and 'wilt' are defined correctly. 'Plush' fabric is luxurious and thick but not coarse. 'Vermillion' is a deep, rich scarlet colour. To 'swoon' means to be overcome by something and faint.

5 The imagery the poet uses in 'Bougainvillea' recreates shapes of the flower dancing 'with summer' and draping itself like 'lace' over 'verandas'. 'Olfactory' refers to the sense of smell.

6 The focus of the poem is the flowers and as a fiesta is a celebration often associated with a parade, the title *Fiesta of Flowers* incorporates the meaning of the poem and its structure, as the stanzas are a parade of one flower after another.

7 The poet creates a celebratory feeling. There is a sense of praise, joy and wonder in the displays created by the flowers.

READING (Real Test)
Understanding narratives Pages 33–34

The Drover's Wife

1 D 2 A 3 written response 4 She is resourceful./Her life is one of hardship. 5 C 6 A 7 incorrect, correct, incorrect, incorrect, correct 8 C

EXPLANATIONS

1 The description of the location of the drover's home is one of isolation: 'Nineteen miles to the nearest sign of civilisation—a shanty on the main road'.

2 Tommy is a mere child. The snake is portrayed as cunning. He can have little understanding of what he intends to undertake.

3 The drover's wife was fearful the snake would get into the bedroom: 'she snatches up some ... bedclothes—expecting to see the snake any minute'.

4 The drover's wife seems to accept the hardship of her life with her husband absent but it is not a life of oppression or exploitation. To survive in the bush she is

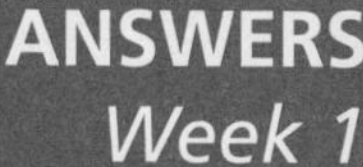

resourceful, making a bed for the children high up on the table fearing the snake may be in the bedroom. She is not lonely having her children to care for. The house is simple and so the family may be poor but she does not live in squalor.

5 Tommy is impulsive. He quickly gets a stick to kill the snake. A task he is not really up to. Tommy feels a strong need to support or help his mother—almost to be the man of the family.

6 Mood refers to the feeling or atmosphere that a writer creates for a reader—the drover's wife's life and location are harsh.

7 The two correct statements are: There are two separate buildings; A primary building material was bark. The home consisted of 'a two-roomed house' and a 'big bark kitchen …larger than the house itself'. The other statements are INCORRECT. Only the kitchen had a dirt, 'an earthen' floor. Floors in the other two rooms were 'rough slab' floors. It is not stated in the text that the veranda surrounds the whole house.

8 The oncoming of night increases the danger. The snake could still attack but it will be harder to see. The amount of light available is extremely limited. The wife will have to stay awake and alert.

WRITING (Real Test)
Persuasive text 1 — Page 39

Tick each correct point.
Read the student's work through once to get an overall view of their response.

Focus on general points

- ☐ Did it make sense?
- ☐ Did it flow? Were the arguments logical and relevant?
- ☐ Did the opinions expressed arouse any feelings/reactions?
- ☐ Was the body of the writing mainly in the third person?
- ☐ Did you want to read on to understand/appreciate the writer's point of view?
- ☐ Were the arguments convincing?
- ☐ Has the writer been assertive (e.g. the use of *is* rather than a less definite term)?
- ☐ Was the handwriting readable?
- ☐ Was the writing style suitable for a persuasive text (objective; not casual or dismissive)?

Now focus on the detail. Read each of the following points and find out whether the student's work has these features.

Focus on content

- ☐ Did the opening sentence(s) focus on the topic?
- ☐ Was the writer's point of view established early in the writing?
- ☐ Did the writer include any evidence to support his or her opinion?
- ☐ Did the writer include information relevant to his or her experiences?
- ☐ Were the points/arguments raised by the writer easy to follow?
- ☐ Did the writing follow the format with an introduction, the body of the text and a conclusion?
- ☐ Were personal opinions included?
- ☐ Was the concluding paragraph relevant to the topic?

Focus on structure, vocabulary, grammar, spelling, punctuation

- ☐ Was there a variety of sentence lengths, types and beginnings?
- ☐ Was a new paragraph started for each additional argument or point?
- ☐ Has the writer used any similes (e.g. *as clear as crystal*) to stress a point raised?
- ☐ Did the writer avoid approximations such as *probably, perhaps* and *maybe*?
- ☐ Did the writer use such phrases as *I know …* and *It is important to …*?
- ☐ Did the writer refer to the question in the points raised (A good way to do this is to use the key words from the question or the introduction.)?
- ☐ Has the writer used any less common words correctly?

- ☐ Was indirect speech used correctly?
- ☐ Were adjectives used to improve descriptions (e.g. *expensive buildings*)?
- ☐ Were adverbs used effectively (e.g. *firstly*)?
- ☐ Were capital letters used correctly?
- ☐ Was punctuation used correctly?
- ☐ Was the spelling of words correct?

Marker's suggestions (optional)

WRITING (Real Test)
Persuasive text 2 **Page 40**

Tick each correct point.
Read the student's work through once to get an overall view of their response.

Focus on general points

- ☐ Did it make sense?
- ☐ Did it flow? Were the arguments logical and relevant?
- ☐ Did the opinions expressed arouse any feelings/reactions?
- ☐ Was the body of the writing mainly in the third person?
- ☐ Did you want to read on to understand/ appreciate the writer's point of view?
- ☐ Were the arguments convincing?
- ☐ Has the writer been assertive (e.g. the use of *is* rather than a less definite term)?
- ☐ Was the handwriting readable?
- ☐ Was the writing style suitable for a persuasive text (objective; not casual or dismissive)?

Now focus on the detail. Read each of the following points and find out whether the student's work has these features.

Focus on content

- ☐ Did the opening sentence(s) focus on the topic?
- ☐ Was the writer's point of view established early in the writing?
- ☐ Did the writer include any evidence to support his or her opinion?
- ☐ Did the writer include information relevant to his or her experiences?
- ☐ Were the points/arguments raised by the writer easy to follow?
- ☐ Did the writing follow the format with an introduction, the body of the text and a conclusion?
- ☐ Were personal opinions included?
- ☐ Was the concluding paragraph relevant to the topic?

Focus on structure, vocabulary, grammar, spelling, punctuation

- ☐ Was there a variety of sentence lengths, types and beginnings?
- ☐ Was a new paragraph started for each additional argument or point?
- ☐ Has the writer used any similes (e.g. *as clear as crystal*) to stress a point raised?
- ☐ Did the writer avoid approximations such as *probably, perhaps* and *maybe*?
- ☐ Did the writer use such phrases as *I know …* and *It is important to …*?
- ☐ Did the writer refer to the question in the points raised (A good way to do this is to use the key words from the question or the introduction.)?
- ☐ Has the writer used any less common words correctly?
- ☐ Was indirect speech used correctly?
- ☐ Were adjectives used to improve descriptions (e.g. *expensive buildings*)?
- ☐ Were adverbs used effectively (e.g. *firstly*)?
- ☐ Were capital letters used correctly?
- ☐ Was punctuation used correctly?
- ☐ Was the spelling of words correct?

Marker's suggestions (optional)

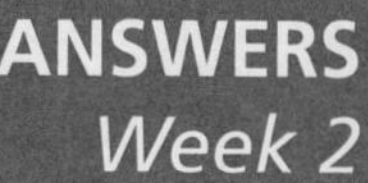

WEEK 2

STATISTICS AND PROBABILITY (Test Your Skills)
Mean, graphs and tables Page 42

1. Mean $= \frac{12 + 18 + 4 + 6 + 10}{5}$
$= \frac{50}{5}$
$= 10$

2. Mode = 8

3. From lowest to highest: 3, 4, 5, <u>10</u>, 11, 18, 50
Median is 10.

4. From lowest to highest: 0, 3, <u>6, 8</u>, 10, 81
Median is the middle of 6 and 8.
The median is 7.

5. Range = highest score – lowest score
$= 25 - (-4)$
$= 29$

6. Mode = 57

7. Median = 52

8. Range = 63 – 41
$= 22$

9. Mode = 2 (tallest column)

10. Number = 1 + 4 + 6 + 3 + 2 + 5
$= 21$

11. 1 walked 0 laps, 4 walked 1 lap, 6 walked 2 laps, 3 walked 3 laps, 2 walked 4 laps and 5 walked 5 laps.
Total $= 1 \times 0 + 4 \times 1 + 6 \times 2 + 3 \times 3 + 2 \times 4 + 5 \times 5$
$= 0 + 4 + 12 + 9 + 8 + 25$
$= 58$

12. Total $= 52 \times 6$
$= 312$ ∴ 312 kg

13. Average in 5 games = 3
Total in 5 games $= 3 \times 5$
$= 15$
Average in 6 games = 4
Total in 6 games $= 4 \times 6$
$= 24$
Goals in 6th game = 24 – 15
$= 9$

14. There are 6 scores which means the median will be the middle of the third and fourth score.
The scores will be 2, 3, <u>5, *x*</u>, 9, 9.
This means that the middle of 5 and *x* is 6.
The value of *x* is 7.

15. The missing number is in the 30s and is at least 34. Considering the scores, 36 has not been recorded. This means the missing number is 6.

16. The median is in the middle of 32 and 34.
The median is 33.

17. $\frac{3 + 6 + 9 + X}{4} = 5$
$3 + 6 + 9 + X = 20$
$X + 18 = 20$
$X = 20 - 18$
$X = 2$

18. Consider each of the choices:
- 2, 4, 6, 6
Range = 6 – 2
= 4
Median = 5 (as middle of 4, 6)
Wrong answer
- 3, 4, 4, 6
Range = 6 – 3
= 3 Wrong answer
- 1, 4, 4, 5
Range = 5 – 1
= 4
Median = 4 Correct answer

19. Could be 2 different answers:
Highest score = 16
Range = 20
Lowest score is 16 – 20 = –4.
(Correct answer is also 22)

STATISTICS AND PROBABILITY (Real Test)
Mean, graphs and tables Page 44

1 A 2 B 3 15 4 C 5 D 6 D 7 9 8 C 9 C 10 B
11 5 12 6.25 13 B 14 27 15 C 16 A, C

EXPLANATIONS

1 Range $= 24 - 9$
$= 15$

Mode = 10

Difference $= 15 - 10$
$= 5$

2 Scores are 9, 10, 10, 16, 17, 19, 24.

The median is 16.

3 $\text{Mean} = \dfrac{10 + 16 + 9 + 24 + 17 + 19 + 10}{7}$

$= 15$

4 Scores are 1, 12, 18, 18, 28, 31, 51, 85.

The median is 23.

5 Mean of 6 scores = 8

Total of 6 scores $= 8 \times 6$
$= 48$

Mean of 7 scores $= 8 + 2$
$= 10$

Total of 7 scores $= 10 \times 7$
$= 70$

7th score $= 70 - 48$
$= 22$

6 Average in 4 games = 3
Total in 4 games $= 3 \times 4$
$= 12$

Average in 10 games = 4
Total in 10 games $= 4 \times 10$
$= 40$

Goals in last 6 games $= 40 - 12$
$= 28$

7 Mode is 67 and Median is 58.
Difference $= 67 - 58$
$= 9$

8 The new score of 44 is one of the lowest scores. This means that the mean will decrease and the mode will remain unchanged at 67.

9 Smallest score is 4 and range is 10 means the largest score is 14; and median is the middle score of 6.

Therefore the scores are 4, 6, 14.

$\text{Mean} = \dfrac{4 + 6 + 14}{3}$

$= \dfrac{24}{3}$

$= 8$

10 5, 5, 6, 6, 7, 7, 7, 8, 9, 10

$\text{Mean} = \dfrac{5 + 5 + 6 + 6 + 7 + 7 + 7 + 8 + 9 + 10}{10}$

$= \dfrac{70}{10}$

$= 7$

Mode = 7
Median = 7
Therefore mean = mode = median.

11 0, 3, 4, 5, 7, 9, 11, 11
Mode = 11
Median = 6 (as middle of 5 and 7)
Difference $= 11 - 6$
$= 5$

12 $\text{Mean} = \dfrac{9 + 0 + 3 + 7 + 11 + 5 + 11 + 4}{8}$

$= \dfrac{50}{8}$

$= 6.25$

13 Number of students $= 2 + 4 + 5 + 3 + 1$
$= 15$

Number of students with 3 laptops = 3

$P(\text{3 laptops}) = \dfrac{3}{15} = \dfrac{1}{5}$

14 Total laptops $= 2 \times 0 + 4 \times 1 + 5 \times 2 + 3 \times 3 + 1 \times 4$
$= 0 + 4 + 10 + 9 + 4$
$= 27$

15 3, 4, 4, 6, 8, 11
Consider each of the choices:
Range: will still be $11 - 3 = 8$
Mode: will still be 4
Median is 5 and will become 4
Mean: will still be 6
The median will change.

16 2, 6, 8, 12, 12
Range is 10, the mean is 8, the mode is 12 and median is 8.
If another 12 is added, the range will remain as 10, the mean will increase, the mode will remain as 12 and the median will increase to 10.
The range and the mode will not change.

NUMBER AND ALGEBRA (Test Your Skills)
Patterns and algebra Page 45

1 The rule is adding 7
Missing number = 26 + 7
= 33

2 Next number = 2 × 58 + 6
= 116 + 6
= 122

3 Rule is subtracting 14.
Missing number = 52 – 14
= 52 – 12 – 2
= 40 – 2
= 38

4 The pattern uses the rule of adding 4.
Tenth number is 6 plus 9 lots of 4.
Tenth number = 6 + 9 × 4
= 6 + 36
= 42

5

Squares	1	2	3
Sticks	4	7	10

The number of sticks = 3 × squares + 1
For 4 squares: Sticks = 3 × 4 + 1
= 13

6 The number of sticks = 3 × squares + 1
For 25 sticks: 25 = 3 × squares + 1
24 = 3 × squares
$\frac{24}{3}$ = squares
8 = squares
This means that 8 squares can be made.

7

Triangles	1	2	3
Sticks	3	5	7

The number of sticks = 2 × triangles + 1
For 6 triangles: Sticks = 2 × 6 + 1
= 13

8 The number of sticks = 2 × triangles + 1
For 25 sticks: 25 = 2 × triangles + 1
24 = 2 × triangles
12 = triangles
This means that 12 triangles can be made.

9 'Multiply the top number by 3 and add 2':
X = 6 × 3 + 2
= 18 + 2
= 20

10 'Multiply the top number by 3 and add 2':
32 = Y × 3 + 2
30 = Y × 3
10 = Y
This means Y = 10.

11

a	0	1	2	3	4
b	3	5	7	9	11

b = 2 times a plus 3
$b = 2a + 3$

12 Substitute $x = 3$ and $y = P$ in
$y = 3x^2 - 4$
$P = 3 \times (3)^2 - 4$
$= 3 \times 9 - 4$
$= 27 - 4$
$= 23$

13 $5a + 3b = 5 \times 2 + 3 \times 4$
$= 10 + 12$
$= 22$

14 $2ab = 2 \times (-3) \times (-4)$
$= 24$

15 $4x^2 = 4 \times (-3)^2$
$= 4 \times 9$
$= 36$

16 $5 - 2y = 5 - 2 \times 3$
$= 5 - 6$
$= -1$

17 $3x + 2y - x + 5y = 2x + 7y$

18 $3(2a + 5) = 6a + 15$

19 $8(2 - 7x) = 16 - 56x$

20 Sum $= x + x + 1 + x + 2$
$= 3x + 3$

21 Perimeter $= 4 \times (x + 3)$
$= 4(x + 3)$
$= 4x + 12$

NUMBER AND ALGEBRA (Real Test)
Patterns and algebra Page 47

1 B 2 C 3 D 4 D 5 B 6 B 7 A 8 20 9 B, D 10 A
11 D 12 18 13 A 14 C 15 B 16 17

EXPLANATIONS

1 Consider each of the choices:
- Multiply by 3 then add 4:
  3, 13 Wrong choice.
- Multiply by 4 then subtract 1:
  3, 11, 43,171, Correct.
- Multiply by 5 then subtract 4:
  3, 11, 51, ... Wrong choice.
- Square and then add 2:
  3, 11, 123, ... Wrong choice.

The correct answer is 'Multiply by 4 then subtract 1'.

2 Continue the pattern: 3, 14, 36, …
4th number $= (36 + 4) \times 2$
$= 40 \times 2$
$= 80$
5th number $= (80 + 4) \times 2$
$= 84 \times 2$
$= 168$ The fifth number is 168.

3 Continue the pattern:

Figure	1	2	3	4	5	6
Dots	1	3	6	10	15	X

The numbers in the second row representing dots follow the pattern: add 2, add 3, add 4, add 5 and then add 6.
This means X $= 15 + 6$
$= 21$

4 $3(6m - 4) = 18m - 12$

5 Suppose the question was 'what is the number 5 less than 8'; we find the answer by using subtraction: 8 – 5.
This means the answer is $p - 5$.

6 $5 - 2x$ is formed from 5, or +5 and $-2x$
This means that $5 - 2x = -2x + 5$.

7 Area = length × breadth
$= (3x + 2) \times 4$
$= 4(3x + 2)$
$= 12x + 8$

8 $5x^2 = 5 \times (-2)^2$
$= 5 \times 4$
$= 20$

9 $ab = 2 \times 4$
$= 8$
$6a + 3b = 6 \times 2 + 3 \times 4$
$= 12 + 12$
$= 24$
$(a + b)^2 = (2 + 4)^2$
$= 62$
$= 36$
$7b - 2a = 7 \times 4 - 2 \times 2$
$= 28 - 4$
$= 24$
The expressions are $6a + 3b$ and $7b - 2a$

10 $\frac{3x}{x+2} = \frac{3 \times 4}{4 + 2}$
$= \frac{12}{6}$
$= 2$

11 $\frac{2x + y}{3y - 2} = \frac{2 \times 3 + 4}{3 \times 4 - 2}$
$= \frac{6 + 4}{12 - 2}$
$= \frac{10}{10}$
$= 1$

12 $(2p)^2 - 2p^2 = (2 \times 3)^2 - 2 \times 3^2$
$= 6^2 - 2 \times 9$
$= 36 - 18$
$= 18$

13

x	0	1	2	3	4
y	–2	0	2	4	6

$y = 2$ times x minus 2
$= 2 \times x - 2$
$y = 2x - 2$

14

x	0	0.5	1	1.5	2
y	2	1.5	1	0.5	0

x plus $y = 2$
$x + y = 2$

15 Difference $= 3x - (2x + 1)$
$= 3x - 2x - 1$
$= x - 1$

16 $x^2 - 5x + 3 = (-2)^2 - 5(-2) + 3$
$= 4 + 10 + 3$
$= 17$

NUMBER AND ALGEBRA (Test Your Skills)
Equations and number plane Page 48

1 Answer is C.

2 Substitute each of the points into $y = 2x + 1$
Try (0, 1): $1 = 2(0) + 1$
$= 1$ Yes!
The point (0, 1) lies on the line $y = 2x + 1$.

3 Substitute each of the points into $y = 3x - 2$
Try (–1, –5): $-5 = 3(-1) - 2$
$= -5$ is on line
Try (0, –2): $-2 = 3(0) - 2$
$= -2$ is on line
Try (1, 1): $1 = 3(1) - 2$
$= 1$ is on line
Try (2, 3): $3 = 3(2) - 2$
$= 4$ is not on line
The point (2, 3) is not on $y = 3x - 2$.

4 Substitute each of the points into $y = 2x - 2$
Try (–3, –5): $-5 = 2(-3) - 2$
$= -8$ not on line
Try (–1, 2): $2 = 2(-1) - 2$
$= -4$ not on line
Try (5, 8): $8 = 2(5) - 2$
$= 8$ is on line
The point (5, 8) is on $y = 2x - 2$.

5 Substitute the point (2, –3) into equations:
$y = x + 3$
$-3 = 2 + 3$ No.
$y = 2x + 1$
$-3 = 2(2) + 1$ No.
$y = 2x - 1$
$-3 = 2(2) - 1$ No.
$y = x - 5$
$-3 = 2 - 5$ Yes.
The point (2, –3) lies on $y = x - 5$.

6 $2x + 5 = 11$
$2x = 11 - 5$
$\frac{2x}{2} = \frac{6}{2}$
$x = 3$

7 $4a - 8 = 4$
$4a = 4 + 8$
$\frac{4a}{4} = \frac{12}{4}$
$a = 3$

8 $3y - 1 = 2y + 4$
$3y - 2y = 4 + 1$
$y = 5$

9 $2a = a - 6$
$2a - a = -6$
$a = -6$

10 $5x + 8 = 3x - 4$
$5x - 3x = -4 - 8$
$\frac{2x}{2} = \frac{-12}{2}$
$x = -6$

11 Substitute each of the values into $A = 3B - 2$
$A = 2, B = 4$ $2 = 3(4) - 2$
$= 12 - 2$
$= 10$ No.
$A = 1, B = 1$ $1 = 3(1) - 2$
$= 3 - 2$
$= 1$ Yes.
$A = 1, B = 1$ satisfy the formula.

12 Substitute each of the values into $P = \frac{24}{Q + 3}$
$P = 6, Q = 0$ $6 = \frac{24}{0 + 3}$
$= \frac{24}{3}$
$= 8$ No.
$P = 12, Q = 1$ $2 = \frac{24}{1 + 3}$
$= \frac{24}{4}$
$= 6$ No.

$P = 2, Q = 9 \qquad 2 = \frac{24}{9+3}$

$= \frac{24}{12}$

$= 2$ Yes.

$P = 2, Q = 9$ satisfy the formula.

13 Substitute each of the values into

$2x - 1 = x + 5$

$x = 3$: $2(3) - 1 = 3 + 5$

$6 - 1 = 8$

$5 = 8$ No.

$x = 4$: $2(4) - 1 = 4 + 5$

$8 - 1 = 4 + 5$

$7 = 9$ No.

$x = 6$: $2(6) - 1 = 6 + 5$

$12 - 1 = 11$

$11 = 11$ Yes.

$x = 6$ satisfies $2x - 1 = x + 5$.

Or, solve $2x - 1 = x + 5$

$2x - x = 5 + 1$

$x = 6$

14 Substitute each of the values into

$3x + 4 = x - 2$

$x = -6$: $3(-6) + 4 = -6 - 2$

$-18 + 4 = -8$

$-14 = -8$ No.

$x = -2$: $3(-2) + 4 = -2 - 2$

$-6 + 4 = -4$

$-2 = -4$ No.

$x = -3$: $3(-3) + 4 = -3 - 2$

$-9 + 4 = -5$

$-5 = -5$ Yes.

$x = -3$ satisfies $3x + 4 = x - 2$.

Or, solve $3x + 4 = x - 2$

$3x - x = -2 - 4$

$2x = -6$

$x = -3$

15 Substitute $P = 20$ and $b = 4$ in

$P = 2a + 2b$

$20 = 2a + 2(4)$

$2a + 8 = 20$

$2a = 20 - 8$

$\frac{2a}{2} = \frac{12}{12}$

$a = 6$

16 Substitute $A = 48$ and $y = 6$ in

$A = xy$

$48 = x \times 6$

$48 = 6x$

$\frac{6x}{6} = \frac{48}{6}$

$x = 8$

17 Substitute $K = 6$ and $x = 2$ in

$K = \frac{V}{3x^2}$

$6 = \frac{V}{3 \times 2^2}$

$6 = \frac{V}{12}$

$V = 6 \times 12$

$V = 72$

18 Substitute $M = 12$, $P = 1.4$ and $v = 10$ in

$M = Pv - L$

$12 = 1.4 \times 10 - L$

$12 = 14 - L$

$L = 14 - 12$

$L = 2$

19 Substitute $T = 10$, $x = 11$ and $y = 14$ in

$T = \frac{B}{\sqrt{x + y}}$

$10 = \frac{B}{\sqrt{11 + 14}}$

$10 = \frac{B}{\sqrt{25}}$

$10 = \frac{B}{5}$

$B = 10 \times 5$

$B = 50$

NUMBER AND ALGEBRA (Real Test)
Equations and number plane Page 50

1 B 2 A 3 D 4 A 5 3 6 C 7 C 8 2 9 10 10 A
11 B 12 B 13 D 14 A 15 C 16 B

EXPLANATIONS

1 The correct graph is B.

Check Your Answers

2 Substitute each of the points into

$$\begin{aligned} & & y &= 3x - 4 \\ x = 0,\ y = -4 & & -4 &= 3(0) - 4 \\ & & &= 0 - 4 \\ & & &= -4 \quad \text{Yes.} \end{aligned}$$

The line y = $3x - 4$ passes through (0, –4).

3 Substitute each of the points into $y = 2x + 1$

$$\begin{aligned} x = 1,\ y = 2 & & 2 &= 2(1) + 1 \\ & & &= 2 + 1 \\ & & &= 3 \quad \text{No.} \\ x = 4,\ y = 2 & & 2 &= 2(4) + 1 \\ & & &= 8 + 1 \\ & & &= 9 \quad \text{No.} \\ x = 0,\ y = 3 & & 3 &= 2(0) + 1 \\ & & &= 0 + 1 \\ & & &= 1 \quad \text{No.} \\ x = 2,\ y = 5 & & 5 &= 2(2) + 1 \\ & & &= 4 + 1 \\ & & &= 5 \quad \text{Yes.} \end{aligned}$$

The point (2, 5) lies on the line $y = 2x + 1$.

4

$$\begin{aligned} 3x + 8 &= 2x - 3 \\ 3x - 2x &= -3 - 8 \\ x &= -11 \end{aligned}$$

5

$$\begin{aligned} 4b - 4 &= b + 5 \\ 4b - b &= 5 + 4 \\ \frac{3b}{3} &= \frac{9}{3} \\ b &= 3 \end{aligned}$$

6 Substitute each of the values into $y > 2x - 1$

$$\begin{aligned} x = 3,\ y = 1 & & 1 &> 2(3) - 1 \\ & & 1 &> 6 - 1 \\ & & 1 &> 5 \quad \text{No.} \\ x = 5,\ y = 4 & & 4 &> 2(5) - 1 \\ & & 4 &> 10 - 1 \\ & & 4 &> 9 \quad \text{No.} \\ x = 2,\ y = 8 & & 8 &> 2(2) - 1 \\ & & 8 &> 4 - 1 \\ & & 8 &> 3 \quad \text{Yes.} \end{aligned}$$

$x = 2$ and $y = 8$ satisfy $y > 2x - 1$.

7 Gradient $= \dfrac{\text{rise}}{\text{run}} = \dfrac{6}{5}$

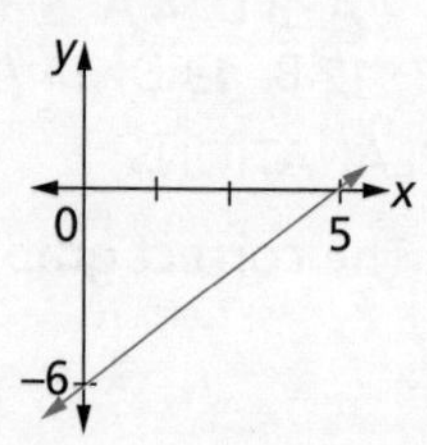

8 Substitute $y = 8$ into

$$\begin{aligned} y &= 2x + 4 \\ 8 &= 2x + 4 \\ 4 &= 2x \\ x &= 2 \end{aligned}$$

9 Substitute $E = 20$ and $v = 2$ in

$$\begin{aligned} E &= \frac{1}{2}mv^2 \\ 20 &= \frac{1}{2} \times m \times 2^2 \\ 20 &= \frac{1}{2} \times m \times 4 \\ 20 &= 2m \\ m &= \frac{20}{2} \\ m &= 10 \end{aligned}$$

10 Opposite sides of a rectangle are equal:

$$\begin{aligned} 3a - 2 &= 2a + 4 \\ 3a - 2a &= 4 + 2 \\ a &= 6 \end{aligned}$$

11 Substitute $r = 4$ and $h = 3$ in

$$\begin{aligned} V &= \pi r^2 h \\ &= \pi \times 4^2 \times 3 \\ &= 150.796\,4474 \end{aligned}$$

The volume is closest to 150 cm^3

12 Substitute each of the values into

$$\begin{aligned} & & 2x + 3y &= 12 \\ x = 1,\ y = 2 & & 2(1) + 3(2) &= 2 + 6 \\ & & &= 8 \neq 12 \quad \text{No.} \\ x = 3,\ y = 2 & & 2(3) + 3(2) &= 6 + 6 \\ & & &= 12 \quad \text{Yes.} \end{aligned}$$

A possible solution is $x = 3$, $y = 2$.

13 Substitute each of the values of a into both equations: $b = 2a - 3$ and $b = a + 4$.

$$\begin{aligned} a = 1: & \quad b = 2(1) - 3 = -1 \\ & \quad b = 1 + 4 = 5 \qquad -1 \neq 5 \\ a = 2: & \quad b = 2(2) - 3 = 1 \\ & \quad b = 2 + 4 = 6 \qquad 1 \neq 6 \\ a = 3: & \quad b = 2(3) - 3 = 3 \\ & \quad b = 3 + 4 = 7 \qquad 3 \neq 7 \\ a = 7: & \quad b = 2(7) - 3 = 11 \\ & \quad b = 7 + 4 = 11 \qquad 11 = 11 \end{aligned}$$

$a = 7$ satisfies both equations.

14 $P = \dfrac{T^2}{M - 6}$

$3.6 = \dfrac{6^2}{M - 6}$

$3.6 = \dfrac{36}{M - 6}$

Now substitute each value of M:

$M = 16$: $3.6 = \dfrac{36}{16 - 6}$

$= \dfrac{36}{10}$

$= 3.6$

Therefore $M = 16$.

15 Rewrite points into a table

x	2	5	6
y	5	11	13

The rule is y is double the x and plus 1.
$y = 2x + 1$
Now substitute each of the points:

(10, 19) $19 = 2(10) + 1$
$= 20 + 1$
$= 21$ No.

(12, 24) $24 = 2(12) + 1$
$= 24 + 1$
$= 25$ No.

(8, 17) $17 = 2(8) + 1$
$= 16 + 1$
$= 17$ Yes.

The line also passes through (8, 17).

16 Both (1, 0) and (3, 8) must satisfy the equation:

$y = 3x - 3$
substitute (1, 0) $0 = 3(1) - 3$
$= 0$ Yes.
substitute (3, 8) $8 = 3(3) - 3$
$= 6$ No.

$y = 4x - 4$
substitute (1, 0) $0 = 4(1) - 4$
$= 0$ Yes.
substitute (3, 8) $8 = 4(3) - 4$
$= 0$ Yes.

This means that $y = 4x - 4$ passes through both (1, 0) and (3, 8).

SPELLING (Real Test)
Common misspellings Pages 53–54

1. approximately
2. independence
3. rebellion
4. currently
5. towered
6. budgeted
7. foregrounded
8. inappropriate
9. proportion
10. reaction
11. proposition
12. peaceful
13. development
14. engagement
15. evaluation
16. reproduce
17. rotation
18. bombarded
19. dissolves
20. uninitiated
21. loiter
22. translates
23. comprehend
24. originated
25. corrupting

GRAMMAR AND PUNCTUATION (Real Test)
Commas, semicolons and apostrophes Pages 57–59

1 A 2 C 3 D 4 C 5 B 6 A 7 C 8 D 9 C 10 B
11 C 12 A 13 D 14 C 15 B 16 B 17 A 18 C
19 D 20 C 21 B 22 A 23 A 24 D 25 C

EXPLANATIONS

1 This is a punctuation question. The correct sentence is: *Yesterday, I went to the promenade for a stroll.*
Tip: The comma comes after the word *Yesterday* to indicate that this is an adverbial clause. An adverbial clause describes when, where, how or why an action has taken place.

2 This is a punctuation question. The correct position for the apostrophe is in the word *it's*.
Tip: The word *it's* is a contraction of *it is* and therefore requires an apostrophe between the 't' and 's' to indicate the missing 'i'. The noun *brothers* is a plural and does not require an apostrophe.

3 This is a punctuation question. The correct sentence is: *"I envy your courage during this difficult time," said George.*
Tip: Only the actual words spoken are enclosed in the speech (quotation) marks (inverted commas). A comma after the spoken words and before the last quotation mark indicates that the dialogue tag is part of a sentence.

4 This is a grammar question. The correct answer is *not.*
Tip: The prefix *un* changes a word to its opposite. This is because the prefix *un* means 'not' or 'the opposite of'.

5 This is a punctuation question. The correct sentence is: *Jason ordered four items from the catalogue: an encyclopaedia of spiders; a pack of playing cards; a poster of the alphabet and a vegetarian cookbook.*
Tip: A colon is used to introduce a list of items. A semicolon is used to separate complex items in the list, not to introduce a list.

6 This is a punctuation question. The correct sentence is: *Florence Nightingale was known as 'The Lady with the Lamp'.*
Tip: The names of people are called proper nouns and must be indicated with a capital letter. The title of a character should be indicated by inverted commas.

7 This is a grammar question. The correct word is the article *a*.
Tip: *A* is an article and precedes words beginning with consonant sounds.

8 This is a punctuation question. The correct sentence is: *There were no cars in Victorian England. People either walked, travelled by boat or used coach horses to move from place to place.*
Tip: Two-part sentences should not be divided by commas. It is more correct to write two separate complete sentences. Sentences begin with a capital letter. Commas are used to indicate a brief pause in a sentence.

9 This is a grammar question. The correct answer is *hyperbole*.
Tip: Hyperbole is a deliberate exaggeration to create an effect. Obviously, chocolate doesn't literally make the world go around.

10 This is a grammar question. The correct use of the colon is to introduce a list.
Tip: A colon (:) is used to indicate the introduction of a list. A semicolon (;) is used to separate complete ideas and commas are used to separate items in a list.

11 This is a punctuation question. The correct sentence is: *Jeff asked for your phone number.*
Tip: This is an example of indirect speech. No actual words are spoken so quotation marks are not needed. No question is actually asked so no question mark is needed.

12 This is a grammar question. The correct answer is *The caterpillar transformed slowly into a beautiful butterfly*.
Tip: The word *slowly* is an adverb to describe the verb *transformed*.

13 This is a grammar question. The correct answer is *what*.
Tip: The word *what* is a pronoun and in this sentence is used to refer to the phrase *an eccentric character*.

14 This is a grammar question. The correct word is the verb *hasn't*.
Tip: *Hasn't* is a contraction of the words *has not*. Singular subjects (nouns) need singular verbs; plural subjects (nouns) need plural verbs. In this case the subject is singular, *Angela*, and needs a singular verb, *hasn't*, and not *haven't*.

15 This is a grammar question. The correct sentence is: *John changed his mind about going to the disco; he's going to go to his friend's house instead.*
Tip: The word *he's* is a contraction of *he is* and the word *his* is a possessive pronoun to show ownership.

16 This is a grammar question. The correct word is the verb *is*.
Tip: The present tense verb *seen* must be used as singular subjects (nouns) need singular verbs and plural subjects (nouns) need plural verbs. In this case, the subject is a skateboard and needs the present tense singular verb *is*.

17 This is a grammar question. The correct answer is *an adverb*.
Tip: An adverb describes the action of a person or thing. Here the adverb *increasingly* is used to describe the action of becoming.

18 This is a grammar question. The correct answer is *an adjective*.
Tip: An adjective is a word used to describe a place, person, event or thing. Here the adjective *vegan* is used to describe a type of diet.

19 This is a grammar question. The correct answer is *an adjective*.
Tip: An adjective is a word used to describe a place, person, event or thing. Here the adjective *mechanical* is used to describe the mill.

20 This is a grammar question. The correct answer is *an adjective*.
Tip: An adjective is a word used to describe a place, person, event or thing. Here the comparative adjective *largest* is used to describe the chocolate.

21 This is a grammar question. The correct answer is the pronoun *she*.
Tip: A pronoun is a word that takes the place of a noun. Examples: *he, she, it, me. The* is a definite article, *had* is a verb and *world* is a noun.

22 This is a grammar question. The correct position for the apostrophe is in the word *frog's*.
Tip: The apostrophe in this sentence indicates possession—the frog owns its ability to move quickly. The possessive pronoun *its* does not use an apostrophe to indicate possession. The word *predators* is a plural noun and does not require an apostrophe.

23 This is a grammar question. The correct answer is the pronoun *He*.
Tip: A pronoun is a word that takes the place of a noun. Examples: *he, she, it, me*. *Built* is a verb and *aphids* is a plural noun.

24 This is a punctuation question. The correct sentence is: *There are three different types of clouds—high, middle and low—that can be seen in our skies.*
Tip: The correct punctuation for this sentence is the use of dashes. These work like brackets as they enclose extra information.

25 This is a punctuation question. The correct sentence is: *Red Cattle Dogs and Australian Kelpies are both energetic breeds; Red Cattle Dogs are also big eaters and can bounce high while Australian Kelpies are good natured and have a slim build.*
Tip: Semicolons are used to connect pieces of information that are different yet related.

READING (Test Your Skills)
Understanding reviews — Pages 60–61

Book Review: That's Why I Wrote this Song

EXPLANATIONS

1 The reviewer thinks the book is exceptional, describing it as 'an outstanding new young adult read' and concluding the review with the comment, '*That's Why I Wrote This Song* is a brilliant book'.

2 The text in italics after the words 'One dream' indicates these are the thoughts of one of the fictitious girls in the band.

3 The word 'pepper' means to 'scatter'. Examples of the lyrics, words from the girls' songs, are to be found in many places throughout the book.

4 A 'collaboration' is the act of working with someone to achieve something. The author, Susanne Gervay, and her daughter, Tory, worked together in writing the book.

5 Angie has 'a perfect life'. The other girls in the band are experiencing difficulties with their parents.

6 The term 'backdrop' can be used as the setting for something. The action in the book is set against the lyrics of songs.

7 The reviewer covers a number of issues that the girls face: 'a tumultuous year of school, boys and family pressures'. She states the band is 'an escape from the real world'. Despite those difficulties, the girls plan to 'make their debut appearance' at the concert, which they think will be 'unreal'. Not all the girls join the band because of dissatisfaction at home, nor do they all believe the band will give them independence.

8 The issues in the book are the exploration of teen issues including parent-child relationships, family roles, boyfriends, friendships and more.

9 The extra bonus is the download of two songs written by Tory. This is stated in the text and is advertised on the image of the book's cover.

READING (Real Test)
Understanding transactions **Pages 62–63**

Interview: Kerri Falls talks to Jon Doust

1 B **2** A **3** difficult, unhappy **4** A, E **5** A **6** C
7 B **8** questions—probing; answers—frank

EXPLANATIONS

1 The story is based on events in Jon Doust's life—he says, 'the starting point was me' and 'I took an event as I remembered it'.

2 Jon Doust's use of the word 'Yeah' indicates he is giving himself some time to think about the question and his answer.

3 Jon's school days were difficult because he was bullied and harshly punished but there was also 'a lot of humour' and he 'survived quite well.'

4 Jon states that some 'bullies are in denial their whole lives', never acknowledging their actions, while others 'feel deeply guilty about what they did in boarding school'.

5 Jon found his need for revenge was 'unexpected'.

6 Jon says he 'survived quite well'. Some of his school associates didn't.

7 Jon was 'scarred' by his feelings for those that didn't survive boarding school. It was unfair what they had to survive. They didn't have his resilience.

8 The interviewer asks very personal questions, probing difficult aspects of Doust's life that *Boy on a Wire* is based on. The questions cause Doust to think about the issues and he gives very frank, honest answers.

READING (Real Test)
Understanding transactions **Pages 64–65**

Letter of invitation

1 four **2** A **3** D **4** C **5** A **6** B **7** B, E **8** D
9 2, 4, 5, 3, 1

EXPLANATIONS

1 Four people are expected to give an address. The official speakers are: Rayma Mathis, the Closing Keynote Speaker; Simon Makepeace, the opening Speaker; the President of the school board who will give 'a short talk'; Mary Geller who will give an address on 'how to interpret external exam marks'.

2 This is a formal letter inviting Rayma Mathis to a formal occasion.

3 Rayma Mathis's position is Director, Public Relations, Educational and Career Opportunities Unit. She has had professional experience in careers advising.

4 'Fly or cry' suggests going out and facing the world bravely or staying unhappily within the security of the home.

5 The principal mentions in his letter: 'the stress families are feeling in these times of global recession and falling employment opportunities'. Parents are anxious to get as much information as they can to secure their children's future.

6 The principal will advise of the content of the other speakers' addresses. This is a courtesy.

7 The writer is the school principal. His tone suggests how important the night is to him and to the school community. The contents of the letter suggest that the event is being carefully organised in advance.

8 By advising Ms Mathis of the earlier speakers' speech content he is ensuring the speeches will be beneficial for the parents.

9 Simon Makepeace 'will be the opening speaker' followed by the President of the board giving 'a short talk'. Then he will 'present the awards'. Ms Geller will follow addressing 'parents and students' about 'external exam marks'. The Keynote speaker will give the 'Closing' address.

READING (Real Test)
Understanding film reviews **Pages 66–67**

Film Review: Samson and Delilah

1 D 2 A alienated; B intriguing; C accepting; D underhanded; E apathetic 3 C 4 C 5 D 6 B 7 written response 8 O, F, F, O, O

EXPLANATIONS

1 The reviewer's opinion is that the film is an honest portrayal of life in the settlement.

2 Samson is isolated from his community due to his petrol sniffing and is 'banned' from joining his brother's band. Delilah is 'rapt' by her grandmother's paintings. Delilah and her grandmother, Nana, 'seem content'. The buyer takes advantage of Nana and her paintings are 'spirited away' because she does not know their true value. The mood at the settlement is one of boredom. People seem 'trapped' and are apathetic, not having the energy to 'make things happen'.

3 The lively sounds of Charley Pride singing Sunshiny Day, contrast with the life in the sunshine experienced by the people of the settlement.

4 Spectators at sporting matches watch from the sidelines. They are not part of the game. In the same way, Samson is not part of Nana and Delilah's life.

5 The location of the settlement is in a magnificent desert location—open and free, but the inhabitants act as if they are trapped.

6 Although the film touches on a number of issues it is addiction (petrol sniffing) that is the main issue. The film opens with petrol sniffing and is 'like all stories about addiction'.

7 Samson takes Delilah to Alice Springs to escape the brutality of settlement life, which culminated in Delilah getting beaten up.

8 Two statements contain factual information and are not based on the reviewer's interpretation of the film. Thornton is an 'Indigenous filmmaker' and the film is about social issues in an 'Aboriginal settlement'. Conventional films have happy endings, whereas the details of the film indicate that *Samson and Delilah* does not. This statement is based on fact, not the reviewer's emotional response to the film and her point of view.

ANSWERS
Week 2

WRITING (Real Test)
Narrative text 1 Page 70

Tick each correct point.
Read the student's work through once to get an overall view of their response.

Focus on general points

- ☐ Did it make sense?
- ☐ Did it flow?
- ☐ Did the story arouse any feeling?
- ☐ Did you want to read on? Did the story create any suspense?
- ☐ Was the handwriting readable?

Now focus on the detail. Read the following points and find out whether the student's work has these features.

Focus on content

- ☐ Did the opening sentence(s) 'grab' your interest?
- ☐ Was the setting established (i.e. where the action took place)?
- ☐ Was the reader told when the action takes place?
- ☐ Was it apparent who the main character(s) is? (It can be the narrator, using *I*.)
- ☐ Was there a problem to be solved early in the writing?
- ☐ Was a complication or unusual event introduced?
- ☐ Did descriptions make reference to any of the senses (e.g. *pink sky, cool breeze*)?
- ☐ Was there a climax (a more exciting part near the end)?
- ☐ Was there a conclusion (resolution of the problem) and was it believable?

Focus on structure, vocabulary, grammar, spelling, punctuation

- ☐ Was there variation in sentence length and beginnings?
- ☐ Was a new paragraph started for changes in time, place or action?
- ☐ In conversations or speaking were there separate paragraphs for each change of speaker?
- ☐ Were adjectives used to improve descriptions (e.g. *hollow sound*)?
- ☐ Were adverbs used to make 'actions' more interesting (e.g. *listened carefully*)?
- ☐ Were capital letters where they should have been?
- ☐ Was punctuation correct?
- ☐ Was the spelling of words correct?

Marker's suggestions (optional)

WRITING (Real Test)
Narrative text 2 Page 71

Tick each correct point.
Read the student's work through once to get an overall view of their response.

Focus on general points

- ☐ Did it make sense?
- ☐ Did it flow?
- ☐ Did the story arouse any feeling?
- ☐ Did you want to read on? Did the story create any suspense?
- ☐ Was the handwriting readable?

Now focus on the detail. Read the following points and find out whether the student's work has these features.

Focus on content

- ☐ Did the opening sentence(s) 'grab' your interest?
- ☐ Was the setting established (i.e. where the action took place)?
- ☐ Was the reader told when the action takes place?
- ☐ Was it apparent who the main character(s) is? (It can be the narrator, using 'I'.)
- ☐ Was there a 'problem' to be 'solved' early in the writing?
- ☐ Was a complication or unusual event introduced?
- ☐ Did descriptions make reference to any of the senses (e.g. delicious chocolate)?
- ☐ Was there a climax (a more exciting part near the end)?
- ☐ Was there a conclusion (resolution of the problem) and was it 'believable'?

Focus on structure, vocabulary, grammar, spelling, punctuation

- ☐ Was there variation in sentence length and beginnings?
- ☐ Was a new paragraph started for changes in time, place or action?
- ☐ In conversations or speaking were there separate paragraphs for each change of speaker?
- ☐ Were adjectives used to improve descriptions (e.g. hollow sound)?
- ☐ Were adverbs used to make 'actions' more interesting (e.g. listened carefully)?
- ☐ Were capital letters where they should have been?
- ☐ Was punctuation correct?
- ☐ Was the spelling of words correct?

Marker's suggestions (optional)

WEEK 3

MEASUREMENT AND GEOMETRY (Test Your Skills)

Time, length, scale and capacity Page 74

1 From 8:30 am to 4:30 pm is 8 hours; then to 4:45 pm is 15 minutes.
The total time is 8 hours 15 minutes.

2 From 7:22 am to 8:00 am is 38 minutes; then 8:00 am to 6:00 pm is 10 hours; then 6:00 pm to 6:08 pm is 8 minutes.
As 38 min + 10 h + 8 min = 10 h 46 min, Praena is away 10 hours 46 minutes.

3 From 7:45 pm to 8:00 pm is 15 minutes; then 8:00 pm to 8:00 am is 12 hours; then 8:00 am to 11:00 am is 3 hours; then 11:00 am to 11:40 am is 40 minutes.
Now, 15 min + 12 h + 3 h + 40 min
= 15 h 55 min

4 From 10:35 am adding 9 hours makes it 7:35 am; then adding another 30 minutes makes it 8:05 am.

5 2.5 metres = 2500 millimetres
= 250 centimetres

6 First, change 2.6 L to 2600 mL
Remainder = 2600 – 140
= 2500 – 40
= 2460
Therefore 2460 mL, or 2.46 L remains.

7 New mass = 940 + 270
= 1140 + 70
= 1210
The new mass is 1210 grams, or 1.21 kg.

8

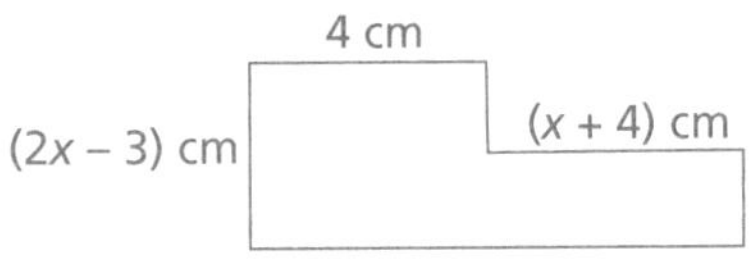

The length is $4 + (x + 4) = x + 8$.
The width is $2x - 3$.
Perimeter = 2(length + width)
$= 2(x + 8 + 2x - 3)$
$= 2(3x + 5)$
$= 6x + 10$
The perimeter is $(6x + 10)$ cm.

9 Use $C = 2\pi r$
$= 2 \times \pi \times 10$
= 62.831 853 07…
= 62.83 (2 decimal places)
The circumference is 62.83 cm.

10 Perimeter = 24 cm
Length + Breadth = 12 cm
The length is three times the breadth.
Breadth is 3 cm and length is 9 cm.

11 Actual distance = 35 × 100
= 3500
The distance is 3500 mm, or 3.5 m.

12 From the table, scale is:
6 cm = 42 km
1 cm = 7 km [dividing by 7]

13 Using the scale 1 cm = 7 km,
Map distance = 154 ÷ 7
= 22
The map distance is 22 cm.

14 Actual distance = 8.9 × 7
= 62.3
The actual distance is 62.3 km.

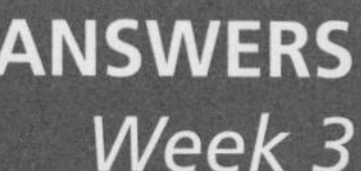

15

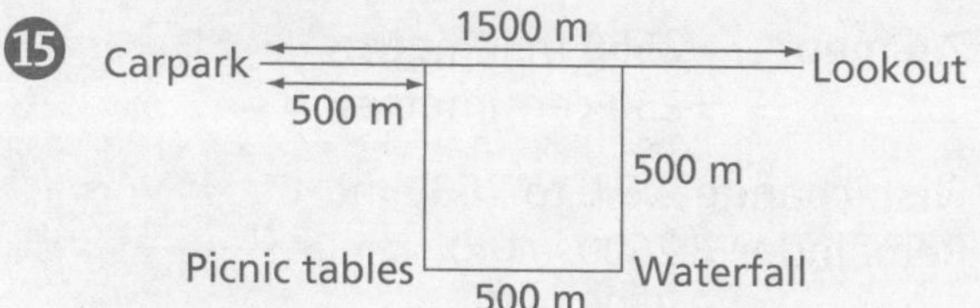

The distance would be about 1500 metres, or 1.5 kilometres.

MEASUREMENT AND GEOMETRY (Real Test)

Time, length, scale and capacity Page 76

1 C **2** B **3** D **4** B **5** C **6** B **7** C **8** 4.5 **9** A **10** A
11 C **12** C **13** B **14** 13.8 **15** 7.5 **16** 1.25

EXPLANATIONS

1 A: 30 min + 6 h 15 min = 6 h 45 min
B: 15 min + 6 h 25 min = 6 h 40 min
C: 5 min + 6 h 50 min = 6 h 55 min
D: 6 h 35 min
Cinema C shows the longest marathon.

2 Total leak $= 15 \times 60 \times 24$
$= 21\,600$
The leak is 21 600 mL, or 21.6 litres per day.

3 1.25 L = 1250 mL
1250 + 50 = 1300
Required milk = 2000 − 1300
= 700
Kelvin needs another 700 mL.

4 If diameter is 8 cm, then radius is 4 cm.
Distance is circumference of the circle.
As π is approximately 3,
$C = 2\pi r$
$= 2 \times 3 \times 4$
$= 24$
The distance is about 24 cm.

5 Perimeter $= 3 + 3 + \frac{3}{4} \times 2 \times \pi \times 3$
$= 20.137\,167...$
$= 20$ (nearest whole)
The perimeter is about 20 cm.

6 Jake and Georgia are 8 units, or 40 km apart. This means the scale used is 1 unit = 5 km. Moni and Sam are 5 units apart. This means they are 25 km apart.

7 Distance is 5 + 2 + 8 = 15 units, or 75 km. As Jake takes 1 hour, his speed is 75 km/h.

8 12 cm = 54 km
1 cm $= 54 \div 12$
$= 4.5$
Therefore the scale is 1 cm = 4.5 km.

9 Distance $= 4.5 \times 8$
$= 36$
Distance is 36 km.

10 Lenfell ⟵⟶ Blight (12 cm) Lochneed

Lenfell to Blight = 12 cm
Blight to Lochneed = 6 cm
The distance is 6 cm.

11 From 10:18 pm to 11:00 pm is 42 min; from 11:00 pm to 7:00 am is 8 hours; from 7:00 am to 7:27 am is 27 minutes.
Total = 42 min + 8 h + 27 min
= 8 h 69 min
= 9 h 9 min

12 Use $C = 2\pi r$ and π is equal to about 3
$60 = 2 \times 3 \times r$
$60 = 6r$
$\frac{60}{6} = r$
$r = 10$
This means radius is 10 cm, and diameter is 20 cm.

13 Distance = 1.5 + 1.5 + 2.3
= 5.3
Daniel walked 5.3 km.

14 10 minutes $= \frac{1}{6}$ hour
Speed = Distance ÷ Time
$= 2.3 \div \frac{1}{6}$
$= 13.8$
His speed was 13.8 km/h.

15 Length of image = 12 cm
Length of original = 8 cm
Enlargement factor $= \frac{12}{8} = \frac{3}{2}$
Width of image $= 5 \times \frac{3}{2} = 7.5$
The width of the enlargement is 7.5 cm.

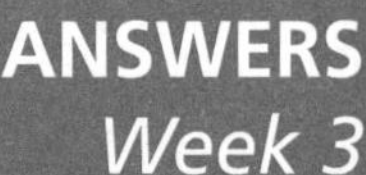

16 First, find the length of the beam.

As 2 + 3 = 5, the shorter length is 2 parts

2 parts = 80 cm

1 part = 40

5 parts = 200

The beam is 200 cm.

As the new cut is 5:3, longer section is $\frac{5}{8}$.

$$\text{Longer length} = \frac{5}{8} \times 200 = 125$$

The longer length is 125 cm, or 1.25 m.

MEASUREMENT AND GEOMETRY (Test Your Skills)
Area and volume — Page 77

1 Area of square = 36 cm^2

Length of side = 6 cm

Perimeter of square = 4 × 6
= 24

The perimeter is 24 cm.

2 $\text{Area} = \frac{1}{2} \times 6 \times 6 = 18$

Area is 18 cm^2

3 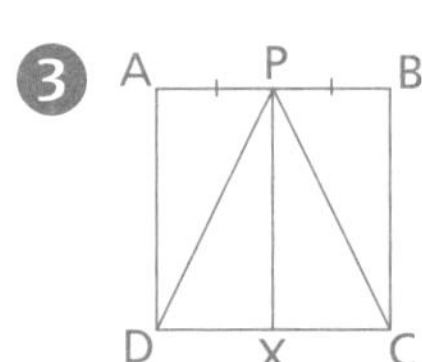

Halve the square by drawing PX. This means the rectangle APXD is half of 36 cm^2, or 18 cm^2. The area of ΔAPD is half of 18 cm^2, or 9 cm^2.

4 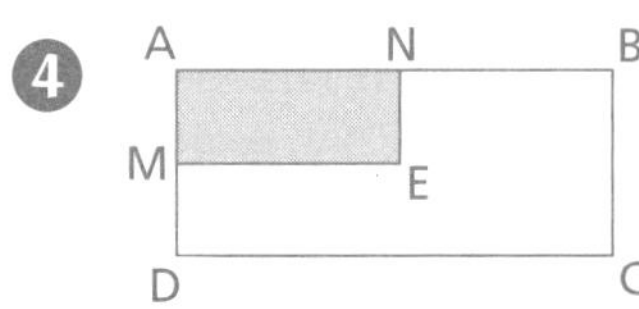

The shaded rectangle is $\frac{1}{4}$ of original.

5 Unshaded area = 3 × shaded area
= 3 × 4
= 12

Area is 12 cm^2.

6 Dimensions are $2x$ and $2x + 2$

Area = $2x(2x + 2)$ cm^2

7 Perimeter = 36 cm

Sum of length and width = 18 cm

As area is 72 cm^2, the dimensions are 12 cm and 6 cm as 12 + 6 = 18 and 12 × 6 = 72. The length is 12 cm.

8 Area = 16 cm^2

Length of side = 4 cm

New length = 4 × 2
= 8

New length is 8 cm

New area = 8 × 8
= 64

New area is 64 cm^2

From 16 to 64, the area will multiply by 4.

9 length × width × height = volume

$$10 \times 6 \times h = 300$$
$$60h = 300$$
$$h = \frac{300}{60}$$
$$h = 5$$

The height is 5 cm.

10 Use $A = \pi r^2$ and π is equal to about 3

$$= 3 \times 5^2 = 3 \times 25 = 75$$

The area is about 75 cm^2.

11 The area of the semi-circle is $\frac{1}{2}\pi r^2$ and the radius is 6 cm.

$$\text{Area} = \frac{1}{2} \times \pi \times 6^2$$
$$= 56.548\,667\,76$$
$$= 56.55 \text{ (2 decimal places)}$$

The area is about 56.55 cm^2.

12 Volume = 8 cm^3

Length of side = 2 cm

Area of face = 2 × 2
= 4

The area is 4 cm^2.

13 Perimeter = 4 × length
= 4 × 2
= 8

The perimeter is 8 cm.

14 Surface area = 2 × 4 × 3 + 2 × 4 × 2 + 2 × 3 × 2
= 52

The surface area is 52 cm^2

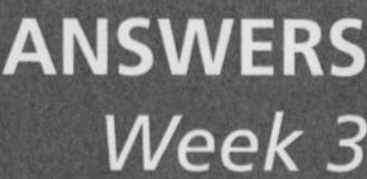

15 Triangular prism has 2 triangles and 3 rectangles.
Area $= 2 \times 18 + 3 \times 24$
$= 36 + 72$
$= 108$ The surface area is 108 cm^2.

16 Area of small square $= 4^2 = 16$
Area of large square $= 12^2 = 144$
Number of small squares $= 144 \div 16$
$= 9$
9 small squares would fit inside the large square.

17 Area $= \frac{1}{2} \times$ base $\times$ height
$= \frac{1}{2} \times 10 \times 8$
$= 40$
The area is 40 cm^2.

MEASUREMENT AND GEOMETRY (Real Test)
Area and volume Page 79

1 7.29 **2** A **3** A **4** C **5** C **6** B **7** C **8** B **9** C **10** C **11** D **12** D **13** C **14** 152 **15** A **16** 24.4

EXPLANATIONS

1 Area $= 2.7^2$
$= 7.29$ The area is 7.29 cm^2.

2 Perimeter = 24 cm
Sum of length and breadth = 12 cm
If length is twice breadth, then length is 8 cm and breadth is 4 cm.
Area of rectangle $= 8 \times 4$
$= 32$
The area is 32 cm^2.

3

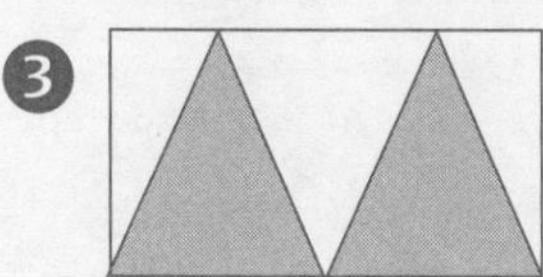

Area of rectangle = 16 cm^2
Sum of areas of triangles = 8 cm^2
Area of one triangle = 4 cm^2

4 New dimensions are 8 cm by 6 cm
Old area $= 4 \times 3$
$= 12$
New area $= 8 \times 6$
$= 48$
Area has increased from 12 cm^2 to 48 cm^2.
The new area is 4 times the area of the original.

5 The shaded square covers 4 units.
This means the scale is 4 units = 8 cm^2
1 unit = 2 cm^2
By counting there are 20 units that are unshaded.
Area unshaded $= 20 \times 2$
$= 40$
The unshaded area is 40 cm^2.

6 Area of remaining shape $= 6 \times 4 - x \times x$
$= 24 - x^2$
The area is $(24 - x^2)$ cm^2.

7 Using $A = \pi r^2$
$A = \pi \times 6^2$
$= 113.097\ 3355$
$= 113$ (to nearest whole)
Area is 113 cm^2.

8 Perimeter = 48
Side length $= 48 \div 4$
$= 12$
The square has side length of 12 cm.
Halving the dimensions: side length is 6 cm.
Area of new square $= 6 \times 6$
$= 36$
The area is 36 cm^2.

9 Surface area $= 2 \times 12 + 2 \times 8 + 2 \times 6$
$= 52$ $\therefore$ 52 cm^2

10 Original square: Area = 16 cm^2
Side length = 4 cm
Perimeter $= 4 \times 4$
$= 16$ $\therefore$ 16 cm
New square: Area = 36 cm^2
Side length = 6 cm
Perimeter $= 4 \times 6$
$= 24$ $\therefore$ 24 cm
Increase in perimeter $= 24 - 16$
$= 8$
The perimeter has increased by 8 cm.

11 Surface area = 600
Area of each face = 600 ÷ 6
= 100
Length of each side = 10 ∴ 10 cm
Volume = 10 × 10 × 10
= 1000
The volume is 1000 cm^3.

12 Consider each of the choices:
10 × 10 × 5 = 500
25 × 50 × 25 = 31 250
20 × 20 × 4 = 1600
40 × 5 × 5 = 1000
Dimensions are 40 m × 5 m × 5 m.

13 Area = Square + Triangle

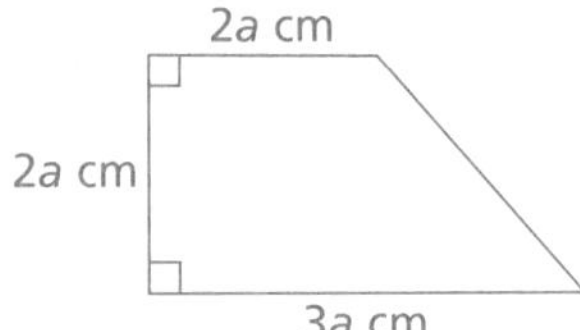

$$\text{Area} = 2a \times 2a + \frac{1}{2} \times a \times 2a$$
$$= 4a^2 + a^2$$
$$= 5a^2$$
The area is $5a^2$ cm^2.

14 The hexagonal prism has 2 hexagons and 6 rectangles:
Surface area = 2 × 16 + 6 × 20
= 152
The surface area is 152 cm^2.

15 Using $A = \pi r^2$ and $\pi = 3$
$A = 3 \times 7^2$
$= 3 \times 49$
$= 147$
The approximate area is 150 cm^2.

16 The diagonals form 6 identical triangles.
Area of hexagon = 73.2
Area of triangle = 73.2 ÷ 6
= 12.2
As the rhombus is made from two triangles:
Area of rhombus = 12.2 × 2
= 24.4
The area is 24.4 cm^2.

SPELLING (Real Test)
Common misspellings Pages 82–83

1 formerly
2 international
3 hypothesis
4 perspective
5 formulae
6 breathe
7 apprentice
8 conscious
9 justice
10 manufacture
11 synchronised
12 prioritise
13 prejudice
14 preference
15 discussed
16 breath
17 accomplice
18 novice
19 cloth
20 percussion
21 sacrifice
22 conscience
23 radius
24 emigrate
25 armistice

GRAMMAR AND PUNCTUATION (Real Test)
Pronouns, prepositions, articles, subject/verb agreement Pages 86–88

1 A **2** B **3** D **4** B **5** B **6** B **7** A **8** A **9** D **10** C **11** B **12** A **13** D **14** C **15** D **16** D **17** D **18** A **19** C **20** A **21** adjective: thrilling; proper noun: Balin **22** A, B, C **23** A, C **24** A **25** B

EXPLANATIONS

1 This is a grammar question. The correct answer is: *The fathers played football in the backyard all day*.
Tip: This is the only sentence with a subject (*The fathers*) and a main verb (*played*) in the active voice that describes an action and who performed it. B, C and D are in the passive voice and do not specify who performed the action (this is either unknown, unimportant or obvious).

2 This is a grammar question. The correct sentence is: *Thinking only of himself, Peter began eating the wrapped chocolates in the box.*
Tip: The comma comes after the word clause *Thinking only of himself* to indicate that this is an adverbial clause. An adverbial clause describes when, where, how or why an action has taken place.

3 This is a grammar question. The correct answer is D.
Tip: The definite article *the* refers to a specific object, group or person that has been previously mentioned. The indefinite articles *a* and *an* refer to an unknown or unspecified object, group or person. We know which old dog is referred to (*the one that is tired*) so must use the definite article. There is no specific bed referred to, so we must use the indefinite article. Note that *an* is used before words beinning with a vowel and *a* is used before words beginning with a consonant.

4 This is a grammar question. The correct sentence is: *Ron and Judy have nothing but admiration for their dog, Juju the star: 'We're just so proud of her. She really is a super dog.'*
Tip: The comma indicates the beginning of the adjectival clause *Juju the star*. An adjectival clause acts like an adjective as it adds more information to a noun.

5 This is a grammar question. The correct sentence is: *Terry felt that had he performed better at school then he would not be feeling so unsatisfied with his career.*
Tip: Singular subjects (nouns) need singular verbs; plural subjects (nouns) need plural verbs.

6 This is a punctuation question. The correct sentence is: *Ellen said that working in the hospital was the best experience she had ever had.*
Tip: This is an example of indirect speech. No actual words are spoken so quotation marks are not needed. No question is actually asked so no question mark is needed.

7 This is a punctuation question. The correct sentence is: *Running swiftly like a gazelle, the young boy caught up to Jamie, his younger brother.*
Tip: The comma in this sentence comes after the adverbial clause *Running swiftly like a gazelle*. An adverbial clause acts like an adverb as it adds more information to an action. Capital letters must be used for the names of people as they are proper nouns.

8 This is a punctuation question. The correct sentence is: *'Don't worry about coming in to work tomorrow,' her boss said, 'the office is flooded.'*
Tip: Only the actual words spoken are enclosed in the quotation marks (inverted commas). A comma after the spoken words and before the last quotation mark indicates that the dialogue tag is part of the sentence. A comma must also come after the dialogue tag to indicate that the second part of the dialogue is still part of the one sentence.

9 This is a grammar question. The incorrect contraction is *you're.*

Tip: Apostrophes can be used to indicate a contraction. The word *you're* is a contraction of the words *you are*. In this sentence the writer wishes to say *you were* (past tense) and therefore the contraction used is incorrect.

10 This is a punctuation question. The correct sentence is: *I certainly wouldn't trust a surgeon who wasn't registered as a professional.*
Tip: There are two contractions in this statement that must be indicated by an apostrophe. There is no direct question asked so a question mark is not needed.

11 This is a grammar question. The correct answer is: *from being hit.*
Tip: *From* is a preposition that indicates a removal or exclusion. In this case, *from* indicates that Madison is being removed from harm.

12 This is a grammar question. The correct word is the verb *was*.
Tip: Singular subjects (nouns) need singular verbs; plural subjects (nouns) need plural verbs. In this case the subject is singular, *JuJu*, and needs a singular verb *was* and not *were*.

13 This is a grammar question. The correct sentence is: *'It's just unbelievable that Maddie didn't get badly hurt.'*
Tip: Singular subjects (nouns) need singular verbs; plural subjects (nouns) need plural verbs. In this case the subject is singular, *Maddie*, and needs a singular verb *get*, and not *got*.

14 This is a grammar question. The correct word is the contraction *could've*.
Tip: This is a contraction of the words *could have*. It is often misspelled as 'could of'. With the irregular verb *could* (past participle of can) you need a 'helper'—another verb to 'help' it. *Have*, *has* and *had* can be helping verbs.

15 This is a grammar question. The correct word is the noun *tourists*.
Tip: *Tourists* is the plural form of the noun *tourist*. The past tense verbs *were happy* indicate that the subject must be a plural, *tourists* and not *tourist*.

16 This is a grammar question. The correct answer is the adverb *Where*.
Tip: An adverb describes the action of a person or thing. The adverb *where* relates to the action and location of the *onions*.

17 This is a grammar question. The correct word is the verb *was*.
Tip: Singular subjects (nouns) need singular verbs. In this case, the singular subject *weather* needs a singular verb, *was* and not *were*.

18 This is a grammar question. The correct answer is the past tense verbs *were tired*.
Tip: The past tense verbs *were tired* must be used as plural subjects (nouns). In this case, the subject is *girls* and needs the past tense plural verb *were* and the past tense verb *tired*.

19 This is a grammar question. The correct word is the verb *wasn't*.
Tip: The past tense singular verb *wasn't* must be used for singular subjects (nouns). In this case, the subject is *he* and needs the past tense singular verb *wasn't*.

20 This is a grammar question. The correct word is the verb *were*.
Tip: Plural subjects (nouns) need plural verbs. In this case, the plural subject *birds* needs a plural verb, *were* and not *was*.

21 This is a grammar question. The correct answers are *thrilling* and *Balin.*
Tip: Adjectives are describing words and can come after the noun. Proper nouns include the names of people.

22 This is a punctuation question. The correct sentence is: *Don't you dare eat that pie, it's Ari's.*
Tip: *Don't* requires an apostrophe because it is a contraction of *do not*. *It's* requires an apostrophe because it is a contraction of *it is*. *Ari's* requires an apostrophe to indicate possession—Ari owns the pie.

23 This is a punctuation question. The correct sentence is: *'It's absolutely unbelievable!' exclaimed Heather. 'Where did you find it?'*
Tip: Only the actual words spoken are enclosed in the quotation marks (inverted commas). The dialogue tag *exclaimed Heather* does not require quotation marks.

24 This is a grammar question. The correct sentence is: *Madison had woken from her daily nap early and had stealthily escaped out of the front door of their home.*
Tip: The adverb *out* indicates the action of the girl as she leaves her house. The other adverbs *into*, *around* and *over* do not fit the passage as effectively.

25 This is a grammar question. The correct answer is: *even though they are expensive.*
Tip: This clause *even though they are expensive* is an adjectival clause. An adjectival clause acts like an adjective as it adds more information to a noun.

READING (Test Your Skills)
Understanding explanations Pages 89–90

Lucid Dreams

EXPLANATIONS

1 Lucid dreams are remarkable for their vividness: 'Lucid dreams can be extremely vivid'. Lucid means clear.

2 The difference between the two types of lucid dreams is the manner in which they commence. One is dream initiated and the other begins from a waking state.

3 The understanding of lucid dreams can be claimed as comprehensive: 'Lucid dreaming has been researched scientifically, and its existence is well established'.

4 Unrealistic feats performed in lucid dreams are taken for granted. The dreamer, although aware he or she is dreaming, readily accepts them as real, unrealistic feats.

5 The correct statement is: 'During lucid dreams the dreamer is aware that he or she is dreaming'. Lucid dreams are 'conscious dreams'.

6 At the highest level of a lucid dream 'the dreamer is fully aware that she or he is asleep, and can have complete control over his or her actions in the dream'.

7 Paragraph 2: the dreamer can 'exert conscious control over the dream characters and environment…'; Paragraph 3: the 'dreamscape' is defined as 'the realm where dreams take place'; Paragraph 4: explains the dreamer's awareness of dream experiences at the 'lowest' and 'highest' levels of lucidity; Paragraph 5: details the 'two ways' in which a 'lucid dream can begin'; Paragraph 6: lists the uses of 'Wake-initiated lucid dreams' including 'what you want to dream'.

8 Lucid dreams can be stimulating—they provide opportunities to explore a fantasy-type world without fear or threat.

READING (Real Test)
Understanding explanations Pages 91–92

Urban legends

1 A **2** D **3** C **4** B **5** an explanation, a narrative
6 B **7** C **8** NO, YES, NO, NO, YES

EXPLANATIONS

1 Urban legends are often regarded as true because they come from a 'teller' with 'narrative skill' who references 'allegedly trustworthy sources, such as a relative or a friend'.

2 Urban legends may gain some acceptance because they can be used as a means of making a warning: 'Sometimes, there's an implied lesson to be learnt: Be careful, this could happen to you!'. The warning for the lovers may well be to avoid isolated places.

3 The writer compares an urban myth to a virus which spreads from one person to another, 'from carrier to carrier' and

mutates, i.e. changes as it spreads. Like viruses, urban legends 'change over time'.

4 After hearing the warning, the teenage boy tried to allay the girl's fears by locking all the car doors.

5 The passage is an explanation of urban legends followed by a short story as an example, which is a narrative.

6 Urban legends are usually passed down by word of mouth. They are not recorded in writing because they have no base in truth. They are rarely reported as news.

7 The teenage boy was not afraid. He wanted to make love to the girl. When this wasn't going to happen he drove off in a fit of irritation.

8 Two conclusions can be drawn. The writer believes urban legends lack 'credibility' and cannot be believed. They do not come from 'trustworthy sources' and are also called 'myths'. The writer also states that urban legends are 'typically…humorous' with 'bizarre humour' being 'characteristic of urban legends'.

READING (Real Test)
Understanding recounts Pages 93–94

A trip to The Tip

1 D 2 a sincere tone; geographical facts 3 A 4 A 5 3, 5, 1, 4, 2 6 1 bumpy; 2 sudden; 3 dry; 4 gushing 7 C 8 D

EXPLANATIONS

1 The writer most likely expected an offer to go to the tip a bit odd (perplexing), expecting tip to refer to a rubbish dump.

2 The writer adopts a sincere tone when describing her experiences, giving insight into her thoughts and emotions. There are geographical facts in the recount including the latitude of Port Moresby and the map of Cape York Peninsula.

3 The sign was predictable, in that it provided basic information for visitors to the tip. It was merely put there as a photo opportunity.

4 You need to look at the map. To go directly from Thursday Island to Seisia you would have to pass between Horn Island and Prince of Wales Island.

5 Paragraph 4: The writer says, 'We passed… the remnants of an Eco Lodge'. Paragraph 5: Then on a climb they passed 'grey nomads'. Paragraph 6: While looking out at the Torres Strait from the summit they saw 'sailing yachts'. Paragraph 7: They left 'the northernmost point' of Australia reluctantly, and 'After lunch' they visited 'air wrecks from World War II'.

6 'Bumpy' is a better description for the road because the 'creek beds' are described as 'rutted' which has a similar meaning. 'Sudden' can only describe the 'pockets of monsoon rain forest'. The best word to describe the 'creek beds' is 'dry' because they could not be 'rutted' if they had water in them. By contrast, 'gushing' describes the deep streams.

7 There was really no obligation to take a picture but the writer felt obliged to have one taken. It's a tongue-in-cheek comment—spoken with gentle irony as a joke.

8 The view at the tip was so appealing it would have inspired a professional photographer. It was good enough to put on a postcard.

READING (Real Test)
Understanding recounts Pages 95–96

Concorde

1 C 2 A 3 CORRECT, CORRECT, INCORRECT, CORRECT, INCORRECT 4 D 5 written response 6 B, D 7 A 8 D 9 A

EXPLANATIONS

1 A top gun is the very best in a particular field. Christian was a top pilot in the Concorde fleet.

2 The Concorde's flight was to have taken the passengers to New York where many of them intended to board a liner and sail to Australia for the 2000 Olympics.

3 The first two statements are CORRECT. On 25 July 2000 Captain Marty 'held back his Concorde flight departure for an hour' then 'taxied…onto runway 24'. The text states, 'Destination: New York'. The next statement is INCORRECT: In 2000 Marty 'had been flying Air France aeroplanes for more than thirty years'. The next statement is CORRECT. In 1982 he was 18 years younger than in 2000 when he was 54. So he was 36 when he went to Senegal. The last statement is INCORRECT. The crash was in 2000.

4 As the Concorde left the ground on take-off, Marty was given chilling information from the control tower: 'Concorde zero... 4590, you have flames... You have flames behind you!'

5 It is not possible to abort a take-off when the plane's speed reaches 380 km/h.

6 The writer feels admiration and regret. The writer values Marty as fit and courageous with a confident personality but regrets what happened to him and the Concorde. What had been 'romantic' and 'adventurous' ended as 'an ugly exclamation'.

7 The term an ugly exclamation mark implies that history of the aircraft ended in a dramatic and disastrous manner. Exclamation marks represent a sudden and often unexpected response from a person.

8 The words the gleaming white bird, starkly underlined with black and crimson smoke draws a stark comparison between a thing of beauty and it's grisly ending. The white of the plane could represent purity and the red and black could represent death and destruction.

9 The writer concludes that the era of the Concorde was an accomplishment not only of Anglo-French cooperation, but a long period of successful flying.

WRITING (Real Test)
Description 1

Page 99

Tick each correct point.
Read the student's work through once to get an overall view of their response.

Focus on general points

- ☐ Did it make sense?
- ☐ Did it flow?
- ☐ Did it arouse your interest?
- ☐ Did you want to read on to understand more about the scene?
- ☐ Was the handwriting readable?

Now focus on the detail. Read the following points and find out whether the student's work has these features.

Focus on content

- ☐ Is the general scene and basic location clearly stated?
- ☐ Has the writer provided some physical general description of scene, landscape?
- ☐ Is the description broken up into parts (e.g. house, tree, pond)?
- ☐ Does the writer try to put the scene in a time frame (e.g. late autumn day)? (optional)
- ☐ Is relevant detail included (e.g. *long verandah*)?
- ☐ Does the language create clear pictures?
- ☐ Does the writer make reference to reactions to the scene through several senses (e.g. *cool water*)?
- ☐ Does the writer convey any feelings created by the scene?
- ☐ Is there a concluding comment, opinion or reaction to the scene?

Focus on structure, vocabulary, grammar, spelling, punctuation

- ☐ Is the description in the present tense?
- ☐ Was there variation in sentence length and beginnings?
- ☐ Are there paragraphs separating different aspects of the scene?
- ☐ Has the writer used any similes (e.g. *reflected as if in a mirror*)?
- ☐ Is there a generous use of adjectives to enhance the writing (e.g. *cool, shady lawns*)?

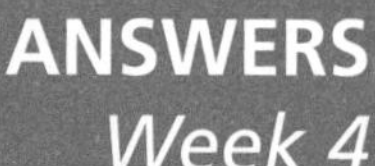

- ☐ Are adverbs used effectively (e.g. *sitting snugly by ...*)?
- ☐ Were capital letters where they should have been?
- ☐ Was punctuation correct?
- ☐ Was the spelling of words correct?

Practical suggestion: ask yourself if you can visualise the scene.

Marker's suggestions (optional)

WRITING (Real Test)
Description 2 Page 100

Tick each correct point.
Read the student's work through once to get an overall view of their response.

Focus on general points

- ☐ Did it make sense?
- ☐ Did it flow?
- ☐ Did it arouse your interest?
- ☐ Did you want to read on to understand more about the scene?
- ☐ Was the handwriting readable?

Now focus on the detail. Read the following points and find out whether the student's work has these features.

Focus on content

- ☐ Is the general scene and basic location clearly stated?
- ☐ Has the writer provided some physical general description of scene, landscape?
- ☐ Is the description broken up into parts (e.g. house, tree, pond)?
- ☐ Does the writer try to put the scene in a time frame (e.g. late autumn day)? (optional)
- ☐ Is relevant detail included (e.g. *long verandah*)?
- ☐ Does the language create clear pictures?
- ☐ Does the writer make reference to reactions to the scene through several senses (e.g. *cool water*)?
- ☐ Does the writer convey any feelings created by the scene?
- ☐ Is there a concluding comment, opinion or reaction to the scene?

Focus on structure, vocabulary, grammar, spelling, punctuation

- ☐ Is the description in the present tense?
- ☐ Was there variation in sentence length and beginnings?
- ☐ Are there paragraphs separating different aspects of the scene?
- ☐ Has the writer used any similes (e.g. *reflected as if in a mirror*)?
- ☐ Is there a generous use of adjectives to enhance the writing (e.g. *cool, shady lawns*)?
- ☐ Are adverbs used effectively (e.g. *sitting snugly by ...*)?
- ☐ Were capital letters where they should have been?
- ☐ Was punctuation correct?
- ☐ Was the spelling of words correct?

Practical suggestion: ask yourself if you can visualise the scene.

Marker's suggestions (optional)

WEEK 4

MEASUREMENT AND GEOMETRY (Test Your Skills)
Angles, lines and polygons Page 102

1 Other angle = 180 – (45 + 65)
= 180 – 110
= 70
The other angle is 70°.

2 $x = 60$ (alternate ∠s, parallel lines)

3 $y = 180 - 40$ (co-interior ∠s, parallel lines)
$= 140$

4 $z = 180 - (60 + 40)$ (∠ in straight line)
$= 180 - 100$
$= 80$

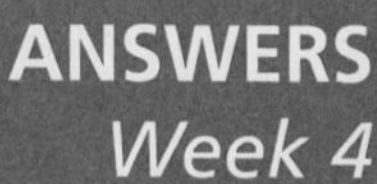

❺ Third angle = 180 – (70 + 40)
= 180 – 110
= 70

The angles are 70°, 70° and 40°.
This means that the triangle is isosceles.

❻ x = 180 – 50 (∠ in straight line)
= 130

❼ y = 180 – (50 + 110) (∠ sum of Δ)
= 180 – 160
= 20

❽ If it is an isosceles triangle, two angles are equal. If one angle is 100°, the sum of the other two equal angles is 80°. This means that the angles are both 40°.

❾ y = 360 – (150 + 70 + 120)
= 360 – 340 (∠ sum of a quadrilateral)
= 20

❿ A hexagon has 6 sides
∠ sum of polygon = 180 × (sides – 2)
Sum of hexagon = 180 × (6 – 2)
= 180 × 4
= 720

The sum of the angles is 720°.

⓫ ∠DBE = 180° – (40° + 90°)
(∠ in straight line)
= 180° – 130°
= 50°

⓬ ∠AEB = 180° – (60° + 40°) (∠ sum of Δ)
= 180° – 100°
= 80°

⓭ Isosceles triangle has 1 axis of symmetry.

⓮ This flag has 2 axes of symmetry.

⓯ If triangle is right-angled then the sum of the two identical angles will be 90°. This means that the angles are both 45°.

⓰ A pentagon has 5 sides.
Sum of polygon = 180 × (sides – 2)
Sum of pentagon = 180 × (5 – 2)
= 180 × 3
= 540

The sum of the angles is 540°.
Size of each angle in regular pentagon
= 540° ÷ 5
= 108°

⓱ One angle is 58°.
Sum of other 2 equal angles = 180° – 58°
= 122°

x = 122 ÷ 2
= 61

⓲ $y = x + 58$ (exterior ∠ of Δ is equal to the sum of the 2 opposite interior ∠s)

MEASUREMENT AND GEOMETRY (Real Test)
Angles, lines and polygons **Page 104**

1 A **2** 140 **3** A **4** D **5** A **6** D **7** A **8** D **9** B
10 85 **11** D **12** A **13** B **14** 72 **15** 2 **16** 30

EXPLANATIONS

❶ x = 180 – (90 + 31) (∠ sum of Δ)
= 180 – 121
= 59

❷ Angle is 140°.

❸ x = 43 (alternate ∠s, parallel lines)

❹ Other angle = 180 – (80 + 25) (∠ sum of Δ)
= 180 – 105
= 75

❺ A hexagon has 6 sides.
Sum of polygon = 180 × (sides – 2)
Sum of octagon = 180 × (6 – 2)
= 180 × 4
= 720

The sum of the angles is 720°.

❻
40°
120° 60° x°

x = 180 – (60 + 40) (∠ sum of Δ)
= 180 – 100
= 80

❼ y = 360 – (50 + 140 + 130)
(∠ sum of a quadrilateral)
= 360 – 320
= 40

8 Total parts = 1 + 2 + 3
= 6
6 parts = 180
1 part = 180 ÷ 6
= 30
3 parts = 30 × 3
= 90
The angle is 90°.

9 One angle is 120°.
Sum of other two equal angles
= 180° – 120°
= 60°
Size of each angle = 60° ÷ 2
= 30°

10
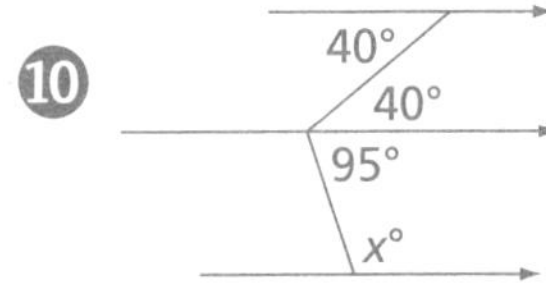

Draw another line that is parallel.
On the diagram we can show 40° (alternate ∠s, parallel lines)
Also another angle is 135° – 40°= 95°.
x = 180 – 95 (co-interior ∠s, parallel lines)
= 85

11 ∠ sum of polygon = 180 × (sides – 2)
= 180 × (10 – 2)
= 180 × 8
= 1440
The sum of the angles is 1440°.
Size of each angle in a regular 10-sided polygon = 1440° ÷ 10 = 144°

12 x = 360 – (140 + 100 + 90)
(∠ sum of a quadrilateral)
= 360 – 330
= 30

13
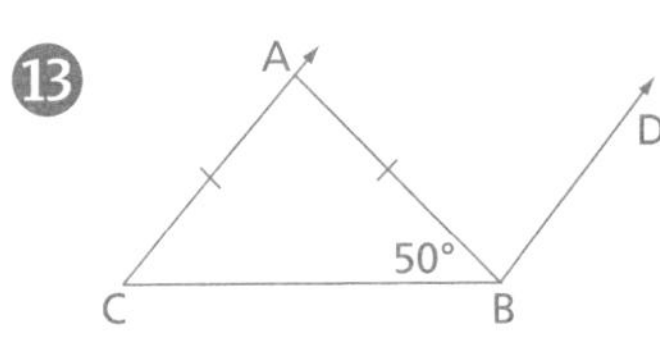

∠ACB = 50° (base ∠s of isosceles Δ equal)
∠CAB = 180° – (50° + 50°) (∠ sum of Δ)
= 180° – 100°
= 80°
∠ABD = 80° (alternate ∠s, parallel lines)

14 ∠ sum of polygon = 180 × (sides – 2)
= 180 × (5 – 2)
= 180 × 3
= 540
The sum of the angles is 540°.
Size of each angle in regular pentagon
= 540° ÷ 5
= 108°
x = 180° – 108° (∠ in straight line)
= 72°

15 A rhombus has 2 axes of symmetry.

16
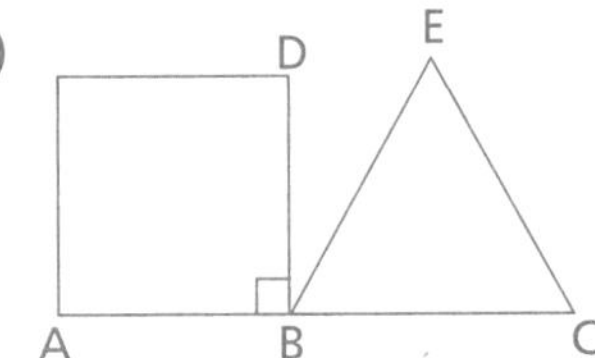

Each angle in a square is 90° and each angle in an equilateral triangle is 60°.
This means ∠ABD = 90°, ∠CBE = 60°.
∠DBE = 180° – (90° + 60°)
= 180° – 150°
= 30°

MEASUREMENT AND GEOMETRY (Test Your Skills)
3D shapes, scale and position — Page 105

1 The cube will be 2 by 2 by 2.
This means that it will have 8 small cubes.
Additional cubes = 8 – 5
= 3
Another 3 cubes are required.

2 A will be opposite C, B will be opposite E, so that D will be opposite F

3 The cubes on the 8 vertices have three painted faces. This means there will be 8 cubes.

4 A triangular prism has two triangles and three rectangles.

5 A square pyramid has 5 faces.
Consider each of the choices:
Pentagonal prism: 7 faces
Pentagonal pyramid: 6 faces
Triangular prism: 5 faces
This means that a triangular prism has the same number of faces as a square pyramid.

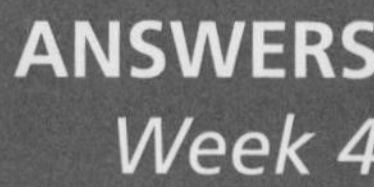

6 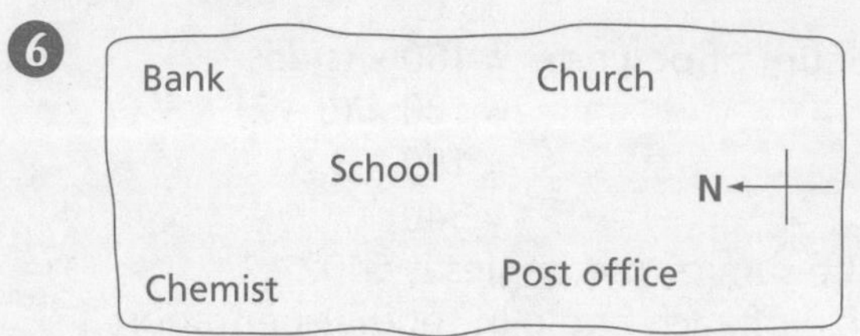

The church is east of the post office.

7 The chemist is north-west of the school.

8 The cross-section would be a circle.

9 The top view is:

10 The image is larger than the original.
In the triangles, 4 and 6 are sides that are opposite the same angle (90°).

Enlargement factor = $\frac{6}{4} = \frac{3}{2}$

11 The two triangles are similar, and the sides with measurements 2 and 4 are opposite the same angle (∠A).

Enlargement factor = $\frac{4}{2} = 2$

12 If the triangles are similar, then AE is twice the length of AC.
AE = 2 × 1.2
= 2.4
Therefore CE = 2.4 – 1.2
= 1.2
Therefore x = 1.2

MEASUREMENT AND GEOMETRY (Real Test)
3D shapes, scale and position Page 107

1 D **2** B **3** D **4** sphere **5** B **6** E **7** B **8** 2.4 **9** 1.5 **10** 9

EXPLANATIONS

1 The view from the top is:

2 A pentagon has 5 sides. This means that the net of a pentagonal prism has 5 rectangles and 2 pentagons. The answer is 5.

3 The shape that cannot be made is

4 If the cross-section is always a circle, the solid must be a sphere.

5 The point on Boa Island is $(3\frac{1}{2}, 4)$.

6 From facing X, Adam turns 270° in a clockwise direction to face point E.

7 B is south-west of C. This means Jannah is south-west of Alysha.

8 A to E is 6 units and E to D is 4 units.
Total units = 6 + 4
= 10
Distance in km = 10 × 6
= 60
Time = Distance ÷ Speed
= 60 ÷ 25
= 2.4
It would take 2.4 hours.

9 The triangles are similar.
From the diagram, matching sides are AB = 4 and AD = 4 + 2 = 6.
The enlargement factor used is found by dividing a side on the image by the matching side on the original:

Enlargement factor = $\frac{6}{4} = 1.5$

10 To find the value of x, we multiply the matching side by the enlargement factor.
$x = 6 \times 1.5$
$= 9$

SPELLING (Real Test)
Common misspellings Pages 110–111

1 erosion

2 constitution

3 immigrant

4 infrastructure

5 pilgrimage
6 principal
7 parallel
8 calculate
9 specification
10 irrelevant
11 agility
12 strategy
13 sauce
14 ingredients
15 invasion
16 scenario
17 laboratory
18 suspiciously
19 incessant
20 exhalation
21 elicited
22 individuals
23 illustrious
24 renowned
25 envisage

GRAMMAR AND PUNCTUATION
Narrative, direct and indirect speech, and clauses Pages 114–116

1 C 2 D 3 B 4 B 5 B 6 A 7 C 8 C 9 C 10 B 11 B 12 B 13 A 14 B 15 D 16 D 17 B 18 A 19 A 20 B 21 C, D 22 B 23 A 24 D 25 C imagery

EXPLANATIONS

1 This is a grammar question. The correct answer is *he was.*
Tip: Singular subjects (nouns) need singular verbs; plural subjects (nouns) need plural verbs. In this case the subject is singular, *he*, and needs a singular verb, *was,* and not *were*.

2 This is a grammar question. The word *core* is a noun.
Tip: Common nouns are the names of things. In this instance, the thing being spoken about is the persona's core. *Core* is a figurative expression for a person's identity or soul.

3 This is a grammar question. The correct word is the verb *felt.*
Tip: *Felt* is an irregular verb. Most verbs in English form their past tenses by adding *ed*. There are a number of irregular verbs where this doesn't happen. We say *felt* instead of 'felted'.

4 This is a question asking about tense. The correct answer is *past tense*.
Tip: The tense of a text is indicated by the form that the verbs take. Look at the form of the verb *spied* (past participle of *spy*).

5 This is a grammar question. The correct answer is *who was older than my mum*.
Tip: An adjectival clause functions just like an adjective in that it gives extra information to a noun or a noun group. In this example the adjectival clause *who was older than my mum* gives extra information about the woman.

6 This is a punctuation question. The correct sentence is: *Although entirely true, people are often surprised when they discover that elephants have no natural predators.*
Tip: The comma in this sentence comes after the adverbial clause *Although entirely true*. An adverbial clause acts like an adverb as it adds more information to an action. An adverbial clause comes at the beginning or end of a sentence. No question has been asked so a question mark is not needed.

7 This is a punctuation question. The correct sentence is: *I went to the local supermarket and collected all of the ingredients required for my Anzac biscuits: sugar, bicarbonate soda, oats, coconut and butter.*

Tip: A colon (:) is used to indicate the introduction of a list. Commas are used to divide items in a list.

8 This is a grammar question. The correct answer is: *three pieces of bread with three toppings.*
Tip: Brackets are used to separate a phrase or clause from the main sentence. This phrase or clause gives extra information. A sentence should be able to stand independently of the words in the brackets.

9 This is a punctuation question. The correct sentence is: *'I am thoroughly impressed by the food preparation in this kitchen!' exclaimed Darrel.*
Tip: Only the actual words spoken are enclosed in the quotation marks (inverted commas). There is no comma needed after the spoken words as an exclamation mark is used to complete the statement.

10 This is a punctuation question. The correct word is *it's*.
Tip: The word *it's* is a contraction of the words *it is* an uses an apostrophe to indicate the missing letter 'i'. The word *its* is the possessive pronoun and is not correct in this sentence.

11 This is a punctuation question. The correct sentence is: *On the night of 14 April 1912, the RMS Titanic collided with a submerged iceberg.*
Tip: The comma in this sentence comes after the adverbial clause *On the night of 14 April 1912*. An adverbial clause acts like an adverb as it adds more information to an action. An adverbial clause comes at the beginning or end of a sentence. No question has been asked so a question mark is not needed

12 This is a punctuation question. The correct answer is *indirect speech*.
Tip: This is an example of indirect speech. No actual words are spoken so quotation marks are not needed.

13 This is a question asking about narrative. The correct answer is *first person*.
Tip: First-person narrative is indicated by the use of the pronouns *I, we, me* and *us*.

14 This is a grammar question. The correct answer is *were pleased*.
Tip: *Were* is the correct plural verb as it has to agree with a subject that is greater than one.

15 This is a grammar question. The correct answer is *should have*.
Tip: With the irregular verb *should* (past participle of *shall*) you need a 'helper'— another verb to 'help' it. *Have, has* and *had* can be helping verbs. *Have* is the past participle of *has*. Singular subjects (nouns) need singular verbs; plural subjects (nouns) need plural verbs.

16 This is a grammar question. The correct word is *was*.
Tip: Singular subjects (nouns) need singular verbs; plural subjects (nouns) need plural verbs. In this case, the subject is the singular plural, *pie*, and needs a singular verb, *was*, and not *were*.

17 This is a punctuation question. The correct sentence is: *Despite the sign warning against it, Amir continued on towards the abandoned house.*
Tip: The comma in this sentence comes after the adverbial clause *Despite the sign warning against it*. An adverbial clause acts like an adverb as it adds more information to an action. The tone of this sentence suggests that it is not an exclamation so an exclamation mark is not needed. No question has been asked so a question mark is not needed.

18 This is a grammar question. The correct answer is *verb*.
Tip: A verb is a word that describes an action or state of being. In this sentence the verb *inspire* describes the attempted action of the team capatain and the effect he wants to have on his team.

19 This is a punctuation question. The correct sentence is: *Your assignment is extremely untidy; you're going to have to complete the task again.*
Tip: Capital letters must be used at the beginning of sentences. Two complete sentences that are closely linked can be joined by a semicolon but not a comma.

20 This is a punctuation question. The correct sentence is: *Phineas danced as the sun's rays rose over the green mountains.*
Tip: The apostrophe is needed to show possession in this sentence. The word *sun's* indicates that the sun possesses the rays. *Phineas* is a proper noun, and *rays* and *mountains* are plural nouns.

21 This is a punctuation question. The correct sentence is: *Marco lost his balance when Morgan, an inconsiderate and selfish child, pushed his way to the front of the canteen line.*
Tip: The two commas used here indicate the inclusion of the adjectival clause *an inconsiderate and selfish child*. An adjectival clause operates like an adjective in that it provides additional information about a noun; in this instance it is the child Morgan.

22 This is a grammar question. The word *amused* is an adjective.
Tip: An adjective is a word used to describe a place, person, event or thing. Here the adjective *amused* is used to describe Sally's grin.

23 This is a grammar question. The correct word is the verb *were*.
Tip: Singular subjects (nouns) need singular verbs; plural subjects (nouns) need plural verbs. In this case the subject is plural, *children*, and needs a plural verb, *were*, and not *was*.

24 This is a grammar question. The correct answer is *there are*.
Tip: Singular subjects (nouns) need singular verbs; plural subjects (nouns) need plural verbs. In this case the subject is plural, *people*, and needs a singular verb, *are*, and not *is*. The word *they're* is a contraction of the words *they are*, and is therefore not correct in this sentence.

25 This is a grammar question. The correct answer is *metaphor*.
Tip: A metaphor is a direct comparison between two dissimilar things. In this sentence the vehicles are being compared to sea creatures in the ocean.

READING (Test Your Skills)
Understanding visual texts Pages 117–118

Resuscitation of children

EXPLANATIONS

1 The frames are arranged in the order in which they should be carried out.

2 The symbol is meant to warn people that a situation may be dangerous or even deadly. A clue is in the heading to the frame.

3 To check if a child is unconscious it is suggested that the lobe of the ear be pinched (Frame 2).

4 A command tells you to do something and can be a single verb. The title of Frame 3 is a verb, 'SHOUT', telling you what action to take. The other titles are nouns, indicating what will be explained in the frame.

5 When you dial 000 (triple 0), the first question that is asked is which service you require (Frame 3).

6 The illustration shows the action required to open the airway (Frame 4). The head is tilted back with one hand on the forehead, and the forefinger and middle finger lift the chin.

7 An unconscious child should not be removed unless the child is in a life-threatening situation (Frame 2).

8 Putting the child into the breathing recovery position is intended to stop the tongue from blocking the airways (Frame 5).

9. The instructions on the Resuscitation of Children poster imply that any adult who arrives on the scene is responsible for initiating an assessment of the situation and, if no other people are present, for administering CPR.

READING (Real Test)
Understanding visual texts Pages 119–120

Example 1: Magic Trick

1 B 2 A 3 CORRECT, INCORRECT, INCORRECT, INCORRECT, CORRECT 4 perform in a showy style 5 C 6 B 7 C 8 NO, YES, YES, NO, NO

EXPLANATIONS

1. The intention of the magic trick page is to provide instructions in a light-hearted, easy-to-follow way.
2. The thought bubble with a question mark is a cartoonist's device to show a puzzled or bewildered character.
3. The act is called a magic trick but is based on an illusion created by changing the cards. The gambit, an act calculated to gain advantage, is what happens when the performer's back is turned. 'None of the three cards shown the second time' are the same. 'Victim' suggests a person can be fooled by the trick. The running spiel (non-stop talking) draws attention away from the magician's hands.
4. The performer should 'ham up' his distracting action to draw attention away from the switch the magician is doing. A ham actor is one that over-acts and performs in a showy style.

Example 2: Comic Strip

5. The series of frames in the comic strip are simply intended to amuse and entertain the reader.
6. The humour is sick humour. It depends upon the reader feeling revulsion at what might have happened—eating worms and meatballs made from the meat of sick sheep.
7. A good title would be The Master Chef. This carries a certain amount of irony as the chef is anything but a master chef.
8. The four people are not drawn as caricatures (exaggerating physical characteristics) of famous people but as stereotypes, representing the idea of a typical magician (hair, suit, smile), surprised volunteer (unkempt hair, casual shirt, facial expressions), bad cook (untidy chef's hat and apron, unshaven) and Australian farm hand (bush hat, shirt). Both have a resolved ending: full explanation of the trick; the disappointed reaction of the farm hand. In Example 1 only the magician speaks, to the reader, not to the volunteer. There is some conflict in Example 2: 'What's the excuse this time?'

READING (Real Test)
Understanding procedures Pages 122–123

How to change a car tyre

1 C 2 D 3 C 4 B 5 A 6 4, 5, 1, 3, 2 7 D 8 written response 9 B

EXPLANATIONS

1. These instructions would be most useful when the driver is in an isolated location and has no-one to call upon for help.
2. Whatever and wherever the situation, it is recommended that the driver turn on the hazard lights.
3. If the car is on flat ground for tyre changing it makes it safer for securing the jack. The car is less likely to roll.
4. The flat tyre should be repaired as soon as possible. There is no knowing when the driver could get the next flat. A flat spare tyre could leave the driver stranded.
5. If the flat tyre is jacked right off the ground before loosening the wheel nuts, it will make the nuts difficult to remove. The wheel will spin.
6. 'As a safety measure place a chock…; Step 3: 'Locate the notch or groove (jacking point)'; Step 5: 'elevate the car's flat wheel right off

the ground'; Step 7: 'Place the spare against the wheel's assembly unit, lining the holes up with the studs'; Step 7: 'Tighten all the wheel nuts … A little extra twist may be given by the brace'.

7. For most people these instructions are only useful in a situation where no help or service is available.

8. Loosening the wheel nuts could be difficult because they could be tight and extra force may be needed to loosen them.

9. The driver should check the spare tyre regularly. The spare tyre can lose pressure, and even become flat, without the driver knowing it. This could result in the driver being stranded on an isolated length of road.

READING (Real Test)
Understanding essays **Pages 123–124**

The silent epidemic

1 B 2 D 3 C 4 A 5 B 6 written response 7 B 8 D 9 OPINION, FACT, OPINION, FACT

EXPLANATIONS

1. The writer objects most strongly to the use of calculators in schools—especially primary schools.

2. This would be a standard excuse by anyone who was totally reliant on a calculator.

3. The writer would be happy to see calculators used for complex operations—calculators 'are permitted, even essential, in many advanced mathematics and science classes because they increase speed and efficiency—both necessary in today's businesses and industries'.

4. An epidemic is an outbreak of a disease that spreads quickly and extensively and often with unpleasant effects. The writer sees the use of calculators in a similar light.

5. Both sugar and salt are not harmful if used when needed and in moderation. Used to excess they can cause serious health problems. As the writer sees it—so can calculators.

6. The skill the writer sees as most useful when using a calculator is to be able to quickly determine if the solution provided is reasonable. The writer gives the example of mistakes made with decimal points.

7. 'Coined' means 'to invent a new word or phrase'. 'Calcuholism' is a combination of calculator and alcoholism, a word created by the writer for this essay.

8. The essay is light-hearted but the writer has some genuine concerns about the misuse of calculators.

9. The writer says parents are partly to blame for letting students use calculators but there is no supporting evidence. It is a fact that phones and desktops have calculators. The amount of work prepared by teachers that is reliant on calculators cannot be quantified and it is an opinion to say it is 'too much'. Because 'speed and efficiency… are necessary in today's businesses', it is a fact that some careers require calculator skills.

WRITING (Real Test)
Recount 1 **Page 127**

Tick each correct point.
Read the student's work through once to get an overall view of their response.

Focus on general points

- ☐ Did it make sense?
- ☐ Did it flow?
- ☐ Did the story arouse any feeling?
- ☐ Did you want to read on? Did the story create any suspense?
- ☐ Was the handwriting readable?

Now focus on the detail. Read the following points and find out whether the student's work has these features.

Focus on content

- ☐ Did the opening sentence(s) introduce the subject of the recount?
- ☐ Was the setting established (i.e. where the action took place)?
- ☐ Was the reader told when the action takes place?

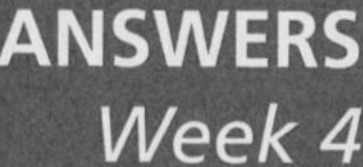

- ☐ Was it apparent who the main character(s) is?
- ☐ Have personal pronouns been used (e.g. *I, we, our*)?
- ☐ Were the events recorded in chronological (time) order?
- ☐ Was the recount in the past tense?
- ☐ Did the writing include some personal comments on the events (surprised, thrilled)?
- ☐ Did descriptions make reference to any of the senses (e.g. *wet rocks, salty air*)?
- ☐ Were interesting details included?
- ☐ Did the conclusion have a satisfactory summing-up comment?

Focus on structure, vocabulary, grammar, spelling and punctuation

- ☐ Was there a variation in sentence length and beginnings?
- ☐ Was a new paragraph started for changes in time, place or action?
- ☐ Were subheadings used? (optional)
- ☐ Were adjectives used to improve descriptions (e.g. *smelly bait*)?
- ☐ Were adverbs used to make 'actions' more interesting (e.g. *yelled loudly*)?
- ☐ Are time words used for time changes (e.g. *later, soon, then*)?
- ☐ Were capital letters used where they should have been?
- ☐ Was punctuation correct?
- ☐ Was the spelling of words correct?

Marker's suggestions (optional)

WRITING (Real Test)
Recount 2 Page 128

Tick each correct point.
Read the student's work through once to get an overall view of their response.

Focus on general points

- ☐ Did it make sense?
- ☐ Did it flow?
- ☐ Did the story arouse any feeling?
- ☐ Did you want to read on? Did the story create any suspense?
- ☐ Was the handwriting readable?

Now focus on the detail. Read the following points and find out whether the student's work has these features.

Focus on content

- ☐ Did the opening sentence(s) introduce the subject of the recount?
- ☐ Was the setting established (i.e. where the action took place)?
- ☐ Was the reader told when the action takes place?
- ☐ Was it apparent who the main character(s) is?
- ☐ Have personal pronouns been used (e.g. *I, we, our*)?
- ☐ Were the events recorded in chronological (time) order?
- ☐ Was the recount in the past tense?
- ☐ Did the writing include some personal comments on the events (surprised, thrilled)?
- ☐ Did descriptions make reference to any of the senses (e.g. *wet rocks, salty air*)?
- ☐ Were interesting details included?
- ☐ Did the conclusion have a satisfactory summing-up comment?

Focus on structure, vocabulary, grammar, spelling and punctuation

- ☐ Was there a variation in sentence length and beginnings?
- ☐ Was a new paragraph started for changes in time, place or action?
- ☐ Were subheadings used? (optional)
- ☐ Were adjectives used to improve descriptions (e.g. *smelly bait*)?
- ☐ Were adverbs used to make 'actions' more interesting (e.g. *yelled loudly*)?
- ☐ Are time words used for time changes (e.g. *later, soon, then*)?
- ☐ Were capital letters used where they should have been?
- ☐ Was punctuation correct?
- ☐ Was the spelling of words correct?

Marker's suggestions (optional)

SAMPLE TEST PAPERS

SAMPLE TEST PAPER 1

LITERACY—WRITING Page 130

Persuasive text

Tick each correct point.

Read the student's work through once to get an overall view of their response.

Focus on general points

- ☐ Did it make sense?
- ☐ Did it flow? Were the arguments logical and relevant?
- ☐ Did the opinions expressed arouse any feelings/reactions?
- ☐ Was the body of the writing mainly in the third person?
- ☐ Did you want to read on to understand/ appreciate the writer's point of view?
- ☐ Were the arguments convincing?
- ☐ Has the writer been assertive (e.g. the use of *is* rather than a less definite term)?
- ☐ Was the handwriting readable?
- ☐ Was the writing style suitable for a persuasive text (objective; not casual or dismissive)?

Now focus on the detail. Read each of the following points and find out whether the student's work has these features.

Focus on content

- ☐ Did the opening sentence(s) focus on the topic?
- ☐ Was the writer's point of view established early in the writing?
- ☐ Did the writer include any evidence to support his or her opinion?
- ☐ Did the writer include information relevant to his or her experiences?
- ☐ Were the points/arguments raised by the writer easy to follow?
- ☐ Did the writing follow the format with an introduction, the body of the text and a conclusion?
- ☐ Were personal opinions included?
- ☐ Was the concluding paragraph relevant to the topic?

Focus on structure, vocabulary, grammar, spelling, punctuation

- ☐ Was there a variety of sentence lengths, types and beginnings?
- ☐ Was a new paragraph started for each additional argument or point?
- ☐ Has the writer used any similes (e.g. *as clear as crystal*) to stress a point raised?
- ☐ Did the writer avoid approximations such as *probably, perhaps* and *maybe*?
- ☐ Did the writer use such phrases as *I know …* and *It is important to …*?
- ☐ Did the writer refer to the question in the points raised (A good way to do this is to use the key words from the question or the introduction.)?
- ☐ Has the writer used any less common words correctly?
- ☐ Was indirect speech used correctly?
- ☐ Were adjectives used to improve descriptions (e.g. *expensive buildings*)?
- ☐ Were adverbs used effectively (e.g. *firstly*)?
- ☐ Were capital letters used correctly?
- ☐ Was punctuation used correctly?
- ☐ Was the spelling of words correct?

Marker's suggestions (optional)

LITERACY—READING Pages 131–143

Minimum-water gardens

1 A **2** C **3** dry riverbed garden **4** A **5** D **6** B **7** A seasonal; B traditional; C vivid; D self-sustaining; E food-producing **8** written response **9** C

EXPLANATIONS

1 The writer is encouraging people to consider gardens that use less water. The writer states: 'In these times of increasing water demands in a period of lower rainfall and a dwindling supply, it may be time for gardeners to think more about drier gardens'.

2 A cacti garden needs a minimum of water. Raising the garden, as shown in the photograph, is a way of getting maximum drainage.

3 The dry riverbed garden is based on a natural dry riverbed which has no water during prolonged dry weather and excessive water when the river is flowing.

4 Dry gardens are becoming increasingly relevant not only because of climate change but because an increased population would require more water for basic living.

5 An important purpose of the Royal Botanic Gardens (Cranbourne) is to display a wide range of plants and habitats. These could be suitable models for many home gardens.

6 A seki-tei garden is often used for prayer, indicating they have a peaceful purpose.

7 The Dry River Bed garden changes 'on a seasonal basis' due to water flow. The Japanese seki tei is a traditional garden, one that has a long history. 'The Japanese have always had their seki tei.' The other gardens are recent innovations at the Botanic Gardens. The 'flower displays' in the Arid Garden 'bring colours' to the landscape. 'Vivid' is a synonym for colourful. The Cacti Garden requires 'little maintenance'. In the Red Sand Garden 'edible berries used for food' are produced.

8 Cacti gardens can fail because they are given too much attention and care—or 'too much love'.

9 The Dry River Bed Garden at the Botanic Gardens is designed with curved lines to represent the bends of a river.

So you want to be an actor?

10 corporate films OR company training films
11 D **12** B **13** 5, 2, 4, 1, 3 **14** C **15** B **16** A
17 see explanation

EXPLANATIONS

10 For an actor, 'a lot of the work' is available in commercials and 'corporate films' or 'company training films'. Immediate money can be made and 'these actually pay better'.

11 Anyone who backs a low-budget film could be considered a gambler. They are taking a risk that the film will make some money—this is not likely with many low-budget films.

12 To make a success of acting, John recommends treating acting as a business. He states: 'remember that it (acting) is a business and treat it as such'.

13 A typical career path for an actor is: extra, 'fifty-worder', featured extra, guest appearance, regular. Not all actors follow this path.

14 John Andrews recommends not only knowing the lines required, but being polite to industry people—'you don't know how much influence they may have'.

15 With a low-budget film many people accept a variety of additional duties. John Andrews acted in a film and later helped edit the film: 'Producing can mean anything from finding the money to put on a play or television show, to finding the actors, directors, venues and getting anything required for the production'.

16 An actor's life is precarious, that is, it is uncertain and insecure: 'You may be the centre of attention one day and almost ignored the next'. He also finds it interesting. He gets opportunities to meet people and do different things as well as act in different media.

17 In 'Minimum-water gardens' the writer sustains a formal tone, avoiding emotive language and using longer sentences and no contractions or colloquialisms. By contrast, the writer of 'So you want to be an actor?' personalises the text and uses informal language, e.g. 'In one budget film I was in'; 'I once read'. Although they write mostly in past tense, both writers include present tense: 'We usually think'; 'This is'. The writer of 'So you want to be an actor?' gives the meanings of some words in parentheses, e.g. 'edit it (decide which parts to use and

throw out)'. The writer of 'Minimum-water gardens' uses parentheses to explain the plural spelling of 'Cacti' and give the biological name of a shrub. The writer suggests 'It is time for gardeners to consider drier gardens…'. The writer of 'So you want to be an actor?' makes a number of suggestions: 'Be professional. Turn up on time'.

Desert Dweller

18 C **19** A **20** B **21** lizard—webbed, sharp, waxed; environment—knotted, searing **22** C, E **23** C

EXPLANATIONS

18 The poet uses 'torpedoes' as a verb, not a noun, to suggest rapid movement across the terrain, i.e. how the lizard moves, rather than a comparison of shape. The lizard is moving across 'rock' and 'sand'.

19 'Splay' means 'spread out, turned outwards'. Therefore 'spread' is closest in meaning because it is the lizard's webbed toes that spread as it runs over rock and sand.

20 The poet describes the lizard's eyes as 'sharp agate'. 'Agate' implies a gemstone or marble quality, a hardness, and in the context of the stanza the word 'sharp' means 'alert'. It adds to the description of the lizard as well equipped to fight off its foes.

21 'Knotted' describes the 'terrain', and 'searing' describes the 'sand'. Both are aspects of the environment. The lizard's toes are 'webbed'. The metaphor, 'dressed in armour' refers to the lizard's skin which is also described as 'waxed leather mail', i.e. the lizard's skin is shiny and leathery. 'Sharp' describes the lizard's eyesight.

22 The poem examines the way the lizard lives and moves (its agility), and how it has adapted to survive in a harsh environment. It is the poet's choice of strong positive imagery ('sharp agate eyes'), which reveals that she does marvel at the ability of the lizard. The lizard is able to divine rock and sand with its feet, it 'dances with the land, a flamenco first and then the tango', which suggests they are partners or equals and it is a 'jousting knight', defending itself against foes with an arsenal of physiological features—'muscle, sinew, instinct'.

23 Throughout the poem the lizard is personified. This is the case even in the title, *Desert Dweller*, which is a term usually used for humans who live in desert environments. The lizard is personified as someone who has the ability to perform divination, as a dancer with a 'repertoire' and as a 'jousting knight'.

Cadaver Dog

24 D **25** 2, 3, 1, 4 **26** A **27** rapid, destructive **28** A **29** B **30** INCORRECT, CORRECT, INCORRECT, INCORRECT, CORRECT

EXPLANATIONS

24 Shane was awakened by the crackling sound. The dog growling would not have been as 'alien' as the crackling sound.

25 Shane became aware of a strange sound (1). Then the dog barked (2) and Shane's father switched on a light (3). Finally Shane's father called the fire brigade on his mobile phone (4).

26 A 'nagging worry' refers to a source of mental discomfort he had. It is irritating like a nagging person. This worry is nagging because Shane cannot think of a reason for the fire. Somewhere in the back of his mind he is aware that someone may have called out.

27 The speed of the fire was rapid. From a flickering of light it soon engulfed the building—'the flames ... turned from a bonfire into an inferno'. The firefighters arrived too late. The fire was also destructive. In a short space of time 'the old school house was little more than a large smouldering heap of burning timber and twisted corrugated iron'.

28 The writer has used a metaphor to describe the shadows. They seemed to twist about like dancers. Grotesque means 'misshapen in a disturbing way'.

ANSWERS
Sample Test Paper 1—Literacy

29 Shane's father swore because he fumbled with the phone: 'His father was fumbling with his mobile phone and swearing impatiently'.

30 During the fire Caddy, the dog, stayed with Shane and his father, at times barking and 'whining nervously' while 'on her haunches near Shane's feet'. Shane and his father watched the firefighters from a distance. After seeing the firemen 'had found something', Shane remembered hearing a cry when he woke up and told his father a 'person had died in the fire'. This is what upset Shane, not the destruction of the old school. Shane's father began to put 'pieces together' but the cause of the fire is unknown.

Book review: Facetime

31 A **32** D **33** C **34** somewhat frightening **35** B **36** C **37** D **38** The reviewer has kept her love of technology a secret; The reviewer positively endorses the novel.

EXPLANATIONS

31 The story is for teenagers: It is 'a fun read for the 16-plus young person (of any age)'. It uses the language teenagers are familiar with.

32 The main theme of the book is a search for true love: 'Is love in a chat room the same as love in real life?' The cover of the book with its love heart and frolicking lovers tends to confirm this.

33 The heavy use of jargon tends to imply that the book was well researched. The author is no longer a teenager: 'The Author, Winnie Salamon, is a writer and freelance journalist who has written about everything from amputee fetishes to Posh Spice. This is her first novel'. This implies she has passed the teenage stage.

34 'Intimidating' means 'to frighten or overawe someone', sometimes making a person do what they might not want to.

35 The graphic on the cover suggests that *Facetime* is a successful dating program. The graphics of the love heart and frolicking lovers supports this expectation. There is an obvious similarity in the name with Facebook.

36 The word 'pixellated' is used to describe an image on a computer screen that is made up of pixels (tiny dots). Esmerelda uses an Internet chat room to meet Jack.

37 Esmerelda's chat room experience results in sharing secrets: 'even passion—so much so that Jack decides to fly to Australia so they can meet'.

38 Someone who has remained in the closet is considered to have kept something secret. The writer has kept being a 'geek', her love of technology, a secret. Because she is a 'geek' she hopes the novelist will write another novel, that *Facetime* 'won't be her last'. Therefore, she is endorsing or recommending the first novel, *Facetime*.

Tying a knot

39 B **40** A **41** C **42** B **43** TRUE, FALSE, TRUE, FALSE, TRUE **44** C

EXPLANATIONS

39 A Windsor knot would be most relevant for professional people: 'the Windsor knot is a wide triangular knot that is preferred for business executives'.

40 The writer's tone shows he or she is very serious about knots and how they should be tied. He or she gives very specific, or accurate, instructions beginning with verbs such as 'drape', 'wrap', 'curl'. Other instructions include 'extending about 30 cm below'; 'draw up the knot snugly'; 'centre the knot precisely'.

41 The writer is most disparaging of the way students treat their ties. This is expressed in the sentence: 'Maybe this is the best solution for school students!'. The writer is suggesting the students would be better off wearing a clip-on tie rather than being disrespectful towards a 'proper' tie.

42 This is a sequencing question. The illustrations may help. 'After looping the tie a second time, pull the wide end across the narrow end (step 5)'.

43 When tying a tie, the wider end is manipulated while the thin end generally just hangs in place. You 'tighten and draw up the knot' (Step 7) after tucking 'the wide end...through the loop a third time' (Step 6). The instructions explain how to get 'the best results' when tying a tie. If the ends are not the same length the instructions are to 'start over'. The other statements are not supported by information in the text.

44 The writer has little regard for the manner in which students treat ties that require tying. They should consider clip-on ties: 'Maybe this is the best solution for school students!'.

Euthanasia—what do you think?

45 C **46** B **47** A **48** first two options **49** D
50 'Tying a knot': to inform and to explain; 'Euthanasia': to inform and to persuade.

EXPLANATIONS

45 The paper is neither supporting nor objecting to euthanasia. It wants informed debate on a contentious issue.

46 The paper offers arguments for and against euthanasia. One point people should consider is the soundness of mind of the person making a decision to volunteer to die.

47 The implication that Dr Phillip Nitschke is 'dicing with the law' suggests that the doctor is prepared to take on the law over the issue of euthanasia. There is an element of contest in the use of the word 'dicing'.

48 The writer uses a number of idioms and expressions that have particular meanings. A 'hot topic' is one that creates debate which is often heated. When you are on a 'slippery slope' you are on a course of action likely to lead to something bad or disastrous. To 'draw the line' suggests thinking about how far the debate should go, not controlling it. The phrase 'sound mind' refers to people who may not have the capacity to make a decision for themselves. Being 'no stranger' refers to Dr Nitschke challenging the law, not to his medical expertise.

49 The main reason for people attending the meeting is to become better informed about the issues involved in euthanasia.

50 'Tying a knot' has a dual purpose. It gives historical information about different types of ties and common mistakes when tying them. The text explains how to tie a tie 'For the best results'. The primary purposes of 'Euthanasia—what do you think?' are to inform readers about various opinions in the euthanasia debate and by doing so persuade people to write to the paper to 'share' their views. The editorial ends with persuasive devices: a rhetorical question and a direction, 'This page is for you'.

LITERACY—CONVENTIONS OF LANGUAGE

Pages 144–147

1 A **2** A **3** C **4** D **5** D **6** D **7** D **8** D **9** D **10** D **11** A **12** B **13** D **14** A **15** C **16** D **17** A, C **18** unbearable **19** A **20** B **21** A **22** C **23** Diving into rock pools **24** A **25** D **26** performance **27** interrupt **28** separate **29** pleasant **30** environment **31** famous **32** guess **33** dangerous **34** human **35** assignment **36** temperature **37** howled **38** aggression **39** unfortunately **40** temporary **41** committee **42** accommodation **43** attention **44** beautiful **45** fascinating **46** definitely **47** parliament **48** weird **49** derived **50** Composting

EXPLANATIONS

1 This is a grammar question. The correct sentence is: *Tan is not a suitable colour for hospitals.*
Tip: Simply put, a noun is the name of a person, place or thing. *Tan* is the name of a colour.

2 This is a punctuation question. The correct sentence is: *Jane told Jenny that the committee has ceased to exist.*

Tip: This sentence is in indirect speech. No speech marks (quotation marks) are required as the actual words spoken are not recorded.

3 This is a grammar question. The correct word is the preposition *in*.

ANSWERS
Sample Test Paper 1—Literacy

Tip: Prepositions put events in position in a time or place. In everyday speech certain prepositions regularly tend to go with certain words. We use *in* with months and years (*in April, 1916*) in order to show when an event took place.

4 This is a grammar question. The correct word is the conjunction *as*.
Tip: Some conjunctions operate as pairs, such as *either—or*.

5 This is a punctuation question. The correct sentence is: *The charismatic Ms P, the nicest teacher in school, was taking our class.*
Tip: *Ms P* is a proper noun—the name of a person must have a capital. All other nouns are common nouns. In this sentence the clause *the nicest teacher in school* is an adjective clause describing Ms P.

6 This is a grammar question. The correct word is the adjective *happiest*.
Tip: Adjectives are compared in degrees. This sentence refers to moments in one's life. One moment would be happy. When comparing two moments, one is happier. When comparing three or more moments, one of the moments is the happiest. *More* (and *most*) are used with words of two or more syllables when it is inappropriate to add *er* or *est*.

7 This is a grammar question. The correct word is the adjective *cleverest*.
Tip: Adjectives are compared in degrees. One girl would be clever. When comparing two girls, one is cleverer. When comparing three or more girls, one of the girls is the cleverest. *More* (and *most*) are used with words of two or more syllables when it is inappropriate to add *er* or *est*.

8 This is a grammar question. The correct word is the verb *waited*.
Tip: Singular subjects (nouns) need singular verbs; plural subjects (nouns) need plural verbs. In this case, the singular subject *Sally* needs a singular verb, *waited,* and not *waits*.

9 This is a grammar question. The correct answer is: *Last year Médecins Sans Frontières sent 27 000 trained medical personnel to help people in need.*
Tip: This is the only sentence with a subject (*Médecins Sans Frontières*) and a main verb (*sent*) in the active voice that describes an action and who performed it. Options A, B and C are in the passive voice and do not specify who performed the action (this is either unknown, unimportant or obvious).

10 This is a grammar question. The correct word is the conjunction *Because*.
Tip: *Because* is a conjunction. It establishes the relationship between the dependent clause and the rest of the sentence. Most conjunctions are located within the sentence and join ideas together.

11 This is a grammar question. The correct sentence is: *'To me it just made sense that I'd go to uni to complete a Bachelor of Science in agriculture so I can learn how to best manage our farms out here,' said Samantha.*
Tip: The word *made* is correct as it is the past tense of *make*. The comment is reflecting on the past so *make* is incorrect.

12 This is a grammar question. The correct sentence is: *Growing up on a 4000-acre farm just north of Dubbo in New South Wales, Samantha has always been a girl devoted to the country.*
Tip: With the irregular verb *always* you need a 'helper'—another verb to 'help' it. *Have, has* and *had* can be helping verbs. The helping verb is always close to the verb it is helping. Also, 'was always' is incorrect as it is in the past tense, when the sentence is in the present tense.

13 This is a grammar question. The correct sentence is: *Samantha will complete her degree in two years time and hopes to use her experience to help her family.*
Tip: Singular subjects (nouns) need singular verbs; plural subjects (nouns) need plural

verbs. In this case, *complete* must be used because there is only one Samantha. *Was completing* is incorrect as it is the wrong tense.

14 This is a grammar question. The correct word is the preposition *to*.
Tip: Prepositions put events in position in a time or place. In everyday speech certain prepositions regularly tend to go with certain words. We use *to* with *similar* (*similar to*) in order to show similarity.

15 This is a grammar question. The correct word is the verb *knows*.
Tip: Singular subjects (nouns) need singular verbs; plural subjects (nouns) need plural verbs. In this case, the single verb, *knows*, goes with the single subject *individual*.

16 This is a grammar question. The correct word is the pronoun *which*.
Tip: Pronouns are used to refer to nouns. *Which* is a common pronoun used to refer to animals or things such as events. *Who* is used to refer to a person, but is incorrect here due to the noun *person*. *What* and *when* are incorrect.

17 This is a punctuation question. The correct sentence is: *You haven't heard, have you? The most important words are in blue. Is that too hard to remember?*
Tip: This passage is made up of three parts: a question, a statement and a question. The locations of the capital letters are clues as to where each sentence starts.

18 This is a grammar question. The correct answer is *unbearable*.
Tip: An adjective is a describing word. In this sentence the adjective *unbearable* describes the novel.

19 This is a punctuation question. The correct sentence is: *Jackson, do you believe in supernatural beings?*
Tip: The comma is used after *Jackson* to separate the person spoken to from the rest of the sentence. Commas indicate pauses.

20 This is a punctuation question. The correct sentence is: *'Nothing is worse than a rainy day,' lamented Todd.*
Tip: Commas are used to separate a quotation (direct speech) from the rest of the sentence. It is situated inside the quotation marks (speech marks).

21 This is a grammar question. The correct answer is *don't*.
Tip: *Don't* requires an apostrophe because it is a contraction of *do not*. The other options are second-person singular verbs and do not require an apostrophe: *belongs, likes, sits*.

22 This is a punctuation question. The correct sentence is: *'I do not believe that the countries will reconcile,' admitted the academic, 'because the hatred it too strong.'*
Tip: Commas are used to separate a quotation (direct speech) from the rest of the sentence.

23 This is a grammar question. The correct answer is *Diving into rock pools*.
Tip: The word *it* is a general pronoun that is often used to refer to objects or experiences mentioned previously.

24 This is a grammar question. The main clause is: *Ghost stories are a lot of fun*. The subject is *Ghost stories*.
Tip: A clause is a group of words that contain a subject. A main clause is a clause that contains a subject and an object. Main clauses make sense on their own.

25 This is a grammar question. The correct word is the abstract noun *frustration*.
Tip: *Frustration* is a noun. Abstract nouns are the names of concepts.

ANSWERS
Sample Test Paper 1—Numeracy

NUMERACY TEST 1 Pages 148–153

1 E **2** C **3** 8 **4** C **5** 272 000 **6** C **7** 4 **8** 55 **9** B **10** A **11** 108 **12** B **13** D **14** 80.4 **15** B **16** D **17** A **18** D **19** B **20** D **21** C **22** 16 **23** 24 **24** B and D **25** B **26** D **27** C **28** 10.8 **29** C **30** C **31** 0.5 **32** B **33** B **34** C **35** 1.202 **36** C **37** C **38** C **39** A **40** D **41** B and E **42** D **43** 5 **44** A **45** 16 m **46** $91 **47** 12 **48** A

EXPLANATIONS

1 Percentage $= \frac{10}{50} \times 100\%$

$= \frac{1}{{}_{1}\cancel{5}} \times \frac{\cancel{100}^{20}}{1}$

$= 20\%$

20% of the cars are red.

2 $86\,400 = 8.64 \times 10\,000$

$= 8.64 \times 10^4$

3 Packets = 85 ÷ 12

= 7, with remainder 1.

This means Lara will have to buy 8 packets.

4 Ratio of blue to yellow is 2.5 : 1 = 5 : 2

5 parts = 800

1 part = 800 ÷ 5

= 160

2 parts = 160 × 2

= 320

Kate needs 320 mL of yellow paint.

5 $1.25 million = $1 250 000

Difference = 1 250 000 – 978 000

= 272 000

The difference is $272 000.

$$\begin{array}{r} 1250 \\ -\ 978 \\ \hline 272 \end{array}$$

6 $4 + 3 \times (12 - 4 \div 2) = 4 + 3 \times (12 - 2)$

$= 4 + 3 \times 10$

$= 4 + 30$

$= 34$

7 Number of blueberry muffins $= \frac{2}{3} \times 48$

$= \frac{2}{{}_{1}\cancel{3}} \times \frac{\cancel{48}^{16}}{1}$

$= 32$

Number of choc-chip muffins $= \frac{1}{4} \times 48$

$= \frac{1}{{}_{1}\cancel{4}} \times \frac{\cancel{48}^{12}}{1}$

$= 12$

Number not blueberry or choc-chip

= 48 – (32 + 12)

= 48 – 44

= 4

There were 4 muffins not blueberry or choc-chip.

8 $1^2 + 2^2 + 3^2 + 4^2 + 5^2 = 1 + 4 + 9 + 16 + 25$

$= 55$

9

Speed
120
60
0
5
10
Time

10 As 3 + 2 = 5, there is a total of 5 parts

Length of BC $= \frac{2}{5}$ of 35

= 35 ÷ 5 × 2

= 7 × 2

= 14

BC is 14 cm.

11 The polygon has 5 sides.

First, find the sum of the angles.

There are 3 triangles so that the angle sum = 3 × 180°

= 540°

As the pentagon is regular, all angles are equal.

$x = 540 \div 5$

$= 108$

12

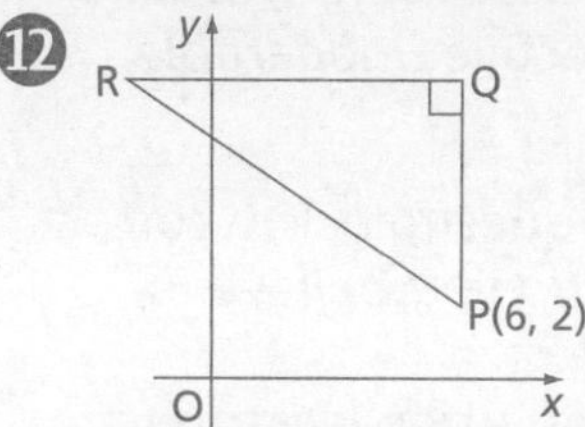

From P(6, 2), the point Q is 5 units away at (6, 7). Also, from Q(6, 7), the point R is 9 units away at (–3, 7). This means the co-ordinates of R are (–3, 7).

ANSWERS
Sample Test Paper 1—Numeracy

13 Range = 19 – (–3)
= 22

14 Increase = 0.5% of 80
= 0.005 × 80
= 0.4
Wednesday height = 80 + 0.4
= 80.4

15 Diameter = 28 cm, radius = 14 cm
Area $= \pi r^2$
$= \pi \times 14^2$
= 616 (nearest whole)
The area is 616 cm^2.

16 Total parts = 2 + 3 = 5
3 parts = 480
1 part = 480 ÷ 3 = 160
5 parts = 160 × 5 = 800
There are 800 students at the dance.

17 Chance is 4 out of 20, or $\frac{4}{20} = \frac{1}{5} = 0.2$

18 $2(3x + 5) = 6x + 10$

19 After drinking 60%, Miriam will have 40% remaining. As 75% is $\frac{3}{4}$, she will have $\frac{1}{4}$ of 40% left.
This means she has 10% remaining.

20 Distance in 3 h = 60 × 3
= 180
In first 3 hours Mitchell drives 180 km.
In the next 2 hours he drives 100 km.
For the entire journey: 280 km in 5 hours.
Average speed = 280 ÷ 5
= 56
Mitchell averaged 56 km/h.

21 There are $(c - d)$ students present. The cost will be $(c - d) \times y$ or $y(c - d)$ dollars.

22 From the middle group we see ✪ = 8. From the first group, ❁ = 2. Then using the third group, ❄ = 7. This means ❄ ❄ ❁ = 16.

23 $(3x)^2 - 3x^2 = (3 \times (-2))^2 - 3 \times (-2)^2$
$= (-6)^2 - 3 \times 4$
$= 36 - 12$
$= 24$

24 If the line passes through a point we can substitute the values of x and y into the equation.
Consider each of the choices for $y = 3x - 4$:
(0, –4):
–4 = 3 × 0 – 4
= 0 – 4
= –4 Yes, –4 = –4
(2, 2):
2 = 3 × 2 – 4
= 6 – 4
= 2 Yes, 2 = 2
The line passes through (0, –4) and (2, 2).

25 Perimeter of square = 12 cm
Length of each side = 3 cm
Length of sides of new square is 6 cm.
Area of new square = 6 × 6
= 36
The area is 36 cm^2.

26

This shape contains 2 triangles.
This shape contains 4 triangles.
This shape contains 16 triangles.
This means the entire shape contains 4 × 16 = 64 triangles.

27 The range of the present scores is 6 – 1 = 5, the mode is 5 and the mean is about 4. By including another 6, the range will remain as 5, the mode will remain as 5 but the mean will increase slightly. The correct answer is 'The mode will remain unchanged but the mean will increase'.

28 $y = 12 - \frac{3x}{4}$

$= 12 - \frac{3 \times 1.6}{4}$

$= 12 - (3 \times 1.6) \div 4$

$= 10.8$

29 On the plan, the stables cover 6 squares.
Scale: 6 squares = 24 m^2
1 square = 4 m^2
Area of garden on plan $= 5 \times 4$
$= 20$
The garden covers 20 squares.
Actual area of the garden $= 20 \times 4$
$= 80$
The garden has an area of 80 m^2.

30 From 11:45 pm to midnight is 15 minutes; from midnight to 6:00 am is 6 hours; from 6:00 am to 6:10 am is 10 minutes.
Total time = 6 hours + 15 min + 10 min
= 6 hours 25 min

31 Distance walked from the car to the signpost, 2.1 km to lookout, 2.1 km back to the signpost, 1.4 km to waterfall, 1.4 km to signpost, back to the car.
Distance = 2 × car to signpost + 2.1 + 2.1 + 1.4 + 1.4
= 2 × car to signpost + 7
If total distance is 8 km,
2 × car to signpost + 7 = 8
2 × car to signpost = 8 – 7
2 × car to signpost = 1
car to signpost = 0.5
The distance is 0.5 km.

32

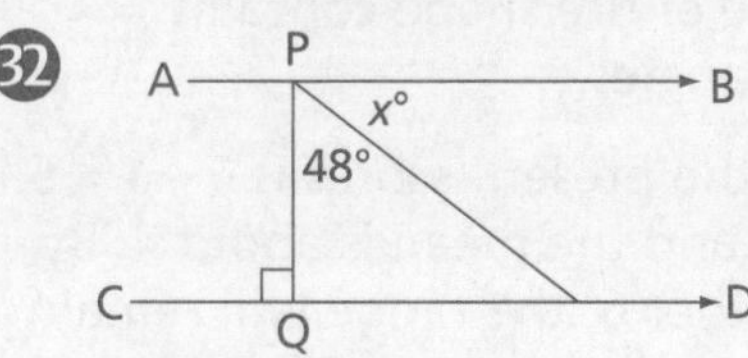

As ∠BPQ and ∠CQP are alternate angles with parallel lines,
$x + 48 = 90$
$x = 90 - 48$
$= 42$

33 The cubes row has the numbers 1, 3, 6, 10, …
The differences are 2, then 3, then 4, so that the next difference will be 5.
This means the missing number is 15.

34 As the lines are parallel, the alternate angles are equal.
$3x - 20 = 2x + 10$
$3x - 2x = 10 + 20$
$x = 30$

35 Halfway between 2 numbers is the average.
Number = (1.004 + 1.4) ÷ 2
= 1.202

36 25% of 8 is 2 and 50% of 16 is 8. This means that 10 out of a total of 24 were born in China. This means 14 were not born in China. This is written as $\frac{14}{24}$ or $\frac{7}{12}$.

37
$T = a + (n - 1)d,$
$32 = 8 + (n - 1) \times 6$
$6(n - 1) + 8 = 32$
$6n - 6 + 8 = 32$
$6n + 2 = 32$
$6n = 32 - 2$
$6n = 30$
$n = \frac{30}{6}$
$n = 5$

38

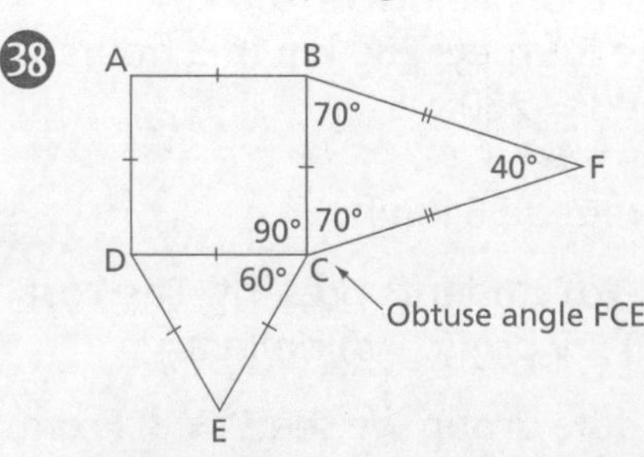

∠BCD = 90° (∠ in a square)
∠DCE = 60° (∠ in an equilateral Δ)
Now, as ∠BFC = 40°,
then ∠FCB = 70° (base ∠s of isosceles Δ equal and ∠ sum of Δ)
Obtuse ∠FCE = 360° – (90° + 60° + 70°)
= 140°

39 First, change each time to minutes.

$$\text{Mean} = \frac{75 + 95 + 48 + 72 + 30}{5}$$
$$= 64$$

The average time is 64 minutes.

40

Number of squares	1	3	5	7
Number of matches	4	10	16	22

'matches' = 3 times 'squares' plus 1.
If there are n squares, then $3 \times n + 1$ or $3n + 1$.

41 $\text{Mean} = \frac{2 + 4 + 4 + 5 + 7 + 10 + 18 + 46}{8}$
$= 12$
Mode $= 4$
Median $=$ middle of 5 and 7
$= 6$
Range $= 46 - 2$
$= 44$
As $6 > 4$, then median > mode.
Also, as $4 < 12$, then mode < median.

42 5th term $= (50 + 3) \times 2$
$= 53 \times 2$
$= 106$
6th term $= (106 + 3) \times 2$
$= 109 \times 2$
$= 218$

43 As both equations equal A, then the equations equal each other:

$$3x - 3 = x + 7$$
$$3x - x = 7 + 3$$
$$2x = 10$$
$$x = \frac{10}{2}$$
$$x = 5$$

44 $\text{Time} = \frac{3}{4} \times 3 = \frac{9}{4} = 2\frac{1}{4}$

Charlotte had $2\frac{1}{4}$ hours in lessons.

45 The diagram shows two similar triangles.
Comparing 1.5 and 24,

$\text{Enlargement factor} = \frac{24}{1.5} = 16$

This means that $h = 16 \times 1$
$= 16$

The height is 16 m.

46 Simple interest $= \$650 \times 0.035 \times 4$
$= \$91$
Ross earns interest of \$91.

47

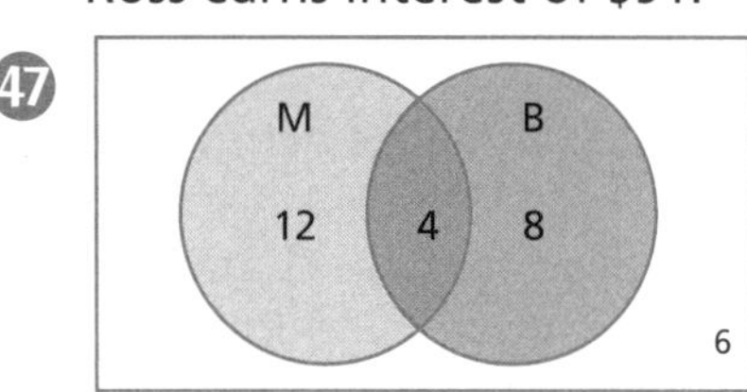

As $16 - 12 = 4$, then 4 students saw a movie and went to the beach. The numbers need to add to 30, so 8 is the other missing number. As $4 + 8 = 12$, then 12 students went to the beach.

48

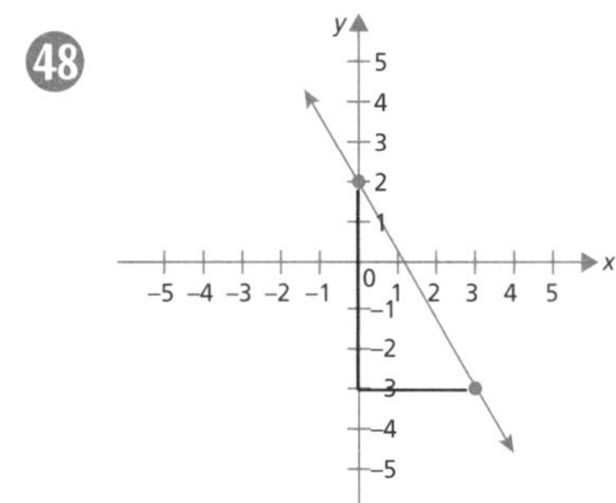

Moving from (0, 2) to (3, –3), you go down 5 units and then 3 units to the right.

This means gradient $= \frac{-5}{3}$.

SAMPLE TEST PAPER 2

LITERACY—WRITING

Page 154

Narrative

Tick each correct point.
Read the student's work through once to get an overall view of their response.

Focus on general points

- ☐ Did it make sense?
- ☐ Did it flow?
- ☐ Did the story arouse any feeling?
- ☐ Did you want to read on? Did the story create any suspense?
- ☐ Was the handwriting readable?

Now focus on the detail. Read the following points and find out whether the student's work has these features.

ANSWERS
Sample Test Paper 2—Literacy

Focus on content

- ☐ Did the opening sentence(s) 'grab' your interest?
- ☐ Was the setting established (i.e. where the action took place)?
- ☐ Was the reader told when the action takes place?
- ☐ Was it apparent who the main character(s) is? (It can be the narrator, using *I*.)
- ☐ Was there a 'problem' to be 'solved' early in the writing?
- ☐ Was a complication or unusual event introduced?
- ☐ Did descriptions make reference to any of the senses (e.g. *pink sky, cool breeze*)?
- ☐ Was there a climax (a more exciting part near the end)?
- ☐ Was there a conclusion (resolution of the problem) and was it believable?

Focus on structure, vocabulary, grammar, spelling, punctuation

- ☐ Was there variation in sentence length and beginnings?
- ☐ Was a new paragraph started for changes in time, place or action?
- ☐ In conversations or speaking were there separate paragraphs for each change of speaker?
- ☐ Were adjectives used to improve descriptions (e.g. <u>hollow</u> *sound*)?
- ☐ Were adverbs used to make actions more interesting (e.g. *listened* <u>carefully</u>)?
- ☐ Were capital letters where they should have been?
- ☐ Was punctuation correct?
- ☐ Was the spelling of words correct?

Marker's suggestions (optional)

LITERACY—READING Pages 155–168

Flying foxes

1 A **2** C **3** B **4** written response **5** B
6 4, 5, 1, 3, 2 **7** D **8** B

EXPLANATIONS

1. The article is a serious, informed article and is intended to inform readers about the Bellingen Island flying foxes.
2. The names are based on size: micro—small and mega—large.
3. The name, flying fox, is inappropriate because they are not foxes. They are not really fruit eaters and fruit bat is not accurate. They are quite different from bats.
4. The most common flying fox in the Bellingen Island area is the Greyheaded Flying Fox.
5. The writer is emphatic that flying foxes do not suck blood: 'They certainly do not suck blood like the "vampire" bats that are found in Central America'.
6. Paragraph 1: It is ironic that flying foxes are called fruit bats because 'their main food' is not usually fruit and they differ 'from other members of the bat family'. Paragraph 2: 'Spooky bat stories' come from 'Europe and the USA', and have 'nothing to do with Australia's flying foxes'. Paragraph 3: Unlike microbats, flying foxes 'have excellent eyesight' and do not use 'echolocation', nor do they 'hibernate in winter, as is common with microbats'. Paragraph 4: The writer suggests two reasons that people call flying foxes 'fruit bats': 'they look like dark fruit hanging in trees' and people are more 'likely to notice' when flying foxes are eating fruit. Paragraph 5: The species of flying foxes called the 'Greyheaded Flying Fox' are 'found only in Australia'.
7. Flying foxes have an unfair reputation of being fruit eaters. They may eat some fruit but they are basically nectar and pollen eaters.

Check Your Answers

ANSWERS
Sample Test Paper 2—Literacy

8 Flying foxes do not like to roost in caves or under cover. They prefer to hang from trees.

Thursday Island timeline

9 B **10** A **11** B **12** 2, 5, 3, 1, 4 **13** C **14** D **15** B **16** 'Flying foxes' B, C, D; 'Thursday Island timeline' B, D, E

EXPLANATIONS

9 The European discovery and settlement of Australia was not coordinated. It involved a number of European countries, over many decades, in a variety of places in Australia that were usually distant from each other.

10 The layout of the information allows for quick cross-references of the dates of events.

11 The '? BC' indicates there is no recorded history in the area prior to the arrival of Europeans.

12 1: In 1627 Francois Thijssen, who was a European, 'sailed along a lengthy section of the Great Australian Bight'. 2: In 1770 Captain Cook sailed through 'the area' which, concluded from the timeline and the map, was the Torres Strait where he noticed islanders who were from the Torres Strait Islands. 3: In 1792 Bruni d'Entrecasteau, sent to find another French explorer, 'explored parts of southern Tasmania'. 4: In 1803, the 'first European settlement was made at Risdon'. This information is in the Tasmania column. It can be concluded that Van Diemen's Land is Tasmania. 5: In 1864 a European settlement where 'Hostilities break out between Europeans and local inhabitants' was established at Somerset. The map shows Somerset is on Cape York Peninsula.

13 Dirk Hartog nailed a pewter (metal alloy) dish to a pole which was later found by another Dutch sea explorer.

14 William Bligh 'visited' the region after mutineers on *The Bounty* set him and a small party adrift in a long boat. He passed through, attempting to return to England.

15 The information suggests that the Torres Strait area was better known earlier by Europeans than other parts of Australia.

16 In both texts, the tone is primarily matter-of-fact. Neither of the writers respond emotionally to their topics and they present information impartially, i.e. the writers do not express any strong view for or against their topics. In 'Flying foxes' the writer describes in the introduction the paradox surrounding the names 'fruit bats' and 'flying foxes'. In 'Thursday Island timeline' the writer says, 'It is interesting to see the comparisons between the various discoveries of Australia…' The purpose of the text is to show how far back, '?BC', Indigenous people were living in the Torres Strait compared with the later discoveries which date from 1606.

A Smuggler's Song

17 A **18** common practice **19** D **20** C **21** D **22** B **23** Stolen goods are stored on their property; Smugglers can rely on them for assistance.

EXPLANATIONS

17 The narrator of the poem is directing his comments to a small girl. This is indicated by the fact that if she is good she will get a doll from France. King George's men were likely to call her 'Pretty maid'.

18 There is evidence in the poem that smuggling is a common practice. The dogs know not to bark. Many people gain from the smugglers' visits, and the line: 'If your mother mends a coat that's cut about and tore', suggests that smuggling is not an unusual occurrence.

19 Calling the smugglers 'gentlemen' is using the word euphemistically. It a respectable way of talking about the smugglers without actually admitting that what they do is illegal.

20 'The dogs lie dumb' is intended to reassure people present that there is nothing to worry about. The dogs aren't up and barking.

21 The language in the poem is friendly and reassuring. It reflects the language of those particular people at the time.

22 King George's men are trying to win the child's confidence by being (falsely) friendly. Most likely if she thinks they are friendly she will happily reveal the information they need.

23 The family involved in the poem's action support the smugglers. They mend their clothes and lend them horses, and hide their contraband: 'if you chance to find / Little barrels, roped and tarred, all full of brandy-wine /... Put the brushwood back again—and they'll be gone next day!'. There is also the suggestion they are prepared to turn a 'blind eye'.

The freak show

24 C **25** B **26** D **27** FACT, OPINION, OPINION, FACT **28** D **29** B **30** unscrupulous; unprincipled **31** C

EXPLANATIONS

24 Freak shows came to an end when people understood that freaks were a result of a disease or genetic defect: 'As mysterious deformities were scientifically explained as genetic mutations or the result of diseases, freaks became the objects of pity then compassion'.

25 An 'archaic term' is one that is no longer in use. Freak shows became politically incorrect.

26 Some people in freak shows were self-made freaks, such as the tattooed man. The less fortunate were those born with or who have developed abnormalities.

27 Two conclusions are not based on fact. It cannot be assumed that people working in freak shows were unable to make their own decisions, although it is highly likely that some could not. It is an opinion that visitors to the Venice Beach Freakshow 'may have been sceptical'. The degree to which people were not convinced that what they were seeing was real cannot be concluded.

28 Freak shows were once a source of fascination. This was followed by disdain and fear as the freaks were little understood. With a growing understanding, 'freaks became the objects of pity then compassion'.

29 The word 'ogled' means 'stare at rudely and blatantly'.

30 The writer states that those in freak shows were 'powerless to protect themselves' against 'exploitation'. The 'operators' who were guilty of exploitation are best described as unscrupulous and unprincipled; they had no scruples or principles and took advantage of unfortunate people for their own gain.

31 The word 'freaks' is in inverted commas to indicate that it carries additional meaning. The word is now politically incorrect, and not really acceptable when referring to people.

Great Expectations extract

32 D **33** A **34** B **35** C **36** B **37** D
38 written response **39** A

EXPLANATIONS

32 Mrs Gargery was looking for Pip. She was not happy with him: 'Mrs Joe [Gargery] has been out a dozen times, looking for you, Pip. And she's out now'.

33 Mrs Gargery was a domineering woman. Her husband, Joe, and Pip were fellow sufferers. Both were 'brought up by hand', meaning they were hit to keep them in line.

34 Tickler is the name given to the rod Mrs Gargery used on Pip and Joe. She used it to keep them under her control.

35 Being 'brought up by hand' suggests that Pip was not handled caringly but was controlled by the open hand, possibly with a smack where it hurt.

36 The Gargerys appear to be reasonably comfortable. He worked in a forge and she looked after the home. Their life might be hard but it was not destitute. It had a working-class simplicity and predictability.

37 A 'fellow sufferer' is one who suffers the same punishment, difficulties or injustices.

38 Pip's action of twisting the one button on his waistcoat indicates he is feeling nervous. Mrs Gargery has the rod out and she is after him. Pip looks 'in great depression at the fire'. He is not happy.

39 Joe Gargery is a quiet, accepting man. He recognises his situation and tolerates it with some sense of fatality. He is friendly to Pip and softly warns him of his misdemeanour—not being home when Mrs Gargery expected him to be home.

Share market returns

40 A **41** B **42** D **43** B **44** A **45** T, T, F, T, F

EXPLANATIONS

40 The important thing is to look at shares over the century. Most years they have provided positive returns, i.e. improved in value. On the information provided this result can be expected as a 'long-term' outcome. There will be a number of years with negative returns.

41 The information on the left of the dividing centre space is the years where shares lost value.

42 In 2008 share values dropped significantly. There had never been a year quite like it.

43 The fall in the value of shares over the two years could be described as dramatic. In 2007 the owners of shares were getting a return of between 10% and 20%. In 2008, the shares had lost value, as much as 40%.

44 Setting out the information in this layout makes it obvious that shares, regardless of the 2008 result, are a good investment. There are many more good years than bad years.

45 T: At the bottom of the table there are no dates listed above the column titled '–40% to –30%. T: During World War II (1939–45) shares gave positive returns in most years and were relatively high in 1942. Only in 1941 were shares in the negative. F: Returns in 1901 were between –10% and 0%, less than 2001 when they were between 10% and 20%. T: 'Most people in Australia' supplement their incomes through shares bought themselves or through 'investment companies or superannuation funds'. F: The average annual return is 13% not 19%.

Teenage drivers

46 D **47** A **48** B **49** A assertiveness; B puzzlement; C overreaction; D anguish; E disbelief **50** E

EXPLANATIONS

46 Teen years are a bit like dog years (one human year equals seven dog years). For Kevin, three months is a long, long time to be without his licence.

47 Parents of teenagers, especially those new to driving would appreciate, or at least understand, what the cartoonist is portraying.

48 Cartoons often depend on making fun of the familiar. The characters and situations tend to be readily recognised by the readers.

49 Frame 1: The exclamation mark after 'speeding!' shows Kevin's disbelief that he could lose his P plates. Kevin's mother's response to Kevin thinking that speeding is not serious is to be assertive, emphasising that for 'Any infringement!' there are severe consequences. Frame 2: The question mark shows Kevin's mother is puzzled by Kevin's reaction to the possibility of being suspended for 'Three months!' Her perspective on time is different to her teenage son's. Kevin covers his face, anguished by the prospect. Frames 2 and 3: The words **'No! No!'** and **'forever'** in bold show Kevin's overreaction because three months is a long time to a teenager.

50 'Share market returns' presents statistical information on positive and negative share-market returns over a long period, '109 years'. There is no attempt to persuade or influence. The information is impartial, presented as fact and there are no suggestions regarding how to respond to the fluctuations over time. 'Teenage Drivers' provides information on the issues facing learner drivers in the

introductory text. The cartoon supports this information and highlights, in a humorous way, the point that young drivers are inexperienced.

LITERACY—CONVENTIONS OF LANGUAGE

Pages 169–173

1 B **2** C **3** B **4** D **5** A **6** C **7** C **8** A **9** A **10** D **11** C **12** B **13** A **14** C **15** C **16** B **17** C **18** C **19** B **20** C **21** D **22** C **23** C **24** B, D **25** B **26** immediately **27** medieval **28** disappointed **29** glistening **30** unfamiliar **31** unbelievable **32** uncomfortable **33** exhaust **34** government **35** imaginative **36** changeable **37** armoured **38** battalion **39** concentration **40** cemetery **41** squadron **42** Graffiti **43** burglar **44** asbestos **45** eccentric **46** silhouette **47** plateau **48** manouevre **49** annihilate **50** therapeutic

EXPLANATIONS

1 This is a grammar question. The correct answer is *a verb into a noun*.
Tip: The suffix *er* changes the verb *preach* (an action) into the noun *preacher* (a person's job; someone who preaches).

2 This is a grammar question. The correct answer is *not*.
Tip: The prefix *un* changes a word to its opposite. This is because the prefix *un* means 'not' or 'the opposite of'.

3 This is a grammar question. The correct answer is: *Three years after Joe began playing guitar, he started at Davidson High School.*
Tip: This question requires you to sequence three sentences in the correct order. Option A fails to mention the three-year time period and option C is incorrect. Option D is grammatically and factually correct but option B expresses the information more succinctly with an adverbial clause.

4 This is a grammar question. The correct answer is: *Sergeant Anderson escorted the children home to their parents.*
Tip: This is the only sentence with a subject (*Sergeant Anderson*) and a main verb (*escorted*) in the active voice that describes an action and who performed it. Options A, B and C are in the passive voice and do not specify who performed the action (this is either unknown, unimportant or obvious).

5 This is a grammar question. The correct word is the conjunction *but*.
Tip: Conjunctions join ideas in a sentence. The conjunction *but* indicates a connection between two different ideas.

6 This is a grammar question. The correct word is the verb *do*.
Tip: Singular subjects (nouns) need singular verbs; plural subjects (nouns) need plural verbs. In this case, the plural subject *children* needs a plural verb, *do*, not *does*.

7 This is a grammar question. The correct sentence is: *'I'm so excited about this project, but I can't wait to put down the books and get onto the land to make a real difference,' stated Samantha*.
Tip: Singular subjects (nouns) need singular verbs; plural subjects (nouns) need plural verbs. In this case, *wait* must be used because there is only one Samantha. *Waited* is incorrect as it is the wrong tense.

8 This is a grammar question. The correct word is the conjunction *Although*.
Tip: *Unless* is a conjunction. It can come at the beginning of a sentence and establishes the relationship between the dependent clause and the rest of the sentence. Most conjunctions are located within the sentence and join ideas together.

9 This is a grammar question. The correct answer is: *had heard*.
Tip: With the irregular verb *heard* you need a 'helper'—another verb to 'help' it. *Have*, *has* and *had* can be helping verbs. The helping verb is always close to the verb it is helping.

ANSWERS
Sample Test Paper 2—Literacy

10 This is a punctuation question. The correct answer is: *Keenan said, 'I love playing the drums'.*
Tip: The full stop must be inside the quotation marks to correctly complete the sentence.

11 This is a grammar question. The correct sentence is: *The mother wrapped the fish in two sheets of newspaper.*
Tip: The word *in* is a preposition. A preposition indicates when, where or how an action occurred.

12 This is a grammar question. The correct answer is *present tense*.
Tip: Look at the form of verbs to help identify tense. In this sentence the verbs *are* and *according* reveal the tense.

13 This is a grammar question. The correct sentence is: *With his heart beating fast, Ryo pulled open the door.*
Tip: In this sentence the adjectival phrase *With his heart beating fast* describes Ryo's nervousness.

14 This is a grammar question. The correct word is the adjective *cleaner.*
Tip: Adjectives are compared in degrees. One beach would be clean. When comparing two beaches, one is cleaner. When comparing three or more beaches one of the beaches is the cleanest. *More* (and *most*) are used with words of two or more syllables when it is inappropriate to add *er* or *est*.

15 This is a grammar question. The correct answer is: *more easily*.
Tip: *Easily* is an adverb and adds meaning to the verb *made*. *Easy* is an adjective.

16 This is a grammar question. The correct word is the verb *wear*.
Tip: *Wear* is a verb and should not be confused with the homonym *where*, which is an adverb.

17 This is a grammar question. The main clause is: *I first met my great aunt in Paris.*
Tip: A clause is a group of words that contains a subject. A main clause is a clause that contains a subject and an object. Main clauses make sense on their own.

18 This is a grammar question. The adverbial phrase is *across the road*.
Tip: Adverbial phrases modify verbs, adverbs and adjectives. *Across the road* tells where the tractor driver *turned*.

19 This is a punctuation question. The correct sentence is: *Deep in the cave, the young boy cried for help.*
Tip: The comma is used after the introductory clause. This clause is called an adverbial clause. Adverbial phrases often don't use adverbs. However, they function in the same way to provide information about how, when, where or to what extent something happened.

20 This is a grammar question. The correct answer is *adjective* and *noun*
Tip: An adjective is a word used to describe nouns and pronouns. In this sentence the adjective *interesting* describes the film. Nouns are things that we can touch, think or feel. In this sentence the noun is *interest*.

21 This is a grammar question. The correct sentence is: *His back was covered in mosquito bites.*
Tip: A noun is the name of a person, place or thing. *Back* is the name of a part of the body.

22 This is a grammar question. The correct sentence is: *The dog catcher tried to hoop the stray around the neck with his rope.*
Tip: A verb is an action word.

23 This is a grammar question. The adverbial phrase is: *For answers to all your questions.*
Tip: Adverbial phrases modify verbs, adverbs and adjectives. *For answers to all your questions* tells what you will find if you *do a Google* search.

24 This is a grammar question. The correct answer is: *Smaug, angry at having been cheated by Bilbo, swiftly and softly flew over the mountains.* OR *Smaug, eager to wreak destruction on the town of Dale, swiftly and softly flew over the mountains.*
Tip: A dependent clause adds more information to an independent clause.

25 This is a grammar question. There are two correct answers. *Mr Anderson, who is the funniest person I know, is my fourth grade teacher.* OR *Mr Anderson, the one with the bushy eyebrows, is my fourth grade teacher.*
Tip: A dependent clause adds more information to an independent clause.

NUMERACY TEST 2 Pages 174–178

1 D **2** B **3** A **4** B **5** D **6** 0.72 **7** 6 **8** 336 **9** C **10** A **11** 4 **12** D **13** A **14** C **15** B **16** 72 **17** C **18** –2 and –3 **19** C **20** 31 **21** A **22** C **23** A **24** C **25** D **26** B **27** D **28** A **29** B **30** C **31** 1250 **32** A **33** 9 **34** 6 **35** 2662 **36** C **37** B **38** C **39** 1:1 **40** 32, 16 **41** A **42** 30 **43** $w(p + t)$ **44** E **45** –6 **46** 896 **47** 59.2% **48** 225

EXPLANATIONS

1 17 hundredths = 0.17
New record = 27.14 – 0.17
= 27.14 – 0.14 – 0.03
= 27.00 – 0.03
= 26.97
The new record is 26.97 seconds.

2 Mean = (12 + 13 + 5 + 10 + 20) ÷ 5
= 60 ÷ 5
= 12
The mean is 12.

3 0.007 68 = 7.68 ÷ 1000
= 7.68×10^{-3}

4 3 parts = 12
1 part = 4
5 parts = 20
4 parts = 16
This means originally 20 red, 16 blue, 12 green.
After the removal of balls: 16 red, 12 blue, 8 green.
New ratio is 16 : 12 : 8 = 4 : 3 : 2.

5 As $\sqrt{0.25} = 0.5$ and $(0.3)^2 = 0.09$, then the correct order is $(0.3)^2$, 0.4, $\sqrt{0.25}$.

6 Total amount of flour $= \frac{3}{4} \times 4.8$

$= \frac{3}{\cancel{4}_1} \times \frac{\cancel{4.8}^{1.2}}{1}$

= 3.6

Amount of flour per loaf
= 3.6 ÷ 5
= 0.72

$5\overline{)3.60}$ = 0.72

Each loaf is made from 0.72 kg.

7 Number given to Kate $= \frac{2}{5} \times 60$

$= \frac{2}{\cancel{5}_1} \times \frac{\cancel{60}^{12}}{1}$

= 24

Balls remaining = 60 – 24
= 36
Number given to Daniel = 18
Difference = 24 – 18
= 6
Kate gets 6 more balls.

8 $\frac{8!}{5!} = \frac{8 \times 7 \times 6 \times 5 \times 4 \times 3 \times 2 \times 1}{5 \times 4 \times 3 \times 2 \times 1}$

$= \frac{8 \times 7 \times 6}{1}$

$= 56 \times 6$

$= 336$

9 The shape is a rectangle with dimensions *a* and *b* minus a square with side *c*.
Area = $(a \times b) - (c \times c)$

10 1000 litres = 1 kilolitre
The correct calculation is 590 ÷ 3 × 7 ÷ 1000

ANSWERS
Sample Test Paper 2—Numeracy

11 Missing number times 6 plus 8 = 32
Missing number times 6 = 32 – 8
Missing number times 6 = 24
Missing number = 24 ÷ 6
Missing number = 4
The number is 4.

12 Consider each of the choices to find the correct rule for $x = 6$ and $y = 2$, and $x = 14$ and $y = 6$
Correct answer is $y = \frac{1}{2}x - 1$, as
(6, 2): $2 = \frac{1}{2} \times 6 - 1$
(14, 6): $6 = \frac{1}{2} \times 14 - 1$

13 Yellow and green are one-quarter of 120. This means yellow = 30 and green = 30. Also red is larger than 30 and blue is less than 30.

Colour	Number of spins
Yellow	30
Red	50
Blue	10
Green	30

14 The possible combinations are
BBB, BBG, BGB, BGG,
GGG, GGB, GBG, GBB
Of these 8 combinations, 3 have 2 boys and a girl: BBG, BGB, GBB
The probability is $\frac{3}{8}$.

15
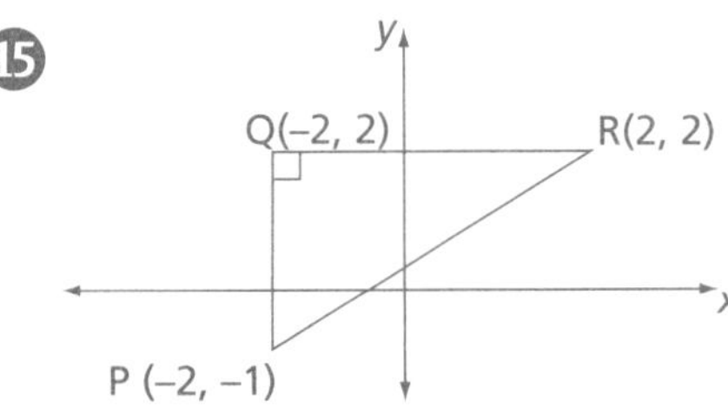

From (–2, –1) move 3 units up is (–2, 2).
Now, move to the right 4 units is (2, 2).
The co-ordinates of R are (2, 2).

16 The lowest common multiple of 4, 2 and 3 is 12. This means that the cube will have a side length of 12 cm. Now, 12 ÷ 4 = 3, 12 ÷ 2 = 6 and 12 ÷ 3 = 4, and 3 × 6 × 4 is 72. The cube holds 72 blocks.

17 The shape of the cross-section is a circle.

18 Two numbers are multiplied to give 6 and added together to give –5. This means the numbers are –2 and –3. As –2 > –3, then square = –2 and triangle = –3.

19 As AD = 3 units, then 3 units = 12
1 unit = 12 ÷ 3
= 4
Now, BF = 4 units: 4 units = 4 × 4
= 16
BF is 16 m long.

20
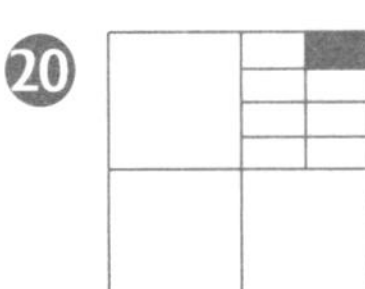

The large square is made from 4 smaller squares which can each be covered with 8 tiles. This means a total of 32 tiles will cover the square. So another 31 tiles are needed.

21 $3(2x + 3) - x + 1 = 6x + 9 - x + 1$
$= 5x + 10$

22 As 1000 mm = 1 m,
25 millimetres = 0.025 metres
Need to know how many 0.025's in 10:
Total number of coins = 10 ÷ 0.025

23
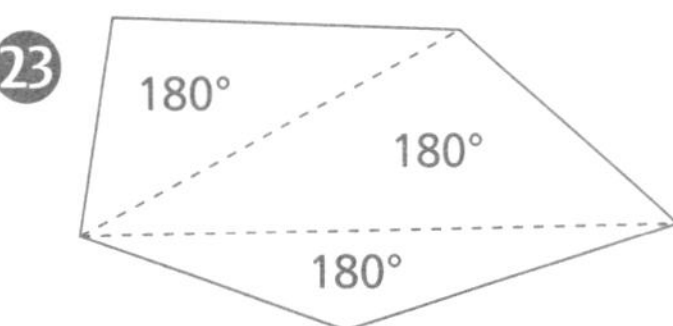

To find the sum of angles in a pentagon we can divide into 3 triangles:
As 180 × 3 = 540, the angle sum is 540°.
$x = 540 - (100 + 130 + 140 + 120)$
$= 50$

24

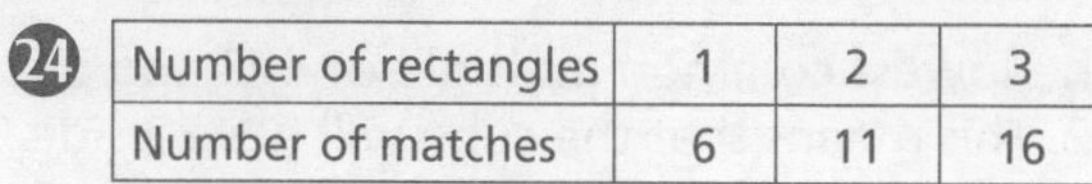

Number of rectangles	1	2	3
Number of matches	6	11	16

Number of matches
$= 5 \times$ number of rectangles $+ 1$

25 Fraction of pink and purple $= \frac{1}{3} + \frac{1}{6}$
$= \frac{1}{2}$

This means $\frac{1}{2}$ of the counters are yellow, and so there are 24 counters in total.

Number of pink counters $= \frac{1}{3} \times 24$
$= 8$

There are 8 pink counters.

26 To purchase 24 cans:
Imran buys 6 packs: Cost $= \$2.40 \times 6$
$= \$14.40$
Kate buys 4 packs: Cost $= \$3.20 \times 4$
$= \$12.80$
Difference $= \$14.40 - \$12.80$
$= \$1.60$

27 $S = 2\pi r(r + h) = 2 \times \pi \times 5 \times (5 + 15)$
$= 628.318\,5307$
The surface area is closest to 628 cm^2

28 As both equations are equal to b, then the equations are equal:
$3a + 1 = 2a - 3$
$a = -4$
OR: Consider each choice by substitution:
$a = -4$: $b = 2a - 3$
$= 2 \times -4 - 3$
$= -8 - 3$
$= -11$
$b = 3a + 1$
$= 3 \times -4 + 1$
$= -12 + 1$
$= -11$
As $b = -11$ in both equations, then the correct value of a is –4.

29 $P = \frac{F}{A}$

$24 = \frac{6}{A}$

Consider each of the choices:

4: $\frac{6}{4} = 1.5 \neq 24$

0.25: $\frac{6}{0.25} = 24$

This means the correct value is 0.25
OR, consider some easy numbers to find how they relate:

e.g. $5 = \frac{15}{3}$ means that also $3 = \frac{15}{5}$.

If $P = \frac{F}{A}$, then $A = \frac{F}{P}$
$= \frac{6}{24}$
$= 0.25$

30 By measurement, the length of the path is about 8 cm.
Using the scale, 1 cm = 400, then
8 cm $= 400 \times 8$
$= 3200$
The path is 3200 metres, or about 3 km.

Time $= \frac{\text{Distance}}{\text{Speed}}$
$= \frac{3}{12}$

Phil will take $\frac{1}{4}$ hour, or 15 minutes

31
$P = 8m - 8500$
$500 = 8m - 8500$
$1500 + 8500 = 8m$
$10\,000 = 8m$
$m = 10\,000 \div 8$
$= 1250$
The value of m is 1250.

32 $2x - x^2 = 2 \times (-3) - (-3)^2$
$= -6 - 9$
$= -15$

ANSWERS
Sample Test Paper 2—Numeracy

33 Area of rectangle $= 6 \times 2$
$= 12$ (12 square units)
Dimensions of the triangle are 2 units and 3 units.
Area of triangle $= \frac{1}{2} \times 2 \times 3$
$= 3$ (3 square units)
The area of remaining shape is $12 - 3 = 9$, or 9 square units.

34 6, 2 and 12 are factors of 24.
Suppose tree A is 24 metres.
This means tree B is 4 metres; tree C is 12 metres and tree D is 2 metres. Tree C is 6 times taller than tree D.

35 First find the value of *B*, then *C*, then *D*.
Now, $B = 2000 + \frac{2000}{10} = 2200$.
Also, $C = 2200 + \frac{2200}{10} = 2420$.
Finally, $D = 2420 + \frac{2420}{10} = 2662$.
The value of *D* is 2662.

36 Comparing 2, 7, 7, 7, 8, 9 and 7, 7, 7, 8, 9
Mode: remains as 7
Mean: increases as 2 is small compared to the other scores
Median: remains as 7
Range: changes from 7 to 2
This means that the range and the mean change.

37 The entire shape ADEH combines 6 identical triangles. As triangle BFH combines 2 small triangles, the area is one-third area of ADEH.

38 If the diameter is 10 cm, the radius is 5 cm.
Use the formula: Circumference $= 2\pi r$
Perimeter $= \frac{1}{2}$ circumference + diameter
$= \frac{1}{2} \times 2 \times \pi \times 5 + 10$
$= 25.707\,963\,27$
Of the choices, the perimeter is closest to 26 cm.

39 Girls $= \frac{3}{8} \times 24$
$= 9$
Boys $= \frac{5}{8} \times 24$
$= 15$
Originally, 9 girls and 15 boys.
Later, $9 + 3 = 12$ girls and $15 - 3 = 12$ boys
Ratio of girls to boys $= 12:12$
$= 1:1$

40 The scale on the grid is 1 unit = 4 cm. Consider the length of the rectangle. It is currently 2 units wide. It can be multiplied by 4 to be 8 units wide. By multiplying the dimensions of the rectangle by 4 we get the enlarged rectangle measuring 32 cm by 16 cm.

41 The 200 motorists who paid $1 also paid 50c. As $350 - 200 = 150$, there are another 150 50c pieces. As $150 \div 3 = 50$, then 50 motorists paid with three 50c pieces.
As $200 + 50 = 250$, then there were 250 motorists.
Percentage $= \frac{50}{250} \times 100\%$
$= 20\%$

42 Each angle in a regular hexagon is 120°.
Each angle in a rectangle is 90°
This means 120° – 90° is 30°.

43 Average after p games $= q$
Total after p games $= pq$
Average after $(p + t)$ games $= w$
Total after $(p + t)$ games $= w(p + t)$

44 Olivia: $\$n$
Cooper: $\$(2n + 20)$
Jack: $\$(2n + 80)$
Mia: $\$(n + 40)$
Total $= \$(n + 2n + 20 + 2n + 80 + n + 40)$
$= \$(6n + 140)$

45 $\frac{2x}{3} + 1 = x + 3$
$2x + 3 = 3x + 9$
$3x - 2x = 3 - 9$
$x = -6$

46 Total area $= 16 \times 16 + 4 \times \frac{1}{2} \times 16 \times 20$
$= 896$
The total area is 896 cm².

47 Discount $= 0.20 \times \$240$
$= \$48$
Discounted price $= \$240 - \$48$
$= \$192$
Cash amount $= \$192 - \$50$
$= \$142$
Percentage $= \frac{142}{240} \times 100\%$
$= 59.166\ 6666\ldots$
$= 59.2$ (1 dec. pl.)
Ella pays 59.2% of the original price.

48 Let n = number of adult tickets.
This means $2n$ = number of child tickets.
Total sales: $2n \times 20 + n \times 30 = 5250$
$40n + 30n = 5250$
$70n = 5250$
$\frac{70n}{70} = \frac{5250}{70}$
$n = 75$, and so $2n = 150$.
Total sales $= n + 2n$
$= 75 + 150$
$= 225$
There were 225 tickets sold.

SPELLING WORDS FOR REAL TESTS

To the teacher or parent

Read the word clearly to the student. Then read the sentence with the word in it to the student. Then read the word again.

Give the student time to write an answer. If the student is not sure of the spelling tell them to make their best attempt but that it is okay to skip a word if it is not known.

Spelling words for Real Test Week 1

Word	Example
1. accommodation	The accommodation was unsuitable for my family, so we left.
2. chemical	The chemical caused horrific burns to the young girl's face and hands.
3. rhymes	I confessed to my best friend that I still enjoy listening to nursery rhymes.
4. temperature	Harry, it is of extreme urgency that you turn the temperature down!
5. separate	Separate those two uncontrollable children at once!
6. chocolate	I was tempted by the chocolate cake that sat on the kitchen table.
7. comfortable	The chair was lovely and comfortable; nothing could move me.
8. movement	The delicate movement of the dancers was seamless.
9. innovation	I was thoroughly impressed by the innovaton of the engineers.
10. puppies	The puppies played happily outside whilst Sejong ate lunch.
11. metaphors	The teacher said to use metaphors to create imagery.
12. ingredients	The ingredients for the pizza looked delicious.
13. boxes	Twenty large boxes arrived at my house, each containing a surprise.
14. poverty	The poverty of the small family made me sad and frustrated.
15. disease	Love is a disease I never want to catch!

Spelling words for Real Test Week 2

Word	Example
1. approximately	The launch will commence at approximately 0800 hours.
2. independence	America was granted independance from the British Empire in 1776.
3. rebellion	Some say the rebellion was a misunderstood protest.
4. currently	The minister is currently under investigation.
5. towered	A giant towered over me as I approached the top of the beanstalk.
6. budgeted	The family hadn't budgeted for meals, so they had to eat plain noodles.
7. foregrounded	The cinematographer foregrounded the little child in the shot.
8. inappropriate	The behaviour of the young man was inappropriate.
9. proportion	The baby's head was out of proportion with its body.
10. reaction	George had an allergic reaction to the bee sting.
11. proposition	Julie was unsure how to respond to the man's proposition.
12. peaceful	The young child looked peaceful as she slept on the lounge.
13. development	The development on the town's foreshore was protested against.
14. engagement	Mary and James celebrated their engagement in June.
15. evaluation	Detailed evaluation of the crime scene was necessary.

SPELLING WORDS FOR REAL TESTS

To the teacher or parent

Read the word clearly to the student. Then read the sentence with the word in it to the student. Then read the word again.

Give the student time to write an answer. If the student is not sure of the spelling tell them to make their best attempt but that it is okay to skip a word if it is not known.

Spelling words for Real Test Week 3

Word	Example
1. formerly	We were formerly residents of Elwood Beach, but now we reside in Bondi.
2. international	The international swimming titles were marred by controversy.
3. hypothesis	The scientist's hypotheses was that too much sunlight killed the plants.
4. perspective	Our perspective of an event is altered by our life experiences.
5. formulae	The numerous formulae confused Jane on her first day of Extension Science.
6. breathe	I struggled to breathe after choking on a boiled lolly.
7. apprentice	Barry became John Turtle's painting apprentice.
8. conscious	To his horror, the boy realised he would be conscious during his surgery.
9. justice	We demand justice for this heinous crime!
10. manufacture	The manufacture of goods in sweat shops should be illegal worldwide.
11. synchronised	I enjoyed the synchronised swimming at the Olympic Games.
12. prioritise	It is important to prioritise your study schedule.
13. prejudice	The Prime Minister will abolish prejudice in his nation.
14. preference	What is your preference, chocolate or strawberry?
15. discussed	The parents discussed their child's future with the principal.

Spelling words for Real Test Week 4

Word	Example
1. erosion	Severe wind storms have resulted in the erosion of the sand dunes.
2. constitution	Amendments can be made to a constitution if enough people support them.
3. immigrant	The life of a new immigrant is often lonely and stressful.
4. infrastructure	The city's infrastructure was meticulously planned by skilled engineers.
5. pilgrimage	Aazim was excited to make the pilgrimage to the holy land.
6. principal	The principal had an impressive vision for the future of his new school.
7. parallel	We noticed the parallel lines on the road that indicated no overtaking.
8. calculate	The shop owner tried to calculate the cost of the water damage.
9. specification	The new product did not meet the company's specification, causing turmoil.
10. irrelevant	What you believe happened, Harry, is irrelevant.
11. agility	The footballer's agility gained him a spot in the Australian team.
12. strategy	What strategy will you use to defeat the ferocious gargoyle Gongala?
13. sauce	The sauce of the lasagne was thick and gelatinous; no-one wanted to eat it.
14. ingredients	Combine the ingredients in the bowl, and add into the food processor.
15. invasion	The invasion of Cyprus by the Turks was inevitable.

SPELLING WORDS FOR SAMPLE TESTS

To the teacher or parent

Read the word clearly to the student. Then read the sentence with the word in it to the student. Then read the word again.

Give the student time to write an answer. If the student is not sure of the spelling tell them to make their best attempt but that it is okay to skip a word if it is not known.

Spelling words for Sample Test 1

Word	Example
26. performance	Another day means another performance for Heather.
27. interrupt	Do not interrupt me when I'm talking!
28. separate	I have made separate meals for each of you.
29. pleasant	The smells of the flowers were pleasant to my nose.
30. environment	Effective waste management will help the environment.
31. famous	The girls became famous for their magnificent hand-made gowns.
32. guess	Can you guess the answer to the questions?
33. dangerous	The squint in the girl's eyes suggested that she was dangerous.
34. human	The most important human emotion is empathy.
35. assignment	It is important to complete your assignment before it is due.
36. temperature	The boy's temperature exceeded 39 °C.
37. howled	The wind howled through the last limp leaves of Autumn.
38. aggression	Huddled on the cracked and faded bench, Jai hides his face from the wind's aggression.
39. unfortunately	Unforunately we have sold out of finger buns.
40. temporary	Remember, this arrangement is temporary.

Spelling words for Sample Test 2

Word	Example
26. immediately	Immediately after the party, James asked Kate out.
27. medieval	In medieval times, knights were considered heroes.
28. disappointed	Never be disappointed—book your holiday early!
29. glistening	Kim slumped in her chair, eyes glistening in the direction of her interrogator.
30. unfamiliar	The sights of Sydney had become unfamiliar to me.
31. unbelievable	That is absolutely unbelievable!
32. uncomfortable	His intense stare was making me increasingly uncomfortable.
33. exhaust	The truck's exhaust smelt terrible.
34. government	Government policy should do more about poverty in our cities.
35. imaginative	Salvador Dali was a surrealist painter known for his highly imaginative works of art.
36. changeable	The girl experienced changeable moods.
37. armoured	The armoured tank roamed the desolate streets.
38. battalion	The first battalion entered the war.
39. concentration	The concentration on Jo's face suggested that the task was difficult.
40. cemetery	The boy walked timidly through the cemetery.

Notes